MINI
MATT
World of Sport

The Daily Telegraph

World of Sport

Orion Books
A division of the Orion Publishing Group Ltd
Orion House
5 Upper St Martin's Lane
London
WC2H 9EA

This collected edition first published by
Orion Books Ltd in 2004

The right of Matthew Pritchett to be identified
as the author of this work has been asserted by him
in accordance with the Copyright, Designs
and Patents Act, 1988

A CIP catalogue record for this book
is available from the British Library

ISBN 0 75285 970 6

Printed and bound in Great Britain by
Clays Ltd, St Ives plc

www.orionbooks.co.uk

FOREWORD

Matt's world is immediately recognisable and all his characters familiar. You always know where you are, and who you are with, in his cartoons. He is a master of the essential, perfect detail; the flowery curtains, the garden fence, the porter's trolley, the tweedy jacket, the unshaven chin, the drystone wall – the list is endless – set the scene with apparently effortless precision.

His characters are sometimes enraged, on rare occasions triumphant, now and then temporarily defeated. But most often they are perplexed, and confront life with a kind of hopeful desperation. And somehow, as you laugh at their comical plight, you feel oddly reassured that you too will make it through.

Nicholas Garland

MINI
MATT
World of Sport

'They're called fences, stop calling them speed humps'

'I've worked out that if Bill Gates followed your racing tips he'd be bankrupt by 2005'

NO
BY-PASS
ROYAL
ASCOT

ASCOT
CRICKET
WORLD CUP

'This should solve the problem of all those wides being bowled'

CRICKET
ACADEMY
GRADUATION

ENGLAND
BOWLERS
DO WELL

ENGLAND
CRICKET
WIN
ELVIS
PRESLEY
NAMED
MAN OF
THE MATCH

ZIMBABWE: CRICKETERS DECIDE

*'Come on . . . NO . . . YES . . .
wait there . . . GO!'*

'It's still deuce – you haven't missed anything'

'Well, judging by how long they lasted, they must be from an England batsman'

'It's good to see an England player catch something for a change'

THEY WON.
IT WASN'T
A DREAM

'We beat the West Indies in 1969 and AGAIN this year – it's getting to be monotonous'

'Would you rather watch the rain at Wimbledon or the rain at Lords?'

'Play is suspended for 25 years until global warming gives us the same climate as the Loire Valley'

WIM
E

WIMBLEDON
MALE STRAWBERRIES £5
FEMALE STRAWBERRIES £3·50

WIMBLEDON
WINKLES
COCKLES
WHELKS

UMPIRE
UMPIRE'S
PUSHY
MOTHER

WIMBLEDON

'Wimbledon?
Follow that cloud'

'Sorry officer, I was just showing my wife how fast a tennis ball travels when served by Greg Rusedski'

'I wish you wouldn't grunt when you use the remote control'

HENMAN

'I can't bear the thought of watching Tim Henman playing until he's 70'

'Oh for goodness sake, get real!'

'If we hurry we can get to Wimbledon before the English are knocked out of that as well'

BACK TO BASICS
GOAL
BALL
FOOT
ENG
ENGLAN
ENGLAND
ENGLAN

'My goodness football is boring when you're sober'

'Zzxllip jjipg klllvvv vcx fjiiikllm David Beckham!'

FOOTBALL:
ENGLAND
INJURY
WORRIES

'For a while, Mr Beckham, you'll only be able to count up to five'

'Do you think both goalies could have been bribed?'

ENGLAND
A YEAR IN PROVENCE

ENGLAND V TUNISIA TICKETS £200
SICK NOTES FOR MONDAY £400

'I had that Dennis Wise in
the back of my cab'

'Maybe you could host the Olympics instead'

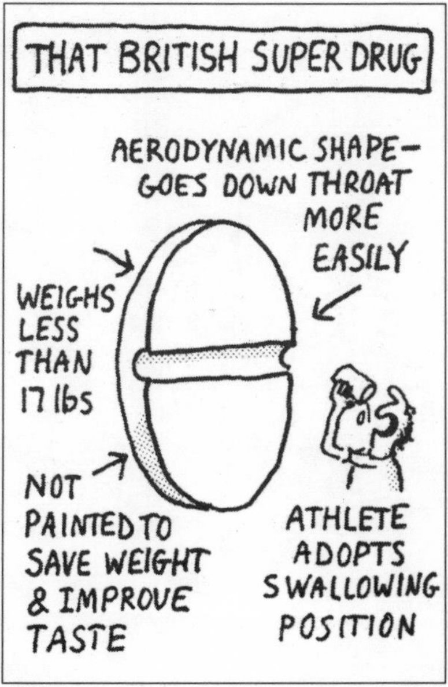

THAT BRITISH SUPER DRUG

AERODYNAMIC SHAPE – GOES DOWN THROAT MORE EASILY

WEIGHS LESS THAN 17 lbs

NOT PAINTED TO SAVE WEIGHT & IMPROVE TASTE

ATHLETE ADOPTS SWALLOWING POSITION

U.K
ARRIVALS
GOLD
SILVER
BRONZE

'If I give you £10 will you go and discuss the Olympic bribes scandal somewhere else?'

OLYMPIC
BALLROOM DANCING
800m RELAY

5.9
5.7
6.0

GRAND PRIX
ESSO
ESSO

'We've put nicotine patches over the names of the tobacco companies'

'If you don't want to know how your marriage ends, look away now'

'I'm willing to work during England's World Cup matches'

'The World Cup makes them terribly nervous – it's best to keep them locked out'

'Come on, gentlemen, haven't you got offices to go to?'

RUGBY WORLD CUP

'If Tony Blair says golf is cool I'm damn well giving it up'

BOWLING
WORLD
ROCKED BY
"HALF OF
SHANDY"
SHAME

BRITISH
SPORTING
ACADEMY
PULL

TOSSING THE TV

SCOTTISH DANCING

TV PUT

BURNS NIGHT

'My name is Rex and I chase foxes'

C000181796

Strong
AT THE
broken places

CWR CWR, Waverley Abbey House, Waverley Lane, Farnham, Surrey GU9 8EP

Scripture quotations are taken from:
NIV, New International Version, © 1975, 1978, 1984, by International Bible Society.
NKJ, New King James Version, © 1979, 1980, 1982, Thomas Nelson, Inc., Publishers.
RSV, Revised Standard Version, © 1972, Thomas Nelson, Inc., Publishers.
Amplified, The Amplified Bible, © 1965, Zondervan Publishing House.
TLB, The Living Bible, © 1971, Tyndale House Publishers.
J.B. Phillips, The New Testament in Modern English, revised edition, © 1958, 1960, J.B. Phillips.
KJV, King James Version, © 1984, 1977, Thomas Nelson, Inc.
Moffat, The Bible. A New Translation, © 1950, 1952, 1953, 1954, James A.R. Moffat.
The Message, © 2002, Christian Art Publishers.

STRONG AT THE BROKEN PLACES
A compilation of excerpts from Every Day with Jesus by Selwyn Hughes 1982, 1984, 1986, 1989, 1993
compiled by Hermanda Steel

Concept development, editing, design and production by
Struik Christian Books Ltd
A division of New Holland Publishing (South Africa) (Pty) Ltd
(New Holland Publishing is a member of the Johnnic Publishing Group)
Cornelis Struik House
80 McKenzie Street
Cape Town 8001

Reg. No. 1971/00972/07

DTP by Bridgitte Chemaly
Cover design by Christian Jaggers
Cover photograph by Photo Access
Cover reproduction by Hirt & Carter Cape (Pty) Ltd
Reproduced, printed and bound by CTP Book Printers
PO Box 6060, Parow East 7501

ISBN 1 85345 262 9

SELWYN HUGHES

GRACE FOR EACH NEW DAY

Quiet Time

Have I sought you,
God,
only in the
pleasant places?
Looked for the
light of your Presence
on just the well lit roads?
Give me strength and
courage to
walk the dark road of
sacrifice and
suffering
leading to the
cemetery of self.
For it is only
there
that I may know
the
True
Brilliance
of
you.

SUSAN LENZKES
EDWJ Nov/Dec 1993

January / February

in a spiritual wilderness

March / April

the wounded healer

May / June

sufficient grace

July / August

strong at the broken places

September / October

live more abundantly

November / December

hinds' feet on high places

Never alone!

FOR READING AND MEDITATION – NEHEMIAH 9:13–21

'Because of your great compassion you did not abandon them in the desert.' (v.19: NIV)

Most Christians at some time or another find themselves in a spiritual wilderness. Who hasn't faced a period when the Christian life seems to go into reverse, prayer is difficult, joy seems to ebb, and the spiritual disciplines are more of a duty than a delight? Why does God allow, or perhaps put us into, such situations? What do we do when we find ourselves going through a 'desert experience'? That is the issue with which we must first come to grips.

I have been through a number of wilderness experiences in my life – times when I thought that God had abandoned me. But although I felt abandoned, in reality that was not so. If there is one thing I have learned in close on half a century of serving Christ, it is that in the case of every wilderness experience I have passed through, I was there because I needed to be there. I had to be willing to let go of a certain part of myself, and because of my unwillingness to lose anything I considered integral to my being, the wilderness was the place I needed to be.

Am I talking to someone who at this moment is in the midst of a wilderness experience? Or just entering it? Then listen carefully – you are there because you need to be there. Those who have never gone through a wilderness experience should keep in mind that at some point in the future they may well find themselves there, or come alongside someone who is there – hence the necessity to understand all we can about this strange spiritual phenomenon. To be forewarned is to be forearmed.

O Father, I realise many of the fears that arise within me are the result of my inability to understand your purposes. Unfold your truth to me daily through these meditations. Help me to learn the lessons of the wilderness. In Jesus' name. Amen.

FOR FURTHER STUDY – 1 Cor. 10:1–13; Ex. 14:14; Isa. 40:3–4, 45:2

1. How are we to view the experiences of the children of Israel?
2. What did God promise to do in the wilderness?

When God is not close

FOR READING AND MEDITATION – PSALM 51:1–19

'Restore to me the joy of your salvation…' (v.12: NIV)

We ended yesterday by referring to the wilderness experience as a 'strange spiritual phenomenon'. Throughout church history this is the exact term that many have used to describe it, and it is interesting to note that almost all of the spiritual giants, from St Augustine to C.S. Lewis, tell of going through such an experience. This leads to the question: what precisely is the 'wilderness experience'? How do we define it and what is its essential nature?

Before focusing on what it is, we pause to consider what it is not. First, it is not the loss and emptiness we feel in our souls when we have committed some grievous sin. I have often spoken to Christians who have told me, 'I am in a spiritual wilderness.' However, upon examination, it became clear that the spiritual barrenness they complained of was really the result of some sin they were unwilling to give up. It stands to reason that if we persist in known sin then a spiritual dislocation is going to take place between God and ourselves. The spiritually sensitive conscience, acting in the capacity of an observer, condemns the ego for wrong actions and a feeling of guilt arises, which produces in the soul a sense of spiritual estrangement. It is not that God moves away from us, but that we move away from God. As one person put it, 'If you no longer feel close to God – guess who moved!'

If persistent sin is involved it will feel as if we are in a spiritual wilderness, but it is important to realise that it is a wilderness of our own making. To get out of that wilderness we simply confess our sin, repent of it, break with it, and spiritual joy is soon restored.

Help me, dear Father, to understand the difference between a wilderness of my own choosing and a wilderness of your choosing. I want no sin to block or damage our relationship. May I ever be on the alert for this. In Jesus' name. Amen.

FOR FURTHER STUDY – James 1:12–15; 1 John 5:17; Num. 32:23

1. What does sin give birth to? / 2. What can we be sure of?

Wrong choices

FOR READING AND MEDITATION – 2 CORINTHIANS 6:1–18
'Do not be yoked together with unbelievers.' (v.14: NIV)

Yet another thing a wilderness experience is not is the hard and difficult time we sometimes go through because of the mismanagement of our affairs or as the result of bad decision-making. Some people I have known have said they were going through a wilderness experience (implying they were put into it by God) when really the difficult circumstances they were in came about because of poor choices.

I remember one young man telling me that his marriage had entered a wilderness experience. On being questioned about it he revealed that when planning to be married he had to make a choice between two women whom he loved equally – one a Christian, the other a non-Christian. He chose the non-Christian because he thought by so doing he could become instrumental in her conversion. That did not happen, however, and a few months after the wedding ceremony the marriage began to deteriorate. I pointed out to him, as gently as I could, that despite his noble intentions he had broken the clear command in Scripture that a believer should not be joined to an unbeliever. The wilderness he was in was a wilderness of his own making. Of course, God did not abandon him because of this, and after a time of genuine repentance he was restored spiritually, even though later his marriage ended in divorce.

If we make mistakes then we must admit to them and seek God's grace and wisdom in correcting them. Let us be careful, though, that we don't spiritualise them and pretend that we are suffering because of the will of God. Sometimes it is because of our own will, not the divine will, that we enter a spiritual wilderness. We must discern the difference.

Father, help me to see the difference between a wilderness experience of my own making and one that is allowed or arranged by you. Give me the strength to face up to my own mistakes or poor choices and to correct them. In Jesus' name I pray. Amen.

FOR FURTHER STUDY – Deut. 30:1–20; Josh. 24:15; 1 Kings 18:21
1. What proposition was put to the children of Israel? / 2. What was Joshua's response?

Developed and dynamic

FOR READING AND MEDITATION – MATTHEW 4:1–11

'Then the devil left him, and angels came and attended him.' (v. 11: NIV)

We must be careful to note that many situations we get into in life cause us a good deal of spiritual concern and perplexity, but not every one of these can be rightly described as a wilderness experience. The true wilderness experience is a prolonged or deeply intense period of trial and testing in which a particular providential purpose is being worked out.

In a sense, of course, and according to Romans 8:28, all situations we get into can be worked out for good, but the wilderness experience has about it distinctive characteristics which mark it out as being specially allowed of God. The wilderness experience is something God either arranges or allows us to enter; not, I hasten to add, because he wants to punish us, but in order to prune us. And he does this because he sees it is the only way he can bring his purposes to pass in our lives.

The passage before us today tells us that Jesus was 'led by the Spirit into the desert to be tempted by the devil'(verse 1). He was there because he needed to be there. Not, I must immediately make clear, in order for some deficiency to be removed (he knew no sin), but in order that what he had might be tested, and to demonstrate to the whole universe that it is possible to be in a wilderness and still not sin. Note, he went in 'full of the Holy Spirit' (Luke 4:1, NIV) and came out 'in the power of the Spirit' (verse 14). Fullness turned to power under the pressure of temptation. He came out different from when he went in. That is the purpose of the wilderness: to come out different from when we went in – different, developed, and dynamic.

Father, something within me shrinks from ever being found in a wilderness experience. The carnal part of me cries out, 'May I never be led into it.' But my spirit cries as did my Saviour, 'Nevertheless, not my will but thine be done.' Amen.

FOR FURTHER STUDY – Eph. 6:10–20; Heb. 4:12; Isa. 11:4

1. How did Jesus combat the devil in the wilderness? / 2. Why is armour alone inadequate?

So few friends

FOR READING AND MEDITATION – PSALM 30:1–12
'... when you hid your face, I was dismayed.' (v. 7: NIV)

Today we ask ourselves: how common is the wilderness experience in the life of God's people? I believe it is more common than we might think. When we open up the pages of the Old Testament, for instance, we see many who were caught up in the wilderness experience, and nowhere does this come through more clearly than in the book of Psalms.

In the psalm before us today, David refers to a time when God appeared to hide his face from him – sometimes a characteristic of the wilderness experience. In Psalm 44 the idea of God withdrawing his face comes across with even greater poignancy when the psalmist cries: 'Awake, O Lord! Why do you sleep? ... Why do you hide your face and forget our misery and oppression?' (verses 23, 24). Jeremiah was another who felt abandoned by God; in Jeremiah 20:7 he actually accuses God of having deceived him. Then of course there is what must be regarded as the classic example of the true wilderness experience – the suffering of God's servant, Job.

There must be some deep, divine purpose in an experience so common to the servants of God as this. What can it be? It cannot (as we said) be God's punishment for sin, as in the case of Job we read: 'In all this, Job did not sin by charging God with wrongdoing' (Job 1:22, NIV). If God withdraws because of sin we know what to do to bring him back again – confess, repent, and claim forgiveness. But if we do not know why he has withdrawn, how do we know how to receive him back again? It was such a moment of confusion that led St Teresa of Avila to say, 'It's no wonder, Lord, that you have so few friends, if you treat so many of them this way!'

My Father and my God, how I long for the kind of faith that trusts you even when it cannot trace you. The heights seem almost unattainable, but I know that grace will be given me to reach the top. Amen.

FOR FURTHER STUDY – Psa. 44:17–26; 2 Cor. 4:17–18

1. What does the psalmist appeal to in God?
2. How did Paul view his different circumstances?

The 'abundant' life

FOR READING AND MEDITATION – PHILIPPIANS 4:10–13

'I can do everything through him who gives me strength.' (v. 13: NIV)

Some Christians believe that the wilderness experience has no place in the life of believers today, as the promise of Jesus is this: 'I have come that they may have life, and have it to the full' (John 10:10, NIV). The whole idea of the wilderness experience, it is argued, is incompatible with these words, for they present a picture of abundant, vibrant, overcoming life that enables us to live in a state of perpetual spiritual exhilaration. We need never be concerned about getting into a spiritual wilderness because if Christ is within, his life will bubble up in constant, effervescent joy.

Well, that is not how I understand our Lord's words. When the Saviour said: 'I have come to give you life to the full,' he meant, I believe, that he would give us a quality of life which would sustain us in the midst of anything that comes.

That the life of Christ can and does exhilarate there can be no doubt, but we make a great mistake when we think that it will insulate us from ever feeling negative emotions. I heard a radio preacher say once that 'the abundant life of Christ operates on our negative emotions so that we just don't feel them any more'. What nonsense! The statement is both spiritually and psychologically naive. The abundant life, as I understand it, does not dampen down our negative emotions (sometimes because of our willingness to face reality we feel them even more keenly). Instead it flows underneath them and upholds us so that though we might experience pain, sometimes even deep pain, we are not destroyed by it, but find the strength and energy always to move on.

Lord Jesus, it was said of you that you were a Man of joy yet also a Man of sorrows and familiar with suffering. Help me understand that the two need not be incompatible. In Jesus' name I pray. Amen.

FOR FURTHER STUDY – 2 Cor. 9:1–8; Eph. 3:20; Phil. 4:19

1. What is God able to do? / 2. What did Paul assure the Philippians?

All things serve

FOR READING AND MEDITATION – JOHN 7:25–44

'Up to that time the Spirit had not been given, since Jesus had not yet been glorified.' (v. 39: NIV)

Another argument often used to refute the idea that Christians can find themselves in a spiritual wilderness is the fact that there are no New Testament evidences of people having to go through such an experience. All the illustrations of wilderness experiences, it is argued, are drawn from the Old Testament where the ministry of the Holy Spirit was occasional rather than perpetual, special rather than general. In New Testament times, say the proponents of this view, the Holy Spirit was given in all his fullness, and when we are baptised in the Spirit, his power and presence are perpetually with us, thus we need not expect any lean or barren times.

It is quite true that the ministry of the Holy Spirit in the New Testament is on a much higher plane than in the Old. This is because the Spirit had a clear channel through whom he could reveal himself and give himself – Jesus Christ. It is also true that we do not see individuals (such as the psalmist) crying out to God because he appears to have hidden his face. Clearly, power was released at Pentecost that seemed to lift people to new heights. However, we have to accept the fact that after a few decades this flood of power subsided, not, I hasten to add, because of a failure of resources, but because of a failure on the part of the Church to receive. When corporately or individually we do not allow the Spirit to invade us in the way he desires, then God has to institute other ways to draw us into the centre of his purposes. The wilderness experience (in my opinion) is one of those ways.

Father, help me grasp this fact that your plans and purposes can never be blocked or stymied. If you cannot bring about your intentions in one way then you will use another. All things serve – even the wilderness. Amen.

FOR FURTHER STUDY – Matt. 3:1–11; Luke 11:13; 24:49; Acts 1:8
1. What did John prophesy of Jesus? / 2. What did Jesus confirm?

Seven clear types

FOR READING AND MEDITATION – 2 CORINTHIANS 1:8–14

'But this happened that we might not rely on ourselves but on God...' (v. 9: NIV)

Now we start to consider in detail the question: what purpose does God have in allowing his children to enter a wilderness experience? As with most perplexing questions, it will help us to step back and try to gain as wide a perspective as possible before attempting an explanation.

Throughout the church's history writers and observers who have made a special study of this strange phenomenon – the wilderness experience – are generally agreed that it can be divided into seven types:

(1) Humiliation – a savage and plausible attack upon one's reputation in which lies are told and imputations made that sear the soul.
(2) Suffering – physical, mental, and spiritual, prolonged and undeserved.
(3) Bereavement – not so much the passing of those who are aged and ripe for heaven (though that can be a heavy trial), but of those who are young and whose deaths appear to be most untimely.
(4) Estrangement – the distance that comes through the breaking of close relationships with one's family and friends.
(5) Doubt – the dark ravine through which some have to pass and where faith often lies torn and bleeding.
(6) Dereliction – the awful sense of being forsaken by God.
(7) Failure – perhaps even the failure of one's life's work.

These seven experiences form the fiercest tests of life, and there can be little doubt that they are the hardest things which mortal men and women are called upon to bear. We shall never understand on earth the full purpose of this type of testing, but even on earth we can understand that purpose lies behind it. Trusting that purpose is not easy, but it is what every child of God is called to do.

O Father, whatever tests you subject me to, help me never to let go in the darkness of what I have discovered in the light. May my trust always be in you. In Christ's name I ask it. Amen.

FOR FURTHER STUDY – Deut. 8:1–20, 13:1–5

1. How did Moses review the wilderness experience? / 2. What was his warning?

Humiliated!

FOR READING AND MEDITATION – ACTS 8:26–40

'In his humiliation he was deprived of justice…' (v. 33: NIV)

We look now at the first of what we called yesterday 'the fierce tests on life' – humiliation. It was said of our Lord that he 'made himself of no reputation' (Phil. 2:7, AV), and many of his servants have been called to follow him there.

Humiliation, according to the dictionary, is 'an injury to someone's dignity or self-respect'. Hardly a person reading these lines has not experienced this to one degree or another, and some may be going through a time of deep and prolonged humiliation at this very moment.

Let me remind you of one of God's servants who knew more humiliation than most – John Wesley, the founder of Methodism. As a young man he was ordained into the Church of England, but after his heart was 'strangely warmed', his evangelistic fervour resulted in him becoming ostracised by many members of the clergy and excluded from the pulpits of a large number of parish churches. He was then faced with the choice of either giving up preaching or preaching in the market places and fields. His biographers say that when confronted by this possibility he went through a torment of soul that is impossible to describe. To his ordered and reverent mind there was something vulgar about taking worship out into the open air. The idea offended him deeply, but he knew that this was the only course left to him. When a friend remonstrated with him and appealed to him not to take his ministry to the public places on the basis that he ought to have some respect for his good name, Wesley replied, 'When I gave my all to God I did not withhold my reputation.' He took to the open air, saying, 'I consented to be more vile.'

Father, I ask myself: have I given my everything to you – including my reputation? Help me be more concerned with bringing glory to your name and less to mine. For Christ's sake. Amen.

FOR FURTHER STUDY – Phil. 2:1–11; 1 Cor. 1:28–29; James 4:10

1. What attitude should we take?
2. What is the difference between humility and humiliation?

There's a saint about!

FOR READING AND MEDITATION – PROVERBS 20:1–13
'Many a man claims to have unfailing love, but a faithful man who can find?' (v. 6: NIV)

Humiliation can be one of the most distressing experiences of life, especially prolonged humiliation. Yet multitudes of men and women who have been followers of Christ have had to endure it.

Have you ever heard of the *Curé d'Ars*? He was a godly French priest who, many years ago, was sent to the little village of Ars. The village had sunk low in its morals and had a bad reputation throughout the whole of the area. Sunday services were ignored by most of the villagers, the dance halls were full, ignorance was widespread, foul language was common in the streets, and drunkenness, blasphemy and lying were all features of the villagers' lives. The faithful priest instantly declared war on this wickedness, but when he did, the villagers struck back by besmirching his reputation. They spread slanderous stories about him, saying he attracted girls to his house for immoral purposes and spent his nights in debauchery. He was the subject of obscene songs and scurrilous letters. A prostitute paraded under his window night after night, accusing him in the filthiest language of being the father of her child.

It was all lies, of course, but the faithful man of God bore it with courage, with dignity and with grace. The humiliation lasted ten years, but eventually he won. God used his unwavering faith in a wonderful way and the time came when the dance halls closed down, foul language was heard no more in the streets and the churches were crowded with worshippers. When congratulated by a visitor from Paris on the atmosphere of the village, a resident said, 'There are some things you cannot do when there is a saint about.'

O Father, how I long that under test I might exhibit a faithfulness such as this. If ever my reputation is besmirched because of my love for you may the same grace be mine. In Jesus' name I ask it. Amen.

FOR FURTHER STUDY – 1 Cor. 4:1–13; 1 Pet. 3:13–22; 1 Tim. 5:14
1. How did Paul describe his humiliation? / 2. How are we to deal with slander?

What's your option?

FOR READING AND MEDITATION – JOB 23:1–17

'I would state my case before him and fill my mouth with arguments.' (v. 4: NIV)

A couple of days ago I said that my words might well be read by some who at this very moment are going through a time of deep and prolonged humiliation. Perhaps there has been a savage and plausible attack upon your reputation and you are reeling under the blows. In such times as this, the question inevitably arises: why? I do not believe it is wrong to ask questions like this when one is under great pressure, as long as we realise that God will not necessarily answer them. This, of course, drives some Christians to even greater depths of frustration and they accuse God of being inconsiderate and uncaring.

Perhaps no one has known more deeply the feelings that one goes through when suffering humiliation than God's servant, Job. He asked one question over and over again: why, God, why? Did God answer his question? Not entirely. In the passage before us today Job has prepared his case to present to God, but later (Chapter 38) he is forestalled by the questions God asks of him. The interesting thing is that God never appears to answer Job's questions. Instead he gives him something better; He rewards him with a richer sense of his presence. This is why Job says subsequently: 'My ears had heard of you but now my eyes have seen you' (Job 42:5).

St Augustine, that great saint of the fourth and fifth centuries, said to a person who was going through some deep waters and wanted God to give him answers, 'If God gave you the option of answering all your questions or giving you a richer sense of his presence, which would you choose?' I know what I would choose. What about you?

Gracious God and Father, to have clear answers satisfies my intellect, but to have your presence satisfies my heart. Help me understand I can handle any darkness or confusion providing I feel you strongly at my side. Amen.

FOR FURTHER STUDY – Isa. 43:1–5; Gen. 28:15; Isa. 54:10

1. What did God promise the children of Israel?
2. What are we promised instead of answers?

Grace in the wilderness

FOR READING AND MEDITATION – MATTHEW 5:38–48

'… I tell you, Love your enemies and pray for those who persecute you…' (v. 44: NIV)

Sooner or later in this hard world everyone experiences a degree of humiliation, but the humiliation that characterises the true wilderness experience is not something that is occasional; rather, it is something deep, constant, and unbroken. I have often heard observers say of a person who was walking through this type of wilderness, 'How can he put up with it?' The answer is, of course, that grace is available to those in such a situation that is not felt (and sometimes not even understood) by those who look on.

Here in Britain many are familiar with the children's homes known as *Barnado's*. However, not many know that Dr Barnado was once a medical student in the East End of London who sold Bibles to help meet his expenses. He was a devout Christian, but his ideas of helping the orphaned didn't go down very well with some sections of the community. They labelled him a 'do-gooder' and continually sought to humiliate him. On one occasion as he entered a public house (beer tavern) to sell Bibles, some drunken ruffians set on him and flung him to the ground. Then they grabbed a table and, placing it upside-down on his prostrated body, began to dance a tattoo. When he was removed unconscious to his lodgings, he was bruised from head to foot and had two broken ribs. It was six weeks before he could move again. However, when pressed by his friends to prosecute his assailants he replied, 'I have begun with the Gospel, and I am determined not to end with the law.' In the wilderness of humiliation he found grace to put the words of our text today into operation.

Father, I see my greatest danger is not anti-Christian but sub-Christian – living below your standards instead of in accordance with them. Help me understand that your grace can never fail, no matter what my circumstances. In Jesus' name I ask it. Amen.

FOR FURTHER STUDY – Prov. 25:1–21; Ex. 23:5; Matt. 5:44; Luke 6:35; 1 Thess. 5:15

1. How are we to relate to our enemy? / 2. What are we to make sure of?

Unrelieved suffering

FOR READING AND MEDITATION – 2 CORINTHIANS 12:1–10
'Three times I pleaded with the Lord to take [a thorn in my flesh] away from me.
(v. 8: NIV)

The second type of wilderness experience we look at is that of suffering. I am referring now to suffering in its broadest categories: physical, mental and spiritual; prolonged, undeserved and bitter. Every kind of suffering has fallen at some time on the people of God, and the way they have endured it is a testimony to their courage and the enabling power of the Holy Spirit.

Take first the question of physical suffering. Can anything be harder to bear? Studdart Kennedy, a World War I army chaplain, used to say that anyone who was undisturbed by the problem of physical sickness and infirmity was showing symptoms of one of two things: a hardening of the heart or a softening of the brain. Recognising the fact that God can and does heal, there are, however, still multitudes of his children who are racked by pain and enduring prolonged sickness. Finding oneself in a wilderness such as this can be a bitter blow. And there are no easy solutions either. Some people simplistically suggest that God would cure disease right away if only the person concerned would 'believe'. Is it possible they do not know that a number of the world's greatest saints have had to walk this way?

Many years ago I experienced a miraculous healing that brought me back from death's door, yet my own wife (a saint if ever there was one) fought a long and painful battle with cancer. All thinking people are disturbed by the problem of physical suffering, but that does not stop us from enjoying the succour of Christ in the midst of the problem. Suffering is a wilderness many would rather not be delivered from if the alternative is to walk through life without him.

O Father, while I am disturbed by the problem of suffering, I am not destroyed by it. My trust in you upholds me in everything. Deepen that trust, no matter what it takes. In Jesus' name. Amen.

FOR FURTHER STUDY – 1 Tim. 5:17–23; Gal. 4:12–14; Heb. 4:15

1. What did Timothy experience?
2. What caused Paul to first preach the gospel to the Galatians?

The pain of the mind

FOR READING AND MEDITATION – JOB 1:1–22

'The Lord gave and the Lord has taken away; may the name of the Lord be praised.' (v. 21: NIV)

Yesterday we looked at what it is like to find oneself in a wilderness of prolonged sickness and physical suffering. Can anything, we asked, be harder to bear? Yes, say some – mental and emotional suffering. Those who suffer in this way maintain they would exchange mental and emotional suffering for physical suffering any day. The great fear that besets people undergoing this type of suffering is the fear that they might lose their mind.

J.B. Phillips, whose translation of the New Testament is one of my favourites, went through serious bouts of depression, which apparently did not result from biological causes; some depression does. On one occasion he is reported to have said that he did not know why God allowed him to suffer in this way, but he knew that the suffering had refined his soul and produced in him a sensitivity of spirit that possibly nothing else could have created. Dr Larry Crabb, a well-known Christian psychologist, in his latest book, *Finding God*, confesses to experiencing occasional bouts of depression, but says he sees it not as something to explain but something to get through with the help of God.

How do Christians handle what is often called 'the pain of the mind' – mental and emotional suffering? They believe God is with them in the suffering – all the time. Because the universe is God's, they regard him as taking ultimate responsibility for whatever happens. They do not see events as happening apart from God, nor put undue stress on the difference between what God actually does and what he allows. They find God even in what he permits, and are convinced that anything that happens, rightly met with God, is productive of good.

O Father, help me lay hold on this strategy your saints down the ages have used to endure all types of suffering, namely that you allow only what you can use. All things, when met with you, can be turned to good. Thank you, Father. Amen.

FOR FURTHER STUDY – Matt. 26:36–46; John 18:11; Luke 22:44

1. What did Jesus pray for three times?
2. How did Jesus describe the experience of his soul?

From the Father's hand

FOR READING AND MEDITATION – MATTHEW 26:36–46

'"My Father, if it is not possible for this cup to be taken away unless I drink it, may your will be done."' (v. 42: NIV)

We have looked briefly at the area of physical and mental suffering; now we look at spiritual suffering. The deepest form of spiritual suffering we can experience in this life, so I believe, is the type our Lord went through in the Garden of Gethsemane. Almost every Christian finds himself or herself at some time or another in a Gethsemane, and while we do not experience exactly what our Lord suffered, we experience something similar, albeit to a lesser degree. I refer to those occasions, brief or prolonged, when one is conscious that God is leading in a direction from which the flesh and one's whole nature shrinks, and when one cries out, 'Father, if it is possible, let this cup pass from me.'

Perhaps this is where you are right now. How are you handling your time in the wilderness? Well, let me remind you of how the Lord handled his time there. After grappling with the issue of how to face the ordeal of Calvary and all that it meant in terms of his separation from God, he eventually said: 'The cup which my Father hath given me, shall I not drink it?' (John 18:11, AV) The principle that sustained him was this: one can transform the contents of a cup if one can see the hand from which one takes it. It was as if our Lord was saying, 'I have a cup of bitterness to drink. If I must drink it, I will not take it from Judas, from Pilate, from Caiphas, from the people … I will take it only from my Father. The cup which my father hath given me …'

However bitter the cup that a life of surrender to the will of God may be, the Christian must learn to take it from the Father's hand. Almost the whole secret of triumph over spiritual suffering lies right there.

O Father, whenever I next find myself in a spiritual Gethsemane, struggling to make the choice between comfort or challenge, hardship or happiness, help me see not just the contents of the cup but the hand that holds it. In Jesus' name I pray. Amen.

FOR FURTHER STUDY – Num. 11:4–15; 1 Kings 19:1–21; Jer. 15:10; Josh. 7:7

1. Who were some of the Bible characters who knew times of spiritual despondency?
2. How did God deal with them?

God's waves and breakers

FOR READING AND MEDITATION – PSALM 42:1–11
'… all your waves and breakers have swept over me.' (v. 7: NIV)

It seems strange to some that God's beloved children have to endure suffering. Surely to be beloved by the Almighty implies safety, security, and protection! Not necessarily so. As God's children we are not kept from suffering; we are kept in it. Every kind of suffering has fallen upon the people of God, physical, mental, and spiritual. Simply to read Paul's catalogue of suffering in 2 Corinthians 11:23–27 is to be lost in wonder, love, and praise. Toils, imprisonments, beatings, stoning, shipwrecks, treachery, hunger, thirst, cold and nakedness – he knew them all. Yet, like the heroes of faith in Hebrews 11, he endured 'because he saw him who is invisible' (Heb. 11:27, NIV).

Early on in my Christian life my pastor pointed me to the text that is before us today and explained it in such a way that it has never left me. He said, 'Notice the psalmist did not declare, "All the waves … have swept over me", but: "All your waves … have swept over me".' He went on to say that when the storm smote the psalmist he refused to accept it just as a storm. He found God in it. With mighty faith he plants God at its heart, and as the icy green waters engulf him he cries: 'All your waves and breakers have swept over me.' Somewhere, in the midst of the awful experience that the psalmist went through, he believed there was a loving and beneficent purpose at work. Hence they were God's waves and God's breakers.

Paul learned the same secret. When in prison he called himself a 'prisoner of Jesus Christ'. In reality he was a prisoner of Nero, but there was much more to it than that. He found God in the situation. After that he could suffer without fretting and endure with patience, even joy.

O Father, how I long to come to the place where I respond to every storm that comes my way with the words and the meaning of the psalmist: 'All your waves and breakers have swept over me.' Help me to get there. In Jesus' name. Amen.

FOR FURTHER STUDY – James 1:1–8; Rom. 12:12; 2 Cor. 1:3–7

1. How does James say we are to handle trials?
2. What can flow to others as a result of our troubles?

Untimely passing

FOR READING AND MEDITATION – 1 CORINTHIANS 15:12–28

'The last enemy to be destroyed is death.' (v. 26: NIV)

Another type of wilderness that Christians sometimes experience is the wilderness of bereavement. The bereavement under consideration here is not so much the loss of loved ones who are well advanced in years and ripe for heaven (though that can be a devastating experience), but more the loss of those whose death, humanly speaking, appears as we say 'most untimely'. I refer to the loss of a child – an only child or one of several – the death of a young man or young woman, or a baby, born or unborn. When our loved ones reach their senior years we are more ready for the parting that death brings. As the poet put it, 'The mellow fruit falls and we have grace to bear the pang.' If they are Christians the blow is softened by the fact that we shall meet again around the eternal throne.

The death of a child or a young person, however, is quite different. To stand at the grave of a young person, to see one's dreams buried and trust God through the gathering dark is not easy. Can Jesus sustain a breaking heart and reeling brain in an hour like that? Yes, he can; I have seen him do it on many occasions. The very first funeral I conducted after coming into the ministry was of a darling four-year-old girl who had been cut down by poliomyelitis. As a young minister I was heartbroken and did not know what to say to the parents, who were also my close friends. In the end they ministered to me. I shall never forget their words, 'But for Jesus, we would want to die at the side of her grave.'

But for Jesus! Ah, that's the secret. When other helpers fail and comforts flee – there is always Jesus!

Father, I marvel at the way you come to us at the crisis hour to comfort us in our disappointments, strengthen us to take the next step and bar the way to cynicism. But for Jesus – where would we be? I am so glad that I am yours and you are mine. Amen.

FOR FURTHER STUDY – Heb. 4:1–16; 1 Cor. 15:54–56; 1 Thess. 4:13–16

1. What is available in times of great need? / 2. How does Paul describe death?

Divine grace at work!

FOR READING AND MEDITATION – HEBREWS 4:1–16

'Let us then approach the throne of grace… that we may… find grace to help us in our time of need.' (v. 16: NIV)

We said yesterday that all bereavement is hard to bear, but the loss of a young child or young adult cut off in the prime of life gets close to being totally unbearable. To live on, when one's hopes have withered and life seems devoid of purpose, is something many find extremely difficult. Difficult, but with God's grace, not impossible. The testimony of God's people in all ages is that even in this wilderness grace can flow in ever-increasing measure.

At the funeral I referred to yesterday – the first one I ever conducted – I was so heartbroken that I was unable to give my prepared address. The words seem to dry up inside me and I wept copious tears. I apologised to the mourners but the parents brushed aside my apology and said, 'Your tears meant more to us than the most eloquent sermon you could ever have given.'

To this day the death of a child is something that I find difficult to come to terms with. Once I watched a couple prepare their little child for death, and the privilege of overhearing their conversation in those last moments is something I will ever be grateful for. As the little one entered the valley of the shadow of death the parents held her hand and said, 'Jesus will be there waiting for you on the other side. Tell him we will be coming soon… look out for us.' Then in the last few moments, when speech was beyond her, the parents held her gaze by their blazing eyes, and with her eyes wide open, the river was crossed. As I heard them pray and utter the words: 'The Lord gave, the Lord has taken away, blessed be the name of the Lord,' I caught my breath and said to myself, 'Divine grace, once again, is doing its wondrous work.'

Gracious God and loving heavenly Father, how can I ever sufficiently thank you that there is no wilderness into which you cannot enter. Especially be with those who are in the wilderness of bereavement this day I pray. In Jesus' name. Amen.

FOR FURTHER STUDY – 1 Tim. 1:1–14; 2 Tim. 2:1; Titus 3:7

1. What did Paul declare to Timothy? / 2. What was Paul's encouragement to Timothy?

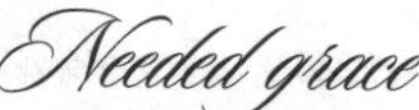

FOR READING AND MEDITATION – 1 THESSALONIANS 4:1–18

'Brothers, we do not want you to … grieve like the rest of men, who have no hope.' (v. 13: NIV)

However fierce the trial that comes when we are called to walk through the wilderness of bereavement, one thing is sure – divine grace follows us every step of the way. We would all prefer not to have to enter such a wilderness, but when we do we have the guarantee that we will find 'needed grace for needed moments'.

It might seem invidious to some to imply that one bereavement is more bitter than another, but it seems to me that no desolation is quite so terrible as that which falls upon a young husband whose wife dies at the price of motherhood. The famous missionary John G. Paton, whom God called to the New Hebrides in the South Pacific, was in this position. He went to the island of Tanna, and there, on a distant station, his wife died in giving birth to a son, and seventeen days later the baby died too. He dug their grave with his own hands, not far from the house, and despite his breaking heart he covered it with coral blocks and made it as beautiful as he could. Did God provide him with grace in such a wilderness? Listen to what he said, 'I was never altogether forsaken. The ever-merciful Lord sustained me, to lay the precious dust of my beloved ones in the same quiet grave dug for them close at the end of the house. Whensoever Tanna turns to the Lord and is won for Christ, men in after years will find the memory of that spot still green, where, with ceaseless prayers and tears, I claimed that land for God in which I had buried my dead with faith and hope.'[7]

Note the words, 'I was not altogether forsaken'. Clearly he was desolated, but not destroyed. And why? He found needed grace for his needed moment.

Dear Father, the hardness and severity of life sometimes overwhelms me. But in such moments hold me close to you I pray, so that I might just feel you there. This is all I ask. In Jesus' name. Amen.

FOR FURTHER STUDY – Psa. 37:1–25; 2. Cor. 4:8–9

1. What was the psalmist's observation? / 2. What was Paul's testimony?

Streams in the desert

FOR READING AND MEDITATION – ISAIAH 35:1–10

'Water will gush forth in the wilderness and streams in the desert.' (v. 6: NIV)

We spend one more day discussing the wilderness experience that comes to those who lose a loved one in what we call 'an untimely death'. The desolation that strikes the soul when called to pass through this type of wilderness is largely unimaginable to those who have never had to walk this flinty way. But neither is it possible to imagine the depth and degree of grace that God provides on occasions like this, for grace can only be experienced, not imagined. C.S. Lewis once said, 'You will never know how much confidence you have in a rope until you are hanging by it.'

Whatever we know or believe about grace, we will never know it in all its fullness until we are obliged to draw upon it as our sole source of sustenance. And the testimony of believers everywhere is that divine grace, like divine love, never fails. Our God is expert at providing streams in the desert. Though we would prefer to avoid hard and desolating experiences, one thing is sure – God always steps in to provide us with the strength to carry on.

If this were simply a theory and not fact then, believe me, I would not have written about it or preached about it for the last forty years. For I am not interested in fine-spun spiritual theories; I am interested only in facts. There are many spiritual facts that cause me considerable, even constant, amazement, but one of the greatest is without doubt the truth, as we said the other day, that God supplies 'needed grace for needed moments'. We don't get 'needed' grace before the event, nor even after the event, but we can definitely count on it being there in the event!

O God, if only I can get hold of this truth, really get hold of it, then I see it will enable me to approach life in the confidence that I am more than a match for anything. For you will never guide me to a place where grace cannot uphold me. Hallelujah!

FOR FURTHER STUDY – Isa. 40:1–31, 41:10; Eph. 3:16

1. What happens when our hope is in the Lord?
2. Echo Paul's prayer for someone struggling today.

I have no son

FOR READING AND MEDITATION – PSALM 27:1–14

'Though my father and mother forsake me, the Lord will receive me.' (v. 10: NIV)

We come now to another type of fiery trial or wilderness experience some Christians are called upon to face – the wilderness of estrangement. By this I mean the severance of close family ties or friendships through treachery or misunderstanding. Everyone knows that the most vulnerable part of human nature is our affections, and some of the sharpest pains we must bear come from those situations when, perhaps from no fault of our own, we are estranged from our family and our friends.

On one of my visits to Madras, India, a saintly old man told me of the pain he experienced when, as the only son, he was cut off from his family after becoming a Christian. He tried to be reconciled and continually kept in touch with them by sending them cards and letters and gifts. One day he heard his mother was dying, and so he made his way from Madras to the town of Trivandrum, hundreds of miles away, determined to make a final attempt at reconciliation. When he finally arrived at his parents' home, the rest of the family blocked his entrance. So in desperation he called out to his mother through the doorway, 'Mother, it's me ... your son.' He paused for a few moments and wondering if he had been heard, shouted even more loudly, 'Mother, it's me ... your son.' Back came the reply that sent a shiver into his soul, 'Go away ... I have no son.'

There will be many reading these lines today who know the pain of estrangement in tender relationships. But most, I imagine, will have found also that painful though such estrangement is, the untrustworthiness of human affection has not filched from them their trust in God.

My Father and my God, the way of estrangement is not the way I would choose to walk. But if because of my commitment to you I am called to walk it, may the promise you gave to the psalmist be true also for me. In Jesus' name I pray. Amen.

FOR FURTHER STUDY – Psa. 23:1–6; Ex. 33:14; Heb. 13:5

1. What assurance did the psalmist carry? / 2. What is the assurance of the believer?

A tough decision

FOR READING AND MEDITATION – MATTHEW 10:32–42

'Anyone who loves his father or mother... son or daughter more than me is not worthy of me...' (v. 37: NIV)

One of the biggest burdens Christians can carry is created when their commitment to Christ brings about a separation between them and their family or friends. It is bad enough to be estranged, but to be the one who provokes the estrangement because of a strong stand for Christ and his principles is particularly hard.

For some reading our text today the lines will have a terrible and solemn meaning: 'Anyone who loves his father or mother ... son or daughter more than me is not worthy of me.' Am I talking to some right now, I wonder, whose commitment to Christ has involved them in estrangement from their loved ones? It's a thorny path to walk, isn't it? Non-Christians find it difficult, even impossible, to understand how any person can take a position that causes disruption in family relationships.

Consider this problem, for example: an unmarried young man or woman brings a boyfriend or girlfriend to the parental home and expects to sleep together, explaining that this is what they do outside the home anyway. What are Christian parents to do? Close their eyes to the situation in the pursuit of good relationships, or insist firmly but lovingly that the home is dedicated to Christ and they cannot permit things to go on that violate his standards? It's a difficult and painful situation for godly parents to face, but in today's moral climate this is the predicament many parents find themselves in. And those who are unwilling to compromise what they believe is an important biblical and moral issue often then find themselves facing an even greater pain – the pain of estrangement.

O God, hold me fast if ever I have to take a stand for you and against those of my loved ones who would encourage me to compromise. Help me see that compromised Christianity is no Christianity. In Jesus' name I pray.

FOR FURTHER STUDY – Matt. 6:25–34; Luke 14:26–33; John 8:31

1. What is the cost of discipleship? / 2. How do we show we are really Christ's disciples?

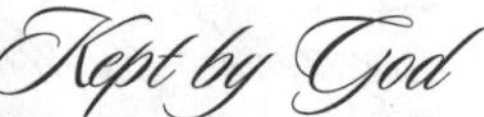

Kept by God

FOR READING AND MEDITATION – LUKE 14:15–35

'If anyone comes to me and does not hate his father and mother, his wife and children ... he cannot be my disciple.' (v. 26: NIV)

We are saying that when Christians commit themselves to giving (as Oswald Chambers put it) 'the utmost for his Highest' and will not compromise with what they know clearly to be sin, it sometimes results in the disturbance of other people's consciences to such a degree that it provokes estrangement. And when that estrangement includes their nearest and dearest, it produces one of the bitterest pangs known to the human spirit.

John Bunyan is a classic example of this. Incarcerated for preaching the gospel, he was told, 'Promise not to preach and you can leave prison today.' He stoutly replied, 'If you let me out today, I shall preach again tomorrow.' But Bunyan's enemies never shook him; it was his friends who came closest to shaking him. Some of them said, 'Your concern about your conscience is very beautiful ... but what about your wife and children? Who has to care for them? And what, in particular, about your blind daughter, Mary?' The decision was not an easy one for John Bunyan to make. Some would argue that his family should have come first and preaching second – and they would have a point. But Bunyan was adamant; he believed that he was at a turning point in history when to compromise on the importance of preaching would have had a deleterious effect on future generations.

It was said by one of Bunyan's biographers that after a visit from a friend who tried to get him to put his family first, Bunyan felt in his cell the shadow of Giant Despair. He fell to his knees, praying that God would keep him faithful. God did keep him faithful, and threw in *Pilgrim's Progress* as well.

O Father, when I see the commitment that some of your past disciples have made to you, I am forced to reconsider the depth and degree of my own. I want to be a worthy follower of you, dear Master. Strengthen me afresh by your Holy Spirit's power. Amen.

FOR FURTHER STUDY – John 6: 53–70; Mark 8:29; Luke 9:20

1. What happened to some of the early followers?
2. How did Peter respond to Christ's question?

Regarded as dead

FOR READING AND MEDITATION – JOHN 12:20–26

'My father will honour the one who serves me.' (v. 26: NIV)

We spend one more day discussing the wilderness of estrangement – the severe testing that some go through when their commitment to the Saviour causes those they love to turn away in feeling or affection.

None know the hardness of this flinty way more than those who turn from Judaism to Christ. In one church I pastored, a young Jewish girl surrendered her life to Christ. When I encouraged her (on the basis of Romans 8:9) to tell someone that she had become a Christian, she asked, 'Does that mean I have to tell my family as well?' I knew what underlay her question, for some Jewish families disinherit family members who become Christians. I said, 'The decision must be yours, but really I don't think you will be happy being one of Christ's secret disciples.' She thought it over for a few days and then decided to tell her family she had become a committed Christian. They were shocked by the news and without even giving her an opportunity to recant, which is the usual response of Jewish families to this problem (though of course she would not have done so anyway), they decided not to disinherit her, but to regard her as dead. They printed funeral cards edged in black and sent them to all the other members of the family, saying that their daughter had died in mysterious circumstances.

Few are called to walk through a wilderness as harsh as this, but this young girl found, as millions of others have found that while there is such a thing as human estrangement, there is no such thing as divine estrangement. Walking hand in hand with Jesus she became an evangelist and has since led hundreds to Christ.

O God, I pray today for all those who because of their commitment to you are estranged by their families and their friends. May the strength of the whole family of God be drawn around them in a special way this day. In Jesus' name I ask it. Amen.

FOR FURTHER STUDY – John 12:37–43, 19:38, 3:1–2; Matt. 10:1–42

1. What does Christ call us to do? / 2. Why did some early disciples seek to remain secret?

Degrees of doubt

FOR READING AND MEDITATION – MATTHEW 28:1–20

'When they saw him, they worshipped him; but some doubted.' (v. 17: NIV)

The next type of wilderness experience we look at is that of doubt. I have discovered over the years that there are different degrees of doubt. First, there is what I call mild doubt. This is the kind that forces people to reflect on things but does not rob them of sleep. Then there is strong doubt – the kind that causes people to ask such questions as, 'Does God really answer prayer?' 'Can the Bible be trusted?' 'Is God really in control of the universe?'... and so on. People generally learn to cope with mild doubts and strong doubts by deciding these things have to be accepted by faith anyway, and they relegate the doubts to a part of the mind where they are temporarily forgotten.

The third category is what I call serious doubts – doubts about the very existence of God, the distinction between right and wrong, the purpose of the universe, the validity of one's own thinking, whether or not there is meaning in all things, one's own separateness and existence as a person, etc. That is doubt – deep, dark, and awful. People who experience mild doubt or even strong doubt may go through some struggles, even deep struggles, but really they are only in the kindergarten of doubt when compared to those whose doubts are serious.

Doubt is not serious when it remains speculative and fleeting; it is serious only when it grips you and holds you prisoner for weeks, and months, and perhaps even years. This is the kind of doubt I am speaking of when I talk of being in a wilderness of doubt. Can God keep us faithful when assailed by serious doubts? I am bold to say that the testimony of the saints down throughout the ages is – he can.

O Father, grant if it be possible that the disease of doubt may never enter my system. But if it does, teach me how to doubt my doubts and believe my beliefs. In Jesus' name I pray. Amen.

FOR FURTHER STUDY – John 1:19–34, 3:22–36; Matt. 11:1–14

1. What did John proclaim? / 2. What point did John reach?

Advocates for honesty

FOR READING AND MEDITATION – PSALM 139:1–24

'Search me, O God, and know my heart; test me and know my anxious thoughts.' (v. 23: NIV)

Those who wander in a wilderness of doubt – serious doubt – walk a hard and difficult path. It is a path that I am grateful I have not had to walk. My own doubts have been mostly mild, sometimes strong, but thankfully never serious.

Some Christians I have come across have told me that they have never had a single doubt about spiritual things since the day of their conversion. I have learned to divide these people into two groups – those in whose hearts it seems impossible for doubt to grow, and those whose personalities are so rigid they never can allow themselves to feel honest doubt. Their faith could never survive doubt so they never allow themselves to feel it.

In recent years I have written frequently about the dangers of pushing things out of awareness and the denial of reality, and I do so again because I think it is one of the most common problems to be found among believers anywhere. Doubt pushed into the unconscious and not faced is harmful. It will most surely leak out and present itself in a hundred different ways, and one of its most obvious guises is that of fanaticism. I like what author H.A. Williams has written about this, 'All fanaticism,' he says, 'is a strategy to prevent doubt from becoming conscious.' When I was a pastor I noticed that the people who tended to be fanatical about their faith, or hysterical in their praise, were the people who confessed in the counselling room to having the deepest doubts. If we don't face our doubts then we live as unreal people. Pretence is never helpful. This does not mean we are advocates for doubt – it means we are advocates for honesty.

O God, help me see that when I have you as my Shield and my Strength there is never anything that goes on inside me that cannot be faced. Make me an honest person – with others and also with myself. In Jesus' name. Amen.

FOR FURTHER STUDY – Psa. 51:1–6; 1 Chron. 28:9; Jer. 17:10

1. What realisation did the psalmist come to?
2. What must we allow God to continually do?

The divine perspective

FOR READING AND MEDITATION – PSALM 73:1–28

'… I entered the sanctuary of God; then I understood their final destiny.' (v. 17: NIV)

Not all Christians, as we have said, find themselves in a wilderness of doubt, but many do. Sometimes they have to toil hard in circumstances God could alter and which on the surface appear to contradict everything they have been told or taught to others. Yet they have to go on working though he gives no sign.

Some time ago I talked to a missionary from Ethiopia who told me some of the awful suffering he witnessed when, during a period of heavy rains, a river changed course and hundreds were swept into eternity. When the weather changes, causing a river to surge in a different direction, and hundreds die, one cannot blame the sins of the people for that. So where does one lay the blame? Is God really as loving as he makes himself out to be? The missionary from Ethiopia, whose task it was to proclaim the love of God after witnessing the death of hundreds, told me, 'I wondered whether I would ever preach again, my doubts were so strong. But God gave me a vision of the cross and it reassured me that the God I served really was Love, and that one day in a bigger framework of reference an explanation would be given me that would satisfy my every demand.'

There will be many reading these lines today in different parts of the world who are being tested in various ways. Some, like the psalmist in the passage before us today, will be tested by the prosperity of the wicked, others with a failure to find a life purpose, and some by the presence of disease and cancers and mental illness. When whipped by doubt, we must do what the psalmist did – go to the place of prayer and ask God to help us see things from the divine perspective.

Father, I know that if I could see everything as you see it then no doubts would ever lodge in my heart. Help me hold on to the cross, for that is the place where you have revealed your heart. A God who would die for me has got to be trusted. Amen.

FOR FURTHER STUDY – 1 Cor. 13:1–12; Zeph. 3:5; Jer. 12:1

1. How does Paul express the way we view things?
2. Why did Jeremiah feel he could question God?

Faith is the victory!

FOR READING AND MEDITATION – ROMANS 3:1–18

'Let God be true, and every man a liar.' (v. 4: NIV)

Today we ask ourselves: how do people keep going when they find themselves in a wilderness of doubt? A study of the biographies of Christians who have been assailed by doubts reveals three things. First, they faced their doubts. They didn't tell themselves, 'Good Christians don't have doubts' and then pretend they were non-existent. No problem can ever be properly dealt with unless it is faced. John Bunyan speaks of 'being much tumbled up and down in [his] thoughts.' He was aware of his doubts and admitted them. This is the first step to the solution of any issue, for a problem has to be exposed before it can be resolved.

Second, they used their doubts. Doubts can be valuable if they force the one who has them to search for deeper and more meaningful answers. Almost all the saints of the past who have been plagued by doubt tell us that as they pursued their doubts and got underneath them, they discovered some exciting beliefs.

Third, they surrendered their doubts. Those who have triumphed over doubt have one great testimony – they laid their doubts alongside the Word of God and surrendered them into his hands. They said in effect, 'Anything that contradicts the Word of God is a lie.' Thus they learned to doubt their doubts and believe their beliefs. The one great answer to doubt is faith in God and in his eternal word. 'No one rises to faith,' said Archbishop William Temple, 'until he first finds it incredible.' When we feel the utter impossibility of what we are asked to believe, the sheer incredibility of it, only then can faith reach up and grasp it and say, 'It is true! Glory! Hallelujah!'

O God my Father, if faith is the victory, then strengthen my faith and confidence in you every hour of every day. Help me first feel the incredibility of what I am asked to believe, and then reach out to hold it in the hands of faith. In Jesus' name I pray. Amen.

FOR FURTHER STUDY – Heb. 11:1–40; Rom. 10:17; James 2:14–19

1. Where does faith come from? / 2. What reinforces faith?

Unresolved mystery

FOR READING AND MEDITATION – GENESIS 50:1–21

'You intended to harm me, but God intended it for good to accomplish what is now being done …' (v. 20: NIV)

It must be crystal clear by now that what characterises and defines the true wilderness experience is not the occasional but the continuous, not the climbing of a short hill, but the walking of a long and rigorous mountain path. It is important to keep this in mind as we look at the next type of wilderness experience – the wilderness of failure.

Now all of us from time to time have to cope with failure, but the failure that characterises the wilderness experience is the failure of one's life work; the falling apart of everything one has dreamed about and built one's hopes upon. I have met many who carry into the latter years of their life a sense of bewilderment as to why the work they believed God called them to do was not rewarded with success.

There was a good deal of mystery in Joseph's life, but in the end the mystery was solved. Sold by his brothers into slavery, slandered by a lascivious woman, thrown unjustly into prison, he might well have wondered whether God had forsaken him. But one day God's watchful care over him was vindicated in the sight of everyone, his brothers in particular, and he was able to say to the men who had dealt with him so treacherously: 'You intended to harm me, but God intended it for good to accomplish what is now being done …'

Joseph lived to see the dark mystery of life cleared up when he discovered that God had allowed everything that had happened to him for a purpose. He was there in Egypt in the providence of God. What about those people, however, who pass out of this world with the mystery of their adverse circumstances unresolved? Their number is greater than we might at first realise.

Gracious God and heavenly Father, I am part of your Body, the Body in which some today will be feeling the pain of an unresolved mystery. As they hurt, so do I. Draw near to all in such circumstances this very hour. In Jesus' name I ask it. Amen.

FOR FURTHER STUDY – Eph. 5:22–32; 1 Tim. 3:16; Col. 1:26–27; Isa. 26:3

1. What is the difference between a mystery and a puzzle?
2. What is it necessary to do in the middle of a spiritual mystery?

Living with deep failure

FOR READING AND MEDITATION – PSALM 69:17–36

'I am in pain and distress; may your salvation, O God, protect me.' (v. 29: NIV)

Failure is not too difficult to cope with when one lives to see the hand of God turn the setback into a springboard. In 1968, just three years after I had started writing *Every Day with Jesus*, there came a moment when it looked as if the writings might have to be discontinued. Money ran out, circumstances took a dire turn, and it appeared that the whole idea of ministering daily to people around the world might have to be abandoned. Failure stared me in the face. Then God intervened, and from the jaws of failure he rescued me and made clear that the 'death of the vision' was his way of making me more dependent on him.

There have been many failures in my life, but I have received an explanation for every one of them. How would I have handled things, I wonder, if there had been no explanations, no turning of the failures into success? That is precisely the wilderness some people find themselves in – they pass out of the sight of men and women unvindicated; apparent failures, with no obvious use made of the sacrifice they offered.

I think as I write of a bishop I met in East Africa, who told me tearfully that he knew God had called him to that part of the world, but he had known nothing but failure. 'In three years I shall retire,' he said, 'but I have nothing to show for my life's work. When I think of how my gifts could have been used in other situations, how many other opportunities I have been offered, the pain is almost more than I can bear. Yet I know I am in the centre of his will.' I tell you, a sense of awe steals over you when you sit in the presence of someone like that – someone who can trust God even when the things for which he has given his life lie broken and apparently purposeless.

O God my Father, again I ask you to bind up the broken-hearted and heal the pain of those who have to end their lives with the mysteries of their failure unresolved. Be with them in a special way this day. In Jesus' name. Amen.

FOR FURTHER STUDY – Matt. 12:15–21; Luke 4:17–21

1. What will Jesus not do? / 2. What will he do?

Absolute trust

FOR READING AND MEDITATION – JOB 13:1–15

'Though he slay me, yet will I hope in him . . .' (v.15: NIV)

An experience that has impressed me over the years is meeting those who, having suffered the apparently complete failure of what they regarded as their God-given plans, were still moving on through life in absolute trust. Some of them have said, like Job: 'Though he slay me, yet will I trust in him' (AV). I can never come away from them without feeling encouraged, heartened and ready to make a deeper commitment to the work of God and the honour and glory of the Lord Jesus Christ.

Some brave souls have even gone into the work of God with their eyes wide open to the possibility that what they would do for God might not meet with success as we define it here on earth. Henry Martyn, missionary to India, was one such. 'Let me labour for fifty years amidst scorn,' he said, 'and never seeing one soul converted . . . the Lord Jesus, who controls all events, is my Friend, my Master, my God, my all.'

It takes a special kind of faith to stand and believe God when one senses that one's spiritual ambitions might never be realised. One thinks of Allen Gardiner and his companions who many years ago sailed to Tierra del Fuego in South America to found a mission. The mission, however, was never founded, for before they got there they ran out of food and one by one they died. The last entry in Gardiner's diary was this, 'Great and marvellous are the loving kindness of my gracious God unto me. He has pre-seen hitherto, and for four days, although without bodily food, without any feeling of hunger or thirst.' Surely in the presence of such awe-inspiring faith our hearts cannot fail to be moved.

O God, I feel I must question my own heart yet again and ask myself: am I more interested in doing the will of God than I am in achieving success? Help me think this through today. For your own dear Name's sake. Amen.

FOR FURTHER STUDY – Dan. 3:1–30; Josh. 23:8

1. How did the young Hebrew men evidence their trust in God?
2. Was it based on 'getting a good result'?

Must we see success?

FOR READING AND MEDITATION – HEBREWS 11:23–39
'These were all commended for their faith, yet none of them received what had been promised.' (v. 39: NIV)

Knowing that one is in the will of God and yet to end one's life without seeing what we describe here on earth as 'the marks of success' is not easy. But this is the wilderness that many have to walk through. Theologians and spiritual advisers have always been at pains to point out that it is a sign of spiritual immaturity if we must see success. A Bible college I used to visit in my teens (not the one I attended) had as its motto, *To be in the will of God is better than success.* By general agreement it was changed to read, *To be in the will of God* is *success* (emphasis mine). That was better because it was more in keeping with reality.

How do you handle life when, even though you know you are doing the will of God, there are no outward signs of success? Well, I can tell you how I handle it – with difficulty. I am growing in this area, however, for I found myself humming these lines the other day in my own daily Quiet Time:

All as God wills, who wisely heeds,
To give or to withhold.

I often meditate on the chapter before us today (it was from this chapter that I preached my very first sermon), and I notice that although here were many who had the mystery of their setbacks explained to them, there were many who did not. Yet they all pressed on in faith. They desired success, but they didn't demand it. They could trust God in the wilderness of failure. And to trust him there is trust indeed.

Gracious God and loving heavenly Father, help me not to rebel when I see no outward signs of success. May I say as the poet, 'All as God wills, who wisely heeds, to give or to withhold.' In Jesus' name I pray. Amen.

FOR FURTHER STUDY – 1 Cor. 15:50–58; Isa. 55:11; Jer. 39:16; Phil. 1:6
1. To what are we to give ourselves fully?
2. What assurance do we have about our work for the Lord?

The soul's dark night

FOR READING AND MEDITATION – PSALM 13:1–6
'How long, O Lord? Will you forget me for ever?' (v. 1: NIV)

We come now to the seventh and last type of wilderness experience and the one most difficult of all to bear – dereliction. By dereliction I mean the sense that one is deserted by God, the feeling that the Almighty is no longer at one's side, that he no longer listens or cares. To be trapped in difficult circumstances is bad enough, but to feel that God is not present in the circumstances is something from which the soul recoils. Yet it is in that dark dilemma that God's servants sometimes find themselves. Ancient writers refer to this experience as 'the dark night of the soul', and one has only to read the biographies of famous Christians to see how many have suffered in this way.

I can recall literally hundreds of times when I have sat with someone in a counselling session and he or she has said, "I can no longer feel God's presence with me. I have committed no sin, yet I feel like a creature banished from his sight.' Intellectually, of course, they knew that God had not departed from them – his promise is: 'I will never leave you nor forsake you' (Josh. 1:5, NIV), but it felt as if he had. And those who might say, 'Stop listening to your feelings and start listening to the Word,' reveal just how little they know about the depth to which the soul sinks when caught in this kind of wilderness.

We are not speaking of a minor mood change here, nor even of a bout of depression; we are talking about a spiritual battle the like of which those who have never entered it cannot conceive. I have had one such experience, and I can say without a doubt that the loss of God's felt presence is the hardest thing one can bear.

Gracious and loving heavenly Father, may I never enter such an experience, but if I do, help me to make sure that what I have been given in the light I will never lose in the dark. In Jesus' name. Amen.

FOR FURTHER STUDY – Job 23:1–12; Psa. 10:1; 89:46
1. How did Job feel? / 2. Where did his steady fortress come from?

When God seems far away

FOR READING AND MEDITATION – LAMENTATIONS 5:1–22

'Why do you always forget us? Why do you forsake us so long?' (v. 20: NIV)

We said yesterday that probably the hardest thing one has to bear in this life is the loss of God's felt presence, the sense that he is no longer there. Intellectually one knows this is not so, but the soul gains no consolation from this fact. And what makes the situation worse is the failure of such activities as prayer, reading the Scriptures and fellowship with other Christians, to make much difference. To feel that God has withdrawn himself because of a grievous sin we may have committed is one matter; to feel that he has withdrawn himself inexplicably is another.

One of the things I am grateful to my parents for is that when I was a child, they encouraged me to read the lives of famous Christians, such as John Bunyan, Mary Slessor, Praying Hyde, and others. It seems tragic to me that young people are not fed on such literature these days. Batman has more appeal than Bunyan, and Madonna more than Mary Slessor. As I was about to begin this page, I remembered how David Brainerd, the famous missionary to the North American Indians, talked about his 'dark night of the soul', and going to my library I found this, 'I have no fellow Christian to whom I might unbosom myself, or lay open my spiritual sorrows, and join in social prayer. But what makes all my difficulties grievous to be borne is that God hides his face from me.' More than once he cried, 'Oh! I mourned after the presence of God.'

To trust God in such darkness, to press on without sight of him, to continue serving when every comfort seems withdrawn, seems impossible – yet the truth is: multitudes have done it. They trusted in the dark what they had received in the light.

O Father, when I see what trust some of your servants have had in you – even when they felt you were no longer with them – I wonder how my own faith would stand such a test. Take me on to a deeper trust in you, dear Lord. In Jesus' name. Amen.

FOR FURTHER STUDY – Matt. 27:32–50; Heb. 4:15; Isa. 53:5; John 5:17–20

1. Why can we find solace in the cross?
2. Why are the two statements Jesus makes not contradictory?

Forsaken!

FOR READING AND MEDITATION – MATTHEW 27:45–56

'… Jesus cried out in a loud voice … "My God, my God, why have you forsaken me?"'
(v. 46: NIV)

There must be some deep divine purpose in an experience so common to the saints as spiritual dereliction. What that divine purpose is we can only conjecture, but we see from the passage before us today that our Saviour went this way too. There on Calvary our Lord himself experienced a moment when he felt abandoned by God. His cry of dereliction shivers to the sky in these piercing and heart-rending words: 'My God, my God, why have you forsaken me?'

There is a sense, of course, in which our Lord's feeling of dereliction was deeper than anything ever experienced by the rest of humanity, either before or after the crucifixion. Human beings may feel abandoned by God, but we know that in reality it is not so. In our Lord's situation, however, Jesus did not just feel abandoned; he was abandoned – literally. I agree with Dr Dale who in his famous book, *Atonement*, wrote, 'I decline to accept any explanation of these words which implies that they do not represent the actual truth of our Lord's position. In the darkness he was absolutely alone … God forsaken.' Christ experienced, not just felt, real abandonment by his Father. But why? Calvin answers that question like this, 'If Christ had died only a bodily death, it would have been ineffectual … Unless his soul shared in the punishment, he would have been the Redeemer of bodies alone. An actual and dreadful separation took place between the Father and the Son … due to our sins and their just reward.'

This is obviously a mystery, and we cannot expect to understand it fully. But what we can understand is this: because our Lord was abandoned by God – we shall never be.

Lord Jesus Christ, what a thought this is – your being abandoned by your Father means that in reality I shall never be. My gratitude will just not go into words. Blessed be your wondrous name for ever. Amen.

FOR FURTHER STUDY – John 14:15–21; Heb. 13:5–6

1. What did Jesus promise his disciples? / 2. What has God said?

Unnecessary suffering

FOR READING AND MEDITATION – PHILIPPIANS 3:1–21

'I want to know Christ and the power of his resurrection and the fellowship of sharing in his sufferings ...' (v. 10: NIV)

We have been saying over the past few days that to feel distanced in one's spirit by the One who has been trusted so implicitly is a harrowing experience. But the life stories of countless Christians show that many have borne it and have come through triumphantly. They follow in the wake of our Lord. Having felt in reality God's presence being withdrawn, subsequently there came a moment, I imagine, when God drew so gloriously near that with confidence, Christ committed his spirit into his hands (see Luke 23:46).

The difference between our Lord's abandonment (as I pointed out yesterday) was that he was actually and literally abandoned, while with us it is only a felt abandonment. What must be understood by every Christian, however, is that all spiritual dereliction is temporary. In every case I have seen it lasts only a few days or weeks and always for a spiritual purpose. We shall move on tomorrow to consider what might be the purpose of all these wilderness experiences, but for the moment let us be content with the fact that God will allow us to go through situations only where he can work for our good.

People often confuse dereliction with depression, and this is why one should talk to a good, biblically minded counsellor to make sure that the one is not being mistaken for the other. All secular counsellors (unless they have uncanny insight) will diagnose dereliction as depression. A talk with a biblical counsellor is imperative because there is no point, I believe, in unnecessary suffering. I share the view of Dr E. Stanley Jones who said, 'Christians have a responsibility to make sure they are not suffering more than they ought.'

Father, help me to be able to discern the difference between that which you are leading me into and that which comes from a natural cause. And when I am unable to discern myself, give me the help I need from another part of your Body. Amen.

FOR FURTHER STUDY – Rom. 8:18–30; 2 Cor. 1:3

1. How did Paul view his present sufferings? / 2. What perspective did this bring to him?

Conflicting views

FOR READING AND MEDITATION – GENESIS 18:16–33
'Will not the Judge of all the earth do right?' (v. 25: NIV)

We turn now to address the question: what possible purpose can the Almighty have in either leading us, or allowing us, to enter into a wilderness experience? Before looking more closely at the divine purpose behind this, we pause to consider whether God brings about the conditions that constitute a wilderness experience or whether he just allows them.

Throughout the centuries theologians have been divided on this issue, and better and more qualified people than I have tried to find a point of general agreement, but have failed. One school of thought says that God engineers difficult circumstances so we can enter into them and learn something for our good. The other school says he does not engineer our difficult circumstances – they come about through the very nature of a fallen universe. However, God allows us to enter into them because he sees that by doing so, he can utilise them for his purposes.

How do we reconcile these conflicting views? I think both views have some truth in them but they must be kept in balance. There are times when God actually brings about situations and steers us into them because he foresees that this is the only way we can know him in the way our souls long to know him. There are other times, however, when he does not purpose things to happen (in the sense that he actually engineers them), but allows them to take place because he sees they can be used for our spiritual advancement and our good. If it were possible to conceive of anything utterly sterile of good then God, I believe, would not permit it to happen. God cannot only be found in what he does, but also in what he allows.

Father, I am not sure whether I can resolve this question here on earth, but give me an ever-growing confidence in the fact that because of who you are, my Saviour and my God, whatever you do is always right. In Jesus' name I pray. Amen.

FOR FURTHER STUDY – John 13:1–11, 6:64, 18:4, 19:28; Heb. 4:13; 1 John 3:20
1. Name one of the characteristics of Christ. / 2. Why is God greater than our hearts?

God is in control

FOR READING AND MEDITATION – PHILIPPIANS 1:12–30

'... I want you to know ... that what has happened to me has really served to advance the gospel.' (v. 12: NIV)

We must spend one more day discussing this question of whether God simply allows things to happen or whether he actively brings about situations for our spiritual advancement and profit.

A catastrophic event happened in the early part of my life that I know without any shadow of doubt was brought about by God, and if he had not done so then I might not be where I am today. It was not pleasant to go through, but I myself am quite sure that God ordered it, planned it, and purposed it. There are other situations I can think of in my life (such as the loss of my wife through cancer) that I believe he did not bring about, but allowed. And he allowed them (so I believe) because he saw that evil though they were in themselves, some good could be brought out of them. I cannot conceive of a God who actively purposes for a missionary family's life to be ended in a plane crash (such as the one that happened some months ago in Nepal), or for innocent children to be mangled by a car driven by a drunk driver. But obviously God allows these things to happen. Why? If in the final sense this is God's universe, must he not take ultimate responsibility for whatever happens?

Some theologians caution us not to put undue stress on the difference between what God does and what God permits, believing that if God allows something then clearly it is his purpose.

We shall not solve this mystery in this life, but in my own mind I am satisfied that there is a difference of intent between what God does and what he permits. He never intends evil, yet he permits it. But – and this is important – only when he sees that he can turn the evil into good.

Father, the deeper I look into the mystery of evil, the deeper my confusion. Help me nevertheless to have a firm and unshakeable trust in the fact that though I may not know what you are doing – you know. Let that be enough. In Jesus' name. Amen.

FOR FURTHER STUDY – Eph. 3:1–6, 4:1; Col. 4:18; 2 Tim. 1:8

1. Who did Paul see himself as a prisoner of? / 2. Who was he actually a prisoner of?

Why the wilderness?

FOR READING AND MEDITATION – MARK 9:14–32
'"I do believe; help me overcome my unbelief!"' (v. 24: NIV)

Finally we come to answer the question: what possible purpose can God have in arranging, or allowing, a wilderness experience? It is for the testing of our faith and the development of our ability to trust God more deeply and more confidently.

The most outstanding Christians of history, it hardly needs to be said, are those who are shining examples of faithfulness; trustworthy in all their commerce with heaven and earth alike, found dependable by God and dependable by others. This will be seen more clearly if we remember that faith or trust is not merely a matter of fact, but a matter of degree. As Christians it is not enough for us to say to ourselves, 'I have faith.' Rather, we must ask, 'How much faith do I have?'

Faith, or faithfulness (I am using the words interchangeably), if we are honest, oscillates in most of us. We are up one day and down the next; we believe today and doubt tomorrow. We are trustworthy and can shout for Jesus when things are going well, but we are not so ready to do so when fiery trials and testings come. People have often told me (and I know this to be true in my own personal experience) that they believe with one layer of their minds and doubt with another that is deeper. Sometimes the oscillations are so swift that we hardly know which is uppermost, and we find ourselves crying out, like the father of the epileptic boy in the story before us today, 'I do believe; help me overcome my unbelief!' One of the greatest qualities that God wants to inculcate in us is the kind of faith that 'works by love'. And if this can be developed and deepened only through a wilderness experience then that is where we must be prepared to go.

Father, forgive me if I am satisfied with merely having faith but am not willing to be questioned on how much faith I have. May the roots of my faith go deeper into the soil of your love, day after day after day. In Jesus' name. Amen.

FOR FURTHER STUDY – Luke 16:1–6; Gal. 5:6; Heb. 11:6
1. What was the apostles' request of the Lord? / 2. What is the only thing that counts?

Faith is the victory

FOR READING AND MEDITATION – 1 JOHN 5:1–21

'This is the victory that has overcome the world, even our faith.' (v. 4: NIV)

We said yesterday that faith (or faithfulness) is not merely a matter of fact, but a matter of degree. God is concerned not only about the presence or absence of faith but its strength as well. Is it insensitive of the Lord to respond to our statement, 'I have faith,' by asking, 'How much faith do you have?' I do not think so. Because faith and trust in God play such an important part in our life and experience here on earth, God is committed to deepening and developing them in every just way that he can.

Everyone in the Christian life may be said to believe – else we would not belong to the Way. However, what God longs for us is that we believe utterly: with every layer of our minds, in shine and shade, in prosperity and adversity, in up times and down times, in winter and in summer. This is the school he is putting us through, and sometimes the lessons in this school include a time alone in the wilderness where we are bereft of our textbooks, our compass, our familiar companions, our drinks and sandwiches, and where we have to rough it for a while. We don't like it and the flesh shrinks from the experience, but we learn there, perhaps more than anywhere, how to take the devil's temptations and our doubts and hack them to pieces in the presence of the Lord.

I tell you, heaven rejoices when it sees a Christian absorb God's grace and stay true to Christ in the midst of the fieriest trials. And there are just no words to describe the scene in glory when a Christian emerges from the wilderness and shouts in triumph: 'This is the victory that has overcome the world, even our faith.'

O God, help me to emerge from every difficult experience – not just a wilderness experience – with a shout of triumph. Grant that my faith will be seen not merely as a virtue but as the way to victory – your victory. In Jesus' name. Amen.

FOR FURTHER STUDY – Rev. 2:1–26, 3:1–12, 21:7

1. What phrase appears seven times in the above verses?
2. What seven rewards are promised?

Trust – or negotiation?

FOR READING AND MEDITATION – MATTHEW 20:1–16

'"I want to give the man who was hired last the same as I gave you."' (v. 14: NIV)

We continue examining the point that the primary purpose God has in either leading us, or allowing us, to enter a wilderness experience is to develop our trust. I have come to the conclusion, after years of pondering this matter, that next to love, one of the most important qualities that God wants to develop in us on this earth is trust. And he will do whatever he has to, to achieve that.

In the chapter before the one that forms our reading for today, Peter asks the question: 'We have left everything to follow you! What then will there be for us?' (19:27). The Lord replied with a story about a landowner who went out early in the morning to hire men to work in his vineyard. He agreed to pay them a *denarius* for the day. He did the same at midday, in the afternoon, and again an hour before sunset. When the day ended the landowner paid everyone the same amount irrespective of whether they had worked a full day, half a day, or just an hour or two. The ones who had worked all day grumbled at the landowner's decision, but the answer was given: '"Don't I have the right to do what I want with my own money?"' (verse 15).

This story, given in response to Peter's question, was intended to make the point that servants should trust their master to do what is right. So many of us are like Simon Peter; we like to say we are trusting God but really what we practise is the art of negotiation. We do trust God of course, but as I pointed out yesterday, it is not the presence or absence of trust we are talking about in the lives of Christians; it is the matter of degree. We trust God, but how much?

O God, forgive me that so often what I say is that I trust you, but what I practise is negotiation. Will I never come to the place of trusting you to do right when it conflicts with my own ideas? Bring me there, dear Lord. In Jesus' name. Amen.

FOR FURTHER STUDY – Job 34:1–19; Matt. 5:45; Acts 10:34–35; Rom. 10:12

1. What characteristic of God is brought out in the above verses?
2. How does this strengthen our trust?

Trusting implicitly

FOR READING AND MEDITATION – HEBREWS 11:1–12

'...anyone who comes to [God] must believe that he exists and that he rewards those who earnestly seek him.' (v. 6: NIV)

The text before us today is probably one of the greatest statements concerning faith in the whole of Scripture. I love the way *The Amplified Bible* translates it: 'For whoever would come near to God must (necessarily) believe that God exists and that he is the Rewarder of those who earnestly... seek him (out).' We are to believe two things when we come to God: one, that he exists, and two, that he rewards those who earnestly seek him. The first is easy, the second difficult.

The truth is that many (perhaps most) of us come to God believing that he is the Rewarder of those who earnestly seek him, but then insist that we be given the rewards we think we ought to receive. Remember the story of the landowner we looked at yesterday? The workers who were taken on in the morning thought that the master was unjust when he paid those who had been taken on later in the day the same amount as them. The point of the story, however, is not whether or not the landowner was just, but that he had every right to do what he liked with his own money. The story was told to illustrate how often we find ourselves in the Master's service and insist that we be given certain rewards – the ones we think we should get. But trust, real trust, has within it no spirit of negotiation. Trust is a condition of the heart that gives us the freedom to ask what we desire but to remain completely content with whatever comes – so long as we have the promise that our Father is there.

The spirit of negotiation has to be taken out of us if we are to know deep trust, and sadly, going through a wilderness experience is often the only thing that can do it.

Father, I see even more clearly that your primary purpose in allowing me to go through the wilderness is to bring me to the place where I will trust you – regardless. But I am a little scared by this. Hold me and strengthen me. In Jesus' name. Amen.

FOR FURTHER STUDY – Psa. 37:1–6, 31:19, 32:10; Prov. 3:5–6

1. What happens when we delight ourselves in the Lord? / 2. What are we not to lean on?

Why sin is so easy

FOR READING AND MEDITATION – JEREMIAH 17:1–11

'The heart is deceitful above all things and beyond cure. Who can understand it?' (v. 9: NIV)

We saw yesterday that we are to approach God believing first, that he exists, and second, that he is the Rewarder of those who earnestly seek him. But what about those times when we earnestly seek him and are not rewarded in the way we think we should be? Can we trust him in such situations?

The following might sound like a strange statement to some, yet it is true: it is possible to approach God not with an already settled confidence in his goodness, but with the desire to test him to see if he is up to his Word. If he rewards us in the way we think we ought to be rewarded, then he is good; if he doesn't, then we can use that as an excuse for not trusting him in the way he asks, or even demands. A discovery I have often made in counselling, and which in the early days used to scare me, is that there lies deep within the human heart, sometimes covered over by a veneer of so-called spirituality and politeness, a thought that if God doesn't come through for me in the way I expect him to, then he can't complain if he doesn't get my absolute trust. I remember the surprise I felt when I first encountered this, and I found through experiment that it is more deeply rooted in the soul than I could have ever imagined. There have been many occasions when I have sat with individuals who, seemingly unconcerned about the gravity of the sin they had committed, were brought to a deep and genuine repentance when they realised the motivation for their sin was rooted in anger and unbelief.

God calls us to trust not because he rewards us but because he is God. To be confident of this is to build a sturdy bulwark against sin.

O God, I realise that deep within I am capable of coming up with many rationalisations and excuses for my sin. Invade the deep parts of me by your Spirit and be the Advocate who presents within my soul a constant argument against sin. In Jesus' name. Amen.

FOR FURTHER STUDY – 1 Kings 19:1–21; Isa. 26:1–3, 50:10

1. What was it that Elijah wanted God to do? / 2. How did he react when it didn't happen?

God is good

FOR READING AND MEDITATION – ROMANS 5:12–21

'…sin entered the world through one man, and death through sin… because all sinned…' (v. 12: NIV)

The point we made yesterday, that we might on occasion approach God not with an already settled confidence in his goodness but with a desire to test him to see if he is capable of doing what he says, is deserving of further examination.

I wonder, is this what went wrong in Adam and Eve's relationship with God in the Garden of Eden? Was the temptation the moment when they began to move away from the settled confidence they had in God's goodness; an attempt to put the Almighty to the test? The nature of Adam and Eve's sin can be understood only when we see that basically it was a refusal to trust. They sinned because deep down they were not sure God could be trusted to have their highest interests at heart – so they acted to protect these. Did Eve say to herself as the temptation proceeded, 'God looks as if he might be keeping something from me, so the best way to enhance my own being is to do what the serpent suggests?' And did Adam say to himself, when invited by his wife to partake of the forbidden fruit, 'God has told us not to eat of this fruit. My wife has already disobeyed that command, but if I refuse her invitation things might be difficult between us. I'm not sure I can trust God to handle such a dilemma so I will yield to the invitation of my wife?'

That may not have been their exact reasoning, but whatever it was, it was reasoning that had within it a lack of trust. The sad thing is that same flaw is now found in each one of us, for we are the recipients of their fallen nature. This is why we hold fast to the truth that God is good, whether it appears to be so or not. Not to do so erodes our ability to withstand temptation.

O Father, help me to be firmly anchored in the thought that you are good whether or not it appears so. Drive it so deeply within me that it becomes not just an opinion but a conviction. In Jesus' name I ask it. Amen.

FOR FURTHER STUDY – Psa. 34:1–8, 25:8; Nahum 1:7; Matt. 19:17

1. What does the psalmist exhort us to do?
2. How did Jesus respond to being called good?

Contempt for God?

FOR READING AND MEDITATION – MALACHI 3:6–18
'But now we call the arrogant blessed...' (v. 15: NIV)

The passage before us today contains some of the most astonishing and disturbing words to be found in the Old Testament. God tells his people that they have said harsh things against him, and when the people ask God what they have said, the Almighty replies: 'You have said, "It is foolish to worship God and obey him... From now on, as far as we're concerned, 'Blessed are the arrogant"' (verses 14-15, TLB).

Catch the import of these remarkably offensive words. The Jews were saying something like this, 'There really is no point in doing things God's way. He can't be trusted to make things go the way they should go. We are better off depending on our own resources than trusting his.' God's attitude towards them for their wrong perception of the situation was severe; he rebuked them for speaking harsh words against him and promised a terrible judgment. God had told an earlier generation of similarly angry and arrogant Hebrews that ' "No one who has treated me with contempt will ever see [the Promised Land]" ' (Num. 14:23, NIV).

What did God mean when he said he had been treated with contempt? By the way they had not believed his Word. Let there be no mistake about this – we treat God with contempt when we do not trust his words. It ought not to go without notice that after the Lord rebuked the Jews of Malachi's day for speaking harsh words against him, the Almighty did not speak any more from heaven for a period of 400 years. We treat God with arrogance when we refuse to trust his words, and when we persist in that arrogance we run the risk of experiencing a long silence in our soul.

O God, forgive me for the arrogance I have displayed when I have been unwilling to trust your Word. Help me understand something of the hurt and pain it brings to your heart when I prefer to trust my own wisdom rather than yours. Amen.

FOR FURTHER STUDY – Psa. 3:1–8, 20:7; Isa. 12:1–6
1. Why did the psalmist say he would not fear?
2. How did he express his confidence in God?

Absolute trust – no sin

FOR READING AND MEDITATION – ROMANS 4:18–25

'...being fully persuaded that God had power to do what he had promised.' (v. 21: NIV)

Without doubt one of the greatest qualities we can have in life is a firm and confident trust in God. More hangs on this than we perhaps realise. Dr Larry Crabb says in the book, *Finding God*, that no one, not even the mature older saint, believes absolutely that God is as trustworthy as the Bible declares him to be. He goes on to say that one who fully believed God's Word and trusted him implicitly would never sin. There is in every sin, he claims, the energy to trust our own resources more than God's. We are like a wealthy man who lives in fear that one day his debts may outdistance his resources.

If we fully trusted God and realised how inexhaustible his resources really are, then there would be no fear of anything life demands of us. No problem could ever destroy us, no tragedy ever cheat us of hope. No agony could extinguish joy, nor loss ever drive us to despair. Trust in God, if we could develop it absolutely, is enough to overwhelm every consequence of sin and cause our hearts to be stayed upon him in every crisis and in every difficult situation.

Of course, no one will develop absolute confidence in God here on earth, even though there may be times (perhaps many times) when trust is strong and firm and deep. Lack of trust in God gives rise to the many struggles we experience in life, for when trust is absent or weak, we fall back on our own energies and strategies to handle life's situations. But our human energies and strategies are often no match for the gigantic problems that come our way. Really we are shut up to trusting God. If we don't trust him, who else can we really trust?

O God my Father, if it is true that I can never trust you as fully and absolutely as you ought to be trusted while I am here on this earth, then help me get as close as possible I pray. In Jesus' name. Amen.

FOR FURTHER STUDY – Hab. 3:1–19; Psa. 23:4, 27:3, 46:1–3

1. What was the depth of Habakkuk's confidence?
2. How did he describe how he sometimes felt?

How trust develops

FOR READING AND MEDITATION – PSALM 55:1–23

'But as for me, I trust in you.' (v. 23: NIV)

Why is it that trust develops so strongly in the midst of a wilderness experience? That is the question that will engage our minds today.

I think the answer must be that when life goes very much as we desire, it is almost impossible to resist a subtle form of pride. We say to ourselves, albeit unconsciously, 'I must be doing things right and am therefore reaping the rewards of obedience.' Pressure and the presence of huge problems such as we experience in a true wilderness experience (or for that matter even in less fierce times of testing) tend to break up our patterns of prideful thinking and we begin to lose confidence in our ability to hold our lives together. We feel the ground is no longer solid beneath us, our feet begin to slip and slide and we look around for a more solid ground of confidence. It is at such times, when trust becomes our only option, that we begin to realise the foolishness of self-dependency, and our confidence in God deepens and grows.

Sometimes the ordinary struggles of life do not shake our confidence in ourselves; we remain self-sufficient, self-centred, even arrogant. What is required if our self-sufficiency is to be disrupted is a degree of trial that has within it the strength and energy to break up our self-centred patterns of thinking and move us from self-dependency to God-dependency. We would wish that the degree of our trust and confidence in God could develop in less painful or traumatic ways, but such is the impact of sin on our souls that regrettably we learn better through pain than we do through pleasure.

O God, may I come through every tribulation and trial with the same conviction as the psalmist. May I too be able to say – and say with conviction: 'But as for me, I will trust in you.' In Jesus' name. Amen.

FOR FURTHER STUDY – Jer. 17:5–10; Psa. 31:24, 33:18, 39:7

1. How is the heart described? / 2. What is the result when man puts his confidence in God?

God's driving purpose

FOR READING AND MEDITATION – ROMANS 8:28–39

'For those God foreknew he also predestined to be conformed to the likeness of his Son…' (v. 29: NIV)

This verse from Romans 8, which I have chosen as our text for today, unfolds for us with perfect clarity the whole purpose of the wilderness experience. Paul, after talking about the fact that God works all things together for good (verse 28), goes on to tell us why God allows us to go through difficult circumstances: 'For from the very beginning God decided that those who came to him – and all along he knew who would – should become like his Son…' (verse 29, TLB).

God's great driving purpose, then, in permitting us to pass through fiery trials is that we 'should become like his Son'. This runs counter to our carnal nature, for our driving purpose is to avoid the fiery trials as we would a plague. But hard and difficult experiences yield more than they cost. Aspects of character are developed in us when we are in the wilderness that could not be developed in a carefree life. God is so excited about the life of his Son, Jesus, that he wants to make us all into his image; and to have the character qualities he possessed, such as love, perseverance, commitment and trust.

I am afraid that in today's Christian culture we have lost sight of the fact that the point of Christianity is not to give us a life free from problems, but to implant deep within us a reality that enables us to pursue God's purposes, regardless of what may have happened to us in the past or may be happening to us in the present. God's great driving purpose, I repeat, is to make us like Jesus, and he will stop at nothing – wilderness experiences included – to reproduce the character of his Son in us.

O God, I see I have to come to terms with the fact that your great driving purpose is different from mine. Work in my heart, I pray, to draw me away from my own designs and deeper into yours. In Jesus' name. Amen.

FOR FURTHER STUDY – 2. Cor. 3:1–18; Phil. 3:21; 2 Pet. 1:4

1. How does Paul describe the ongoing change in our lives?
2. What does God want us to be partakers of?

Facing reality

FOR READING AND MEDITATION – EPHESIANS 6:1–20

'Stand firm then, with the belt of truth buckled round your waist…' (v. 14: NIV)

We touched yesterday on a thought that I suspect does not go down well with many Christians, namely that the point of Christianity is not to give us a life free from problems, but to implant deep within us the trust that pursues God's purposes, whether we understand them or not. But many modern-day Christians (thankfully not all) don't want to hear this message. They prefer the emphasis of those who claim that prosperity and freedom from problems are what the Lord appoints for those who love him.

It's an idea that is very attractive to our carnal nature, but there's just one thing wrong with it – it isn't true. Of course God gives prosperity to some, and of course many live lives that are apparently free from huge and distressing problems. But that is not the general picture, either historically or in the present. The Christian life, someone said, is like a hurdle race – we run on the flat for a little while and then before we know it we are up in the air, trying to get over a hurdle. Another person has described a Christian as being like a tea bag – he is not much use until he has been through some hot water.

There are those who take the attitude that if we see a problem coming, we should turn our back on it, pretend it is not there, and it will then go away. That is the most nonsensical advice I think I have ever heard. Pretence and denial are not Christian virtues. Denial is the very opposite of honesty and integrity, and Christians are supposed to be people who are open and honest in all things. Integrity requires that whatever is true must be looked at. It doesn't have to be embraced, but it does have to be faced.

O God, deliver me I pray from the false notion that I can have heaven now whilst I am here on earth. Show me that though I can have a little bit of heaven to go to heaven in, struggles will not cease until I arrive in glory. In Jesus' name. Amen.

FOR FURTHER STUDY – Mal. 2:1–17; 1 Peter 2:9; Rev. 1:6

1. What complaint did the Lord have against the priests?
2. What was the Lord's testimony of Levi?

Giving God glory

FOR READING AND MEDITATION – 1 CHRONICLES 16:7–36

'…ascribe to the Lord the glory due to his name.' (v. 29: NIV)

We must reflect further on the thoughts that have been engaging our attention over the past couple of days. This, I believe, is something the Church must come to grips with, namely that God's glory is what is most important in the universe.

To some it might seem that I am simply stating the obvious and that all Christians want to see God being glorified. This may be true in theory, but it is not always true in practice. What is the first thing we think of when we are plunged into a fiery trial? Isn't it how to find a way out? It's natural to prefer comfort to challenge, pleasure to pain, and not many of us, if we are honest, will say when entering a fierce trial, 'Lord, in this I am far more interested in your glory than I am in my own well-being.'

It may sound as if I am being very critical of the contemporary Christian church, but these things have to be said, for modern-day Christians (generally speaking) appear to be far more interested in their own reputation than in the reputation of God. God's glory is the most important thing in the universe, and if he arranges or allows me to go through some difficult experiences because it brings honour to his name, then who am I to disagree? God is not here for my ends; I am here for his. If our purpose in life is to get God to co-operate with our designs and desires rather than to co-operate with his, then our attitude towards him will swing between two extremes, depending on how well things are going. Either we will only praise him when he blesses us or we will become angry towards him when he disregards our desires. God's interests must ever be first.

Lord, your knife is going deep into my soul, I wince, yet I gladly consent, for I never want to get to a place where I am resistant to your challenges. Help me be more interested in your reputation than I am in my own. In Jesus' name. Amen.

FOR FURTHER STUDY – Psa. 19:1–14; Ex. 33:18, 40:34

1. What do the heavens declare? / 2. What was Moses' prayer?

The high-water mark

FOR READING AND MEDITATION – ISAIAH 42:5–17

'I am the Lord; that is my name! I will not give my glory to another…' (v. 8: NIV)

I feel compelled to linger for one more day on the point we have been making, namely the need to put God's reputation ahead of our own. John Piper, in his book, *The Pleasure of God*, says something which I think will make clearer what I am trying to express, 'God's commitment to the cause of his people is grounded not in his people, but in himself. His passion to save and to purify feeds itself not from the shallow soil of our value but from the infinite depth of his own.' Powerful words!

When we realise that God's chief aim is for us to magnify his name and not ours, then we are cut down to our proper size. Our trouble is that we are too arrogant; we think God is here for our ends and purposes, rather than us being here for his. Modern-day Christianity can't receive this too well as it cuts across the present emphasis of, 'How can I improve my self-image?' 'How can I be more assertive?' 'How can I solve all my problems?' and so on. We fail to see that God uses fiery trials to reduce us to humility and worship and get us to focus our eyes on how wonderful and glorious he is.

But isn't this rather self-centred of God? Is He using us to get an ego stroke? Of course not, and to linger here and indulge in such thinking borders on blasphemy. God is interested in us pursuing his glory because in glorifying him we become more fulfilled. We are made in such a way that when we glorify God, we reach our highest potential. When we focus on how we can bring God glory and contribute more to his reputation than our own, we are getting close to the high-water mark of Christian living.

Father forgive me I pray that so often I am more concerned with my reputation than I am with yours; with my glory rather than the glory of the Trinity. Deepen my understanding of this truth, hour by hour. Amen.

FOR FURTHER STUDY – John 13:18–32, 14:13, 17:4; 1 Pet. 4:11

1. What did Jesus view as his purpose? / 2. What was he able to say?

A Person to trust

FOR READING AND MEDITATION – 1 PETER 2:1–12

'... the one who trusts in him will never be put to shame.' (v. 6: NIV)

Today we ask ourselves: how deeply do we trust? It might help us to evaluate the depth and degree of our trust if we examine the feelings we experience when we are not in control.

Some psychologists claim that the desire to be in control is one of the strongest drives in the personality. I see no reason to disagree, for I know when I look into my own heart, the thing that I hate the most is to feel out of control. Yet this is precisely what trust demands; it is being willing to face those feelings of helplessness, and assert in the midst of them that God is on the throne. Have you noticed how often when something goes wrong or your life is wrapped in mystery, you search desperately for some understanding of why things are the way they are? Then, when you arrive at an understanding, you feel a good deal better, for your life seems slightly more under control. Now you have something to work on to make things better; by thinking hard and working hard you might develop a plan that will get you out of the difficulties. A friend of mine says, 'When Christians are in a crisis they are far more interested in finding a plan to follow than a Person to trust.'

The desire to be in control is one of the greatest enemies of trust. And of course it must be said that there are times when it is right to be in control. But we must watch this desire very carefully, for it might well militate against the trust that God is trying to develop in us. The desire to be in control is not necessarily wrong; it becomes wrong if we use it to provide us with a plan to follow when God invites us just to trust.

Father, as I look into my heart I sense this strong urge always to be in control. And I see that sometimes it can be a help but sometimes a hindrance. Help me to understand and know the difference. In Jesus' name. Amen.

FOR FURTHER STUDY – Psa. 62:1–12; Prov. 14:32; Heb. 6:18–19

1. What important phrase did David use?
2. How did the writer of Hebrews describe our hope?

The law of opposites

FOR READING AND MEDITATION – ROMANS 5:1–11

'…we also rejoice in our sufferings, because we know that suffering produces perseverance…' (v. 3: NIV)

We will not develop the kind of trust that God wants us to know as long as the energy of our lives is directed towards attaining constant and continuous control. I pointed out yesterday that the greatest enemy of trust is the desire to be in control. We have to learn as growing Christians not to insist that God provide us with answers for everything, but to walk on in times of darkness, content that although we are not in control – he is. One of the principles of effective Christian living (as our text for today makes clear) is that whenever God sees a quality that is lacking in us and sets out to develop it, he puts us in a situation where the opposite conditions prevail.

Let me explain. If God wants to develop patience and perseverance in us then he will make sure we have opportunities to learn how to do so by sending (or allowing us) to have more than our usual share of tribulation. If he wants to develop joy then he will allow us to become involved in circumstances that cause sorrow. If it is peace he wants to develop then we will find ourselves in a situation akin to being in the midst of a war. It is the same with trust. To develop trust there is no better way than putting us in a position where we feel we are not in control, where no masterplan can be drawn up that will get us out of it, and where we simply have to fall back on the grace that God provides and believe that he and he alone will bring us out of it.

I can think of no better place for a deep and confident trust in the Almighty to be developed than in the wilderness. And as I have said before, if that is where it has to be developed, then God will not shrink from arranging it.

O God my Father, I bring this strong desire for control that resides within me and place it at your feet. Help me clearly discern the time when it is right to be in control and when it is right to sit in dependent trust. In Jesus' name. Amen.

FOR FURTHER STUDY – John 12:20–26; Luke 6:38; Acts 20:30; Luke 14:11; Matt. 20:26

1. List some of the laws of opposites found in Scripture.
2. What are some of the differences from modern-day thinking?

Jesus' own wilderness

FOR READING AND MEDITATION – PHILIPPIANS 2:1–13

'... [he] made himself nothing... And being found in appearance as a man, he humbled himself...' (vv.7–8: NIV)

Today we remind ourselves that in coming to this earth, our Lord knew more deeply than anyone the agony of the wilderness experience. If we look at the seven types of wilderness experience we listed earlier, we can see, with the exception of doubt and the failure of one's life work, that Christ knew the others to a degree that we will never know.

Take the first – humiliation. It began for him the moment he left his home in glory. 'It took more humiliation for Jesus to become a man,' said C. H. Spurgeon, 'than for an angel to become a worm.' And once he arrived here it was humiliation all the way. Then what about suffering? No one has ever suffered more than he – physically, mentally, and spiritually. His sufferings on the cross consisted of all three – physical, mental, and spiritual – and they must have combined to produce such agony that it is quite beyond our imagination to conceive of it. There was bereavement also. How stricken he appeared to be when hearing the news of the death of his cousin, John the Baptist. He knew estrangement and treachery too. A man who walked with him for three and a half years sold him for thirty pieces of silver. Then finally – dereliction. No one, as we said earlier, has experienced such dereliction as Jesus. His cry: 'My God, my God, why have you forsaken me' (Matt. 27:46) is one of the saddest cries in the history of the universe.

To those who may find themselves caught up in some fiery trial I would say – remember your Saviour went this way too. Because of this he knows, and feels, and cares.

O God, I am so thankful that when I come to you for comfort I come to One who has worn my flesh, walked in my shoes, measured all of my frailty, and knows exactly what I am going through. What joy and consolation this gives me, dear Lord. Amen.

FOR FURTHER STUDY – Gal. 4:4; Isa. 53:1–12; 1 John 4:2

1. What are some of the elements of suffering found in Isaiah 53?
2. What does Paul attest to?

He dwelt among us

FOR READING AND MEDITATION – LUKE 1:57–75

'Praise be to the Lord, the God of Israel, because he has come and has redeemed his people.' (v. 68: NIV)

We stay with the thought that our Lord, in coming to this world entered into a wilderness experience, and by so doing was tempted in all points as we are – yet without sin.

Our text today reminds us that he has come and redeemed his people. He did not come without redeeming us, and he did not redeem us without coming. The only way to redeem us was to become like us. He didn't sit on a cloud and utter a command, or pick us up with celestial tongs and take us to heaven, not soiling his fingers with the messy business of living. No, he dwelt among us, amid our poverty, amid our temptations, amid our problems and our choices and disappointments. He lived among us and showed us how to live by living.

I want to stay with that word 'dwelt' a little longer, as there is much truth to be drawn from it. We need to keep in mind that the revelation of God in Jesus was not a momentary rift in the clouds that surround the mystery of the Deity – a swift and sudden insight into what God is like. It was more than a fleeting vision of the Godhead that Jesus came to give us – it was as full a revelation as possible. Hear the words once more: he dwelt among us.

Jesus lived on earth for only thirty-three and a half years, but this was long enough for him to reveal God's character in operation. And he revealed it in the same surroundings in which you and I have to operate. The power he called upon is the same power that is available to every one of us. He has walked in our shoes, worn our flesh, measured its frailty, and understood every one of life's challenges. He became like us in order that we might become like him.

Lord Jesus, when you speak it is Deep speaking unto deep. We know that you know us, and knowing how you love, how can we help but love in return? We do so with all our ransomed beings. We love you, dear Lord. Receive our worship and our praise. Amen.

FOR FURTHER STUDY – Col. 1:1–14; Eph. 1:7; Gal. 3:13; 1 Pet. 1:18

1. What is the meaning of 'redemption'? / 2. What has Christ redeemed us from?

Your way, Father!

FOR READING AND MEDITATION – PSALM 25:1–22

'To you, O Lord, I lift up my soul; in you I trust, O my God.' (vv. 1–2: NIV)

It was Oswald Chambers who said, 'We are more likely to come to terms with reality when we understand that life in a fallen world is more tragic than orderly.' How we would love to have our days go by with order and predictability and make everything come out the way we would like it. However, as Oswald Chambers points out, this is a fallen world, and we have no way of knowing when a disaster is going to strike, when a loved one is going to die, or when a business is going to collapse.

The fact that the world is more tragic than orderly strikes a deep blow at our desire for control. We are terrified of vulnerability, of being overcome by something we didn't foresee, because it puts us in the position of being out of control and having to trust someone bigger and stronger than ourselves. It goes back to what I was saying earlier, that our carnal nature abhors the feeling of helplessness, which in turn puts us in a position where we have to trust. And until we recognise this, we are unlikely to do anything about it.

But what can we do? We can come before God and surrender to him our strong desire to be in control. We can say, as I heard one of my counselees once pray, 'Lord, I like this feeling of being in control of my life. I just love being in the driving seat all the time. But today I surrender that right to you. I will drive when you want me to drive, or sit back contentedly when you want to drive.' She ended rather quaintly but not petulantly, 'Have it your way, Father.' Hardly anything matters more in a disorderly universe than trust. The sooner we realise it the better.

Father, as I learn more about the importance of trust, help me not to be satisfied with just theoretical knowledge. Lead me on to an experiential knowledge. This is so right; forgive me that very often I have got it so wrong. Amen.

FOR FURTHER STUDY – Phil. 4:1–12; 1 Tim. 6:6–8; Heb. 13:5–6

1. What was Paul able to say? / 2. What was his advice to Timothy?

Lord, love me less

FOR READING AND MEDITATION – JAMES 1:1–18

'Consider it pure joy, my brothers, whenever you face trials of many kinds ...' (v. 2: NIV)

Don't be surprised if, as you have followed these meditations day by day, you have found yourself thinking occasionally that God expects too much of you. St Augustine went through periods in his life when he wished that God would lower his expectations, so that he could go about living the Christian life more comfortably. His goal at those periods was comfort, not Christlikeness. Later he came to see the foolishness of this position and moved on into a wonderful and deep relationship with the Lord.

When I talk about joyfully entering a wilderness experience because we know we are going to come out of it purified and refined and with a greater ability to trust, I can imagine some of my readers finding this difficult and saying, 'Selwyn is ploughing too deep for my liking.' Let me say a word to such people because I am sure many will be struggling with the theme I have been expounding over these past few weeks. God loves you too much to lower his expectations of you. C.S. Lewis referred to God's unwillingness to settle for anything less than the best in us, as 'the intolerable compliment'. We are glad that he takes an interest in us and in our spiritual development, but sometimes, when it necessitates us travelling along the route of pain we would prefer it if he took just a little less interest.

A friend of mine whom God took along a very flinty path heard the Lord whisper to her heart, 'I love you.' 'Well, Lord,' was her response, 'do you think you could love me just a little bit less?'

Father, I confess there are times when I feel like this too. But when the dust has settled and my heart has had time to reflect, I know that your way is always best. Help me absorb that so thoroughly that it becomes instinctive, not just a reflective reaction. Amen.

FOR FURTHER STUDY – Psa. 91:1–16, 34:7

1. What confidence did the psalmist display? / 2. Why will the Lord rescue him?

A good dose of trouble

FOR READING AND MEDITATION – 2 CORINTHIANS 1:1–7

'…the God of all comfort, who comforts us in all our troubles…' (vv. 3–4: NIV)

Have you ever noticed that those Christians whose lives draw you closer to Christ with a sweet and compelling force are those who know what it is to enter and come through a wilderness experience?

It used to strike me in the days when I was a pastor that, more often than not, the people who demanded my attention were not those with serious difficulties but those with what I used to call 'little personal niggles'. They were consumed with such matters as improving their self-image, forgetting the hurts of the past, or making their existence more pleasant. Sometimes (not always) I would say to myself, 'What this person could do with is a good dose of trouble.' For there is nothing like trouble and trials to bring into focus the real and important issues. The people with major difficulties and those who were enduring hardships such as humiliation, loneliness, estrangement, and so on, seemed to have an aura about them that was powerfully attractive. I came to the conclusion that the attractiveness was due to the fact that they were finding grace in the wilderness and it rubbed off them onto others.

Haven't you stumbled across the path of someone in your own Christian fellowship or community whose life provokes you with a sense of feeling small and somewhat behind schedule; someone whose way of talking about the Lord reflects the warm familiarity of a deep, ongoing relationship? I can almost guarantee that if you sat down with that person and encouraged the story, you would discover that he or she knew a lot about the wilderness. It is between the hardest rocks that the sweetest water flows.

O Father, when I see how trouble can produce in my soul a radiance and a fragrance that ministers to others, my natural tendency is to say the cost is too great. But help me see that you share that cost. And that makes all the difference. Amen.

FOR FURTHER STUDY – 1 Thess. 5:1–11, 5:14; John 16:33

1. What did Paul admonish the Thessalonians to continue in? / 2. What did Jesus promise?

No higher place

FOR READING AND MEDITATION – 2 TIMOTHY 1:1–18

'…I know whom I have believed, and am convinced that he is able to guard what I have entrusted to him …' (v. 12: NIV)

We are now almost at the close of our meditations on the wilderness experience – a theme that I know has been deeply challenging, yet immensely important to our understanding of spiritual things. We might wish there was no such thing as a wilderness experience, or that it were unnecessary to Christian growth and development, but that is not the reality. 'The worst thing God could ever do for us,' said the great Reformer John Knox, 'is to make our journey through this world comfortable and without trial.' Those who can enter a wilderness experience and trust God even though they can't trace him are blessed indeed.

There are some who are so strong in trust they believe God is good even though he gives them no word. Corrie ten Boom used to tell the story of a woman who had a dream in which she saw the Lord standing before three nuns in a convent. He came to the first and spent a few minutes talking to her before moving on. He did the same with the second, but the time spent with her was just a little less. The third he appeared to ignore altogether, and he simply walked on by without even a glance or a smile. The woman thought to herself in her dream – the Lord must be sorely displeased with that third person. But then a voice came from somewhere above her and said, 'No, that is not the explanation. The first woman was weak in her faith and love for the Lord and needed much encouragement. The second had a little more faith and love and so that is why the Lord spent less time with her. The third was strong in trust and love and could continue serving whether the Lord ministered to her or not.'

O Father, how I long to be in the place where my trust in you is so firm and absolute that though I never saw another sign or heard another word from you, it would not alter my confidence. Bring me there, dear Father. In Jesus' name. Amen.

FOR FURTHER STUDY – Phil. 1:1–6; Heb. 12:2; Phil. 4:12–16

1. What was Paul confident of? / 2. What attitude did he maintain?

The end of the beginning

FOR READING AND MEDITATION – PSALM 56:1–13

'When I am afraid, I will trust in you.' (v. 3: NIV)

Now that we have concluded our meditations on the theme of the wilderness experience we ask ourselves: what have we learned? This: although Christians are called to go through many trials and difficulties which they often describe as a 'wilderness experience', the true wilderness experience is a period of deep and prolonged testing which God either arranges or allows. Observers of this strange phenomenon down through the ages are almost unanimously agreed that the true wilderness experience can be divided into seven types: (1) humiliation, (2) suffering, (3) bereavement, (4) estrangement, (5) doubt, (6) failure, and (7) dereliction. Some of God's people have met them all, but not everyone has all to meet.

We learned how God's people mastered these assaults on their faith by clinging to Christ. This is the purpose of the wilderness experience – to deepen and develop our faith so that it comes through the fires of testing as polished gold. Next to love, faith and trust are regarded by God as the prime qualities. The Almighty delights to see us trust him in the dark; perhaps this is why he keeps so many of us in the dark.

Our Lord himself has endured the same wilderness experiences through which we are called to go. He was humiliated, he suffered, was bereaved, estranged, and experienced the deepest dereliction possible. He is the supreme example of trust and confidence in God, and when we follow him we will emerge from every wilderness as he did, with the words trembling on our lips: 'This is the victory that overcomes the world – even our faith.'

Gracious and loving heavenly Father, I have learned the theory: now for the practice. Take me on in this coming year to a deeper understanding of what it means to trust you – in everything and for everything. In Jesus' name. Amen.

FOR FURTHER STUDY – 1 Pet. 2:1–25; John 13:15; Heb. 3:1

1. What did Christ leave us? / 2. What are we to do?

His wounds answer our wounds

FOR READING AND MEDITATION – HEBREWS 4:1–16
'For we do not have a High Priest who cannot sympathise with our weaknesses …'
(v. 15: NKJ)

We embark today on a theme which I trust will not only deepen your love for the Lord Jesus Christ, but will help you understand in an even greater way the truth of his ability to enter into and sympathise with every phase of human need. Let it be said at once – our Lord is a wounded healer. That is to say, his ability to heal our wounds flows from the fact that he himself has experienced our wounds. The God we see in Jesus has been in our condition. He has gone through everything we have to go through. His wounds answer our wounds.

Throughout time, men, in manufacturing their gods out of their imaginations, made them appear aloof from the hurts and sorrows of life on earth. They thought that to show them as being affected by the problems of men would make them appear weak and inadequate. Their strength (so they believed) lay in their aloofness. They had to be always strong, always victorious. But how different is the truth about the real God. As Edward Shillito puts it in *Jesus of the Scars*:

The other gods were strong, but Thou becamest weak
They rode, but Thou didst stagger to a throne
But to our wounds only God's wounds can speak
And not a god has wounds, but Thou alone.

No other god can speak to my condition because no other god has been in my condition. Nothing can be more wonderful in earth and heaven than to know that when we come to Jesus, we come to One who has worn our flesh, measured its frailty and knows exactly how we feel.

God, how can I sufficiently thank you that you left your throne to stagger under a cross. Forever you have the marks of your descent upon you. And those marks are not mere scars – they are sacraments of your love. I am eternally grateful. Amen.

FOR FURTHER STUDY – Matt. 26:36–46; Psa. 103:13; Isa. 63:9

1. How do we see Christ's humanity displayed in the Garden?
2. How many times did Jesus make his request?

The humiliation of God

FOR READING AND MEDITATION – PHILIPPIANS 2:1–11

'... but made himself of no reputation, taking the form of a bondservant, and coming in the likeness of men.' (v. 7: NKJ)

We saw yesterday how men, through the ages, in manufacturing gods out of their imaginations, had to make them always appear to be victorious and strong. There was never to be a sign of weakness because that would betray their earthliness.

How different from the picture of the true God presented to us in the Scriptures. There we are told, as in our text for today, that the Creator of the universe took upon himself the form of a servant and was made in the likeness of men. Only the strong can dare to become weak, and so strong was our Creator that he subjected himself to the most astonishing humiliation and became a human being – just like us. Charles Spurgeon, the great preacher of a bygone age, put it like this, 'For God to become a man was more humiliation than for an angel to become a worm.'

Why did he do it? There are many reasons, but listen to what the great writer Dorothy Sayers has to say about it, 'For whatever reason God chose to make man as he is – limited and suffering and subject to sorrows and death – he had the honesty and courage to take his own medicine. Whatever game he is playing with his creation, he has kept his own rules and played fair. He can exact nothing from man that he has not exacted of himself. He himself has gone through the whole of human experience; from the trivial irritations of family life and the cramping restrictions of hard work to the worst horrors of pain and humiliation.' Because God came and put himself in our condition, he now fully understands our condition. How amazing! I don't know about you, but a God who gave himself to me in this way is a God who can have my heart any day.

Lord Jesus, I cannot fully understand the reasons that lay behind your humiliation, but I love you for it nevertheless. May my love be kindled by the flame of your love this day. In your dear name I ask it. Amen.

FOR FURTHER STUDY – 2 Cor. 8:1–9; Matt. 27:38; Luke 2:7

1. How was Christ's humiliation seen in his birth and death?
2. How did Paul express Christ's humiliation to the Corinthians?

The highest honour

FOR READING AND MEDITATION – JOHN 13:1–17

'If I then, *your* Lord and Teacher, have washed your feet, you also ought to wash one another's feet.' (v. 14: NKJ)

Yesterday we touched on the thought that only the strong can dare to be weak. Permit me to develop that thought a little further and take you to one of my favourite scenes in Scripture – Christ washing the disciples' feet.

Look first at how the sacred Scriptures focus on our Lord's consciousness of his greatness: 'Knowing that the Father had given all things into his hands, and that he had come from God and was going to God' (v. 3: NKJ).

Notice that before our Lord stooped to wash the disciples' feet, he had a clear sense of his dignity and status – he knew who he was. If we did not know the events that followed and were asked to fill in the next sentence, our minds would probably come up with something like, 'Knowing that the Father had given all things into his hands, and that he had come from God and was going to God … he invited the disciples to wash his feet.'

How different is the true text: 'Jesus, knowing … that he had come from God and was going to God, rose from supper and laid aside his garments, took a towel … poured water into a basin and began to wash the disciples' feet.' The consciousness of his greatness was the secret of his humility, for, as you see, only the great can afford to stoop. A famous Indian swami is reported to wash his feet in milk and then pass the milk around to his disciples to sip in a kind of pseudo-communion service. How different from the Saviour who washed his disciples' feet. Christians worship at the feet of a God who washes their feet.

O Father, help me see that one of the highest honours is to be girded with a towel. Give me a vision today of my own greatness in you, so that I, too, will dare to be weak. In Jesus' name I ask it. Amen.

FOR FURTHER STUDY – Isa. 52:13–53:12; Zech. 9:9; Matt. 8:20, 11:29

1. List several aspects of Christ's humility. / 2. How did Jesus describe his lifestyle?

God the more!

FOR READING AND MEDITATION – HEBREWS 2:5–18

'Because he himself suffered when he was tempted, he is able to help those who are being tempted.' (v. 18: NIV)

I don't know about you, but the more I contemplate the wonder of God taking on human form, the more I want to throw myself at his feet. Only the God whom we see in Jesus could ever think of doing a thing like this. The poet Browning put it this way:

> To herald all that human and Divine
> In the weary, happy face of him, half God,
> Half man, which made the God-part, God the more!

I have a little problem with the phrase, 'half God, half man', because the merging of the divine and human in Christ cannot be explained in such simplistic or equal terms, but I fully endorse the thought that God, in taking upon himself the constraints of our humanity, 'made the God-part, God the more!' In other words, God never acted more like God than when he became man. He did what we would expect of him.

What if God had not condescended to wear our flesh and enter into our sins and sorrows? Then he would have violated his own principle: 'To him who knows how to do good and does not do it, to him it is sin' (James 4:17, NKJ). You see, there is not one set of principles for God and another for man. The Creator of the universe acts on the same principles he requires of us.

> By all that God requires of me,
> I know that he himself must be.

Solemnly and reverently I say it: the Almighty was never so much God as when he became man.

O Father, what security it gives me to know that you act on the same principles you hold out for me. I am in the hands of a God who is loving, truthful, and consistent. Thank you, Father. I am lost in wonder, love and praise. Amen.

FOR FURTHER STUDY – John 1:1–14; Gal. 4:4; 1 Tim. 2:5–6

1. What happened in the fullness of time? / 2. How does John put it?

Ever the same

FOR READING AND MEDITATION – HEBREWS 13:7–21

'Jesus Christ is the same yesterday and today and for ever.' (v. 8: NIV)

The willingness of our Creator to subject himself to the conditions under which we live must surely spell out one thing – God is intensely interested in the hurts and sorrows that attend the human condition. He did not pick us up with a pair of celestial tongs and hold us before his gaze in order to study and understand our sufferings – he wrapped himself in our flesh and experienced our pains in the same way we experience them. And his interest flows, not to some of his creation but to all his creation.

You may be familiar with the famous painting by Charles E. Butler, entitled *The King of Kings*. It is a fine and beautiful painting depicting Jesus Christ standing at the foot of his cross and receiving the homage of the crowned heads of the world. In the background is the defeated Prince of Darkness who watches as the monarchs of the world press in to do Christ honour. Altogether 158 portraits are included and only two are not royal personages – George Washington and Oliver Cromwell.

The intention of the painter to depict Christ as the King of kings is to be commended, but some have criticised it on the grounds that it implies Christ is interested only in the noble and great. That was not Butler's intention, of course, but I can see how some might draw that deduction. The truth is that the eye of Jesus is held, not by the crown on a person's head but by the ache in their heart. When he was here on earth, he had a special concern for those whom life had wounded. Did that concern end when a cloud received him out of their sight? Our text for today settles it. What he was he is, and what he is he was, and what he is and was he ever will be.

Lord Jesus Christ, Son of God and Son of Man, I am grateful beyond words that the same compassion that filled your heart when you were here on earth is there right now as you sit on the eternal throne. Blessed be your glorious name forever. Amen.

FOR FURTHER STUDY – John 8:43–59; Micah 5:2–4; John 17:5–24; Rev. 22:13

1. What did the prophet declare about Jesus? / 2. What did Jesus declare regarding himself?

Pity, sympathy and empathy

FOR READING AND MEDITATION – LUKE 24:36–53

'"... It is I myself! Touch me and see; a ghost does not have flesh and bones, as you see I have."' (v. 39: NIV)

We continue meditating on the truth that our Lord is not just a healer but a wounded healer. He is able to help us with our hurts because he has experienced our hurts and by reason of this, he is able, as the hymn puts it, 'to soothe our sorrows and heal our wounds'. One of the definitions of Christianity I have come to appreciate is this: 'Christianity is that religion which puts a face and flesh on God.' Suppose there were no flesh in the Godhead, no face like our face – would the Godhead be attractive and approachable? Could we come to him in confidence, knowing that he truly understands? Hardly. He would certainly be able to understand our condition from an objective viewpoint but he would not have been able to empathise with us, for empathy flows only from involvement.

There are three main words used to describe the action of feeling for someone who has been hurt or wounded – pity, sympathy and empathy. Pity is feeling for someone; sympathy is feeling like someone; empathy is feeling with someone. Pity says, 'There, there, don't cry.' Sympathy says, 'I will cry with you.' Empathy says, 'It really hurts, doesn't it? I have cried those same tears too, but let me show you how I found the strength and power to deal with them.'

I think myself that there is a small degree of pity and sympathy to be found in all true empathy, but the thing that makes empathy so much more helpful than pity and sympathy is that while it feels so deeply, it is able to maintain its objectivity and not be overcome with the plight of the person for whom it feels. Our Lord's heart is like this; his sojourn among us enables him to feel, not only for us and like us, but with us.

Blessed Lord Jesus, again I come to you with thanksgiving in my heart for the fact that you meet me in the midst of my need. You have lived amid my needs and thus you can feel for me in my needs. I am so deeply, deeply grateful. Amen.

FOR FURTHER STUDY – Psa. 113; Matt. 9:10–11, 27–34

1. What did the psalmist understand? / 2. What could the Pharisees not understand?

It lays no hold on my heart

FOR READING AND MEDITATION – JOHN 3:1–17

'For God so loved the world that he gave his only begotten Son, that whoever believes in him should … have everlasting life.' (v. 16: NKJ)

We continue with the thought we touched on yesterday: suppose there were no flesh in the Godhead, no face like our face – would the Godhead be attractive and approachable? If God had just given us the principles for living without having put himself in our condition, those principles would have made little impact on our lives.

Take the statement: 'A new commandment I give you, that you love one another; as I have loved you, that you also love one another' (John 13:34, NKJ). The thing that gives this statement such power is the phrase: 'as I have loved you'. The principle of loving has been exemplified in a person – and a person who is not just like God, but is like us. Principles are powerful, but they become even more powerful when they are expressed through a person. Suppose a child is crying for its mother and you say, 'Don't cry, little child, take comfort that there is a principle in this world called the principle of motherhood.' The child would continue to sob, 'But I want my mother.'

The great Indian poet Tulsi Das, when contemplating the many gods of India and realising how unable they were to understand what went on in the inner depths of his being, said, 'The Impersonal lays no hold on my heart.' The Impersonal is too cold and unresponsive. The principles of living become power only as they are embodied in a person, and in a person who is not immune to the sufferings and woes that plague the human condition. Otherwise those principles fall faintly upon the human heart. God has given us more than principles; He has given us himself. Now he knows us – from within.

Father, I am bowed in wonder as I contemplate the idea that you thought so much about my condition that you would not rest until you had tasted my condition. My person responds to your Person. Blessed be your name forever. Amen.

FOR FURTHER STUDY – Rom. 5:1–8; Jer. 31:3; Eph. 2:4–5

1. How did Paul say God shows his love for us? / 2. What is the depth of God's love?

God's credibility rating

FOR READING AND MEDITATION – JOHN 1:1–18

'And the Word became flesh and dwelt among us, and we beheld his glory… full of grace and truth.' (v. 14: NKJ)

Dr Cynddylan Jones, one of Wales' greatest revival preachers and a famous theologian, once said, 'The only way for God to maintain his credibility in the midst of a human race that was ravaged by sin was to taste for himself the conditions under which we live. This he did in the act of the Incarnation, and so before he gave himself for us, he gave himself to us.'

Powerful words, but the text before us today puts it even more powerfully: 'The Word became flesh and dwelt among us'. I love the phrase: 'and dwelt among us'. The visit of God to our world was not a momentary rift in the clouds, giving us just a fleeting glance of the Deity. No, He dwelt among us, from the cradle of the manger to the grave of the tomb; amid our poverty, amid our temptations, amid our problems and our choices, amid our oppositions and disappointments.

Thirty-three years on planet earth was not long, but it was certainly long enough for him to sweep aside all charges that might be levelled against him by both sinners and devils that God was aloof and insensitive to the plight of his creation. He met life as you and I meet it. He called on no power not at our disposal for his own moral battles. He performed no miracle to extricate himself from any difficulty. He had power to restrain power, holding it only for the meeting of human need in others. He never performed a miracle just to show power or confound an enemy. And don't think (as many do) that because he was God in human form, his divine nature prevented him from feeling just as keenly as we do the hurts and sorrows that from time to time are the experience of every single one of us. He feels for us because he has felt like us.

O Father, help me to snuggle up to your heart today and contemplate the wonder of the fact that you are a God who knows exactly how I feel. Believing – I nestle. Amen.

FOR FURTHER STUDY – Rom. 1:1–7; Isa. 7:14; Matt. 1:1; Luke 1:31; Rom. 8:1–3

1. What did Isaiah declare? / 2. What does Paul declare?

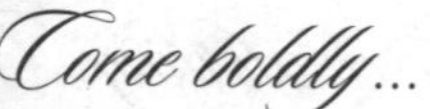

Come boldly...

FOR READING AND MEDITATION – HEBREWS 5:1–14

'...though he was a Son, yet he learned obedience by the things which he suffered.' (v. 8: NKJ)

We continue discussing the point that because Christ has worn our flesh and has experienced the conditions under which we live, he is able to enter into our sufferings and our sorrows in a real and personal way. It is because of this that we are bidden by the writer of the book of Hebrews to 'come boldly to the throne of grace, that we may obtain mercy and find grace to help in time of need' (Heb. 4:16, NKJ).

Over the years I have been astonished at the way in which this text has been misused and misapplied. I have sat in hundreds, if not thousands of prayer meetings in my time and heard Christians pray something like this, 'Father, we are thankful that we don't have to tiptoe into your presence, but as your Word says, we can come boldly. And we come boldly because the veil has been torn away and there are no obstacles on our path to the eternal throne.'

Now I have no problem with these or similar expressions, and I'm sure God doesn't either, but when I hear them I wonder whether those who refer to this text really understand what it is saying. We are encouraged to come boldly to the throne of grace, not just because the way has been opened up for us, but because One sits on the throne who knows exactly how we feel. The thought in the text is this: don't stand there timidly, hesitantly, fearfully – wondering whether God really understands what is going on inside you or not. He knows and feels and cares. He knows the whole gamut of your human emotions. And so come into his presence boldly; he really is a sympathetic and understanding God. Can anything be more wonderful on earth or in heaven?

O Father, the more I ponder the truth that you know everything I feel, the more my heart bows in awe before you. Your understanding helps me stand. I am so grateful. Amen.

FOR FURTHER STUDY – Eph. 3:1–12; Heb. 10:19; 1 John 4:17
1. Where did Paul's boldness come from? / 2. How will this boldness help us?

The comforting Christ

FOR READING AND MEDITATION – ISAIAH 53:1–12

'... a Man of sorrows and acquainted with grief ...' (v. 3: NKJ)

Today we examine a question that is often asked by those passing through deep emotional trauma: how can Christ enter into my feelings when he did not experience the same kind of situation I am going through at present? A man once said to me when I tried to offer him the comfort of Christ at the death of his three-month-old baby, 'Jesus didn't know what it was to lose a child, for he was never a father. How can he really understand what my wife and I are feeling at this moment?'

The answer I gave him was this: although the problems we face in our world are varied and different, those problems produce a pain in our hearts that is shared in the same way by everyone. I asked, 'How would you describe the pain you are feeling in your heart at this moment?' Without hesitation he replied, 'Desolating grief and sorrow.' I pointed out to him that although Christ had not passed through the identical circumstances, he most certainly had felt, and felt equally keenly, the pain of 'desolating grief' in his heart. That truth appeared to comfort as it has comforted many others with whom I have shared. I hope it might comfort you today.

The problems on the surface of our lives may have different wrappings, but deep down in our hearts the pain we experience has the same labels – hurt, sadness, grief, emptiness, despair and disappointment. The problems in our world lead to pain in the heart and it is that pain, whatever its label, that Christ has touched somewhere on the journey between his birth and his death. No wonder our Lord is referred to by so many as 'the comforting Christ'.

Jesus, my blessed Redeemer, how can I ever thank you enough that you know and understand every pain I may feel? My pains are your pains. This makes you more than just the 'Truth'; it makes you the warm, tender, compelling Truth. I am eternally grateful. Amen.

FOR FURTHER STUDY – Heb. 2:1–10; Isa. 50:6; Mark 15:34; Luke 22:44

1. How was Christ made perfect? / 2. How does Luke describe Christ's suffering?

The blight of loneliness

FOR READING AND MEDITATION – GENESIS 2:15–25

'The Lord God said, "It is not good for the man to be alone ..."' (v. 18: NIV)

Now that we have seen how necessary it was for Christ to have worn our flesh, we turn to consider in detail some of the circumstances and situations which occurred in his life and which make it possible for him to know exactly how we feel. Take first the fact of loneliness. He knew loneliness as no one has known it – before or since. Someone has said that greatness is always lonely, and there are multitudes of biographies which clearly confirm that – even Christian biographies.

As the word 'loneliness' may mean different things to different people, let me define how I am using the word. Loneliness is the feeling of being bereft of human companionship, the sadness that comes through the loss of a loved one or the failure to find a close and loving friend. Some Christians hold the view that all loneliness is a sin. One Christian writer says of loneliness, 'If a Christian is lonely, then it means he or she is not walking with the living God; if they were, then they could never feel lonely. Loneliness is therefore a sin – a refusal to accept the companionship of God.'

Personally I find such reasoning unacceptable. It is possible to walk with God and yet feel bereft of human companionship – thus lonely. Adam walked with God and although we do not read that he was 'lonely', God clearly saw the possibility of this and, as our text for today points out, provided a companion and a helper for him. Christians can walk with God, even have a rich relationship with him, yet at times feel incredibly lonely. This is a simple empirical fact – to refuse to face it is to live in denial.

Father, I see that if I am to be helped and come to maturity, then I must face things as they are, not as I would like them to be. Deliver me from any form of denial and make me a realist. In Jesus' name I ask it. Amen.

FOR FURTHER STUDY – Psa. 38:1–11, 102:7, 142:4; 2 Tim 4:16

1. How was the psalmist feeling? / 2. What did Paul share with Timothy?

Can all loneliness be resolved?

FOR READING AND MEDITATION – ROMANS 8:12–30

'… even we ourselves groan within ourselves, eagerly waiting for the adoption, the redemption of our body.' (v. 23: NKJ)

We ended yesterday with the statement that Christians who refuse to face the fact that a Christian can sometimes feel incredibly lonely are living in denial. One of the things that concerns me deeply about much of modern-day church life is the tendency of some to practice denial. I have written a good deal about this lately, so forgive this further emphasis. Let me remind you once again what denial is all about – it is looking at things, as one would like them to be rather than as they really are.

Let us face this question together as realistically as possible: can loneliness (in the sense I have already defined it) be completely resolved while we are here on earth, or merely relieved? My own view is that for some it may never be fully resolved, but only relieved. There are those, it must be said, whose loneliness is really of their own making. The circumstances of life may have compelled them to live alone, but instead of fostering fellowship with others by hospitality and service, they have grown critical and self-pitying and unconsciously drive folk away. Others find themselves unnecessarily lonely because of bitterness and unforgiveness.

My concern, however, is for those who through no fault of their own find themselves in situations where they feel desperately lonely – can this type of loneliness be completely resolved? As I have said, it can be relieved but it may never be fully resolved. The grace of Christ can flow in to ensure that the loneliness is not incapacitating or disabling, but it may be that one has to live with the sharpness of it until the day when faith is lost in sight.

Father, I know there is a clear ring about truth, but sometimes that ring is not what I want to hear. Help me, therefore, to keep my heart open, even though I hear things that may shake my previously held ideas. In Christ's name I ask it. Amen.

FOR FURTHER STUDY – John 15:1–15; Prov. 17:17, 18:24

1. How can we express friendship? / 2. How can we gain friendship?

Heaven now?

FOR READING AND MEDITATION – 2 CORINTHIANS 6:1–18

'... by honour and dishonour... as sorrowful, yet always rejoicing... as having nothing, and yet possessing all things.' (vv. 8,10: NKJ)

We are discussing the thought that for some, a sense of loneliness may be a fact of life that will never be removed this side of heaven. This, I know, runs counter to the teaching in many sections of the church, saying we can confidently expect complete spiritual satisfaction to be ours this side of heaven. There is a view in many Christian communities that can be expressed like this, 'Christ's joy can eliminate loneliness, not just support us in it. It simply isn't necessary to struggle with any form of loneliness, for the reality of Christ's presence can so thrill our souls that the pain of loneliness is never felt.'

The effect of this teaching is to assume that Christ's presence promises to take all the struggles out of the Christian life and give us heaven now. This is why our churches are full of Christians who pretend to feel now what they are not able to feel until they get to heaven – complete and total satisfaction. This is what they are taught, so whenever they struggle they say to themselves, 'Christians are not supposed to have struggles, so when someone asks me how I am, I had better not let the side down – so I will pretend things are fine.'

Can you hear the denial going on in those words? Those whose integrity will not allow them to pretend often worry that they are not making it spiritually and think to themselves, 'Something must be wrong with my Christian life.' Churches tend to reward those who can create the illusion of having it all together by holding them up as examples of what a Christian should be, while actually, in some cases, such people may be less spiritual than those whose integrity compels them not to deny their struggles.

Father, help me to grasp the point that although I cannot expect to have heaven now, through your Spirit's presence in my heart, I have a little bit of heaven to go to heaven in. Thank you, dear Father. Amen.

FOR FURTHER STUDY – Matt. 11:7–19; Luke 7:34; James 2:23

1. What was said of Jesus? / 2. What was Abraham called?

It's OK to hurt

FOR READING AND MEDITATION – 2 CORINTHIANS 12:1–10

'… "My grace is sufficient for you, for my power is made perfect in weakness."' (v. 9: NIV)

We continue meditating on the thought that some forms of loneliness may remain part of our human condition until we die and go to heaven. Is this watering down the effectiveness of the Holy Spirit or the joy that Christ gives to us? I believe not. No one is more confident of the power of Christ to work miracles and overcome problems than I, but there are some issues that will never be fully resolved until we get to heaven – and loneliness may be one of them.

Some might never struggle with loneliness, for they will be surrounded with love and affection until the day they die, but others will not be so favoured. What about such people? They can either pretend they are not lonely and refuse to grapple honestly with their condition, or accept the fact that they may continue through life with a groan in their heart, a groan that is relieved by the presence of Christ but not always eliminated. A friend of mine who is a counsellor tells his counselees, 'It's OK to hurt.' He says that sometimes they appear relieved that they are given permission to feel that way.

Some hurts are part of the human condition and they may be with us until the day we die, but remember this – Christ's presence can be there to relieve and support so that the pain is not incapacitating. We are not absolutely sure what Paul's 'thorn in the flesh' was (some think it was a physical problem, others a spiritual problem, such as constant harassment from Satan) but the important thing to remember was that while God did not deliver him from it, he was certainly there with him in it. God always gives enough grace to carry on.

Father, help me see that though some of the problems in my life may not be fully resolved while I am here on earth, I can always count on your grace seeing me through. Glory and honour be to your name forever. Amen.

FOR FURTHER STUDY – 1 Tim. 1:1–14; 2 Tim. 2:1; Titus 3:7

1. What did Paul tell Timothy? / 2. What was Timothy's testimony?

The awful loneliness of God

FOR READING AND MEDITATION – MARK 3:20–34

'… they went to take charge of him, for they said, "He is out of his mind."' (v. 21: NIV)

Today we ask ourselves: did Jesus experience loneliness? I think he knew loneliness as no one has known it before or since. As a child, he must have felt a little apart – not superior (though he was superior), but a sense of being different. At the age of twelve he knew that he must be about his Father's business.

When his ministry began, it caused concern among some of the members of his family. Other men have known what it was like to have the entire world take up arms against them, but usually they had someone at home who would take up arms beside them against the world. Jesus lacked even that. The other children born to Mary and Joseph and who formed part of Christ's earthly family came to believe that he did not know what he was doing and were astonished by his actions. In what remained of his earthly life, it was to his disciples he looked for understanding and companionship – but he looked in vain. On the eve of his crucifixion, they argued about precedence, they slept while he agonised in the Garden and ran away at the moment he was arrested.

Many of the world's martyrs knew at the moment of their death that there were some in the world who sympathised with them and understood the cause for which they died. But Jesus had little sympathy and little understanding. His sacrifice mystified the people who were closest to him. As Dr Sangster, the famous Methodist preacher, put it, 'It mattered to all the world that he died for love, but no single soul in the world understood that he was doing it. He was lonely with the awful loneliness of God.' Can it be doubted that he is able to sympathise with anyone who is engulfed by loneliness?

Blessed Lord Jesus, as I realise that no one could ever have been as lonely as you, I see with fresh insight into the truth that you are a sympathetic and compassionate Saviour. And I am grateful more than these faltering words can convey. Amen.

FOR FURTHER STUDY – Matt. 26:39–50; Mark 14:32–42

1. Where were Christ's disciples when he needed them?
2. How did Christ express the depths of his loneliness?

I can resist anything but temptation

FOR READING AND MEDITATION – 1 CORINTHIANS 10:1–13

'... God is faithful, who will not allow you to be tempted beyond what you are able, but ... will also make the way of escape ...' (v. 13: NKJ)

We look now at another situation and experience in which Christ found himself and one which, from time to time, we are called on to undergo – strong and vigorous temptation. No one has experienced such a depth or degree of temptation as our Lord.

However, before we focus on his temptations, let's consider the subject of temptation in general. Why is temptation so 'successful'? What makes it work? How can we handle it? These are questions that constantly appear in my correspondence. Mark Anthony, you may remember, was known as 'the silver-throated orator of Rome'. He was a brilliant statesman and magnificent in battle. He had, however, the fatal flaw of moral weakness and one day his tutor confronted him with these words, 'O Marcus ... able to conquer the world, but unable to resist a temptation.' That indictment, I'm afraid, applies not just to Mark Anthony but to almost everyone. When I was young, a close Christian friend of mine used to say facetiously, 'I can resist anything but temptation.'

It is important, I believe, to differentiate between a trial and a temptation. Generally speaking, a trial is an ordeal or a test of our faith, while a temptation is a deliberate enticement to do evil. God cannot tempt us, but he can and does test or try us (see James 1:13 and Job 23:10). Normally there is nothing immoral involved in experiencing a trial. It is a hardship, an ordeal, but not an enticement to evil. Temptation involves a definite enticement to do wrong. The dictionary says, 'To tempt someone is to beguile them to do wrong, by promise of pleasure or gain.' Temptation motivates a person to be bad by promising something that appears to be good. Isn't that just like the devil?

Lord Jesus, can it really be possible that you know how I feel when I am under the intense pressure of temptation? It must be so – for your Word clearly states it. Teach me more of this, dear Lord, so that I can lean more on you. In your name. Amen.

FOR FURTHER STUDY – Gen. 3:1–11; Matt. 4:1–11; 2 Cor. 11:3

1. How did Satan tempt Eve? / 2. How did Satan tempt Jesus?

The answer to temptation

FOR READING AND MEDITATION – GALATIANS 5:16–26

'…the fruit of the Spirit is love, joy, peace, longsuffering, kindness, goodness, faithfulness, gentleness, self-control …' (vv. 22–23: NKJ)

We spend another day looking in more detail at the difference between a trial and a temptation. Take, for example, Job's trials. He lost his family, his home, his cattle, his health – everything. There was nothing immoral involved in those trials, although, of course, in Job's case we have to recognise that they were not just natural disasters but were brought about by sinister intent.

A clearer illustration of a trial might be that of John on the Isle of Patmos. He was banished to the island because of his commitment to Jesus Christ and was forced to live in isolation – removed from all those things that he would have held most dear. It was a trial. The same applies to Elijah who, in the midst of difficult circumstances, became depressed. When his life was threatened, he went away to hide and pleaded with God: 'It is enough! Now, Lord, take my life, for I am no better than my fathers!' (1 Kings 19:4, NKJ).

Temptation is different, for it has to do with more than circumstances – it contains a deliberate enticement to commit sin. It is not just experiencing an ordeal (though temptation can be an ordeal) but involves being solicited by evil. How do we resist temptation? The Biblical answer is so simple that many stumble over it. It is found in the text before us today, and the word I want to focus on is self-control. The Greek word literally means 'in strength', and that's exactly what happens when the Holy Spirit resides in us – he comes in to strengthen us on the inside. In other words, God promises that through his Spirit, we will be able to master our turbulent feelings in the moment of temptation. Pause and let that sink in.

Father, this sounds so simple that it is almost simplistic. But I have learned that your Word can never be that. Teach me more on this issue, for anything I can learn about how to combat temptation scratches where I am itching. In Christ's name I ask it. Amen.

FOR FURTHER STUDY – Rom. 6:1–14; Prov. 16:32; 1 Peter 1:3–7; 2 Peter 1:5–7
1. What did Paul write to the Romans? / 2. What are we to add to our faith?

Shouting a thunderous 'No' to sin

FOR READING AND MEDITATION – 2 PETER 1:4–7

'… make every effort to add to your faith goodness; and to goodness, knowledge; and to knowledge, self-control …' (vv. 5–6: NIV)

We pick up from where we left off yesterday when we looked at the answer to temptation – self-control. Now some may be saying at this stage, 'Wait a minute – dealing with temptation is not something I have to do, but something God does for me. I am not able to do anything about temptation and unless he does it in and through me, I am sunk. God is the active one and I am the passive one.'

Now there is a grain of truth in this, for it is true that the more we allow God to work in and through us by his Holy Spirit, the more power we have at our disposal, but ultimately we have to put it to work though deliberate choice and conscious action. It is like engaging the clutch in a manually controlled car. The engine may be running at a very fast rate, but there will be no forward or backward movement of the car until the driver makes a conscious decision to avail himself of the power of the engine by engaging the clutch.

Whatever view we might hold about the work of the Holy Spirit in our lives, the bottom line is this – God holds us responsible for shouting a thunderous 'No' to sin. I am to decide, whenever I am faced with the possibility of yielding to sin, that I will not do so because I reject sin even as God does. Victory depends upon believing and accepting the fact that God's power is sufficient to resist the seemingly overwhelming rush of internal feelings and urges and deciding not to yield. If you try to deal passively with temptation and turn the responsibility over to God, then you will fail. Self-control comes from God, but we have to carry it out. He supplies the power – we supply the willingness.

Father, I must confess that I struggle with this question of responsibility. Something in me wants to be a passive spectator in the battle, but I know I have to be active. Help me put this whole thing together – once and for all. In Jesus' name. Amen.

FOR FURTHER STUDY – Rom. 8:1–14; Prov. 1:10, 4:14

1. What are we not to follow? / 2. What are we to do when enticed?

Let go and let God

FOR READING AND MEDITATION – JAMES 4:1–12

'Submit yourselves, then, to God. Resist the devil, and he will flee from you.' (v. 7: NIV)

We continue thinking through the issue of how to combat temptation. The view that says if temptation is to be overcome, then we must passively wait on God and let him do it for us, is responsible for more failures and difficulties in the Christian church than almost anything else.

Some years ago, when talking to a Christian man who told me he had homosexual inclinations and found himself at times yielding to those desires, I was not surprised to find that his view of temptation ran something like this, 'Whenever I have been tempted, I try to "let go and let God" as I have been taught, but my urges always seem to carry me to my homosexual partner.' (Let me make it clear that despite the woolly thinking in some parts of the Christian church, I regard homosexual practice as sin.) Further conversation revealed that he was looking for victory from two sources: either that the desire would be weakened or that greater strength would be given to him by God to resist the desire. Notice, neither option depended on him at all. He was responsible for nothing. He was passively saying, 'Lord, I don't really want to sin; help me.'

I pointed out that his responsibility was to decide assertively not to sin, then to trust God to work in him both to will and to act according to his good pleasure. The strength to resist was there in his life in great abundance (as it is also in yours if you are a Christian), but victory depended on his assuming responsibility for what he could control – making a clear and clean-cut decision to obey God by not sinning. The same basic supply of the Spirit is given to every child of God, but it is our responsibility to carry out the action of self-control before victory can be seen in our lives.

Father, drive this truth deeply into my spirit today that victory over temptation involves a team effort – you and me together. Help me to work out all the implications of this in my life day by day. In Jesus' name. Amen.

FOR FURTHER STUDY – Eph. 4:17–27, 6:11; 1 Peter 5:8–9

1. What did Paul admonish the Ephesians about?
2. How did Peter put it?

Our Lord's temptations

FOR READING AND MEDITATION – MATTHEW 4:1–11
'Then Jesus was led up by the Spirit into the wilderness to be tempted by the devil.'
(v. 1: NKJ)

Today we ask ourselves: did our Lord know what it was to be tempted? Was our Lord put through the same pressures that we go through when we are tempted to go another way than God's? No one has ever experienced such a depth and a degree of temptation, as did Jesus. In the film, *The Last Temptation of Christ*, our Lord is depicted engaging in sexual fantasies. What blasphemy! The argument goes: how can Christ understand our feelings unless he knew what it was to experience all our feelings?

In answering that question, I must remind you of what I said earlier about Christ meeting us, not at the surface of life where there are so many differences, but in the depths where we are all the same. Underneath all temptations the basic issue is this – an enticement to act independently of God. Hold that in your mind and you will not go wrong in understanding Christ's involvement with our human nature.

Did he experience the temptation to take an easier road – to act independently of God? I have no doubt myself that the three temptations levelled at Christ in that rigorous and severe encounter in the wilderness were the most powerful temptations a human being has ever experienced on this earth. But our Lord showed that obedience to God is possible even in the most difficult of situations. As I have said on a previous occasion, the first Adam failed in a garden feasting, but the second Adam triumphed in a wilderness fasting. Can Jesus succour those who are passing through the fires of temptation? I know of no one better – do you?

Blessed Lord Jesus, the more I contemplate your humanity, the more I see that you came to me at awful cost. You know how I feel – even when I am tempted. I am grateful beyond words. Thank you, dear Lord. Amen.

FOR FURTHER STUDY – Luke 4:1–13; 1 Cor. 10:13; 2 Cor. 2:11
1. What comes with every temptation? / 2. How did Jesus demonstrate this?

Trust my love

FOR READING AND MEDITATION – JEREMIAH 15:10–21

'Why is my pain perpetual and my wound incurable, which refuses to be healed . . . ?' (v. 18: NKJ)

We turn now in the days that lead up to Good Friday and Easter to focus on another aspect of the way in which Christ has identified with our humanity – the aspect of suffering and pain. No one has suffered more than our Lord and his experience in Gethsemane and on the Cross are evidences of this fact.

How do we begin to deal with this difficult problem of suffering and pain? It keeps raising its head, regardless of the most erudite attempts to explain it away. Even C.S. Lewis, who offered perhaps the most articulate explanation of pain this century, saw his arguments wilt as he watched the onslaught of bone cancer in his wife's body. Sharing his feelings some time after the event, he wrote, 'You never know how much you really believe anything until its truth or falsehood becomes a matter of life and death to you.' I know something of what he meant, having watched my wife die in a similar way. Like Hercules battling against the Hydra, all our attempts to chop down the arguments of the atheists and the agnostics in relation to suffering and pain are met with writhing new examples, each one seemingly worse than the others.

Is suffering and pain, as some philosophers claim, God's big mistake? I do not believe so myself. I remember as a child having to have my tonsils removed and when the moment came to enter the hospital, I clung to my mother, pleading with her to save me from the ordeal. The look she gave me said, 'I must not save you from it. You will understand some day. You must trust my love.' This is how God deals with us in the presence of suffering and pain. He says, 'What I permit may not make much sense to you now. . . but there is a purpose. Trust my love!'

O Father, in my moments of perplexity when I struggle with this issue of suffering and pain, help me realise that the One who asks for my trust is the One who gave himself for me on Calvary. In the light of this, how can I hold back? Amen.

FOR FURTHER STUDY – Psa. 34, 118:8; Prov. 3:5

1. What was the psalmist's conviction? / 2. What is our natural tendency?

If you were God ...

FOR READING AND MEDITATION – GENESIS 1:1–31

'Then God said, "Let us make man in our image, according to our likeness ..."' (v. 26: NKJ)

We continue thinking through the issue of suffering and pain. Omnipotence, of course, could have easily avoided the problem but only at the price of making us marionettes. Can anyone who is not utterly engulfed in sorrow regret that God did not take that path; that his love would not compromise with sin; that nothing would thwart him in his purpose of giving us freedom of will? But by giving us free will, God had to take the risk that we would misuse and misapply our freedom.

One writer uses this analogy to describe the situation. God made wood, which is a useful product as the branches of a tree bear fruit, support leaves that provide us with shade and shelter birds, squirrels and other forms of wildlife. Even taken from the tree, wood is useful. Men use it to build homes, make furniture and many other useful things. Wood, however, is hard and by reason of that fact is potentially dangerous. You can put a piece of wood in a man's hand and he can either use it to make something useful or break open the skull of another man. Of course, God could reach down each time a man hit another with a heavy piece of wood and turn the wood into a sponge so that the wood would bounce off lightly – but that is not what freedom is all about.

Months after C.S. Lewis's wife had died, a friend said to him while out walking, 'If you were God, would you make a man like a machine or with the freedom to choose?' He paused for a while and his sharp mind saw right through to the core of the issue. If he were a machine, he would not feel the intense pain he was going through at the time, but then he realised he would not feel joy either. His reply was short but filled with deep understanding, 'I would do as God did.'

O Father, if I were a machine I would not be able to have fellowship with you. To commune with you is worth far more than any pain or suffering I may have to go through. I would have it no other way – even though seven deaths lay in between. Amen.

FOR FURTHER STUDY – Heb. 11:23–29; Isa. 66:3; Psa. 119:30

1. What was the testimony to Moses' life? / 2. What path did the psalmist choose?

Pain – God's megaphone

FOR READING AND MEDITATION – REVELATION 21:1–8

'And God will wipe away every tear from their eyes …
There shall be no more pain, for the former things have passed away.' (v. 4: NKJ)

In the days prior to my conversion, one of the things that used to impress me about Christianity was its willingness to meet the issue of sin and suffering head on. Other religions set out to deny that pain exists or encouraged their adherents to deal with it stoically. Many dodged the issue of pain – Christianity looked it squarely in the face. Someone has described suffering and pain as 'God's megaphone'. It is an appropriate phrase because it shouts to us that something is wrong.

It was this aspect of Christianity that made G.K. Chesterton say, 'The modern philosopher told me I was in the right place but I still felt depressed, even in acquiescence. Then I heard that I was in the wrong place and my soul sang for joy.' What did he mean? The optimists of his day told him that this world was the best of all possible worlds and he should make the best of it. Christianity came along and told him that this is a stained, marred planet.

This perspective then led him to say, 'It entirely reversed the reason for optimism. And the instant the reversal was made, it felt like the abrupt ease when a bone is put back in the socket. I had often called myself an optimist to avoid the too evident blasphemy of pessimism. But the optimism of the age was false and disheartening because it tried to prove we have to fit into the world.' Suffering and pain, God's megaphone, can either drive us from him or draw us to him. It can make us angry with God for allowing such conditions in his universe, or make us appreciative of God for building a new environment in which sin and sorrow will have no place.

Gracious and loving Father, I see I do not have to fit into this world, for you are preparing for me a new world where everything fits. Because of this I am a true optimist – one who sees things from your point of view. Thank you, Father. Amen.

FOR FURTHER STUDY – John 14:1–7; Psa. 30:5, 34:19–20
1. What did Jesus promise his disciples? / 2. What comes in the morning?

God has suffered too!

FOR READING AND MEDITATION – HEBREWS 12:1–13

'For consider him who endured … lest you become weary and discouraged in your souls.' (v. 3: NKJ)

On a Good Friday, it seems almost fatuous to ask the question: did Christ experience suffering and pain? In keeping with our theme, we must ask it nevertheless. Linger with me today at the foot of Calvary. One writer says of it, 'The scene, with its sharp spikes and bleeding death, has been told so often that we, who shrink from a news story on the death of baby seals, flinch not at all at its retelling.' How sad.

The physical and mental sufferings of Christ began in Gethsemane when his sweat was as great drops of blood. One doctor says, 'Though rare, this is the phenomenon of hematidrosis where, under great emotional stress, tiny capillaries in the sweat glands break, mixing blood with sweat. This process alone could have produced marked weakness and shock.' After the arrest in the middle of the night, Jesus was brought before Caiaphas the high priest, at which point a soldier struck him across the face. The palace guards then blindfolded him and mockingly taunted him to identify them as they each passed by and struck him in the face.

In the early morning, battered, bruised, dehydrated and exhausted from a sleepless night, Jesus is taken across Jerusalem to the Praetorium, where he is stripped naked and scourged. Then a heavy beam is tied to his shoulders and for a while he is forced to carry his cross until relieved of the ordeal by Simon of Cyrene. At Golgotha, he is skewered to that cross by iron nails and strung up like a dog to die. If you still struggle over the mystery as to why God allowed pain and suffering into his world, then I point you to an even greater mystery – God has suffered too!

O Father, the mystery of your own suffering may not satisfy my reason as to why you allowed pain and suffering in your world – but it satisfies my heart. Help me to trust you even when I cannot trace you. In Jesus' name. Amen.

FOR FURTHER STUDY – Matt. Ch. 27; Isa. 50:6; Heb. 2:10

1. List at least six elements of suffering Christ endured on Good Friday.
2. Sit quietly for five minutes and contemplate the events of Good Friday.

God came incredibly close

FOR READING AND MEDITATION – LUKE 23:33–49
'And when they had come to the place called Calvary, there they crucified him…' (v. 33: NKJ)

Those who may have wondered what I meant when I said earlier, 'God's wounds answer to our wounds', might find the story of what happened to Joni Eareckson helpful and enlightening. One day, during the summer of 1967, Joni dived off a raft in Chesapeake Bay near Baltimore and struck her head on a rock, breaking her neck. She was instantly paralysed and, were it not for the quick thinking of a friend, might have drowned there and then. Joni was rushed to hospital and several weeks later learnt that her condition would be permanent.

Joni's spirits fell to great depths and turning to her friend Jackie, she said, 'Help me die. Bring me some pills or a razor blade, even. I can't live inside a grotesque body like this.' Of course, Jackie couldn't bring herself to do what Joni asked, which served only to increase Joni's sense of helplessness. Some time after this, one night, while Cindy, her newfound friend, sat reading with her, Cindy blurted out, 'Joni, Jesus knows how you feel – you aren't the only one – why, he was paralysed too.' Joni asked, 'What do you mean?' 'It's true,' said Cindy. 'Remember, he was nailed on a cross. His back was raw from beatings and he must have yearned for a way to move, to change positions or redistribute his weight. But he couldn't. He was paralysed by the nails.'

The thought went deep into Joni's spirit. It had never occurred to her before that God had felt the exact piercing sensations that racked her body. 'At that moment,' said Joni, 'God came incredibly close.' This is always the effect upon those who realise that the God they serve knows exactly how they feel. May he come close, incredibly close, to you today.

Father, I am convinced of one thing, no matter how many mysteries I face in this world – you are worthy of my trust. Knowing you is worth all enduring. Thank you, my Father. Amen.

FOR FURTHER STUDY – 2 Cor. 1:1–7; 1 Peter 2:21, 3:18; Heb. 13:12
1. What is the result of Christ's sufferings? / 2. What should be the result of our sufferings?

What if there were no resurrection?

FOR READING AND MEDITATION – 1 CORINTHIANS 15:12–28

'If in this life only we have hope in Christ, we are of all men the most pitiable.' (v. 19: NKJ)

Easter Sunday focuses on the glorious fact of our Lord's resurrection. It might seem to some that in drawing attention to the resurrection in the midst of this theme on the humanity of Christ, I am simply paying respect to the day, but believe me, there is much more to it than that.

Consider what our situation would be like if there were no resurrection. Elie Wiesel, who was a victim of the Holocaust, tells in his book, *Night* about an occasion in the concentration camp when he watched a child being hanged. He describes the child as having the face of a sad angel and as, along with others, he watched the brutal spectacle take place, he heard a voice behind him groan, 'Where is God? Where is he? Where can he be now?' Wiesel goes on to say that as a result of the things he witnessed in the concentration camp, he became a pessimist. He writes, 'Can words like hope, happiness and joy ever have meaning again?'

I say, 'Yes, they can.' And here's why – Christ, too, went through a time when he cried: 'My God, my God, why have you forsaken me?' He knew what it was to identify fully with the pain and suffering which sometimes racks our bodies and our souls, but it didn't end there – it ended in resurrection. That's the hope the resurrection brings – the hope that sin, pain, suffering and death are not the end. Life is the end – glorious, everlasting, abundant life. The resurrection adds another layer to human experience and lets us know that, whatever the reasons God allows pain and suffering, they are beaten enemies. Difficult though it may be to believe, good will come out of them. The resurrection is the pledge that it will.

Gracious and loving Father, I am so thankful that in everything, you have the last word. And your last word is not death – but life. Lift my heart on this resurrection day to appreciate and revel in this fact. In Christ's name I ask it. Amen.

FOR FURTHER STUDY – Psa. 30; Isa. 61:1–3; John 16:20

1. What did the psalmist testify? / 2. How did Isaiah put it?

However deep the pit…

FOR READING AND MEDITATION – GENESIS 50:14–26

'…you meant evil against me; but God meant it for good…' (v. 20: NKJ)

We continue meditating on the great truth of our Lord's resurrection. Yesterday we referred to the story of Elie Wiesel who, in his book, *Night*, came to the conclusion that God didn't care about his universe and, as a result, developed hard and bitter feelings toward the Almighty.

How different from the story told by Corrie Ten Boom in *The Hiding Place*. All the pain and suffering of *Night* are present in Corrie's gripping story. She, too, saw people murdered, watched her sister die, felt the pain of a whip and sensed all around her the dissolution of virtue. But there is another element present that only a Christian mind can understand – the element of victory and hope. Time and time again, she refers to the ways in which God turned the evil to good. If you have read the story, you will remember the many miracles that took place, the secret Bible studies, prayer times with other believers, acts of great sacrifice and compassion, and so on. Wiesel's book leads to unyielding despair, but Corrie's book leads to triumphant hope.

What is the reason for this difference? It is the resurrection of our Lord. The resurrection is like a lighthouse in a storm-tossed sea of pain and suffering, beaming out a powerful message of life and hope. It says, 'Sin, pain and suffering are not the final answer – God is the final answer.' So have confidence in the confidence of God. His Son overcame everything life threw at him, and he sits once again on the throne of the universe, having himself endured the deepest agonies of human suffering. As Corrie Ten Boom puts it in The Hiding Place, 'However deep the pit, God's love has gone deeper still.'

Gracious and loving Father, it is obvious that you have confidence in your ability to turn everything that is negative in this universe into something that is positive and good. Pour into me that selfsame confidence too. In Jesus' name I ask it. Amen.

FOR FURTHER STUDY – Gen. 37:1–36; Jer. 38:1–20; Acts 16:19–34

1. What was true of Joseph, Jeremiah, Paul and Silas?
2. How did God use these experiences?

He showed them his hands

FOR READING AND MEDITATION – JOHN 20:19–31

'... in his hands the print of the nails ...' (v. 25: NKJ)

Today we ask ourselves: what practical effect does Christ's identification with our pain and suffering have upon those who go through dark and depressing experiences? Christian literature fairly bulges with the truth that those who have suffered, and suffered deeply, derived enormous strength from the fact that the God they served has also endured pain.

One of the most moving stories I have ever read comes from the book, *Ten Fingers for God* by Dorothy Clarke Wilson, in which she tells the story of Dr Paul Brand, who worked among leprosy patients in Velore, India. One evening Paul slipped in late to a patients' gathering, where the air was heavy with the stench of crowded bodies, stale spices and treated bandages. The patients implored him to speak to them and reluctantly, because he had nothing prepared, he stood up in the midst of them. Pausing for a moment, he looked at their hands, some with no fingers, some with only a few stumps, and said, 'I am a hand surgeon, so when I meet people I can't help looking at their hands.'

He went on to say that he would have liked to have had the chance to meet Christ and study his hands! He said, 'It hurts me to think of a nail being driven through his hands, for that would have made them appear horribly twisted and crippled.' As he said these words, the effect on the patients was electrifying. They looked at each other as if to say, 'Jesus was crippled like us; he too, had clawed hands like ours.' Tears flowed down their cheeks. Suddenly they lifted their hands (or what was left of them) to heaven as if with new pride and dignity. God's own response to suffering made theirs so much easier.

Lord Jesus, what a mystery – the God of the stars becomes the God of the scars. All this you have done for me, yet what have I done for thee? I give myself and all I am afresh to you this day. Receive me – in your name. Amen.

FOR FURTHER STUDY – Matt. 4:13–16; Psa. 23:4, 107:9–10

1. What was David's testimony?
2. What does Christ bring to those in the shadow of death?

The powerful hands of Jesus

FOR READING AND MEDITATION – MATTHEW 8:1–17
'He touched her hand and the fever left her …' (v. 15: NIV)

We pause in our meditations on the nail-pierced hands of Jesus to think for a few moments on the importance of the hands. In a way, our hands are no more important than any other part of our bodies – each part depends on the others – but for some reason, the hands have a special significance.

No part of the body has so worked its way into common speech as the hands. Think of just a few of the sayings that have to do with hands: to lend a hand, to come cap in hand, to be an old hand, to rule with a heavy hand, to take a thing in hand, hands off, hands up, all hands on deck – and there are at least a dozen more. When I was ordained to the ministry, hands were laid on my head. Our five senses may in some ways be inferior to those of the lower creatures (our eyes are not as sharp as an eagle's, for example) but we all outsoar all other creatures with relation to our hands. Not even the ape can claim to have our amazing dexterity with hands.

As I have meditated on the hands of Jesus in preparation for what I am now writing, my heart has been deeply moved and stirred. I thought of how his hands caressed the heads of the little children; touched to life the daughter of Jairus; plucked the fever from the throbbing brow of Peter's mother-in-law; touched the lepers and made them clean. I feel moved by the Spirit to say to those of you who are sad at heart and sorely needing the tender touch of your Saviour – kneel before him in the quietness and ask for his help in your hour of need. Be unhurried. Wait before him filled with just that longing – to find him near. I promise you – he will honour your faith. He will touch you with his tender hands.

Jesus, my Lord and my Master, let me feel afresh this day the touch of your hands upon my entire being – spirit, soul and body. Touch me, my Saviour – and make me whole. Amen.

FOR FURTHER STUDY – Neh. 2:1–18; Psa. 37:24, 104:28; 1 Peter 5:6
1. What was Nehemiah's testimony? / 2. What result did this have on the people?

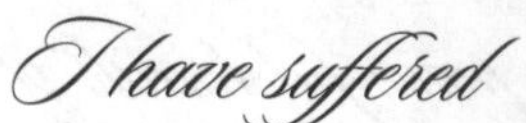

I have suffered

FOR READING AND MEDITATION – 1 PETER 3:8–22

'For Christ also suffered once for sins, the just for the unjust, that he might bring us to God …' (v. 18: NKJ)

We spend another day meditating on the pierced hands of Jesus. Have you ever seen a pierced hand? Really looked at it? W.E. Sangster, in one of his Westminster Sermons, tells how he had a little sister who was smitten with a vicious disease. She had been operated on so many times that her face 'was marred more than any man's' and had to be hidden from the sight of all but the brave.

Among her many disfigurements was a pierced hand. He tells how many times as a lad he would take her hand in his, and it struck him that it looked like a poor, dumb mouth. What would it say if it could speak? He found himself in his boyish perplexity amending Shakespeare and murmuring, 'I would there were a tongue in every wound …' If you and I could at this moment have the privilege of holding in our hands the hands of Jesus, and look long and steadfastly at the nail prints and if somehow there was 'a tongue in every wound' of Jesus, what, I wonder, would they say? I think I know, 'I have suffered.'

Those of you who are experiencing pain and suffering at this moment – reflect on that. The hardest part of suffering is the temptation to believe God is not with us in it – the idea that he reigns in some far-off splendour, untroubled by our woes. It is not true! Whenever we are in need of succour in our lives and Jesus comes alongside, the first thing that impresses itself into our consciousness is the fact that he has pierced hands. There is a kinship among those who suffer which others cannot share. They understand each other! In moments of trial, our Lord has no need to say anything. It is enough that he shows us his hands.

Blessed Redeemer, I am so thankful that you are not just the leader of a scarred community – you have been scarred yourself. You fully comfort me because you fully understand me. Blessed be your wondrous name forever. Amen.

FOR FURTHER STUDY – Matt. 9:18–31; Mark 9:27; Acts 3:7, 9:41

1. How did Jesus respond to Jairus' daughter, the blind men and the child?
2. Why not reach your hand out to someone today?

For ever one

FOR READING AND MEDITATION – REVELATION 5:1–14

'And I looked, and behold, in the midst of the throne … stood a Lamb as though it had been slain …' (v. 6: NKJ)

I cannot explain why but I feel compelled to spend one more day putting before you some further thoughts on the pierced hands of Jesus. As we have seen, when Jesus met with Thomas the doubter, the first thing he said to him was: 'Come, look at my hands.' Have you ever wondered why, in his resurrection body, Christ still bore the marks of the nails? I think it was that he wanted to carry back to heaven an eternal reminder of the fact that he had hung upon a cross. Not that he could ever forget it, of course, but it was his way of saying (so I believe) that he wanted to be forever one with us. Think of that, those of you who have suffered and those of you who suffer still. A hymn writer has put it thus:

The dear tokens of his passion
Still his dazzling body bears;
Cause of endless exultation
To his ransomed worshippers:
With what rapture
With what rapture
Gaze we on those glorious scars!

When Paul was cast into prison, chained hand and foot, it must have seemed a deep mystery to him that God should allow such a thing, especially as Paul's great ambition was to preach Christ wherever he went. I often wonder if Jesus appeared to him in his cell and showed him his hands. I cannot be sure, but I know if he did – that would have been enough.

Dear Lord Jesus, to know that you, too, have suffered binds me to you in a way that nothing else can. Through your wounds I see into the heart of God – and what I see is beautiful. Thank you, my Saviour. Amen.

FOR FURTHER STUDY – Rev. 13:1–8; Isa. 53:7; John 1:29; 1 Peter 1:19; Gen. 22:7–8

1. What was the lamb prepared for? / 2. What did Abraham's experience depict?

Cruel and unjust criticism

FOR READING AND MEDITATION – MARK 8:1–21

'And he groaned and sighed deeply in his spirit . . .' (v. 12: *Amp. Bible*)

Another set of experiences Christ faced and which we often find ourselves in is that of coping with cruel and unjust criticism. I think I am drawn to write this morning on this subject because I have experienced a little of this myself. When I first began to write, I used to receive many letters of criticism, most of which, I have to say, were helpful and constructive. Some, however, were devastatingly negative and hurt me deeply.

Over the years, as I have learned to express myself more clearly and have taken pains to make plain my meaning, the destructively critical letters have dwindled and become just a trickle. Over the past few days, however, I have had several letters of criticism, one constructive and the others destructive. I am trying to analyse my reactions as I write these lines, and I have to admit that the ones that are destructive and which are clearly based on spite and spleen have the effect of producing within me feelings of deep hurt.

I know that I must accept some responsibility for my hurt feelings because I am a rational being and my feelings follow my perceptions and the meaning I give to an event. By that I mean the way I evaluate a situation determines my feelings, not necessarily the event itself – hence I have a responsibility to evaluate things correctly and put them in their right perspective. Allowing for all that, however, I still feel hurt. Does Jesus know how I feel? I would feel utterly bereft and alone (and so, I am sure, would you) if I did not believe that he does.

Blessed Lord Jesus, nothing really human was alien to you. You touched every feeling I touch – yet without sin. I move in a world that has been hallowed by your personal involvement. And for that I am deeply grateful. Thank you, Lord. Amen.

FOR FURTHER STUDY – Matt. 9:1–13, 12:1–8, 15:1–9

1. Why did the Pharisees criticise Jesus as they did?
2. How did Jesus respond to their criticism?

A right response to hurt

FOR READING AND MEDITATION – MATTHEW 13:44–58

'And they took offence at him. But Jesus said to them, "Only in his hometown and in his own house is a prophet without honour." ' (v. 57: NIV)

We continue pondering the question: does Jesus know how we feel when we are hurt by cruel and unkind criticism? Some would say that no one can ever hurt you by cruel or unkind criticism – you hurt yourself by responding to it incorrectly.

Here, for example, is the conclusion of one psychologist, Dr Albert Ellis, in this connection, 'No one can ever hurt you by their criticisms of you. No matter how vicious or vituperative their criticism, the words they use do not have the power to produce within you the teensiest bit of discomfort. If you are hurt, the problem arises because of the value and meaning you give to the words the person uses. Only one person has the power to put you down – you yourself. Cruel or unjust criticism hurts because it triggers off in your head ideas that are in harmony with the way you see yourself. If you didn't see yourself this way, the criticism would wash over you and fail to affect you.'

Now there is a good deal of truth in this, of course, but it is not all the truth. Dr Albert Ellis is widely known for his stoical approach to life – the approach that advocates developing indifference to both pleasure and pain. The Christian approach, as I have said many time before, is to face and acknowledge your feelings and recognise they are there. It is not a sin to be hurt. This is a very human response to the instinct for self-preservation that is within all of us. It is a sin only when we harbour a hurt. In my opinion, cruel and unjust criticism would have hurt our Lord deeply, but he made sure that the hurt would be quickly offered to God and not allowed to develop into bitterness in his soul.

O Father, teach me how to handle my hurts, for I see that a wrong reaction here can soon poison my entire being. You have given me yourself; now give me your secrets. For Jesus' sake. Amen.

FOR FURTHER STUDY – Matt. 5:43–48, 7:1–6

1. What did Jesus teach in these parts of the Sermon on the Mount?
2. How are we to respond to those who treat us badly?

The University of Adversity

FOR READING AND MEDITATION – 1 PETER 4:12–19

'Yet if anyone suffers as a Christian, let him not be ashamed, but let him glorify God . . .' (v. 16: NKJ)

We said yesterday that it is not a sin to be hurt; it becomes a sin when we harbour a hurt and allow it to distort our judgment or provoke us into unrighteous anger. One cannot make his way very far along the road of life without experiencing hurt. Whether we like it or not, life ensures that everyone one of us is enrolled in the University of Adversity, where the school colours are black and blue. Someone has said that if you had a coat of feathers as white as snow and a pair of wings as shining as Gabriel's, somebody, somewhere, would have such a bad case of colour blindness that they would mistake you for a blackbird and shoot you.

Listen to our text for today as it appears in the *Amplified Bible*: 'But if one is ill-treated and suffers as a Christian, let him not be ashamed, but give glory to God that he is deemed worthy to suffer in this name.' Notice the phrase: 'and suffers as a Christian'. Peter faces the fact that ill treatment produces pain and hurt. He does not dodge or evade the issue and say, 'But if one is ill-treated, ignore your feelings and give glory to God.' The implication is that we get hurt and we should not ignore that hurt but look beyond it to gain a wider perspective.

I know some Christian counsellors (may their tribe decrease) whose approach to those who are hurting is to say, 'You are a Christian – you shouldn't feel like that.' I am glad that Christ does not deal with us on that basis. He says, 'I see you are hurt. I know what it is like, for I have been hurt too. Let me show you how to deal with it so that it does not infect your soul.' No wonder he was called 'the Wonderful Counsellor'.

O Jesus, Lover of my soul, let me to thy bosom fly. For no one understands me the way you do. Teach me how to look beyond all my hurts and gain that wider perspective spoken about today. For your own dear name's sake. Amen.

FOR FURTHER STUDY – Mark 11:20–26; Luke 17:1–4; Eph. 4:32

1. How did Jesus teach the disciples? / 2. How often did Jesus teach them?

God's absolute justice

FOR READING AND MEDITATION – 1 PETER 2:11–25

'... when he suffered, he did not threaten, but committed himself to him who judges righteously.' (v. 23: NKJ)

If there is any doubt remaining in our minds about Jesus experiencing hurt when critical or insulting things were said about him, then the text before us today must settle the issue once and for all. Permit me once more to quote you the *Amplified Bible* translation: 'When he was reviled and insulted, he did not revile or offer insult in return; when he was abused and suffered, he made no threats of vengeance; but he trusted himself and everything to him who judges fairly.'

I pose the question once again: did Jesus experience hurt when reviled and insulted? The text says so: 'when he was abused and suffered'. Because our Lord was human, he was affected by what people said about him – he suffered – but he never allowed his hurt feelings to develop into bitterness or resentment. Why was Jesus so successful in allowing himself to feel hurt but not allowing the hurt to develop into a root of bitterness? I think the answer is to be found in: "... he made no threats of vengeance; but he trusted himself and everything to him who judges fairly.'

When we get hurt, our natural (and sinful) reaction is to hurt the one who has hurt us. We cry out for justice – 'I have been hurt, now let the one who hurt me be hurt too.' That is the only perspective our carnal nature knows. Christ's attitude, however, was to transfer the whole matter into the hands of God and trust himself and everything to him who judges fairly. He handed responsibility for retaliation over to God: ' "Vengeance is mine, I will repay," says the Lord' (Rom. 12:19, NKJ). God's absolute justice heals wounded spirits.

Gracious and loving Father, help me to handle my hurts in the way your Son did – by transferring the responsibility for justice and retaliation over to you. I know this requires trust – something I often struggle with. But help me, Father. In Jesus' name. Amen.

FOR FURTHER STUDY – 1 Peter 3:1–9; Col. 3:13

1. What should we do when we are attacked by evil?
2. Do you have a quarrel with anyone that needs resolving?

Guilt by association

FOR READING AND MEDITATION – LUKE 15:1–10
'... the Pharisees and scribes complained, saying
"This Man receives sinners and eats with them."' (v. 2: NKJ)

Today we look at some specific examples of how Jesus was unjustly and unfairly criticised. Our passage today tells us that when the tax collectors and sinners came to hear Jesus speak, the Pharisees and scribes complained that he received sinners and ate with them. Their criticism implied that because he associated with sinners and tax collectors, he was just like them – guilt by association.

How did Jesus react to this? He would have been hurt by it, but as we learned yesterday, the way he reacted to hurt was to turn everything over to God. The account says: 'So'- note the 'so' – 'he spoke this parable to them', and then gave the parables of the lost sheep, the lost silver, and the lost son, all revelations of the seeking, redemptive God. What a reaction to an accusation – he turned it into a revelation.

Take another occasion when the Pharisees watched him to see whether he would heal a man with a withered hand on the Sabbath, so that they might criticise and condemn him. The Scripture says: 'He ... looked around at them with anger, being grieved by the hardness of their hearts' (Mark 3:5, NKJ). In this action, our Lord defined the nature of righteous anger – grief at what is happening to another rather than a grudge at what is happening to oneself. That reaction, too, was a revelation – a revelation of the nature of righteous anger. When next you are the subject of cruel and unjust criticism and the hurt penetrates deep into your soul, draw comfort from the fact that not only does Christ know how you feel, but he can help you make your reactions a revelation too.

O Father, is this really possible? Can I, too, handle my hurts so that my reactions turn into a revelation? Your Word says: 'All things are possible to him who believes.' I believe – help thou my unbelief. Amen.

FOR FURTHER STUDY – Matt. 5:21–26; Prov. 20:22, 24:29; Rom. 12:17–19
1. What are we to do with our adversary? / 2. What did Paul write to the Romans?

Bigots!

FOR READING AND MEDITATION – LUKE 5:17–26

'... the scribes and the Pharisees began to reason, saying, "Who is this who speaks blasphemies? Who can forgive sins but God alone?"' (v. 21: NKJ)

The issue we come to now is one that I have thought long and hard about before bringing it before you – the issue of bigotry and prejudice. This, too, was something our Lord experienced, for he was outlawed from the beginning by the religious leaders and teachers of his day. So bigoted were the Pharisees that not long after our Lord appeared on the scene, they came to desire his death and, at an appropriate moment, set about working to achieve it: 'The Pharisees went out and plotted against him, how they might destroy him' (Matt.12:14, NKJ).

Who were these men who were so caught up in bigotry and prejudice that they actually conspired to bring about the death of the Son of God? The Pharisees were deeply religious men. An authority on the subject says, 'They had grown up as a school of thought and a body of teachers during the centuries between the Testaments. But for their conserving work, it is possible that the Jews would have been lost in the welter of pagan peoples long before Christ was born at Bethlehem.' As you know, in the centuries immediately preceding the birth of Jesus, the noble line of Hebrew prophets had ceased to be. There was no Isaiah, Jeremiah, Amos or Ezekiel – and the Pharisees, as a body, partly filled the gap left by their absence. They were not priests – or only very rarely. Nobody could be a priest who was not descended from a priestly family. Some commentators say the Pharisees became the conscience of the Hebrew people. How do you think our Lord felt, being outlawed by the acknowledged representatives of those he came to save?

O Jesus, my Lord and Master, when I think of how much you endured when you were here on earth, my heart is bowed in the deepest gratitude and the profoundest awe. Such love can have my heart forever. Thank you, my Saviour. Amen.

FOR FURTHER STUDY – Mark 6:1–6; Luke 4:16–32; John 1:46

1. Where else did Jesus meet bigotry?
2. Why were these people not helped by Jesus?

Christ's clear note of authority

FOR READING AND MEDITATION – LUKE 4:31–44

'Then they were all amazed ... saying, "What a word this is! For with authority and power he commands the unclean spirits ..."' (v. 36: NKJ)

Today we ask ourselves: why did the most religious men of Christ's day become so poisoned by bigotry and prejudice that they became involved in the foulest crime ever committed by the human race? One reason was that they were deeply upset by his note of authority. We who are Christians can look back into the Old Testament and have a clear understanding about Christ's authority. He came from God the Father and spoke for God the Father. He did not suggest or recommend – he announced. The common people noticed immediately that 'he taught them as one having authority, and not as the scribes' (Matt. 7:29, NKJ).

Inevitably, that note of authority angered the Pharisees. As educated men and leaders of the people, they were accustomed to receive from the uneducated masses (among whom they placed Jesus) a certain deference and respect. Now they were witnessing that respect being undermined. The people were following Jesus from one place to another, and were obviously impressed with his clear exposition of the Scriptures. No doubt the Pharisees said amongst themselves, "Who is he, anyhow? Isn't he just a carpenter from Nazareth? He speaks with a Galilean accent and has never been properly educated. He has never been to one of our synagogue schools and has never sat at the feet of one of our Rabbis.'

While they were discussing these things amongst themselves, the voice of Jesus was booming out all across the land: 'I am the Bread of Life', 'No man comes to the Father but by me', 'I and the Father are one'. The tremendous note of authority in the message of Jesus was something bigotry could not stand.

Lord Jesus, I see more clearly than ever that you are not an evader, a by passer of our problems. You faced everything I am called to face – so that I can overcome it too. I am so deeply thankful. Amen.

FOR FURTHER STUDY – John 6:30–52, 8:37–59

1. How did Jesus expose their bigotry? / 2. How did they react?

Disliked because different

FOR READING AND MEDITATION – MATTHEW 23:1–23
'Woe to you, scribes and Pharisees, hypocrites!' (v. 15: NKJ)

We continue examining the bigotry and prejudice of the Pharisees. Another reason why they were angry with Christ was because of his declared interest in the Gentiles. While it was true that the Jews were God's chosen people, our Lord made it equally clear that although he had come to them first, it was not to them only. The implication of his message was universal. Beginning at Jerusalem, it was to encompass the whole world. He had time for the Samaritan woman at the well; He had time for the Syrophoenician woman also. This greatly angered the Pharisees, for they saw in his actions an attempt to belittle the separateness and spiritual superiority of their race.

Another thing that angered them was Christ's indifference to their Puritanism. The Pharisees would never have eaten with tax collectors and sinners – but Jesus did! On one occasion, he invited himself to the home of a tax collector (Luke 19:5). If the tax collectors and sinners had a party and asked Jesus, Jesus went. When Matthew forsook his old life to follow Christ and gave a farewell feast for his friends, Jesus was there.

But perhaps the biggest cause of their anger was the fact that sometimes Jesus verbally lashed them. Yes, I mean lashed. He called them hypocrites to their faces. Five times in a few verses he utters woes upon them. He calls them 'blind guides' and 'whited sepulchres'. 'Whited sepulchres'! It is not in human nature to like people who talk about us in this way. Well, there it is. These were the things that brought about their animosity. They disliked Christ because they were so unlike him.

Father, help me to understand this principle, that the world doesn't know what to do with those who are different – hence it persecutes them. Make me like Christ, dear Father – no matter how much antagonism I may have to bear. In Jesus' name. Amen.

FOR FURTHER STUDY – Matt. 6:1–18, 12:2; Mark 2:9
1. How was Pharisaism displayed? / 2. How are we to conduct ourselves?

When bigotry banishes love

FOR READING AND MEDITATION – LUKE 9:46–62

'… "Do not forbid him, for he who is not against us is on our side."' (v. 50: NKJ)

There can be no doubt that bigotry and prejudice were abhorrent to Jesus Christ. He was hurt when he was on the receiving end of it, and he was hurt also when he observed others being subjected to it.

Our passage today shows John turning to him and saying: 'Master, we saw someone casting out demons in your name, and we forbade him because he does not follow with us' – and Jesus rebuked the Son of Thunder in no uncertain way. One wonders what John might have expected Jesus to say. It seems he made the announcement in the manner of a man who was rather pleased with his promptitude. Casting out demons! In your name! Jesus soon sets the record straight and says: 'Do not forbid him, for he who is not against us is for us.'

The spirit of bigotry and prejudice did not die with apostolic times – it is with us still. All down the ages, one group of Christ's disciples has been forbidding another group of Christ's disciples on no more serious grounds than 'they do not follow with us'. Some years ago, I was invited to preach at Westminster Cathedral, London (not in the actual church but in an adjoining hall) by a group of Catholics. Some months later, while preaching at a rally in the Westminster Central Hall, I happened to refer to the fact that I had preached at Westminster Cathedral. Within a few days, I had a letter from a group of Christians taking me to task for what I had done. I was deeply saddened, not for myself but for them; saddened because bigotry had banished love.

O Father, help me to see that even though my perception of truth may cause me to differ with my brothers, this need not, nor should not, bring about a lapse in my affection. For when I fail in love, I fail – period. Amen.

FOR FURTHER STUDY – James 2; James 1:26–27

1. How does James depict bigotry? / 2. What two things go together?

We must go on loving

FOR READING AND MEDITATION – JOHN 17:6–26
'… "that they may be one just as we are one." ' (v. 22: NKJ)

No one familiar with history and jealous for the honour of Jesus Christ can help feeling unutterably sad when he or she reads the stories of how one section of Christ's church has persecuted another; the burning and torturing of Protestants in one generation and the burning and torturing of Roman Catholics in another. And all this undertaken in the name of Christ, who said: 'By this all will know that you are my disciples, if you have love for one another' (John 13:35, NKJ).

Nor is it all ancient history. Even today, poisoned words are still flung about between one Christian group and another. Men and women wound each other in the most tender parts of their souls and think that they do God service in so doing. In bigotry and prejudice, there is almost always the disposition to persecute. Circumstances may prevent it finding any fiercer expression than through barbed or sarcastic words, but then words can sometimes wound more deeply than swords.

The hateful heart of a bigot's sin is that he or she fails in love. People often ask me, 'What are we to do when others fail in love towards us; when they speak contemptuously of our particular viewpoint; when they deride our doctrines; when they say we are not really part of Christ's Bride; when they pour scorn on our sincerity?' The answer is – we must go on loving. We must meet slander with affection, scorn with service, ostracism with the right hand of fellowship. We are followers of him who said: 'He who is not against us is on our side (Luke 9:50, NKJ). If it is hard, then remember Jesus knows exactly how you feel. He, too, was the victim of bigotry and prejudice. Let his wounds heal your wounds.

O Father, forgive us for the fact that we, your people, the people called by your name, have so fragmented your image in the world by our bickering, our bigotry and our lack of love. Forgive us and restore us – in Jesus' name. Amen.

FOR FURTHER STUDY – Acts 10:34–48; Rom. 10:12; 1 Tim. 5:21; Gal. 3:28
1. What did Peter declare? / 2. What did Paul teach?

Grief is inescapable

FOR READING AND MEDITATION – JOB 1:1–22

'In all this, Job did not sin by charging God with wrongdoing.' (v. 22: NIV)

We look now at yet another area of life and feeling which our Lord touched on when he was here on earth – grief over the loss of a loved one. I am thinking particularly of Christ's sorrow over the death of Lazarus, but before focusing on that I want to spend a few days looking at the painfully familiar story of Job. Generally speaking, loss falls into two categories – loss of people and loss of things – the loss of a job or the loss of personal necessities and benefits. Job lost both people and things.

It is so easy to glamourise and immortalise the man who is known for his great patience, but I want you to try to feel some of the emotions he must have experienced as he came face to face with loss. Look at the list of Job's possessions. First of all, he had godliness and character (Job 1:1). Second, he had a large family. Seven sons and three daughters were born to him – ten children in all. That's quite a 'quiver full' (see Psalm 127:3–5). Third, he had abundant possessions: seven thousand sheep, three thousand camels, five hundred yoke of oxen, five hundred donkeys and servants by the dozen. Suddenly they were all taken away.

How did he respond? Some think that because he acknowledged God's sovereignty in it all (1:21), Job did not grieve, but the rest of the book shows that he did. The natural reaction to deep loss is that of grief, and any attempt to avoid this can lead to all kinds of spiritual and psychological problems. So don't try to escape grief by any illusions or subterfuges, for the illusions and subterfuges will in the end turn out to be worse than the grief itself.

Gracious and loving Father, help me to see that the way to deal with life is always to go 'through' and not 'around'. I surrender to you now all my impulses to escape. Give me the spirit of reality – the will to go through. In Jesus' name. Amen.

FOR FURTHER STUDY – Job 14:1–22, 5:7; Eccl. 2:22–23; 1 Cor. 15:57–58

1.What feelings did Job express? / 2. What response can the Christian make?

Grief involves work

FOR READING AND MEDITATION – JOB 2:1–13

'… no one spoke a word to him, for they saw that his grief was very great.' (v. 13: NKJ)

We continue examining Job's situation, particularly as it relates to the matter of grief. Some Christians teach that the way to deal with all the troublesome issues of life (even the loss of a loved one) is to lift your heart to God in thanksgiving and focus only on him. If you dwell on the negatives, they say, you will allow the seeds of doubt to invade your heart and this will undermine your spiritual life and bring you into bondage to doubt and unbelief.

All error is truth out of balance, and this error, like so many others, has a kernel of truth – but it is not truth in balance. It is true that when calamity strikes, we should focus on God, but it is not true that we should seek to escape from the feelings of loss and grief that are the natural reaction of the soul. Yesterday we saw that Job's initial reaction to his loss was to lift his heart to God, but today we see him working through his grief. Notice how those who shared the experience with him said nothing, but simply sat in silence.

Joe Bayly, a Christian writer who unexpectedly lost three of his teenage children through death, says in his book, *The View from the Hearse*, 'One of the best contributions we can make to a person going through intense suffering and loss is our presence without words, not even verses of Scripture dumped into the ears of the grieving.' An individual reeling from the blow of a calamity like the loss of a loved one usually has a broken heart. The soil of the soul is not yet ready for the implanting of the heavenly seed. It will be ready later, but not right away. Never forget that, for many a soul has been damaged by well-meaning Christians who said the right thing, but at the wrong time.

Father, now I see why it was that when I have grieved in the past, before giving me words you gave me your presence. Help me to follow this principle when next I am called upon to sympathise with others. For your own dear name's sake. Amen.

FOR FURTHER STUDY – 1 Thess. 4:13–18; Matt. 5:4

1. Is Paul saying we should not grieve? / 2. What is he saying?

The walk to Emmaus

FOR READING AND MEDITATION – LUKE 24:13–35

'As they talked and discussed these things with each other, Jesus himself came up and walked along with them …' (v. 15: NIV)

We spend another day meditating on the fact that when calamity strikes and grief arises in the heart, the first thing one needs is not words, but a loving presence.

One writer puts it like this, 'I was sitting, torn by grief, when someone came and talked to me of God's dealings, of why it happened, of hope beyond the grave. He talked constantly; he said things I knew were true. I was unmoved except to wish he'd go away. He finally did. Another came and sat bedside me. He didn't talk. He didn't ask leading questions. He just sat beside me for an hour or more, listened when I said something, answered briefly, prayed simply, left. I was moved. I was comforted. I hated to see him go.' Did you notice, in the reading today, how when Jesus met the two on the way to Emmaus who were so obviously overcome by grief, he did not immediately expound the Scriptures to them, but walked alongside them for a while, asking gentle questions, until he knew that they were ready for what he wanted to share with them?

Two years after the death of my wife, I could look back upon the event with a little more objectivity than before. The people who most helped me and encouraged me in those early days, when grief was tearing at my soul, were not those who told me that God would use this to deepen my ministry and greatly extend my influence and service for him (though that was certainly true), but those who simply said, 'We know you are hurting, and for what it is worth we want you to know – we hurt for you too.' The first thing a person who is grieving needs to know is not that something good will come out of the experience, but that someone cares.

O Father, make me a person who is deeply sensitive to the needs of others, and teach me the art of knowing what to say and when to say it. In Jesus' name I pray. Amen.

FOR FURTHER STUDY – Heb. 3:1–15; Phil. 2:1–2; 1 Pet. 5:7; 1 Cor. 12:25

1. What did Paul say to the church at Corinth? / 2. What are we to do daily?

FOR READING AND MEDITATION – ISAIAH 61:1–11

'To console those who mourn in Zion, to give them beauty for ashes, the oil of joy for mourning …' (v. 3: NKJ)

It seems appropriate, when talking about the subject of grief, that we give some consideration to the subject of excessive grief. As we know, grief comes to us all; it is part of mortal existence and it is inherent in our nature and the world in which we live. Nobody escapes grief – not even our Lord when he walked here on earth.

How are we to avoid excessive grief? First, see clearly that at some time, grief is bound to come to you. This attitude will save you from feeling, when grief does come, that you are being singled out for persecution. If you don't do this, you will have a persecution illusion, a martyr complex. Say to yourself, 'Grief is the lot of everyone on this earth; I am not an exception.' Second, don't try to escape grief through illusions and subterfuges. I knew a man once who, though almost blind, insisted he wasn't and refused to wear glasses. He thought the wearing of glasses was a sign that he lacked faith, and because he wanted to appear deeply spiritual went around half blind, until one day he walked into a lamppost and ended up in hospital with some serious injuries. Fortunately the jolt jolted him into reality.

Third, surrender all bitterness and resentment into the hands of God, for it is this, more than anything that is responsible for grief staying with us longer than it should. Finally, get alongside someone else who is grieving, and see what you can do. Meister Eichart said, 'God's every affliction is a lure' – a lure to help you to help others. You are made tender by your sorrow and that tenderness can make your service for Christ tenderly protective and effective.

Father, I see that I must grieve, but help me not to hold within me any excessive grief. And help me to lighten my own burdens by taking up the burdens of others. In Jesus' name I ask it. Amen.

FOR FURTHER STUDY – Heb. 12:1–15; Eph. 4:31; James 3:14

1. What are we to look out for? / 2. What does the writer to the Hebrews advise?

No denial in Jesus

FOR READING AND MEDITATION – JOHN 11:17–44
'Jesus wept.' (v. 35: NIV)

Today we ask ourselves the question: is our Lord able to sympathise with us when we experience grief? Did Christ experience the same feelings that we go through when we lose a loved one? The verse before us today leaves us in no doubt. Why did our Lord shed tears? Was it out of sympathy for Mary and Martha? I think that may have been part of the cause for his tears, but the main reason (so I believe) was his personal sense of loss.

I cannot be absolutely sure about what I am now going to say, but I feel that what Jesus was doing here was allowing himself to feel the grief that swept through him at the thought of his friend being swallowed up by death. One might think that as Jesus knew he was about to bring him back from the dead, he would not have experienced grief, but he was wise enough to know that to deny what he was feeling at the moment – grief, because of what he was about to feel in the hours that lay ahead – joy, would not have been in harmony with the way the personality best functions.

You see, no matter how positive and optimistic our outlook may be, we must never deny what we are feeling at the moment. We need not be dragged down by our feelings into a whirlpool of despair, but we must be willing to face and feel those emotions. That is the principle of mental and emotional health that Jesus knew, understood and practised. So standing by the tomb of Lazarus, he allows his grief to find expression. The tears start from his eyes. He really feels, does this man of Galilee. Remember, when next you grieve, that he who wept at the grave of his dearest friend not only knows how you feel, but will impart to you his unfailing strength and power.

O Jesus, how grateful I am to know that your heart, too, has felt the deepest grief and sorrow. Help me to share my griefs with you, for 'a grief shared is a grief halved'. I ask this in and through your peerless and precious name. Amen.

FOR FURTHER STUDY – Luke 7:11–17; John 11:36
1. What did the onlookers say when Jesus grieved? / 2. What does grief express?

The paralysing sting of humanity

FOR READING AND MEDITATION – MATTHEW 8:18–27

'But Jesus told him, "Follow me, and let the dead bury their own dead." ' (v. 22: NIV)

Another earthly circumstance our Lord was called to pass through was that of being misunderstood. Few things are more difficult to live with than being misunderstood. Sometimes it's downright unbearable. One author calls it, 'the paralysing sting of humanity'. When I first read that description of misunderstanding, I felt the writer was overstating the issue, but the more I have thought about the feelings that are generated through misunderstanding, the more I have come to agree. When you are misunderstood, you have no defence.

Perhaps you have been in such a situation recently – or you may be passing through such a phase at this very moment. Have you noticed how, when you are misunderstood, no matter how hard you try to correct the misunderstanding, it doesn't seem to get you anywhere? Usually, it gets worse. You get all your facts lined up; ready to make things clear, and all you get are blank looks of incredulity and unbelief. The harder you work to make your motives clear, the worse it gets and the deeper it hurts. Yes, the sting of being misunderstood can be truly 'paralysing'. I don't think there is a person alive who has not at some time or another felt misunderstood.

When analysed, misunderstanding can be seen as having two elements: one, an innocent remark or statement that is misinterpreted, and two, the offence that arises in the heart of another due to the mistaken interpretation. Jesus was constantly being misunderstood. Every statement and utterance that fell from his lips came from a heart of love, but still he was misinterpreted and thus maligned. Believe me, no one knows better than our Lord what it means to be misunderstood.

Loving heavenly Father, once again I want to express my thanks for the fact that when I am misunderstood, you not only know how I feel but can help me keep my spirit intact. I am deeply grateful. Thank you, dear Father. Amen.

FOR FURTHER STUDY – John 6:60–71; Matt. 19:23–30

1. How did some of the disciples respond to Christ's teaching? / 2. How did Peter respond?

Learning how to be a king

FOR READING AND MEDITATION – 1 SAMUEL 16:1–13

'Then Samuel took the horn of oil and anointed him … and the Spirit of the Lord came upon David …' (v.13: NKJ)

Yesterday we saw that misunderstanding arises from an innocent word or implication. Nothing was meant by it, but it was misread and an offence was created. Apart from Christ, one of the most misunderstood men in Scripture was King David, and a brief examination of his life and circumstances will illustrate for us the dynamics of misunderstanding. After David killed Goliath, and had been anointed with oil by Samuel, the statement was made to Jesse's family, 'Your youngest is going to be king.' But learning how to be king included learning how to endure being misunderstood.

Saul, the current king of Israel, had problems in his life, which became apparent soon after he had been appointed. He was a deeply insecure person, and like all insecure people, tried to compensate for his failings by such things as people-pleasing, attention-getting and so on. One day, when returning from a battle with the Philistines in company with David, he heard the women singing a song they had put together in honour of the victory: 'Saul has slain his thousands, and David his ten thousands' (1 Sam. 18:7). Saul was deeply upset. It was not just the nine thousand difference that bothered him, but the fact that David was getting the glory. Notice what he said: 'What more can he have but the kingdom?'

But David was not after the kingdom. He was Saul's man, and amongst other things his personal musician. The innocent acts of David were so misinterpreted by Saul that thereafter David's life became almost unbearable. If it's any comfort, being misunderstood has always been the standard operating procedure for those whom God appoints to special service. You do not grow fully or completely without being misunderstood.

Father, I see that though misunderstanding sometimes causes me to groan, it also causes me to grow. Help me to come through all my own misunderstandings a better, not a bitter person. For your own dear name's sake. Amen.

FOR FURTHER STUDY – Prov. 15; Eph. 4:29; Prov. 18:21, 25:11

1. List six things Proverbs 15 says about the use of words.
2. To what end does Paul say we should use our words?

How to handle misunderstanding

FOR READING AND MEDITATION – PSALM 140:1–13

'I said to the Lord, you are my God; give ear to the voice of my supplications, O Lord.' (v. 6: *Amp. Bible*)

Many Bible commentators believe that the Psalm before us today was written by David following the events we discussed yesterday. David is now on the run and is being hunted by an angry King Saul. An explanation of this Psalm brings out some principles that ought to help us next time we are misunderstood.

The first thing to notice is that David recognised his predicament had been caused by exaggeration. When people misunderstand you, they exaggerate what you said or what you did and make it mean something you did not intend. Look how exaggeration affected David's enemies: 'They devise mischiefs in their heart; continually they gather together and stir up wars' (verse 2: *Amp. Bible*). Often misunderstanding starts with a slightly wrong interpretation and then gradually builds up to where a person is willing to believe out-and-out lies.

Next, David got in touch with his feelings and acknowledged his sense of vulnerability: 'Keep me, O Lord, from the hands of the wicked' (verse 4). These are the words of a person who feels vulnerable and exposed. Vulnerability is one of the things that reverberate inside us whenever we are misunderstood. We are caught off our guard, we are not prepared or ready to deal with it; we feel trapped, naked, exposed. What do we do when this sort of thing happens? Look at the passage again: 'I said to the Lord, you are my God (verse 6). Notice, he said this to the Lord, not just thought it. Our dependence on God must be verbalised if it is to be realised. Talking to him not only gets something out of us; it opens us up to God so that he might get something into us.

O Father, help me see the importance of talking to you about my problems. Show me even more clearly how verbalising my thoughts opens up my inner being and prepares me to receive. In Jesus' name I pray. Amen.

FOR FURTHER STUDY – James 3; Psa. 34:13; Prov. 21:23; 1 Peter 3:10

1. What does James say about the power of the tongue? / 2. What are we to refrain from?

We are not orphans

FOR READING AND MEDITATION – PROVERBS 16:1–16

'When a man's ways please the Lord, he makes even his enemies to be at peace with him.' (v. 7: NKJ)

We return today to the thought that we actually grow through misunderstanding. It hurts when it happens, but it causes us to depend on the Lord in a way that perhaps we have never quite done before. Once we give the situation over to God and say, 'Lord, I have done what I know is right, but I feel defenceless and misunderstood', then we must wait and let him vindicate us. His ability to vindicate, as our text for today suggests, is one of our Creator's specialities!

Are you misunderstood in your home or your place of work? Is someone in your school or college causing you hurt through an innocent remark that you might have made? Then ask the Lord to be your defence. Don't just think it – talk to him about it. Ask him to take care of you and then you can lie down at night knowing that although the tongue of your accuser might be busy, God is taking care of the situation. Far too many of us forget that when we become Christians, we enter into the family of God. We have a new Father who delights in taking care of our needs and becoming involved in every detail of our lives. We are not orphans; we are children of the living God. So learn to bring all your misunderstandings to him.

Early in my ministry I was involved in a situation where I was so misunderstood that I thought the pain would never go away. Crushed and bruised, all I could do was wait. The memory of the event is still there, but the sting has gone and something very beautiful has come out of it. I would not give a penny for the pain, but I would not take a million pounds for what has emerged in my life because of it.

O God my Father, help me to grow gracefully, beautifully and creatively. Let everything that happens to me be used to increase your likeness in me. For Jesus' sake. Amen.

FOR FURTHER STUDY – John 8:25–30; 1 Thess. 2:4; Heb. 13:16

1. What did Jesus always do? / 2. What is God pleased with?

When other helpers fail...

FOR READING AND MEDITATION – JOHN 14:1–14

'Philip said to him, "Lord, show us the Father, and it is sufficient for us."' (v. 8: NKJ)

Probably no one in the history of the world was more misunderstood than Jesus Christ. He came to earth offering love, pouring it out passionately and prodigally on all who were in need, but the more he ministered, the more he was misunderstood. The people among whom he had been brought up misunderstood him. His own immediate family misunderstood him. Even his disciples, who spent so much time in his presence and knew him more closely than any others – they, too, misunderstood him.

Although the text before us today cannot strictly be put under the category of misunderstanding, it must have grieved our Lord greatly that even though Philip had been with him almost from the first day of his public ministry, he had not really understood the Master's purpose in the world or who he was. 'Show us the Father,' said Philip, 'that is all we ask; then we will be satisfied' (verse 8: *Amp. Bible*).

How these words must have hurt the heart of Jesus. Philip had listened to his words, witnessed the many miracles he had performed, seen firsthand the demonstration of Deity, yet he still had not grasped the relationship of Christ to God. It's like an art student studying under the tutorship of an art master for three years, then suddenly turning to him at the end of the time and saying, 'Please show me the principles of art.' Let me make the point once again – when it comes to the issue of being misunderstood or not being understood (there is a slight difference between the two), remember that no one has touched this as deeply as Jesus. Take comfort in the thought that when other helpers fail and comforts flee – there is always Jesus.

Blessed Lord Jesus, forgive me that so often I look to you as the last resource for comfort rather than the first. Help me to be a more dependent person – God-dependent. In your name I ask it. Amen.

FOR FURTHER STUDY – Matt. 16:13–23, 15:16; Luke 18:34

1. What didn't the disciples understand? / 2. What did Peter understand?

Never forsaken

FOR READING AND MEDITATION – HEBREWS 13:1–15

'... For he himself has said, "I will never leave you nor forsake you."' (v. 5: NKJ)

As we approach the close of our meditations on the theme of the wounded healer, I want to focus your attention on a feeling that Christ experienced that I hope you will never know, but which nevertheless you may encounter at some point in your life. I have in mind the experience of feeling abandoned and forsaken by God. Perhaps no feeling is as intolerable and disabling as that of feeling deserted by God. But even this darkest of dark hours, our Lord knows. His piteous cry of dereliction on the Cross makes him kin to all those who feel themselves deserted by the Almighty, and of course his glorious resurrection (we must not forget that) proves beyond all cavil that:

Behind the dim unknown
Standeth God within the shadow
Keeping watch above his own.

All men to whom are entrusted the care of souls are familiar with fine Christian people who, at times, feel their prayers go unheeded or who pray for something that seems of certainty to be within the will of God and yet find the heavens as brass, and thus are tempted to believe that God has forgotten or abandoned them. It must be made clear right at the outset, however, that although a Christian may feel abandoned by God, the feeling is the result of illusion, not reality. We are never really abandoned, even though we may feel abandoned. He could no more abandon one of his blood-washed children than he could tell a lie!

O Father, let the wonder of this fact sink deeply into my spirit today – that no matter what my feelings tell me, the truth is that I am yours for all eternity. You forsook your Son in order that you might not forsake me. Thank you, dear Father. Amen.

FOR FURTHER STUDY – Josh. 1:1–5, 9; Isa. 41:17, 42:16, 54:10
1. What was God's promise to Joshua? / 2. What was God's promise to Israel?

Feeling forsaken

FOR READING AND MEDITATION – MATTHEW 27:45–54
'… "My God, my God, why have you forsaken me?" ' (v. 46: NKJ)

All men to whom is entrusted the care of souls are familiar with people who feel forsaken by the Lord. When I first entered the Christian ministry, I remember being deeply perplexed by the fact that, from time to time, I would meet good and sincere Christians who told me they felt deserted by God. I remember walking on the Welsh mountains one day in company with a well-known evangelist, a man greatly used of God, who confessed to me that he felt that God had abandoned him. His confession shook me to the depth of my spiritual foundations. I wondered how it could be that a man so close to God could feel forsaken by him.

I have not gone through an experience like that myself, but I have known hundreds who have. J.B. Phillips, best known for his translation of the epistles into modern English, *Letters to Young Churches*, which he subsequently extended to a translation of the whole New Testament, went through such an experience. His wife, Vera, and a close friend Edwin Robertson have compiled a selection of letters he wrote which reveal the pain he underwent as he passed through what theologians call 'the dark night of the soul'.

Dr Leslie Weatherhead, well-known minister of the City Temple, London, tells of a similar experience also. In a letter to J.B. Phillips, he said, 'I felt concerned about what you describe … because I went through the same hell thirty years ago.' Teresa of Avila knew the experience too. In fact, Christian history is filled with the record of men and women who went through 'the dark night of the soul'. It happens to the choicest saints – something you ought to struggle to remember should it ever happen to you.

O Father, I feel today as your Son must have felt when he prayed: 'If it is possible, let this cup pass from me.' Help me to understand this strange phenomenon, so that either it will not overtake me or I shall be adequately prepared to meet it. In Jesus' name. Amen.

FOR FURTHER STUDY – Psa. 22, 23, 24
1. At what point does David start in Psalm 22? / 2. What happens in Psalm 23?
3. At what point does he finish in Psalm 24?

The physical affects the spiritual

FOR READING AND MEDITATION – 1 THESSALONIANS 5:12–28

'May your whole spirit, soul and body be kept blameless at the coming of our Lord Jesus Christ.' (v. 23: NIV)

We continue looking at the issue of deeply committed Christian men and women experiencing times when they feel as if God has abandoned them. How can this be? If God wants to have fellowship with them and they want to have fellowship with God – what hinders the meeting? Why is there no sense of 'getting together' – no close communion? Clearly the fault cannot be in God; therefore it must be something unsuspected in them. If they are not deliberately indulging in some known sin, or consciously resisting God at some point where he has a plain controversy with them, the barrier must be hidden.

Sometimes the barrier is a fault in the person's physiology. When something goes wrong with our physical functioning, it can soon affect our inner condition and make us feel spiritually bereft. Elijah is a case in point. This great man of faith came to a time when he wanted to die: 'It is enough! Now, Lord, take my life…' (1 Kings 19:4, NKJ), but part of his problem lay in the fact that he was overtired and overworked. He had been busier than he should have been, so God had to slow him down so that his body could catch up with his spirit.

In my time, I have dealt with literally hundreds of people whose low spiritual condition was influenced by a physical malfunction such as a glandular problem, a viral infection, or some other type of chemical disturbance. In many of these cases, proper medication was all that was needed to restore the body to a position of balance, and thus take pressure off the soul. Never forget that the physical can deeply affect the spiritual.

Father, help me to see that you have made me in such a way that what affects me on the outside can affect me on the inside – and vice versa. Give me wisdom to take this into account when next I am feeling spiritually low. In Jesus' name. Amen.

FOR FURTHER STUDY – 1 Cor. 12:12–18, 6:19, 9:27; 2 Cor. 6:16

1. How does Paul describe the body? / 2. How did Paul treat his body?

Telling yourself the truth

FOR READING AND MEDITATION – ROMANS 12:1–13
'And do not be conformed to this world, but be transformed by the renewing of your mind …' (v. 2: NKJ)

We saw yesterday how faulty physical functioning can affect our spiritual condition and bring about the feeling that God is not interested in us or is far away. This feeling can also be brought about through psychological malfunctioning, such as having a faulty concept of God, unrealistic expectations, perfectionist standards, irrational fears and so on. In fact, J.B. Phillips (whom we referred to earlier on) kept a diary of the thoughts that went through his head day by day, and found on reflection that they were almost all filled with negativism and gloom.

Here is a list of some of those thoughts taken directly from his diary, which, as you see, come across as rambling and confused: '…seems I cannot get rid of colossal fantastic demands'; '… have discovered my own limitations but still feel the demand to give 130 per cent'; '… rather die than be ordinary'; '… the centre of my worship and my energies is – I'll show them'; '…the God I have been looking for is not a grown-up God at all'; '… I want to be colossal or soon die'; '… if I left the world a great light would go out'; '… nearly all that I call God is my father magnified.'

Is it any wonder then, with thoughts like that buzzing around in his head that God seemed to be far away? When the feeling of being abandoned by God comes mainly from the thoughts in our head, then good Christian counselling can show you how to deal with them. Take my advice, if you cannot solve this problem yourself; discuss the issue with a mature Christian friend.

Father, help me to understand how what I tell myself greatly influences and affects the way I will feel. Teach me how to stop believing lies and believe the truth. In Jesus' name. Amen.

FOR FURTHER STUDY – Rom. 12:1–5; Eph. 4:23; 2 Tim1:7
1. What did Paul exhort the church at Rome to do? / 2. What did he affirm to Timothy?

The cry of dereliction

FOR READING AND MEDITATION – PSALM 22:1–24

'"My God, my God, why have you forsaken me? …"' (v. 1: NKJ)

Today we look in detail at an issue I touched on a few days ago – 'the cry of dereliction'. The phrase is used by theologians to describe the feelings of abandonment which our Lord appeared to have had when he cried out from the cross: 'My God, my God , why have you forsaken me?'

Throughout the history of the Church, great debates have taken place on this matter of our Lord's cry of dereliction. Some believe he was not actually abandoned by God but felt abandoned, while others take the view that it was much more than a feeling and that on the cross he actually was forsaken by God. I find myself in agreement with the latter of these two beliefs. R.W. Dale, in his book, *The Atonement*, convinced me of this when he wrote, 'I decline to accept any explanation of these words which implies that they do not represent the actual truth of our Lord's position. I cannot believe that Jesus was uttering a false cry.'

Just imagine it – our Lord, who had been forsaken by men, was now being forsaken by God. As he began to experience in his soul the suffering of sin (not his own sin, but ours) and proceeded through his sufferings to pay the terrifying debt that sin had built up in the universe, God, who could have nothing to do with sin, had to turn his back upon him. Our Lord plunged into the darkness of sin and endured the awful suffering of the atonement entirely on his own. Jesus experienced on the cross not just a felt, but a real abandonment – something those who are Christians will never experience. Let this solemn but glorious truth take hold of you today – because he was abandoned, you will never be abandoned.

O Jesus, my Lord and my God, I bow my head and my heart in deepest gratitude for the fact that you were willing to be forsaken by God so that I might be at one with him for ever. May my life reflect this gratitude, not just today but every day. Amen.

FOR FURTHER STUDY – Matt. 28:16–20; John 10:28; Rom. 8:38–39

1. What was Christ's promise in the great commission?
2. What ten things did Paul say are unable to separate us from Christ?

How to avoid infection

FOR READING AND MEDITATION – EPHESIANS 4:17–32

'... forgiving one another, even as God in Christ forgave you.' (v. 32: NKJ)

We have been saying over the past few weeks that out of the many things that endear Christ to his church, one of the chief reasons must be that he has worn our flesh, measured its frailty, and knows exactly how we feel. Our Lord is a wounded healer; his ability to heal our wounds flows from the fact that he has experienced our wounds. Christ has taken the entire range of our emotions with him into the Godhead so that now our Creator feels as we feel. What a mystery!

It is important now to note the way Christ responded to the wounds he received compared to the way, generally speaking, we respond to our wounds. When we are wounded, our natural response is either to nurse our hurt in an attitude of self-pity, or flare up in unrighteous anger. Comb the record of our Lord's days on this earth and you will not find one ounce of self-pity. When the daughters of Jerusalem wept over him on his way to the cross, he said: '... do not weep for me, but weep for yourselves and for your children' (Luke 23:28, NKJ) – no self-pity.

Neither did he harbour unforgiveness. When men laid his weary body upon a cross and transfixed him to the wood, the cry that rose from his heart was not for justice, but forgiveness: 'Father, forgive them, for they do not know what they do' (Luke 23:34, NKJ). That was the most sublime prayer that was ever prayed, for it embodied the most sublime spirit ever shown. The cross shows us how Jesus dealt with hate. He held it to him and quelled it in his mighty heart of love. The boomerang lost its power because the venom which flew toward him at the crucifixion did not fly back again in revenge. He freely forgave those who hurt him – so must we.

Blessed Lord Jesus, help me to avail myself of your grace and power so that I, too, might be free from corroding hate and cancerous resentments. Save me, not from hurt but from infected hurts. In your dear name I pray. Amen.

FOR FURTHER STUDY – Luke 7:36–50; Matt. 6:14–15; Psa. 130:4

1. What is the key to knowing God's forgiveness?
2. What was Jesus teaching Simon the Pharisee?

Go home and suffer

FOR READING AND MEDITATION – 2 CORINTHIANS 1:1–11

'… the one who so wonderfully comforts and strengthens us … so that when others are troubled … we can pass on to them this same help and comfort …' (vv. 3–4: TLB)

There is a sense in which not only is our Lord a wounded healer, but we are called to be wounded healers also. Just as our Lord's wounds give him a special empathy for us in our struggles and sorrows, so our own wounds can be used to soothe and strengthen those who hurt. For example, it is a well-known fact in the field of counselling that the best helpers are those who have suffered the most hurts.

Some time ago, I saw a video tape of Rollo May, a well-known counsellor in the United States, and I remember being deeply impressed with a statement he made which I cannot quote verbatim but which went something like this, 'Whenever I interview anyone who wants to join my team as a counsellor, the first thing I have to know is how much they have suffered. If they cannot convince me that they have experienced some suffering, then I tell them I have no use for them at the moment and to come back when they have really suffered.'

Strong words – but understandable. The more we have suffered, the more our sufferings can speak to others. And remember, you don't have to be a trained counsellor to help others. Every Christian has something he or she can offer to a brother or sister who is hurting if, as our text for today points out, we let God comfort us and then pass on the same comfort to others. Shakespeare put it well when he said, 'He jests at scars who never felt a wound.' Believe me, there is no more powerful ministry than to come alongside someone who is suffering and share the fact that you have felt that self-same hurt too. Your weakness, under God, becomes someone else's strength.

Father, through all these meditations you have been teaching me to understand – to understand by undergoing. I could never understand otherwise. I want to enter into the hurts of others. So when I hurt, let me hurt – good. In Jesus' name. Amen.

FOR FURTHER STUDY – John 14:25–31, 15:26–27, 16:5–7

1. What was Jesus' promise to his disciples? / 2. What is one of the titles of the Holy Spirit?

Suffering versus miracles

FOR READING AND MEDITATION – JOHN 5:16–30

'... the Son can do nothing of himself, but what he sees the Father do ...' (v. 19: NKJ)

The emphasis we have been making over the past few days, that we are to welcome suffering and see it as an opportunity to take the sympathy we receive from Christ and pass it on to others, may raise the question in some people's minds: where is the place for miracles in all this? Is life all suffering? Doesn't God promise to deliver us from some things and work supernaturally on our behalf?

Of course he does. There are many situations where faith in God brings great deliverance, so don't hear me discounting the place of prayer and miracles in Christian life. After all, God is a big God and delights in answering prayer. That said, however, it is clear that even in the most charismatic of churches, where miracles and supernatural happenings abound, there is still a good deal of suffering. People get hurt, things go wrong, and troubles come, as Shakespeare said, 'not in spies but in battalions'.

What do we do when, despite the most positive and energetic intercession, we continue to experience hurt and anguish and sorrow? We turn to God and draw from our great *El Shaddai* (the phrase literally means 'the Breasted One') the strength and encouragement we need. If you do not get these two things in perspective – miracles and suffering – you will finish up greatly confused. God does work miracles in answer to prayer, but at times he chooses to let us pass through something so that he can use it in our lives to deepen our understanding and enrich our ministry to others. As Alan Paton puts it in his book, *Cry, the Beloved Country*, 'Christ suffered, not just to save us from suffering, but to teach us how to use it.'

Loving and gracious heavenly Father, help me to have a clear perspective on this issue of suffering versus miracles. Help me to know when you want to keep me from something and when you want to keep me in something. In Christ's name. Amen.

FOR FURTHER STUDY – Heb. 11; James 1:2–3, 5–7

1. What two aspects of faith are depicted in Hebrews 11?
2. What is said of those who suffered?

Turning pains into pearls

FOR READING AND MEDITATION – REVELATION 21:9–27

'…each gate made of a single pearl.' (v. 21: NIV)

It is quite clear from what we have been seeing over the past few days that Christians are to follow in the steps of their Lord and turn their sufferings to good account. The way in which this is to be done is beautifully illustrated by the experience of the oyster, into whose shell there comes one day a grain of sand. This tiny piece of quartz lies there imposing pain and stress – so what shall the oyster do?

Well, there are several courses open. The oyster could, as so many men and women have done in times of adversity and trouble, openly rebel against God. The oyster, metaphorically speaking, could shake a fist in God's face and say, 'Why should this happen to me?' But it doesn't. Or it could say, 'It can't be true; this is not happening to me. I must not permit myself to believe it.' It doesn't do that either. It could say also, 'There is no such thing as pain. It is an error of the mind. I must think positive thoughts.' But that is not what the oyster does.

What, then, does it do? Slowly and patiently, and with infinite care, the oyster builds upon the grain of sand layer upon layer of a white milky substance that covers every sharp corner and coats every cutting edge. And gradually… slowly… by and by, a pearl is made. The oyster has learned – by the will of God – to turn grains of sand into pearls. And that is the lesson we must learn along this pilgrim way. Surely it is something more than a simile when the Bible says that the entrance into the New Jerusalem is through a gate made of pearl. It is pointing out that the way into the city of God is through a wound that has been healed. Let God help you turn your pains into pearls, so that others can walk through them into joy and encouragement.

O Father, help me to turn every wound in my life into a 'pearly gate' – something through which others can pass to find faith, hope and love. In Christ's peerless and precious name I ask it. Amen.

FOR FURTHER STUDY – 2 Cor. 11:22–12:10, 4:8

1. List some of the sufferings of Paul. / 2. What was his testimony?

He's been there!

FOR READING AND MEDITATION – HEBREWS 12:1–11

'... looking unto Jesus ... who for the joy that was set before him endured the cross ...' (v. 2: NKJ)

In *Migrants, Sharecroppers and Mountaineers*, Robert Coles tells the story of a migrant worker whose daughter was seriously ill, and one morning in church he strode up to the minister, lifted up his daughter to the minister and shouted, 'My daughter is sick and we have no money to help her. How can you talk about a God who loves when he takes good care of some and not of people like us?'

That migrant worker summed up the dilemma of suffering as well as it can be expressed. Why does God allow a world of sick children, of poverty and little hope? I don't have a clear answer and nor, I suspect, do you. But I know one thing; the God who made the world has been here and seen what it is like to suffer. He took on the same flesh that you have. His nerve fibres were not bionic – they screamed with pain when misused. There is nothing known to us which he has not felt. And that makes all the difference. G.R. Solomon sums up the whole issue in these powerful words:

When we come to the place of full retreat
And our heart cries out for God
The only person whose heart ours can meet
Is the one who has likewise trod
Others may offer a word of cheer
To lift us from despair
But above the rest, the one we hear,
Is the whisper, 'I've been there.'

Take heart, beloved fellow traveller. No matter what your struggles, your Lord has been there! Hallelujah!

O Jesus, Master of the inward wound, teach us the same mastery. Help me to go on when wounded by life, knowing that your wounds are answering my wounds. And may my wounds answer someone else's wounds. For your own dear name's sake. Amen.

FOR FURTHER STUDY – Phil. 2:1–11; Rom. 8:3; John 13:15; 1 Pet. 2:21–23

1. What mind is to be in us? / 2. How did Peter sum it up?

Grace in the dungeon

FOR READING AND MEDITATION – JEREMIAH 30:18–31:3

'For this is the Eternal's promise: "Those who survive the sword shall find grace in the dungeon." ' (31:2: Moffatt)

Our theme for the next two months of the year is one that brims over with optimism and encouragement – finding grace in the dungeon. The people to whom this passage was addressed did 'find grace in the dungeon' – they were purified in the Exile and became, in God's hands, the instruments of truth and righteousness. The dungeon of difficulty – banishment and exile – became, through God's grace, a place of thrilling revelation.

I feel, as I write, that over the next two months I will be talking to thousands of you who are caught up in a variety of difficult and perplexing circumstances, and my main thesis is this – if you are not able to get out of the dungeon, then the only thing to do is to get the dungeon out of you – to find grace in the dungeon. Some of the most beautiful words ever penned by the apostle Paul are these: 'This salutation is in my own hand, from Paul. "Remember I am in prison. Grace be with you" ' (Colossians 4:18, Moffatt). We might have expected Paul, after being incarcerated for the sake of the Gospel, to write, 'I am in prison. God give me grace.' But no, he puts it the other way round: '... "I am in prison. Grace be with you." ' Paul is saying, 'I have found grace in the dungeon – enough to pass on to you.'

A dungeon experience can make or break us. Some it shatters; others it strengthens. When our souls are open to the grace that constantly flows toward us from heaven then every limitation, every difficult situation and every perplexing circumstance can be the setting for a new discovery of God and a new revelation of his love.

O Father, help me to fasten onto this truth, that when my circumstances become a dungeon, I can, like the apostle Paul, find grace there. Make this a reality – for Jesus' sake. Amen.

FOR FURTHER STUDY – 2 Cor. Ch. 12; Phil. 4:19; Eph. 2:6–7

1. What was Paul's strength? / 2. How did he respond?

Grace enough – and to share

FOR READING & MEDITATION – COLOSSIANS 4:7–18
'...Remember my chains. Grace be with you.' (v.18: NIV)

I feel led to speak today to those who may have just come into the Christian life and are a little fearful of the fact that standing up for Christ brings persecution. Perhaps you were drawn to Christ through the idea that he promises to give us life – far more life than before. How, you might be saying to yourself, can I have full life while being persecuted?

In answer to that question let me invite you to look at yesterday's verse again: 'For this is the Eternal's promise, those who survive the sword shall find grace in the dungeon' (Jer. 31:2, Moffatt).

If you are caught in the dungeon of persecution and can't get out, then the only thing to do is to find grace in that very dungeon. Look again at the text for today: 'Remember my chains. Grace be with you.' If I might refer to James Moffatt's translation again, this is the wording he gives: 'Remember I am in prison. Grace be with you.' Paul found grace in the dungeon. When you find yourself in the dungeon of persecution then remember this: there are enough resources not only for you, but even to share with others!

Father, if my circumstances make me feel as if I am trapped in a dungeon, help me avail myself of your grace. Save me from complaining. Instead may I focus on finding resources, enough even to share. Amen.

FOR FURTHER STUDY – 2 Cor.12:9–10; Phil. 4:23
1. Why did Paul plead with the Lord? / 2. What was the Lord's response?

Strengthened for everything

FOR READING AND MEDITATION – LUKE 22:39–53

'He ... prayed, "Father, if you are willing, take this cup from me; yet not my will, but yours be done."' (vv. 41–42: NIV)

We continue our theme of finding grace in the dungeon. All our limitations, our difficult circumstances, our dungeons can be places where we find grace. I shall focus therefore on particular issues that most of us face from time to time in our Christian pilgrimage, and attempt to give some helpful advice on how to turn that issue to good advantage.

The first I want to examine is what I am going to call the dungeon of hostile opposition. Are you caught up in an environment in which others are bitterly opposed to you, and it seems you are imprisoned in a dungeon from which you cannot escape? Have you prayed to be delivered, and yet no deliverance has come? Then, take heart, for if God does not answer your prayer to take you out of the dungeon, he will most certainly take the dungeon out of you. The answer is found in the passage before us today: 'He withdrew about a stone's throw and knelt in prayer, saying, "Father, if it please thee, take this cup away from me. But thy will, not mine, be done." And an angel from heaven appeared to strengthen him' (vv. 41–43, Moffatt). Here, God's answer was not to take away the cup but to give strength to turn that bitter cup into a cup of salvation, which later he would put to the thirsty lips of humanity. So God's answer to Jesus was not to exempt him from the Cross but to give him added strength so that he was able to experience it and make his suffering redemptive.

There are times when God's way of deliverance is not to deliver us from a situation but to deliver us in it. And when he does the latter, it is no less a deliverance.

O Father, help me not to whine to be released when it is your will to let me remain where I am, but help me to lay hold upon your strength and turn the hell into a heaven. For Jesus' sake. Amen.

FOR FURTHER STUDY – 1 Ki. Ch. 19; Psa. 91:11; Heb. 1:13–14

1. How did God minister to Elijah? / 2. What is the promise to the 'heirs of salvation'?

Crazy logic

FOR READING AND MEDITATION – LUKE 6:1–16

'This filled them with fury ... It was in these days that he went off to the hillside to pray.' (vv. 11–12: Moffatt)

We are studying the Christian way to respond when we find ourselves surrounded by hostility, criticism and opposition. Jesus, in the passage before us today, was surrounded by a hostile group of people, but he turned the situation to good advantage by going out into the hills to pray. It was after that prayer that he summoned his disciples, choosing 12. We see from this that the fury of the hostile group furthered him. It led to his decision to choose the 12 with whom he could entrust his message of individual salvation.

The same principle was at work in the hearts of the apostles who had caught the secret from Jesus. We read in Acts 14:2–3: 'But the unbelieving Jews ... poisoned their minds against the brethren. So they remained for a long time, speaking boldly' (RSV). This is what one writer terms as 'crazy logic'. Listen to it again: '... the unbelieving Jews ... poisoned their minds against the brethren. So they remained for a long time, speaking boldly.' One would have thought it might have read, 'They poisoned their minds against them, so they left.' But no, they remained, and 'remained for a long time, speaking boldly'. The poison produced persistence, and the persistence produced results.

Take another illustration from Acts 18:6–8: 'And when they opposed and reviled him ... he left there and went ... next door to the synagogue. Crispus, the ruler of the synagogue, believed ... and many of the Corinthians hearing Paul believed ...' Here Paul was opposed but he turned the opposition into opportunity. When one door was shut a bigger one opened. The epistles to the Corinthians came out of that opposition. When you can produce such a chapter as 1 Corinthians 13 out of opposition and criticism, then you are incorrigibly victorious.

O God, teach me more about this way of life that can turn all my oppositions into opportunities and all my disabilities into doors. For Jesus' sake. Amen.

FOR FURTHER STUDY – Matt. 5:1–16; 2 Tim. 2:12; 1 Pet. 2:20

1. How should we respond to persecution?
2. How would you interpret the word 'exceeding'?

Every project a prisoner

FOR READING AND MEDITATION – 2 CORINTHIANS 10:1–18

'... I take every project prisoner to make it obey Christ.' (v. 5: Moffatt)

We are seeing that when God allows us to be shut up in a dungeon of opposition, we can, by his grace, turn it into a dungeon of opportunity. Are people against you? Are you the victim of spite and spleen? Then ask God to help you turn the situation to advantage – for you and him.

We noted yesterday that the apostles, when opposed at Iconium, stayed where they were and preached the Gospel. Later on, however: 'When an attempt was made ... to molest them and to stone them, they learned of it and fled to Lystra ... there they preached the gospel' (Acts 14:5–7, RSV). They stayed a long time in Iconium but in the end they fled. In both cases – staying or fleeing – they preached the Gospel. You see, the end result was not staying or fleeing but preaching the Gospel. There was no stubborn adherence to one particular mode or method – they could stay or flee – but their aim was to achieve their main purpose, that of preaching the Gospel.

Agnes E. Meyers is reported to have said, 'The principal quality of exceptional women is the capacity to accept the triumphs of life without pride and the sufferings of life without despair.' The sufferings of life can be met without despair, not by gritting our teeth and saying, 'I'll grin and bear it,' but by seeing that God's grace enables us to use everything that comes our way. The Swedish have a saying, 'Blessed is he who sees a dawn in every midnight.' And there is a dawn in every midnight – so expect it before it comes. Paul learned how to 'take every project prisoner to make it obey Christ' – even the 'projects' of injustice and wrong. And so, my friend, can you.

Yes, Father, as an aeroplane rises against the wind, so I shall rise against the resistances of this day, and, through your grace, make every opposition serve to deepen my character and teach me more of your infinite resources. Hallelujah!

FOR FURTHER STUDY – Jas. Ch. 1; Job 23:10; 2 Cor. 4:17; Heb. 12:11

1. Why is our faith tried? / 2. What is the reward?

Making all things serve

FOR READING AND MEDITATION – JOHN 14:16–31

'... the Prince of this world is coming... his coming will only serve...'
(vv. 30–31: Moffatt)

We continue examining ways in which we can turn a dungeon of opposition into a dungeon of opportunity. Someone said that, 'The prelude to every discovery is a pain in the mind.' When there is a pain anywhere in life, it is the prelude to discovery.

A mother and her daughter came up to me at the close of a seminar session and said, 'We are the only two Christians in a family of seven. We were discouraged because we have had to take the scoffs and taunts of the rest of the family, but we have seen tonight that the opposition we have been experiencing has served only to deepen our trust in God and our faith in his purposes. We might have been much weaker Christians if it hadn't been for the opposition.' They were both 'made' by something that could have 'unmade' them. I have said it many times before, and I will probably say it many times again before I die: it is not what happens to us but what we do with it that determines the result.

A young woman I met recently told me that her hair turned grey when she went through a family crisis. She said to her doctor, 'What am I going to do with my grey hair?' And the doctor promptly said, 'Admire it.' That's it! If circumstances put a white crown on your head, then wear it as a crown and not a complaint. If you glory in everything, then everything will be glorious. In contrast, consider this: a woman I know lost £5,000 on the stock market and as a result her throat closed up so that she couldn't eat. She is choking herself to death with grief. And she is choking to death the happiness of those around her. It's not a joyful experience to lose £5,000, but even that can be turned to advantage by God's grace.

Lord Jesus, as you made all things serve you when you were here on earth – even Satan's coming – so I, too, will make everything serve, including those who ridicule me and oppose me. For your own dear name's sake. Amen.

FOR FURTHER STUDY – Dan. 3:13–30; Eccl. 7:8; Rom. 12:12

1. How did the Hebrew young men turn a setback into a springboard?
2. What did they declare?

Healing with ease

FOR READING AND MEDITATION – HEBREWS 12:1–13

'If you want to keep from becoming fainthearted and weary, think about his patience as sinful men did such terrible things to him.' (v. 3: TLB)

We continue studying how to turn a dungeon of opposition into a dungeon of opportunity. Many years ago, when I was less experienced and made more mistakes, I passed through a time when it seemed as if the whole world was against me. Almost daily I received the bitterest criticism from people whom I considered had my interests at heart. My critics seemed as numerous as the sand on the seashore, and although some of their criticisms were merited, most were not. I remember, however, waking up one morning and thinking to myself, 'I feel so wonderfully happy; I wonder, are my critics as happy as I am?' I doubted it. Those who criticise you are often their own worst enemies. Why add to their inner discomfiture by retaliating? Better to take the grace that flows in through the chinks in the door of the dungeon of opposition, and use it to make you more like the One who exhibited such patience when 'sinful men did such terrible things to him' (verse 3, TLB).

A letter I received recently says, 'My friends seem to make me their special target – I am the bull's eye for their criticisms. But every time they score a hit, I seem to heal with as much ease as they pull the trigger.' I happen to know that this lady is not a thick-skinned individual who cares for nothing and nobody, but a person who is highly sensitive and easily hurt. Her critics are becoming more and more frustrated as she responds in this way, but because she knows how to utilise the grace God gives, she is becoming more and more fruitful.

O God, give me the flexibility and the strength of the bamboo so that I bow and don't break before the opposition that from time to time I encounter. For Jesus' sake. Amen.

FOR FURTHER STUDY – Lk. 6:20–30; Matt, 10:22; 1 Pet 2:19

1. How are we to retaliate? / 2. What quality is essential?

How to live in a dungeon

FOR READING AND MEDITATION – 1 PETER 2:20–25

'This suffering is all part of the work God has given you. Christ, who suffered for you, is your example…' (v. 21: TLB)

We have been seeing over the past week that by God's grace every dungeon of opposition can be turned into a dungeon of opportunity. So if you find yourself surrounded by hostility, criticism and disapproval, turn it to your own and God's advantage by doing these things:

(1) Analyse the situation to see that you are not contributing to the problem by your own insensitivity or self-centredness. Some Christians bring about a negative reaction in those they meet or work with, not because of their stand for Christ, but because of their own unsanctified dispositions.

(2) Remind yourself that if God does not take you out of a dungeon of difficulty, his plan is to take the dungeon out of you. The Christian answer to life is to use whatever comes – justice or injustice, pain or pleasure, compliment or criticism. Everything God allows can be used.

(3) Surrender any frustration that arises into God's hands – don't keep it bottled up within. Whatever you do, don't try to deal with it yourself. You and God together can make something out of it.

(4) Expect strength from God – to transform everything that comes into the central purpose of your life. 'Everything is grist to the Christian's mill,' said an acquaintance recently. Do you remember the words of Joseph: '…you sold me … God sent me …'? (Gen. 45:5, Moffatt)

(5 Now that God and you are working together, look for the good that is to be rescued out of the situation. Doing that will turn your mentality from useless complaint to expectancy. So begin to thank him for the problem, for through it you are going to discover a new dimension of living. God can do anything with a thankful heart, but he can do little for a complaining one. It is closed to his grace.

O Father, now I know that nothing can come which does not contribute, I am able, by your grace, to turn everything into something better. Every Calvary can be an Easter morning. Amen.

FOR FURTHER STUDY – Gen. 37:23–36, 45:1–15; Eph. 4:32

1. List five responses of Joseph. / 2. What might have been a natural response?

The dungeon of temptation

FOR READING AND MEDITATION – 1 CORINTHIANS 10:1–13

'…for he has promised this and will do what he says.
He will show you how to escape temptation's power …' (v. 13: TLB)

We turn now to consider another dungeon in which Christians sometimes find themselves confined – the dungeon of temptation. Perhaps at this very moment you are surrounded by a host of powerful temptations that threaten to engulf your soul. But, take heart, our text for today tells us that God is committed to giving you the strength to face the fiercest of temptations. You will find grace in the dungeon.

Note what the text says: 'He has promised this and will do what he says.' God owes it to himself, his Word, his character and his love to succour you in any temptation that threatens to overwhelm your soul. He knows that you can do nothing without him, and that you will certainly fail if he abandons you. The truth is that if God was to remove himself from you in the critical moments when you are overtaken by a strong and fierce temptation then he would not be true to himself. So drop your anchor right now into the depths of this reassuring and encouraging revelation: 'He has promised this and will do what he says.' Or, in other words, you will find grace in the dungeon.

The faithfulness of God's promise does not consist in delivering us from the dungeon of temptation but in never allowing the temptation to go beyond our power to resist. God knows infinitely better than we do just how much strength we have, and in the most amazing way he moderates the activities of the Tempter, and will never permit him to attack us with more strength than we have to resist. This is not all – he will increase the power of his assistance in proportion to the strength of the temptation. And that's a promise!

O Father, I am so thankful that I am not alone in this battle against temptation. I see that success in meeting temptation comes, not by mastering certain techniques, but in being mastered by certain convictions – the conviction that you will support me in every temptation. Thank you, Father. Amen.

FOR FURTHER STUDY – Matt, 4:1–11; Heb. 2:18; 2 Pet. 2:9

1. How did Jesus handle temptation? / 2. What was the Father's response?

Unbeatable and unbreakable

FOR READING AND MEDITATION – ISAIAH 54:11–17
'…no weapon turned against you shall succeed …' (v. 17: TLB)

We continue examining the subject of finding grace in the dungeon of temptation. We saw yesterday that God is committed to strengthening us to face every temptation that comes our way, and he has promised that he will not permit one temptation to come to us that we cannot handle. Temptation, though we may not think so when we face it, has a useful purpose. As we grapple, we grow. Goethe said, 'Difficulties prove men.' They do. We must learn to do more with temptation than just bear it – we must learn to use it. Using temptation, and turning it to our advantage, is one of life's greatest secrets. Once we have learned this we are unbeatable and unbreakable.

A Christian schoolteacher once told me that when she was talking to her class about the Cross, one little girl raised her hand and said, 'Jesus didn't just carry his Cross – he used it.' 'Out of the mouths of babes and sucklings'! What a powerful truth lies in the words of that little girl. God doesn't want us just to bear the cross of temptation: He wants us to use it. You can't bear a cross for long unless you use it. A stoic bears a cross; a Christian uses it and makes it bear him.

We must, therefore, make a decision before we go any further: are we simply going to bear temptation or are we going to use it? When we view temptation with the right attitude, and face it with the strength and grace that God provides, then the things that oppose us contribute to our advancement. I once heard the singer, Sammy Davis Jnr, take words that were shouted to him from the audience and set them to music. Someone read out a shopping list that he promptly set to a tune! It's not what comes; it's what you do with it that matters.

O Father, I see so clearly that when I am in you, and you are in me, then everything can be used – even temptation. Your grace enables me to be unbeatable and unbreakable. I am so thankful. Amen.

FOR FURTHER STUDY – 1 Jn. Ch. 5; Rev. 12:9–11; 2 Cor. 2: 11, 11:3; 1 Thess. 3:5
1. What is the victory that overcomes the world? / 2. What are two aspects of this?

It hurts good

FOR READING AND MEDITATION – JAMES 1:1–8

'… is your life full of … temptations? Then be happy, for when the way is rough, your patience has a chance to grow.' (vv. 2–3: TLB)

We are saying that when we find ourselves in the dungeon of temptation, God finds a way of supplying us with sufficient grace that makes the temptation, not a groaning point, but a growing point. Everything, temptation included, can be taken and used for higher ends when God is in it. That is why a true Christian ought not to be nonplussed, for everything can be made to work towards favourable ends. A young army officer, involved in the Falkland Islands dispute, was asked by a television reporter, 'But isn't the weather unfavourable?' He replied, 'Weather in war is always favourable – providing you know how to use it.' That is the point – everything can contribute if you know how to use it.

Philosophers have told us repeatedly that life is determined more by our reactions than by our actions. Temptation sweeps in upon us and forces its way into our lives without our asking (and sometimes without our acting), and it is then that reaction plays an important part. We can react in self-pity and frustration or we can act with confidence and with courage, and make the temptation work to improve our character and deepen our hold upon God. Temptation may contain an evil design but by the time you have finished with it, the evil has been turned into good.

The South American Indians like bitter medicine. They don't consider it beneficial unless it has an acrid taste. 'It hurts good,' they say. You can make temptation 'hurt good' when you see in it the possibilities of increasing your dependency upon God and developing your character by moulding it into the image of Jesus Christ.

Lord Jesus, you who faced the bitterness of temptation and of the Cross, and used that bitterness to make me better, strengthen me by your grace so that I, too, can follow your example and turn every temptation into a triumph. For your own dear name's sake. Amen.

FOR FURTHER STUDY – Jas. 4:1–8; Eph. 6:11; 1 Pet. 5:8

1. What is the five-point plan to overcome temptation? / 2. What does God supply?

Why God allows it

FOR READING AND MEDITATION – JAMES 1:9–20

'Blessed is the man who perseveres under trial, because when he has stood the test, he will receive the crown of life . . .' (v. 12: NIV)

Today we examine the question: why does God allow temptation? In order to answer that we must look at the Greek word for temptation used in the New Testament – *peirasomos*. It means 'to test, to try or to prove'. The Biblical use of the word (unlike the modern use of it) does not contain the idea of seduction or entrapment, but rather the putting of people to the test for the purpose of deepening their personal qualities. The purpose, then, behind every temptation is the development of our character.

One writer says, 'The conversion of a soul is the work of a moment, but the making of a saint is the work of a lifetime.' Oswald Chambers, expressing the same truth but in a different way, said, 'God can, in one single moment, make a heart pure, but not even God can give a person character.' Character would not be the precious thing it is if it could be acquired without effort, without combat and without contradictions. 'Virtue that has not been tried and tested,' said one great theologian, 'is not worthy of the name of virtue.' It is essential, in a world such as this, that temptation comes to try the people of God, for without temptation there can be no advancement, no development, no growth in character.

The question may arise in your mind: 'What is character?' 'Character,' as someone aptly put it, 'is what we are in the dark.' Reputation is what other people think of us – character is what we are on the inside. Character is the strength and refinement of soul that we develop as we stand against the tide of temptation. As I said the day before yesterday: as we grapple, we grow. And out of the growing comes character.

O Father, if character is something achieved rather than acquired, then help me in the achieving. And if temptation is the way by which you deepen my character, then I welcome it – in your name. Amen.

FOR FURTHER STUDY – Job Chs. 1, 2, 13:15, 17:9, Ch. 42

1. What was Job's attitude? / 2. How did it develop character?

Why fear it?

FOR READING AND MEDITATION – 1 PETER 1:1–9

'These have come so that your faith … may be proved genuine …' (v. 7: NIV)

To many people the idea of God allowing his children to be tempted by the devil is inconsistent with his omnipotence. 'If God is almighty,' they reason, 'then he should intervene in Satan's attempts to seduce us and prevent him from having access to our personalities.' However, it is because God is omnipotent that he permits us to be tempted.

F.P. Harton says, 'A conquering nation that is not sure of its own strength, refuses to allow the people it subjects any kind of independence at all, and keeps control with a strong hand – but the real reason is fear.' God does not control his universe through fear but through eternal love and justice. Although God allows men and women to be tempted for the express purpose of building character, he ensures that to each one there flows a stream of grace that, when received, enables the person to overcome the temptation and use it to higher ends.

One of the devil's strategies in attacking God's children is to attempt to persuade them that God is not able to help them in time of temptation. God is well able to help them, and he helps, not so much by extricating them from the temptation, but by supplying them with sufficient grace to use it and overcome it. Temptation is part of God's purposes for us here on earth so why fear it? If humility does not allow us to desire temptation, because that would be to presume on our own strength, then zeal for our Christian development does not allow us to dread it, still less to be unhappy when it comes. Holiness and purity of soul would not be as awesome to our carnal nature if they could be acquired without effort.

Lord, I see that you seek to deliver me from all that would stain my soul and sour my spirit. And temptation is one way that this can be achieved. So help me to face it in your strength, and recognise that it has a beneficial purpose. Amen.

FOR FURTHER STUDY – Zech. Ch. 13; Job 23:10; Psa. 66:10; Isa. 48:10; 1 Pet. 4:12–13

1. How should we respond in the day of refining? / 2. What is the result?

Making our problems his own

FOR READING AND MEDITATION – HEBREWS 2:5–18
'Because he himself suffered when he was tempted, he is able to help those who are being tempted' (v. 18: NIV)

We continue thinking through this matter of why God allows us to be tempted.

When God designed us in the beginning he made us with the awesome power of choice – with the possibility that we might go astray and break our own hearts as well as his. What if God had made us without the power of choice, or with the power to choose only the good? Well, this would not really have been choice, because choice obviously involves choosing between one thing and another. If we could choose only the good, then there would be no such thing as character, for character involves freedom of choice – the freedom to choose either the good or the evil. Kant said, 'There is nothing in the world, or even out of it, that can be called good, except a good will.' You see, if there is no will, there is no personality, and where there is no personality, there is no sense of goodness and badness.

In a way, God, in desiring to give man freedom of choice, embarked upon a risky project. Yet, as one theologian points out, 'Parents take the same risk when they bring a child into the world. The child may go astray and crush their lives – and his own.' But parents assume that risk. And why? Because they determine that they will do their best for their child, and make that child's problems their very own. Parents accept the fact that having children involves suffering and pain, especially when the children decide to go contrary to their expectations and wishes. However, parenthood accepts this cross – it cannot do otherwise. So it is with God. In creating us, he knew he would have to make our problems his own; and this he did, all glory to his wonderful name, when he wore our flesh, endured our temptations and gave himself for us on that blood-soaked tree.

O Father, how can I ever sufficiently thank you for making my problems your very own. You are truly a wonderful Parent – and I am grateful more than words can convey. Amen.

FOR FURTHER STUDY – 1 Pet. Ch. 2; Isa. 53:12; Heb. 9:28, 4:15–16
1. What did Jesus do when reviled? / 2. Why can we approach his throne boldly?

The highest petition

FOR READING AND MEDITATION – MATTHEW 6:5–15

'"... lead us not into temptation ..."' (v. 13: NIV)

We must face one more question before we finish discussing the dungeon of temptation: should we take any steps to prepare ourselves to meet temptation or should we just go into it head-on, trusting God to help us overcome it? Well, the text before us today suggests that we ought to pray to be kept from all temptation. However, is that what it is really saying? I get more letters about this one text than any other in the Bible. The phrase is the last petition in the *Lord's Prayer*. I used to think it an anti-climax but now I see it as the highest petition of all.

We know, from what we have seen, that temptation can be a means in God's hands of refining our souls and enriching our characters; why then should we ask not to be led into it? I am convinced that what Jesus meant by these words is that we should think in terms of being kept from unrecognised temptation. When temptation is recognised it can be resisted, for as we absorb the corresponding stream of grace that God has promised accompanies all temptation, we can overcome it and even use it.

However, temptation is not always easily discerned. Simon Peter is an example of this. In the Garden of Gethsemane he was over-confident, but Jesus warned him: 'Watch and pray so that you will not fall into temptation' (Matt. 26:41, NIV). But Peter didn't heed that word, and later, when temptation came in the form of a little maid, he cursed and swore and denied his Lord. Peter had not done what the Lord had advised him: 'Watch and pray so that you will not fall into temptation.' We must recognise our human tendency to stumble on in blind folly, and so we need always to pray, 'Lead us not into [unrecognised] temptation.'

Lord Jesus, help me to avoid Simon Peter's mistake, and to be ever prayerful and watchful so that I recognise temptation whenever it comes, and whatever form it takes. For your own name's sake I pray. Amen.

FOR FURTHER STUDY – Psa. 91:1–16; Lk. 10:19; 2 Cor. 2:10–11; Heb. 2:18

1. What are some 'fowler's snares'? / 2. How can we guard against Satan's devices?

The dungeon of sickness

FOR READING AND MEDITATION – 2 CORINTHIANS 9:6–15
'And God is able to make all grace abound to you …' (v. 8: NIV)

We move on now to consider yet another dungeon in which some Christians sometimes find themselves confined – the dungeon of physical sickness. What happens if, after praying for healing from a sickness, nothing happens, or we take an unusually long time to recover? We can find grace in the dungeon! Let me make myself clear about this important subject of physical sickness.

Whenever we are attacked by sickness, disease or infirmity, I believe it right to take a positive approach in the matter and seek to be free of it. We can do that by calling on the elders of the church to anoint us with oil as the Scripture advises (James 5:14) or by taking advantage of the benefits of medical science by seeing a doctor. We know from experience, however, that some sicknesses and disabilities stubbornly remain after the most intensive prayer and the most expert medical attention – so what do we do then? We must do with a stubborn sickness what we do with the other problems of life – make it serve.

A girl of twenty was confined to bed with a bad heart. The first week was spent in bitter rebellion. Then she read a book in which the author opened up the possibility of not merely bearing suffering and frustration but of using them. The remaining fifty-one weeks of that year were beautiful – the best year of her life. She read, studied and prepared herself for a college education. When she was able to lead a normal life again, she attended college, and became one of the most promising and useful women in the community. She found grace in the dungeon. The frustration became fruitfulness.

O God, when my circumstances become a dungeon then help me to find grace there – grace enough to turn a tragedy into a triumph. For Jesus' sake. Amen.

FOR FURTHER STUDY – Rev. Ch. 21; Psa. 30:5, 34:19; Isa. 43:2
1. What is the 'hope of the believer'? / 2. What is the promise for the present?

God gives – we receive

FOR READING AND MEDITATION – GENESIS 17:1–8

'... the Lord appeared to Abram, and said ... "I am Almighty God ..." ["I am God – the Enough..."]' (v. 1: NKJ)

We are seeing that when, after treatment or prayer, a physical sickness remains, we do not have merely to suffer it – we can use it. God gives grace, not just to bear things, but to transform things. This motto was on the desk of a high-school principal in Pusan, Korea, when I visited him during the course of a crusade I held in that city a number of years ago:

For every evil under the sun
There is a remedy, or there is none,
If there be one, try and find it,
If there be none, never mind it.

The suggestion regarding an evil that had no remedy was good, but not good enough. The problem might be so acute and insistent that you cannot help but mind it. Sometimes sickness can be so upsetting that the iron of it enters the soul, producing great gloom and melancholy. What is to be done?

Open your being to the grace of God. First, recognise that God has promised to provide grace for every problem (2 Cor. 12:9). This is not just wishful thinking. The eternal God stands behind his Word. Next, focus on the fact that God has more than enough grace to meet your need. Many American offices have wall-plaques and desk-stands bearing the words, 'We talk abundance here.' And when we talk about the grace of God, as spoken of in the Scripture, 'we talk abundance'. God, as I have said before, is the great *El Shaddai* or 'God, the Enough'. Finally, visualise God's grace streaming toward you. Picture yourself standing under a waterfall, the waterfall being God's grace. Make a conscious effort to open your being to all that God offers you. When you open the doors of your being, I promise you, God will flow in – Grace.

O Lord, just as thousands of our children down the ages have found grace in the dungeon, help me to experience it too. Show me how to visualise it, to receive it, to absorb it. In Jesus' name I pray. Amen.

FOR FURTHER STUDY – Isa. 41:1–13, 25:4; Psa. 23:5, 57:1

1. What is God's promise to the believer? / 2. How are you going to 'talk abundance' today?

Using even an illness

FOR READING AND MEDITATION – GALATIANS 4:1–14

'... it was because of an illness that I first preached the gospel to you.' (v. 13: NIV)

When Paul was thrown aside at Galatia by a sickness, was he frustrated? No. He says: 'It was because of an illness that I first preached the gospel to you.' Thrown aside by an illness, he used that frustrating time to preach the Gospel. Through the illness, he raised up a Christian church, and wrote a letter to it – a letter which has greatly enriched the ages. Now that is victory!

When Paul asked God to take away the 'thorn in the flesh, the messenger of Satan to buffet me', he received the reply: 'My grace is sufficient for you: for my power is made perfect in weakness' (2 Cor. 12:9, NIV). He was promised, not deliverance, but grace to use the infirmity. He then arose and said, 'Most gladly therefore will I rather glory in my infirmities ... for when I am weak, then am I strong' (verses 9, 10). If the 'messenger of Satan' were there to buffet him, then he would determine the direction in which the blows would send him. We can't be certain that the 'thorn in the flesh' was a physical sickness because there is no clear evidence for that. Some think it was a demonic spirit sent to harass the adventurous apostle. However, the principle remains – everything can be used.

Someone asked a man who had been sick for some years, 'How's your constitution?' meaning, of course, his physical constitution. 'Oh,' he said, 'that's gone long ago – now I'm living on the by-laws.' Some people live better on their by-laws than most people on their constitutions. A friend of mine who is a preacher of the gospel certainly does. He has one lung, and he does more with that one lung than most people do with two! Paul, the apostle, said: 'I am no speaker' (2 Cor. 11:6, Moffatt); but did that lack of oratorical ability stop Paul? No – it only spurred him on to success.

O Father, slowly it is dawning upon me that no matter what my circumstances, I am never beaten until I am beaten within. And with you I am not beaten there. Abide with me and I can then abide with anything. Thank you, Father. Amen.

FOR FURTHER STUDY – Psa. 84:1–12; Isa. 41:10, 40:31; Eph. 3:16

1. What is the reward of the upright? / 2. Read verse 6 of Psa. 84 in the RSV.

The problem of pain

FOR READING AND MEDITATION – EPHESIANS 4:1–16

'But to each one of us grace has been given ...' (v. 7: NIV)

We continue meditating on finding grace in the dungeon of physical sickness. For many, sickness is not so much of a problem as pain. Studdert Kennedy used to say that a man who was undisturbed by the problem of pain was suffering from one of two things; either from a hardening of the heart, or a softening of the brain. Kennedy was right. Everyone who is mentally alert and alive, especially if they believe in a God of love, finds this problem difficult to solve. To sit at the bedside of a loved one who is sick, and unable for a while to carry out their usual tasks, is one thing, but to see that person twisted with pain is another. Some sicknesses are bad enough; but pain ...!

Is Christ able to succour a person who is struggling with pain? Yes. His grace is available even for that. I have talked with many Christians throughout the 32 years of my ministry, who have been racked with pain, and they have told me that just below the level of their physical pain, they have been conscious of a power at work supporting, sustaining and upholding them.

Sometimes it is harder for a person to look at a Christian loved one who is suffering, because the one who stands by as a mere observer is unable to experience the same grace that God provides for the sufferer. You see, God only provides needed grace for needed moments. He provides grace for the sufferer, and although he provides grace in a general way for those Christians who might look on, it is not the same degree of grace, Someone said, 'You only get dying grace at a dying moment.' How thankful we ought to be, even in the face of inexplicable pain, that God gives grace to cope with it.

O Father, what a comfort it is to know that you give grace to cope with physical pain. Help me to avail myself of this grace whenever I need it. In Jesus' name. Amen.

FOR FURTHER STUDY – Mk. Chs. 14, 15; Heb. 4:15–16

1. List ten aspects of pain Christ suffered. / 2. How was he able to face it?

The purpose of pain

FOR READING AND MEDITATION – JEREMIAH 51:45–58
'…and pagans waste their pains.' v. 58: Moffatt)

We continue meditating on the problem of pain. Some Christians say that while they can accept the reasons for sin and sickness being in the universe, they find it difficult to understand the reasons for pain. However, had there been no pain in the world, we would not have survived as a race. For instance, were there no pain attached to disease, we should probably allow disease to eat on – it doesn't hurt, so why bother? But pain is the monitor of human health. It draws our attention to issues by saying, 'Look out! There is something wrong here – better attend to it.' 'Pain,' said a Christian doctor, 'is God's red flag run up to warn of underlying danger.' We can, then, thank God for pain.

However, it is difficult to thank God for pain unless we can do something with it other than bear it stoically. Unless pain is working towards some end, it frustrates us by its meaninglessness. Jeremiah tells us in our text today that the 'pagans waste their pains'. Whether the pain referred to here is physical or spiritual makes no difference; the principle is the same – pain must be used, not wasted. Those who live without God – i.e. the pagans – don't know what to do with pain; they waste it. Their pain ends in dull, fruitless, meaningless suffering. It gets them nowhere. Only when we see redemption in pain can we have any release while experiencing it – purposeless pain is paralysing.

So whenever you next feel pain, continual pain that wears you down, ask God to help you to turn it into something redemptive. He can make it work to deepen your sensitivity to others, increase your awareness of his presence, or a dozen other different things. But, whatever happens, don't waste it. Only the 'pagans waste their pains'.

O Father, when bowed down with pain, it is not always easy to pray, so I ask you now – help me turn pain to redemptive ends. For Jesus' sake. Amen.

FOR FURTHER STUDY – Job Ch. 19; Psa. 27:1–14; Mal. 4:2
1. What was Job's affirmation despite his pain? / 2. What was the psalmist's declaration?

There is no God

FOR READING AND MEDITATION – 2 CORINTHIANS 12:1–10

'But he said to me, "My grace is sufficient for you ..."' (v. 9: NIV)

We are meditating together on the subject of finding grace in the dungeon of physical sickness. In one of the first churches I pastored, there was a young couple who had a child, an angel child, who lived only until she was seven. The child was born with a strange disease, and despite skilful medical treatment, she never recovered. Fifteen times in seven years she was operated upon, and she became so disfigured that the parents had to hide her away. Only the strong-nerved could look at her and what was left of her dear, disfigured body. Some of the neighbours, knowing of the child's condition, wrote on the walls of their home in letters three feet high, 'There is no God.' I could understand their confusion even though I could not agree with their conclusions. The amazing thing is though, that not once did I ever hear the parents complain. They found grace in the dungeon.

At the funeral of that little child, I cried so much that I had to hand over to one of the church elders. What moved me was the way the parents responded to the grace that God gave them, for I knew that if I had been in their position, I might not have come through with such Christian heroism and fortitude. As a minister I had no answer, at least no complete answer, to explain the situation; but I learned from sharing that couple's predicament that no matter how dark and dismal the dungeon, God finds a way of getting his grace through. This is why, as someone said, 'When the world is at its worst, Christians are at their best.' The dungeon can only do for a surrendered and victorious Christian what the fire did for the Hebrew children – burn off the fetters.

O Father, I am so thankful to you for showing me the indomitable way. Whatever comes, it is possible for life to be held together by poise that leads to calmness and victory. I can find grace in the dungeon. I am so thankful. Amen.

FOR FURTHER STUDY – Psa. 34:1–22, 30:5; Matt. 10:29–30; 1 Pet. 5:7

1. What was the psalmist's response amidst affliction?
2. How did Jesus illustrate God's care?

Either way we win!

FOR READING AND MEDITATION – HEBREWS 4:12–16

'… so that we may … find grace to help us in our time of need.' (v. 16: NIV)

Dungeons of various kinds often lead to our finding grace. Milton wrote his *Paradise Lost* when blind. Clifford Beers was once in a mental asylum, but later recovered and wrote a book entitled *A Mind That Found Itself*. He went on to become the founder of the National Commission for Mental Hygiene. Carlyle, the famous author, said that he wrote with 'a sickness constantly gnawing at his stomach'. Someone I know became an artist after being confined to bed with a prolonged sickness. Hours of looking at the wallpaper in his bedroom gave him the idea of becoming a sketch artist. He tried his hand and became an extremely successful one. He found grace in the dungeon.

When sickness or disability come, and despite prayer and medical treatment, stubbornly remain, be on the alert for the grace of God flowing into your 'dungeon'; and use it to make your life even more purposeful and productive. A Christian, you see, can never be defeated. If the sickness goes, then he is free to follow his usual routine; but if it doesn't go, then he is promised grace to cope with it, and even to transform it. So, as Christians, either way we win!

In 1958, in the city of Sheffield, I suffered a physical breakdown that brought me to death's door. The doctors told my wife that I was about to die, and as I waited for death to take me, I turned to the Scripture and saw in its pages that I had been pursuing the wrong type of ministry. I asked the Lord to spare my life so that I might fulfil his purpose – and he did. I was miraculously healed, and came up from that bed to a new and exciting ministry. I found grace in the dungeon.

Gracious and loving heavenly Father, I come to you with my dungeon life. You can either free me or give me grace to make the dungeon into a place of new and thrilling revelation. So either way I win. Hallelujah!

FOR FURTHER STUDY – 1 Cor. Ch. 1; 2 Cor. 12:9; Heb. 11:33–34

1. How can God use our weaknesses?
2. List several things God can do with our weaknesses.

The dungeon of limitation

FOR READING AND MEDITATION – PHILIPPIANS 4:4–13

'... I can do everything God asks me to with the help of Christ who gives me the strength and power.' (v. 13: TLB)

This week we examine together a further variation of our theme – finding grace in the dungeon of limitation. Many people feel themselves to be greatly limited in life, limited in their education, limited in their intellectual capacity, limited in their ability to express themselves and so on. However, all our limitations can be places where we find grace.

When I entered the ministry 32 years ago, I felt myself to be greatly limited both in my education and in my intellectual ability. Due to my father's ill health I had to leave school earlier than I planned and go to work to help out with the family budget. Later, when called to the ministry, I attended an obscure college that didn't cater for theological degrees. When I left, I felt unprepared and inadequate. I was in a dungeon of limitation, but did I find grace? Most assuredly. God has helped me to gather from every moment, every occasion and every conversation something that will help educate me. My mind has become like a magnet so that I draw from every person I meet, and every situation I come across, some information, some truth that will further me. Such has been the supply of grace flowing into my dungeon that through my writings, preaching and counselling, I have been able to help people who are far above me educationally and intellectually. Jesus has been my Counsellor, and he has kept me alert and alive to life.

On the tombstone of a man were these words: 'He died climbing.' I would like to have this inscription on mine: 'He died discovering.' What I considered a limitation, through God's grace, became liberty. I found grace in the dungeon. And so, my friend, can you.

O Father, how grateful I am that whatever the restrictions life places upon me, the dungeon of limitation can, through grace, be a place of new and thrilling discovery. I am so thankful. Amen.

FOR FURTHER STUDY – 2 Cor. Ch. 3, 4:1; Lk. 10:19; Rom. 14:4

1. Where was Paul's sufficiency? / 2. Of what was Paul a minister?

Limited – yet adequate

FOR READING AND MEDITATION – JOEL 2:25–32

'I will restore to you the years which the … locust has eaten …' (v. 25: RSV)

We continue meditating on the subject of finding grace in the dungeon of limitation. Some people feel themselves greatly limited in life by reason of a physical handicap or some such disability.

A friend of mine I knew in West Wales was struck down in his early twenties with infantile paralysis. He was a farmer but, no longer able to work on the farm, he turned his thoughts to consider what contribution he could make to life and to his family. He decided that as his working experience had been mainly on the farm, he would utilise his farming knowledge and become a farm seed salesman. Week after week he turned up in an invalid carriage at the cattle marts in such towns as Carmarthen, Llandeilo, Haverfordwest and so on, until eventually he made enough money to purchase a hand-operated car. I travelled hundreds of miles with him in that car, and saw him not only sell seeds with a skill I have never seen before, but witnessed him lead hundreds of souls to Christ. He contributed more to the kingdom of God than he could ever have done on a farm, and his life affected mine in many ways.

He died the other day, and his wife told me that he had lived far beyond his expected lifespan. Like the man I referred to yesterday, 'he died climbing'. He found grace in the dungeon. This man illustrates what I am constantly emphasising in all my writings – that it is not what happens to you but what you do with it that matters. When the worst happens, we have, through God's grace, the resources to be able to turn it into the best.

Lord Jesus, despite all my limitations, help me to be confident. Even if the worst should happen, we can turn it into the best. I say 'we' for I cannot do it alone. But with you I can do anything, bear anything and use anything. All praise be to your wonderful name. Amen.

FOR FURTHER STUDY – Jer. Ch 1; Ex. 3: 11–12; Mk. 1:7; 1 Cor. 15:9

1. What sort of people does God use? / 2. How did he change Jeremiah?

Handicaps have handles

FOR READING AND MEDITATION – 1 SAMUEL 16:1–7

'...man looks on the outward appearance, but the Lord looks on the heart' (v. 7: RSV)

Some people feel greatly limited in life because of a plain appearance, a lack of good looks. One young woman in a Bible college told me, 'I see little hope of achieving anything in life because I am a "plain Jane". If I looked a little more attractive then perhaps I might achieve more for God and his Kingdom.' I pointed out to her the fallacy of her argument. God uses people, not because of their looks or appearance, but because of the inward qualities that supersede outward beauty – qualities such as love, patience, empathy, understanding, the ability to listen and so on.

Many great beauties (not all) have nothing but physical beauty. The reason is obvious – they get so caught up with their appearance that they cannot free themselves from it to pass on to constructive achievement. Sometimes a person who thinks of herself as being plain, looks in the mirror and says, 'I am not much to look at,' so she goes out and accomplishes something worthwhile. I knew a girl who worked in a Christian organisation, whom everyone considered to be physically uninteresting and unattractive. Yet people flocked round her like bees round a honey pot. She had an inner beauty that shone out of her soul. She found grace in the dungeon. Such was the evidence of the fruit of the Spirit in her life that it superseded anything good looks could achieve. When she left everyone cried because they recognised that she would leave a gap that would be difficult to fill.

I think often of the words of a man I regard as my spiritual mentor, Dr E. Stanley Jones, 'Remember, a secondary failure may make you a primary success, whereas a secondary success (like beauty) may make you a primary failure.'

Father, what I lack by nature I shall make up for by grace. I may not be able to draw heavily upon nature's endowments, but I can draw heavily on you. Make my weakness into a strength. In Jesus' name. Amen.

FOR FURTHER STUDY – 2 Cor. Ch. 5; Matt. 23:27; Jn. 7:24

1. What is God's standard of beauty? / 2. What was the Pharisee's problem?

Breaking through

FOR READING AND MEDITATION – PHILIPPIANS 2:1–11

'So by all the stimulus of Christ …' (v. 1: Moffatt)

We continue meditating on the subject of finding grace in the dungeon of limitations. Some people feel that their greatest limitation in life is a lack of creativity. 'I feel like I'm in a prison cell,' said a woman in her early fifties to me some years ago. 'Everything is a dull routine. I get up, do the same things day after day … nothing changes. Life is one endless round of chores.' I pointed her to the text at the top of this page, '… by all the stimulus of Christ …' and suggested that she make it a matter of definite prayer to ask God to enable her to draw on the creativity he had placed within her so that she could become a fully creative and fully expressive person. She did just that – and within a year from that date, she had painted five beautiful pictures, formed a women's group and started a nursery school. She wrote to me and said, 'A month hardly goes by without my breaking through another horizon.'

That is what happens if we avail ourselves of the grace that flows into every dungeon of limitation – we break through one horizon after the other. God's grace, as focused in Jesus Christ, stimulates the creative centre in our beings, making it first aware of God and then of the infinite possibilities in God.

One young boy said, 'I was at the bottom of my class until I met Christ, and then I said to myself, "This is no place for a Christian," and left it.' People cannot open their beings to God's grace for long without feeling an irresistible urge to roll up their sleeves and say, 'Where do I start?' No matter what happens to you, it is never too late to become a creative person. You can find grace in the dungeon.

Lord Jesus, you stimulated me into life at my conversion, now come, I pray, and stimulate every nerve and fibre of my being, that I might be a truly creative person. For your own name's sake. Amen.

FOR FURTHER STUDY – 2 Tim. Ch. 1, 2:15; 1 Tim. 4:12–16, 6:20–21

1. What were Paul's exhortations to Timothy?
2. How can we 'stir up the gift' that is within us?

I never had a chance

FOR READING AND MEDITATION – ISAIAH 53:1–12
'Surely he has borne our griefs, and carried our sorrows …' (v. 4: RSV)

We continue examining the area of personal limitations – things that have happened to us which make us feel we are not as free as others, and that life has confined us to a dark, depressing dungeon.

Today we consider the problem of bad heredity. 'I can never rise very high in life,' said a woman to me a few years ago, 'because I had a bad start – my heredity is against me.' When I pressed her for details, she said, 'My parents were immoral. I was born out of wedlock and there is a streak of mental instability in my family.' Well, I admit that these considerations can weigh heavy on some people's hearts – nonetheless it is possible to find grace even in this dungeon.

Think for a moment of the genealogy of Jesus, for remember he was human as well as divine. His ancestors are listed twice in the New Testament (Matthew 1:1–17 and Luke 3:23–38). I realise there is a difference between the two lists, and I recognise also that the main purpose is their application to Joseph. However, no one can look at the family tree of Jesus without spotting the names of some pretty unsavoury characters. Rahab, the harlot, is there, and so are David and Bathsheba (Matthew 1:5–6) – we know what depths to which they descended in their desire for one another. Other names are included that give no ground for boasting. If your complaint is that you have been born into a family with a past, then I ask you to consider Jesus. The Scripture says of him: 'Surely he hath borne our griefs, and carried our sorrows.' All your difficulties are known to him. The grace that enabled him to walk through the world, overcoming every obstacle and difficulty, is flowing now to you. Never again say, 'I never had a chance.'

Gracious Father, I realise that life is made or broken at the place where I meet and deal with my obstacles. My heredity may be against me, but, by your grace, I can overcome it, and pass on to others the blessings of the new heredity I have in Christ. Amen.

FOR FURTHER STUDY – Gal. Ch. 4; Jn. 1:12; Rom. 8:15; 2 Cor. 6:18
1. What does 'adoption' mean? / 2. What is the significance of being able to cry 'Abba'?

Life begins at fifty-four!

FOR READING AND MEDITATION – HOSEA 14:1–9

'… he shall blossom as the lily, he shall strike root as the poplar.' (v. 5: RSV)

Some people feel greatly limited by their age. It was Shakespeare who said that there are seven ages to man, but I heard a preacher some time ago say that there were not seven ages but three: youth, middle age and 'you are looking very well'. You may have arrived at stage three of this group and wonder whether you are much use to the Kingdom. You may think that as your age advances, it limits your effectiveness in the work of God. Don't believe it! Don't fight the fact that you are getting old – use it!

I am fifty-four and I love it! I wouldn't be twenty-four for anything; fifty-four is too interesting and too full of adventure for me to want to return to my early twenties. I am simply tingling with interests; and in the midst of all that goes on around me, there is a calm and a poise that I did not have in my younger days. Life begins at fifty-four! An old Quaker said, 'After fifty I found a freedom and a calm and an interest in people, not merely as sex beings.'

You may think that advancing age is like the clang of a dungeon door, hemming you in and restricting your contribution to God and his world, but nothing is further from the truth. Grace flows in under the door to help you discover a new dimension of living. Some discover, with advancing age, that they are no longer pressed down by obsessive sexual thoughts, and thus they enjoy a freedom they never thought possible. So with the restrictions come also the liberties. It is possible to love others, really love them, without thoughts of sex muddying the waters. And never retire. Change your work, but never retire. The human personality is made for creation, and when it ceases to create, it creaks and cracks. So create, otherwise you will grow tired resting. Create! Create! Create!

O Father, I see that growth goes on forever. Let your Spirit so dwell in me that it may flatten out the wrinkles and counteract decay. May I die growing. In Jesus' name. Amen.

FOR FURTHER STUDY – Titus Ch.2; Eccl. 12:1; Isa. 46:4

1. How can you use your age to be spiritually productive? / 2. What was Paul's advice?

Limitation to liberty

FOR READING AND MEDITATION – 2 CORINTHIANS 5:1–10

'For we must all appear before the judgment seat of Christ, that each one may receive what is due to him for the things done while in the body…' (v. 10: NIV)

We come now to the end of the subject of finding grace in the dungeon of personal limitations. Have you some personal limitation that makes you feel inadequate and ineffective? Then while I am not unsympathetic to your predicament, I would not have you ignorant of the fact that there is a day, scheduled for the future, when you will stand before the heavenly judge and give an account to him of your service here on earth. Nor is there any doubt as to the identity of the Judge. John tells us that all judgment has been committed to the Son (John 5:22).

How are you preparing for the judgment? Are you polishing your excuses? Will you plead the problem of physical disability with people like Helen Keller standing at his side? Will you whisper, 'I was illegitimate,' with Dr. Alexander Whyte, the famous preacher from Edinburgh who was a nameless child, also standing there? Will you step up and say, 'I didn't have a good education,' when in the background you will catch sight of thousands who didn't have a college or university education, yet who made their mark for God on the world?

My friend, I beg you to see that all your personal limitations can become liberties if you will open up your life to the grace that flows into your situation. There is power with God to enable you to overcome every limitation. The man or woman who has everything is not the person to envy. Those who get everything they want also get something they don't want – hardness of heart or a flaw in their personality. The greatest university is the 'university of adversity' where the school colours are black and blue.

O Father, in that day when you gather together your precious jewels, grant that the shine I have gained in the polishing shop of adversity might rebound to your eternal praise and glory. For your own dear name's sake. Amen.

FOR FURTHER STUDY – Matt. 25:14–30, 12:36; Lk. 12:48; Rom. 14:12

1. What was Jesus teaching in this parable? / 2. Why had the servant buried his talent?

The dungeon of shattered hopes

FOR READING AND MEDITATION – LUKE 8:26–39

'... So he got into the boat and left.' (v. 37: NIV)

We continue examining the various dungeon experiences we face in life, and now we will look at the dungeon of shattered hopes and plans. This is probably one of the most difficult things to face – the frustration of the plans we have for our life. It throws confusion into everything, for so much is geared to those plans. However, again, grace will flow even into this dungeon.

Consider how Jesus reacted to the blocking of his plans in the incident that is before us today. After he had healed the man possessed with devils, the people came to see what had happened, and found the man 'sitting at the feet of Jesus, clothed, and in his right mind' (verse 35). The passage goes on to say: 'and they were afraid.' Afraid of what? Sanity? The people begged Jesus to depart from them and leave the area. His presence had cost them too much. Here was a man who thought more of men than he did of swine. Anyone with such an idea could be dangerous! Part of their fear arose from the fact that they couldn't understand Jesus. We are usually afraid of something we can't understand. However, I am convinced that their biggest fear was the fear that he might do something else to upset their values.

How did Jesus react to this blocking of his ministry? Utilising the grace that flowed toward him from God his Father, he turned in another direction. He was not blocked but redirected. Following this, he did some of the greatest miracles of his ministry, as we can see from the rest of the chapter and the next one, and so he turned the blocking into a blessing. If he couldn't do this, then he could do that. The frustration turned to fruitfulness. So when your plans are upset, do what Jesus did – utilise the grace of God, and turn in another direction.

O Father, help me not to be deterred by the blocking of my plans. Give me the resilience of spirit that sees a purpose in everything. When my plans are broken up, then, by your grace, I will make new and better ones. Thank you, Father. Amen.

FOR FURTHER STUDY – Lk. 24:1–35; Job 3:20; Rom. 15:4

1. Why were the disciples discouraged? / 2. How was their shattered dream restored?

Isolation becomes revelation

FOR READING AND MEDITATION – REVELATION 1:4–20
'... I was on the island of Patmos, exiled there for preaching the Word of God ...'
(v. 9: TLB)

Yesterday we saw how the ministry of Jesus was not deterred but deflected by opposition and frustration. The deflection became, for him, a spur. There is grace to be found in every dungeon – even that of one's shattered hopes and plans. Perhaps you find yourself, at this very moment, sitting in such a dungeon. You feel cramped and confined because so much of what you planned seems to have gone wrong. Lift up your heart; there is grace flowing from God right to where you are, and if you avail yourself of it, then you can turn the blocking into a blessing, the frustration into fruitfulness and the opposition into an opportunity.

When John found himself on the isle of Patmos, incarcerated for the sake of the Gospel, it must have seemed that his ministry and his plans had all been rudely shattered. He says: 'I ... found myself on the island called Patmos, for adhering to God's Word' (verse 9, Moffatt). However, he continues: 'On the Lord's day I found myself rapt in the Spirit, and I heard a loud voice ... calling, "Write your vision ..."' (verses 10–11, Moffatt). Isolated from men, and prevented from preaching the Gospel, he wrote his revelation. The place of isolation became the place of revelation. This is what can happen to you today, if you turn from an attitude of self-pity, receive the strength that God waits to pour into you and 'write out' the vision of coming victory.

Philip Brooks, better known perhaps on the other side of the Atlantic, wanted to become a schoolteacher but failed – and failed miserably. He turned to preaching, and became one of the world's greatest preachers. When powerless to change your circumstances, grace can help you change your attitudes. And sometimes that is the greatest miracle.

O Lord Jesus, impart to me the secret of making my circumstances the whetstone on which my life shall be sharpened for your purposes. For your name's sake. Amen.

FOR FURTHER STUDY – Gen. 12.1–4,15:1–6, 18:1–15, 21:1–8
1. How were Abraham's plans shattered? / 2. What was the end result?

Working with a wound

FOR READING AND MEDITATION – MATTHEW 14:1–14

'When Jesus heard it, he withdrew by boat to a desert place in private …' (v. 13: Moffatt)

We continue meditating on the thought that when our plans are shattered and broken, the grace of God, flowing into our lives, can enable us to build bigger and better ones.

Look at the picture before us today. Jesus had just heard that John the Baptist, his cousin and forerunner, had been beheaded, and the account says: 'When Jesus heard it, he withdrew by boat to a desert place in private.' No doubt he wanted to be alone to let the wound in his heart heal a little, 'but crowds heard of it and followed him on foot from the towns' (verse 13: Moffatt). They broke up his plans. Now what did Jesus do? Did he turn on the people and reprimand them for invading his privacy? No: 'So when he disembarked, he saw a large crowd and out of pity for them he healed their sick folk' (verse 14: Moffatt). He responded to the situation with tenderness and compassion.

If anyone thinks that I am not unmindful of the hurt and torn feelings one experiences when hopes are shattered or plans are thwarted, then let me pause to make this point clear. I am not saying that when things go wrong we won't feel shaken. We most certainly will. However, what I am saying is that by utilising the grace that flows towards us in those moments of shattered hopes and plans, we can turn the situation to good, and make it work for us – even though there may be wounds in our hearts. Just before she was to speak in a church I once pastored, a missionary friend of mine received a cable telling her that her father had died. She said nothing to us, but went on to give a talk that reached deep into every soul. She worked with a wound, but that wound became healing for others.

O Father, you know what it means to wince when wounded, for you have worn my flesh. Help me to remember that your wounds are healing my wounds, and my wounds will heal someone else's. Make my hurts healing. For Jesus' sake. Amen.

FOR FURTHER STUDY – Jn. 21:1–17; Matt. 26:75; Acts 2:14 –36

1. How did Peter use his failure? / 2. What did he almost allow it to do?

The show will continue

FOR READING AND MEDITATION – PHILIPPIANS 4:4–13
'I can do all things through Christ who strengthens me.' (v. 13: NKJ)

We are seeing that there is grace to be found in every dungeon, even the dungeon of shattered hopes and plans. When things don't go the way you had planned, it seems as if your life lies in pieces all around you. Well, God's grace and strength can enable you to pick up those pieces and reconstruct them into an even better pattern than they were before.

Someone has spoken of 'getting meaning out of life's remainders'. Sometimes life leaves us with nothing but 'remainders'. However, you can gather up those remainders and make meaning out of them. 'A Christian,' said Oral Roberts, an American evangelist, 'is a person who, when he gets to the end of his rope, ties a knot and hangs on. Another evangelist I know, now gone to be with the Lord, said that the passage in Revelation where it says that there was silence in heaven for the space of half an hour, was God moving the scenery for the next act. Can you see that the silent suffering space in your life when your shattered hopes and plans lie all around you, may be God getting you ready for the next great act? So hold steady – the show will continue. In the meantime, get meaning out of life's remainders.

I met a person the other day who told me that a year ago all his plans to emigrate and start a new life with his family evaporated at the last moment. 'I was shattered,' he said, 'and thought my life was at an end.' However, he held steady, and slowly, as he picked up the pieces, God gave to him in such a way that within three months he had shaped for himself a new career – one that exceeded his wildest dreams. As I have said before, an upset can sometimes set us up.

Gracious heavenly Father, because your grace is flowing into my dungeon of shattered plans and hopes, it teaches me that I may bend, but I will never be broken. Help me to be equal for anything – by your strength and power. For Jesus' sake. Amen.

FOR FURTHER STUDY – 1 Ki. Ch. 19; Jn. 16:33; Isa. 43:19
1. What was the shattered dream of Elijah? / 2. How did God deal with him?

His heart went out to them

FOR READING AND MEDITATION – MARK 6:30–44

'When he came ashore, he saw a great crowd; and his heart went out to them …' (v. 34: NEB)

We said yesterday that the silences we fall into when our plans are held up, or lie shattered in pieces around us, could be God's way of getting us ready for the next act. One of the most distressing experiences we can face in life is when our plans are interrupted for no apparent reason. We plan something well in advance, and then something upsets those plans – and us. We react by thinking our work is spoiled; but it may be that the interruption is our work.

One of the things that fascinate me about the life and ministry of our Lord Jesus Christ is the fact that whenever his plans were interrupted, he made the interruption an interpretation. Some of his finest statements, his greatest deeds, the most glorious revelations came out of those times when something, or someone, upset his plans. He looked upon the things that came, as God thrusting human need across his path, and he responded to these interruptions with dignity and grace.

Once when he was so pressed by human demands, and his disciples didn't even have enough leisure time to eat, he retreated with them to 'a lonely place. But many saw them leave and recognised them, and came round by land, hurrying from all the towns … and arrived there first … and his heart went out to them' (verses 32–34: NEB). I love those words: 'His heart went out to them.' Those who broke into his plans and interrupted his rest, he taught and healed. Those six words: 'His heart went out to them,' are probably worth more than all the volumes men have produced on the subject of patience and love. They are 'window words' that open out into the heart of our Saviour. That interruption was an interpretation of his inner attitudes.

Lord Jesus, teach me the art of recognising in all my upset plans and interruptions, a way to demonstrate your grace in a new facet. For your own dear name's sake. Amen.

FOR FURTHER STUDY – Lk. 7:1–17; Matt. 9:36, 20:29–34; Mk. 1:40–42
1. How did Christ respond when interrupted? / 2. What were the results?

The hidden better

FOR READING AND MEDITATION – JOHN 16:5–16

'...It is for your good that I am going away.' (v. 7: NIV)

We continue examining the subject of finding grace in the dungeon of shattered hopes and plans.

How it must have upset the plans of the disciples when they were told by Jesus that he was about to leave them. After three years it seemed that his ministry was just beginning to make its mark. Their hearts must have sunk within them with a strange sense of spiritual orphanage: they would be alone in the world without him. Those disciples had given up their jobs to travel with him. Peter had turned from his fishing nets, Matthew from his tax gathering, and so on. It must have seemed like an anti-climax, or worse, when Jesus announced that he was leaving them. It was the collapse of all their hopes and expectations. However, he said in effect, 'My going is for your good. I will take away my presence and give you my omnipresence. I will come back to you in the Spirit and be closer to you than I am now. Now I am with you, but then I will be in you.' And that actually happened. He did change his presence for his own omnipresence. In the presence of the Spirit he came back, not merely to be with them, but in them, burningly, blessedly near. They had but to drop into the recesses of their heart, and there he was.

Those disciples were to learn, as you and I must learn, that God never takes away the good unless he is going to replace it with something better. The disciples of Jesus must have said to each other after Pentecost, 'He has truly gone, but he is nearer than ever.' Meditate on this thought through the day, and I will not be surprised if, at the end of it, you come to recognise that your shattered plans are but the prelude to the advancement of his.

Gracious Father, when some earthly good is taken away, and it leaves me feeling bereft, help me to see the 'hidden better'. For Jesus' sake. Amen.

FOR FURTHER STUDY – Jn. 18:1–11, 7:33, 14:27–31

1. How did Peter react? / 2. What had he misunderstood?

Grace – 'tis a charming sound

FOR READING AND MEDITATION – PSALM 84:1–12
'Blessed are those whose strength is in you …' (v. 5: NIV)

Whenever in the past I have written on the subject of God's enabling in human predicaments, I have received letters from some who say something like this, 'Your emphasis on divine aid to cope with problems destroys a person's initiative, weakens their fibre and turns them into clinging, dependent people.' But does it?

God's grace does not weaken our personalities but strengthens them. In John 4:14 Jesus said: 'But the water that I shall give him shall be in him a well of water springing up into everlasting life.' Now note: 'the water that I shall give … shall be … a well … springing up.' The gift produces spontaneity and self-expression. Many gifts do not – they weaken rather than strengthen. Indeed, it is hard to give to some people because you know that by so doing you weaken rather than reinforce them. But the grace of God is a gift that strengthens and develops a person, and brings them to a place of independent dependency.

When we receive the gift of God's grace, it is not a gift that demands nothing on our part. It is, perhaps, the most expensive gift we can ever receive – expensive to us. For when we take it – fully take it – we have to give our all in exchange. Once we give ourselves to God, then comes mutuality. We are no longer nonentities – we are co-operating persons. 'At the very moment we bend lowest,' said a famous theologian, 'we stand straightest.' Those who depend most on the grace of God develop the strongest personalities. So when we receive God's grace, and allow it to pulse through our personalities, we become, not clinging, dependent types, but men and women who, as John Powell puts it, are 'fully human and fully alive'.

Blessed Lord Jesus, may this well of spontaneous life ever spring up within me, for I cannot be fully alive until I am alive in YOU. Thank you, dear Jesus. Amen.

FOR FURTHER STUDY – Acts Ch. 16; Matt. 19:26; Lk. 1:37
1. How did Paul respond to God's grace? / 2. What was the result?

The dungeon of loneliness

FOR READING AND MEDITATION – JOHN 14:16–27

'No, I will not abandon you or leave you as orphans in the storm – I will come to you.' (v. 18: TLB)

This week we turn to consider yet another dungeon into which many are thrust by life's jailors – the dungeon of loneliness. The good news of the Christian faith is that there is grace provided for this dungeon, too.

Preachers are at pains to point out that there is a difference between loneliness and aloneness. It is possible to be alone and yet not lonely. Loneliness has in it a mixture of deprivation, worthlessness and inner emptiness. Rupert Brooke, the poet, records how, when he was sailing for New York on the S. S. Cedrick on May 22nd 1913, he felt terribly lonely because no one had come to see him off. Everyone else had friends waving goodbye – but not he. He alone was alone. Looking down from the deck he saw a scruffy little boy, and swift as thought he ran down the gangway, and said to him, 'Will you wave to me if I give you sixpence?' 'Why, yes,' said the boy. The sixpence changed hands, and Rupert Brooke wrote in his diary, 'I got my sixpence worth and my farewell – dear, dear boy.'

Those who have never felt lonely find it hard to understand a story like that. But to others it carries a whole world of meaning. It is awful to be lonely. However, can grace reach us when we are imprisoned in a dungeon of loneliness? It can. It can! Grace can flood your inner being with such a consciousness of the divine presence that, even though you may still ache for a human companion, it will warm your heart, and wrap itself around you so that even though you are alone – you will never feel lonely.

O Father, I know with my intellect that when I have you I need never feel lonely. But drive this truth deep into my being so that it takes hold of my heart as well as my head. For Jesus' sake. Amen.

FOR FURTHER STUDY – Matt. 26:36–75; Psa. 102:7; Jn. 16:32

1. How was Christ's loneliness magnified? / 2. Which lonely person will you befriend today?

No one as lonely as he

FOR READING AND MEDITATION – MATTHEW 26:36–56
'Then all the disciples deserted him and fled.' (v. 56: NIV)

We said yesterday that there is a difference between loneliness and aloneness. It is possible, we said, to be alone yet not lonely. Loneliness is a feeling of bereft, companionless isolation. It is, as we said, quite terrifying to feel lonely. Nor is that feeling of loneliness diminished when one is in the heart of a crowd, or, for that matter, in a Christian church. Someone described some churches as 'places where lonely people go so that everyone might be lonely together'. One can be in a crowd and not of it.

Did Jesus ever feel lonely? Bearing in mind that he was sinless, and would not, therefore, have felt worthless, there were times, especially as he drew near to the Cross, when he would have felt bereft of human companionship. The disciples were not able to enter into his feeling as he agonised in his soul about his impending torture on Calvary. On the eve of his death, they argued about precedence; they slept while he wrestled in prayer in the Garden of Gethsemane, and when he was arrested, they ran away.

Most who have been willing to die for a cause could comfort themselves that there were those who sympathised with them, and understood the cause for which they were prepared to die. But even this was denied Jesus. His sacrifice mystified the people who were his closest companions. Not one single soul understood why he allowed himself to be taken to the Cross. This is why, whenever you feel lonely, you have the assurance that Jesus knows how you feel. He knew loneliness as no one knew it – before or since. And because he has felt as you feel, he is able to succour you with empathy and an understanding that no one else on earth can comprehend.

Lord Jesus, I see that no one ever touched the same depths of loneliness as you. Draw close to me in those moments when I feel lonely, and build my spiritual life so that I might use even this to my spiritual profit. Amen.

FOR FURTHER STUDY – Isa. Ch. 53, 50:6; Matt. 27:46; Psa. 37:25
1. Why did the Father forsake the Son?
2. How does this mean that we will never be forsaken?

A trifle to talk about

FOR READING AND MEDITATION – MATTHEW 28:16–20

'... and be sure of this – that I am with you always ...' (v. 20: TLB)

We continue focusing on the issue of finding grace in the dungeon of loneliness. To those of you suffering the pains of loneliness, it might sound trite and insensitive of me to say that the lonelier you feel, the closer Christ will come; but nevertheless it is true.

F. W. Robertson, the prophetic preacher of Brighton, proved this. He was bitterly attacked by fellow Christians for views which he held, and as his brief life sped away, his friends seemed to become fewer and fewer. It was in one of these dark periods, when it seemed that all his friends had left him, that he wrote, 'I am alone, lonelier than ever, sympathised with by none, because I sympathise too much with all, but the All sympathises with me ... I turn from everything to Christ. I get glimpses into his mind, and I am sure that I love him more and more. A sublime feeling of his presence comes about me at times, which makes inward solitariness a trifle to talk about.' Consider that last sentence once again: 'A sublime feeling of his presence comes about me ... which makes inward solitariness a trifle to talk about.' What a glorious testimony! He found grace in the dungeon.

With the assurance of Christ's presence vouchsafed to every Christian, there need not be utter loneliness in the hearts of God's children. Christ walked that way so that no man might walk it again. No old man, struggling to eke out an existence in one room, no old woman in a bed sitter, no widow, no single parent, indeed, no single person need feel the desolation of desertion. God will live intimately with his children in any circumstances, and give them such an inward glow that it will make 'inward solitariness a trifle to talk about'.

O Father, what a prospect! The lonelier I feel, the closer you come to me. Show me how to drop all my barriers so that your presence can come in and make this truth a reality in my life and experience. For Jesus' sake. Amen.

FOR FURTHER STUDY – Acts Chs. 23–24; Phil. 1:1; Eph. 3:1, 4:1; Col. 4:2–3

1. How did Paul view his solitary confinement? / 2. How did he use it?

Pause – and consider

FOR READING AND MEDITATION – ROMANS 12:1–21

'When God's children are in need, you be the one to help them out. And get into the habit of inviting guests home …' (v. 13: TLB)

The subject of finding grace in the dungeon of loneliness cannot be properly discussed without making the point that some people bring loneliness upon themselves – they are lonely through their own fault.

Although the purpose of these studies is to focus on issues in which we find ourselves through little or no fault of our own, I feel compelled to pause today to consider the fact that some forms of loneliness are self-generated. Those whose circumstances have compelled them to live alone must not permit themselves to become morose, critical, self-pitying and inward looking. These attitudes will only reinforce even the slightest feelings of loneliness, and will unconsciously drive others away from them. 'In a needy world like ours,' said Dr W.E. Sangster, 'anybody can have friendship who will give it.' And Emerson said, many years ago, 'The only way to have a friend is to be a friend.' And millions knew that before Emerson.

When one says, 'I am friendless,' it comes dangerously near to self-condemnation. It begs the rejoinder: 'Have you been a friend?' The Greek word charis, usually translated in the New Testament as 'grace', also means 'charm'. God's grace flowing into the dungeon can not only cheer the heart, but also add charm to unlovely sinners. Have you ever noticed how two people in love sometimes become radiant? They not only become loving to each other, their love spills over to others as well. So if your loneliness is self-induced, then let God's love flow into your life until it irradiates your human nature and heightens your attractiveness. Christ's presence in your heart will help you to be a friend, and being a friend means you will never have to concern yourself about having a friend.

Father, I needed this challenging word. If my loneliness is self-induced, help me to realise this and to change it. Fill me so full of your love that it will illuminate my life. For Jesus' sake. Amen.

FOR FURTHER STUDY – Lk. 7:31–35; Jn. 11:1–17; Prov. 18:24, 27:10, 17

1. How did Jesus look upon Lazarus? / 2. Who will you befriend today?

Alone – yet not alone

FOR READING AND MEDITATION – JOHN 16:17–33

'You will leave me all alone. Yet I am not alone, for my Father is with me.' (v. 32: NIV)

Those who find themselves confined to the dungeon of loneliness should reflect on the fact that one of the ways in which God's grace flows in to meet the situation is by bringing to our attention the Word of God. One of the ministries of the Holy Spirit is to draw our attention to certain passages of Scripture, for these, when meditated upon and absorbed into the personality, are often the solution to our problem.

How did Jesus cope with his loneliness? The passage before us shows how. He says: 'You will leave me all alone. Yet I am not alone, for my Father is with me.' Can you see what Jesus is doing here? He is telling himself that he is alone, yet not alone. The thoughts we entertain in our minds, as I have pointed out before, greatly affect the way we feel. If your minds hold the idea that God is with you, and that his presence is all around you and in you, then this message will gradually seep through to your emotions. God's grace (or strength) is often distilled through Scripture, and there is no dungeon that life, or Satan, has ever designed which can keep God's Word from getting through to your heart. Trust God to get his Word through to you, and when he does, meditate upon it, roll it around on your 'spiritual' tongue, so to speak, as you would a sweet, and suck every precious drop of refreshment from it.

Start with the text: 'For in him we live, and move, and have our being' (Acts 17:28); and say to yourself, 'In him I live and move and have my being.' Then when you lie down to sleep tonight, say to yourself again, 'Today I have lived and moved and had my being in God, and while I sleep I still live and have my being in him. He will guide and purify me even in my sleep and in the morning, when I awake, he will be here still.'

O God, you know the temptation that faces me, to be a hearer and not a doer of your Word. Help me to hold your Word in my heart until its message of peace and hope spreads into every one of my emotions. For Jesus' sake. Amen.

FOR FURTHER STUDY – Psa. 139:1–12, 18:35; Ex. 19:4; Deut. 33:27; Isa. 41:10

1. What was the psalmist's confidence? / 2. Write your own psalm.

So is God with us

FOR READING AND MEDITATION – HEBREWS 13:1–8

'"Never will I leave you; never will I forsake you."' (v. 5: NIV)

We said yesterday that when you are alone it is good to remember that you are not alone – Christ has promised to be with you and in you wherever you go. At the time of seemingly greatest loneliness, he is closest, watching over you and carefully scrutinising every move you make on the chessboard of life.

The American Indians used to train their children in gaining courage by making them spend a night in the forest with the wild animals. This was an ordeal that few children looked forward to experiencing, and they would enter the forest with great apprehensiveness and trepidation. Through the long hours of the night they would wait, longing for the moment when dawn would break, but when the dawn came, they would see their father behind a nearby tree with drawn bow. Without the child's knowledge, the father had been there all night, making sure that no harm would come to his son. So is God with us.

John Wilhelm Rowntree tells how, when he left his doctor's surgery, where he had been told that his advancing blindness could not be stayed, he leaned heavily on some railings for a few moments to collect his thoughts and steady himself. He wrote, 'Suddenly I felt the love of God wrap about me as though an invisible presence enfolded me, and a joy filled me such as I had never known before.' Our Lord will manifest his presence to us when we most need it. Thomas á Kempis says, 'Jesus will come unto thee and show thee his consolation, if thou prepare for him a worthy abode for him within thee. When Jesus is present all is good and nothing seems difficult, to know how to keep Jesus is great wisdom.' It is true. If you prepare to receive him, he will come.

O Father, wrap yourself around me as the atmosphere wraps itself around my body, and let me respond to you as my physical body responds to its environment and lives. I breathe it now – deep breaths of you – into every pore and fibre of my being. In Jesus' name. Amen.

FOR FURTHER STUDY – Jon. 1:17–2:10; Isa. 54:10, 43:2; Jn. 13:1

1. Why had God prepared a 'dungeon' for Jonah? / 2. What did God teach him?

I live in God

FOR READING AND MEDITATION – ACTS 17:22–34

'For in him we live, and move, and have our being.' (v. 28: NIV)

The main thrust of my thesis, as no doubt you are realising, is this – everything, loneliness included, can be used. God gives us grace in the dungeon. A psychologist, by the name of Clark Moustakas, suggests that we ought to see loneliness as something positive. He claims we ought to look for the good in loneliness, for it can bring deeper perception, greater sensitivity and increased insight.

According to Romans 8:28, God permits problems to arise for our own good; he will never allow anything to come into our lives unless it can be used. This doesn't mean that we look upon loneliness as something wonderful, because that would be pretending that it is something other than it is; it would be an escape into unreality. Loneliness can be painful, hurtful and sometimes almost unbearable. But if we recognise that God only allows what he can use, then instead of focusing on the problem, we will begin to focus on the advantages.

And what are the advantages? The hurt brings deeper sensitivity to the problems of others, greater awareness of God's tenderness and nearness, increased self-understanding and the realisation that you can find grace in the dungeon. God will draw close to those who are lonely, no matter what their circumstances. A visitor to an Old People's Home saw a man he knew, a Christian, and said, 'I'm sorry to see you living in this Old People's Home.' The old man drew himself up to his full height, and with measured tone and dignity befitting the occasion, said, 'My friend, I do not live in this Old People's Home; I live in God. – What about you, my lonely friend? Where do you live? In a single room – or in God?'

O Father, sweep into my soul with such a consciousness of your presence that I shall never again feel lonely. Help me to open my heart to the grace that is flowing right now into the dungeon. In Jesus' name I pray. Amen.

FOR FURTHER STUDY – Psa. 42:1–11, 71:5; Jer. 17:7

1. What was the psalmist's predicament? / 2. What was the psalmist's conclusion?

Unhappy home circumstances

FOR READING AND MEDITATION – 1 PETER 3:1–12

'... heirs together of the grace of life ...' (v. 7: NKJ)

We turn now to consider another dungeon in which some Christians find themselves confined – the dungeon of unhappy home circumstances. It may be that you have an unhappy marriage, or a bad relationship with your parents. Perhaps you are a parent whose teenage children are becoming rebellious, and causing you deep concern. You can find grace in the dungeon.

What is to be done? First go over the whole matter anew. See if some of the reasons for your unhappy home circumstances are not in you. Be objective and relentless with yourself. Remember, grace flows to help you live with a problem, but if you are the problem, then it's not grace you need, but courage to face up to it. If, in looking at yourself, you find things that need putting right, then confess this to God and to those whom you may have hurt. Leave it to others to confess their faults. Don't try and confess another person's sins. When you have done this, then you can sit back and relax, for you are in a position to receive the grace that God provides for such situations.

I know many Christians who are caught in the dungeon of unhappy home circumstances, and I observe them day by day doing what the oyster does when it gets an irritating grain of sand in its shell – it forms a pearl around the irritation. Whenever you are unable to get free of a situation, then God gives grace to enable you to throw 'the pearl of character' around the problem. The dungeon, then, becomes a trysting place where daily you and the Lord work out life together in spite of the irritation. No matter how difficult the problem, how unhappy the circumstances, how depressing the situation; you can find grace in the dungeon. Not just today, but every day!

O God my Father, I come to you with my dungeon life. I know, when I can't get out of a dungeon, that I am not blocked, for I can make my circumstances make me. Help me to avail myself of your grace to do just this. For Jesus' sake. Amen.

FOR FURTHER STUDY – Psa. 127:1–5; Gen. Ch. 4; Matt. 5:23–24

1. What was the problem of the first home? / 2. What was Jesus' solution?

Don't correct by disapproval

FOR READING AND MEDITATION – MATTHEW 7:1–5

'For you will be judged by the way you criticise others ...' (v. 2: J.B. Phillips)

Today we begin asking ourselves a pertinent question: how does God's grace enable us to live securely in the midst of unhappy home circumstances? Well, for one thing, it enables us to cope with the situation without resorting to nagging complaints. Remember the Pharisees in the New Testament? They thought the only way to change people was by showing disapproval. They tried it, and only ended in being disapproved of themselves. Once they journeyed all the way from Jerusalem to Galilee, and what did they see? The astonishing miracles of God's only begotten Son? The gates of life being thrown open to stricken souls? Oh, no! They saw only the fact that the disciples ate with unwashed hands. They overlooked the tremendous and saw only the trivial. They belittled themselves by what they saw.

Attempting to correct others by nagging complaints is a failure – and always will be. The offending people react by justifying their actions. They say, 'Look how unloving and misunderstanding my family are. I'm justified in finding love and understanding somewhere else.' The Pharisees tried to correct the world by disapproving of it, but it didn't work. The one who is hypercritical usually turns out to be hypocritical too.

There are two ways to get rid of a block of ice. One is to try to smash it with a hammer, in which case you only succeed in scattering it; the other way is to melt it, in which case you really do get rid of it. God's grace, flowing into an unhappy home situation, is there to enable you, not to smash the situation, but to melt it. The way of the Pharisees is not the Christian way; the Christian way is the way of grace. And grace, like love, never fails.

O Father, help me to see that the way of disapproval – the way of the Pharisees – is not a way that works, enable me to use your grace and power to take the Christian way in everything – the way of caring. For Jesus' sake. Amen.

FOR FURTHER STUDY – Ex. 15:20–16:3; Deut. 1:19–35; Jn. 6:43; 1 Cor. 10:10; Phil. 2:14

1. Why did the Children of Israel murmur? / 2. What fruit did these seeds bring?

The key to all doors

FOR READING AND MEDITATION – ROMANS 13:1–10

'Let no debt remain outstanding, except the continuing debt to love one another …' (v. 8: NIV)

We said yesterday that the way of the Pharisees – the way of disapproval – is not the way to change people. What then is the way? It is the way of Christ, the way of grace, the way of love. Love melts rather than smashes. It has power to open up the human heart in a way no other force could accomplish.

Perhaps you have gathered by now something of my fondness for the Moffatt translation of the Bible. It is not as accurate as some (he takes astonishing liberties with some passages), but, nevertheless, he sets some texts in a fascinating light. Take this, for example, from Revelation 5:5: 'He (Jesus) has won the power of opening …' The passage here talks about Christ winning the power to open up the seals of the scroll by his life, death and resurrection. Jesus won the power of opening, not just by those acts themselves, but because of the love that went into those acts. He was the Lord of love become flesh. Where other reformers of humanity failed, he succeeded. E.S. Jones said, 'Where knowledge knocks in vain, love enters in by lowly doors. Where other keys get jammed, love opens all the doors, for love fits the heart – every heart.'

Love, if it is the love of Christ, gets rid of deficiencies of most kinds, for a loving person succeeds where a purely efficient and correct person fails. The love is the success. A management engineer reported that he could increase the output of a plant by ten per cent, with no change of machinery, by straightening out the relationships between the men. Goodwill puts oil in the machinery; ill will puts sand in the machinery. Love is efficient and effective. Love never fails – it never fails, for even if it is not received, the person who loves is more loving for having loved.

Lord, help me to be as gracious and loving in my home as you were in your home in Nazareth. Today, by your grace, I shall try the key of love to unlock those hearts that are not open to me. In your name. Amen.

FOR FURTHER STUDY – 1 Jn. Ch. 4; Jn. 15:9–13; 1 Thess. 3:12

1. What is the basis of our love for each other? / 2. Write out your definition of family love.

Compliments change things

FOR READING AND MEDITATION – LEVITICUS 19:1–18

'Do not seek revenge or bear a grudge … but love …' (v. 18: NIV)

We continue examining the importance of being gracious and showing love in the midst of unhappy home circumstances. Another thing that grace enables us to do in the midst of difficult relationships in the home is to give sincere and genuine compliments to the other members of the family. If I have learned one thing in my years of counselling families who are in trouble, it is this – compliments, sincere compliments, have the power to transform human relationships. A famous psychologist said in my presence, 'I have never counselled anyone with serious emotional problems who can remember being complimented by his parents.' Can you see what he meant? Every emotionally ill-adjusted person he had counselled couldn't remember ever being complimented.

Compliments are to the personality what food is to the body. You must have heard of the Sunday school teacher who, upon asking a new Sunday school scholar for his full name, was told, 'I'm Johnny Don't.' 'Are you sure that's your full name?' queried the teacher. 'Well, that's what my mother and father call me when I'm at home,' was his reply. Poor Johnny must have responded to that with an attitude of inner resistance and rebellion. It reminds me of the boy who said, 'My father told me to sit down, but I was still standing up on the inside.'

Take this example, however. A little boy sat down at the table and began to eat before his parents had said grace. When gently reprimanded by them, he said, 'Well anyway, I didn't chew.' His wise mother and father complimented him for that much restraint! Then they appealed for full restraint. Bring into the home genuine compliments and appreciation, and the hearts of all in it will open up to their genial warmth.

O Father, help me to compliment people sincerely especially my family, and when I can't appreciate them for what they are, help me to appreciate them for what they can be. Amen.

FOR FURTHER STUDY – Rev. 2:1–7; 2 Tim. 4:8; Matt. 25:23; 1 Pet. 5:4

1. How did the Lord deal with the Church of Ephesus?
2. What was the response to the faithful servant?

Prompted by her mother

FOR READING AND MEDITATION – DEUTERONOMY 6. 1–12

'These commandments that I give you today are to be upon your hearts. Impress them on your children.' (vv. 6–7: NIV)

It is a well-known fact that children in a home catch the attitudes of their parents rather than their words. The child is much like the subconscious mind – he learns by what he sees people acting on, rather than by what they say. The account concerning the daughter of Herodias dancing before Herod, reads: 'Prompted by her mother, she said, "Give me …" ' (Matt. 14:8, NIV). What did the daughter want? She wanted what her mother wanted – the head of John the Baptist.

Some people wonder at the undisciplined youth of this generation. I don't. We have only to look back over the previous generation and we have the answer. This generation has been 'prompted' by the parents of today. Those who express surprise at the state of affairs amongst modern-day youth say, 'We told our children of the importance of morality and religion; why didn't they listen?' Well, perhaps it's because this generation of parents repeated the sanctions of morality and religion with less conviction and example. The generation before today's parents, having undergone a wave of evangelical awakening at the end of the last century and the beginning of this, had some deep convictions. The next generation lived on the afterglow of that, but with little personal experience.

A child learns not so much from what parents say, but from what they do; and if parents contradict, by their own actions and attitudes, what they say, the child structures himself on what they do. The influence of actions and attitudes is far more powerful than words. The prodigal son came back because he had a good father. The prodigal daughter (the daughter of Herodias) never came back because she had a bad mother.

O God, help your Church to bring into the home such a flame of pure living that the young might be supplied with a torch that will never go out. In Jesus' name I pray. Amen.

FOR FURTHER STUDY – 1 Sam. Ch. 2; Prov. 22:6; 2 Cor. 12:14; Eph. 6:4

1.Who did God hold responsible for sin in the temple? / 2. What is the Biblical principle?

Facing an affair

FOR READING AND MEDITATION – HEBREWS 12:1–15

'Be careful that none of you fails to respond to the grace of God, for if he does there can spring up in him a bitter spirit …' (v. 15: J.B. Phillips)

At this point in my writing I received a letter from a distressed woman who said, 'My home is breaking up due to my husband's affair with another woman. What can I do?' How do we maintain spiritual poise when a partner is involved in an affair? I feel compelled to share a précis of my answer to this dear woman with you.

Firstly, remind yourself that there is grace even in this dungeon. Throw yourself on God. Others have received grace to face this problem – and so can you. Secondly, ask yourself, 'Why did it happen?' Often (not always) an affair begins out of the desire for companionship and love that is not found in the home. If there is a deficiency here, recognise it and decide what can be done to correct it. Thirdly, face any anger you might feel and don't repress it. While the Bible exhorts us not to express anger, it is not wrong to acknowledge it. If you are angry, admit it to yourself, and ask God to help you deal with it. Fourthly, confess your deficiencies to your partner, not for the purpose of winning them back, but because it is right. Confess your own faults, and never confess your partner's – that is fatal. Let your partner confess his own if he wishes. Fifthly, don't alternate between tongue lashing and fawning over your partner. No one is corrected by nagging – no one. Some who find that nagging doesn't work then turn to an affectation of devotion and love. They overdo it, and it comes across as a device to win back the partner. It defeats itself. Sixthly, keep believing in your partner in spite of their actions. The very belief will create the thing you believe in. And lastly, lift up your partner in constant prayer. Affairs are often temporary; they grow fast and can wither fast. Prayer can help dissolve them.

O God, I am so thankful that you have an answer to every problem. For this, and every other problem, help me to affirm always: God is my answer. For Jesus' sake. Amen.

FOR FURTHER STUDY – Jn. 8:1–11; Psa. 78:38; Col. 2:13

1. How did the Pharisees respond to the woman? / 2. How did Jesus respond?

Holding all things together

FOR READING AND MEDITATION – MATTHEW 5:13–16
'"You are the salt of the earth."' (v. 13: NIV)

An observer, during the days of the Early Church, said, 'These Christians hold the world together.' Christians do, and they also hold the home together.

Isn't it interesting that a homeless, unmarried Man becomes the power that graces a couple in marriage and helps them hold their home together. His power was never more needed than in this present generation. For the home is being assailed from many directions. Did you know that Satanists in this country are praying and conducting rituals designed to break down the home? If the home survives, it will be because the Christians save it. Christians who know how to avail themselves of God's grace do not fall to pieces when trouble hits the home; they know how to hold situations together. A Christian knows how to forgive when wronged, knows how to apologise when necessary and knows how to conduct life on Biblical principles.

Jesus said, 'Have salt in yourselves, and be at peace with each other' (Mark 9:50, NIV). Note: 'Have salt in yourselves.' Don't be dependent on your environment – have springs from within, then the ups and downs of home life will not mean that you go up and down. You are fed and inspired from within. Your home may have in it a partner, a child, a mother, a father or an in-law whose actions may cause you great hurt, but don't let their actions determine yours. There is enough grace flowing into your heart and life to enable you to transform everything, and turn the dross into gold. You can hold your home together because you partake of a grace that holds you together. And when you are held together, then the things that are around you can be held together too.

O God, give me that inner fortitude that your grace provides that enables me to be held together. And when I am held together, then all things outside of me can be held together. I am so thankful. Amen.

FOR FURTHER STUDY – Jn. Ch. 13; Lk. 23:34; 1 Cor. 7:16; 1 Tim. 4:12; Titus 2:7
1. What example did Jesus show? / 2. How can we follow this example?

The terrible twins

FOR READING AND MEDITATION – 2 CORINTHIANS 4:1–15

'…we may be knocked down but we are never knocked out!' (v. 9: J.B. Phillips)

At some time most of us have met the 'terrible twins' as they have been called – sadness and grief. It is all part of existence – nobody escapes. Even Jesus wept at the grave of a loved one. 'My son,' said an ancient philosopher to one of his students, 'the world is dark with griefs and graves, so dark that men cry out against the heavens.'

If, at this moment, you are confined in a dungeon of grief and sorrow, then take heart – there is grace flowing out of heaven right to where you are. Since grief and sadness come to us all, how they affect us determines the results. Some seem to take grief and sorrow more or less in their stride. Others, unaware of God's grace that flows alongside every problem, or unable to grasp it, are badly affected by grief.

How are we to meet sorrow and grief? Well, before answering that, let me first define the terms. By sorrow and grief, I am referring to those troubled emotions which occur after loss – the loss of a loved one, a divorce, a financial collapse, redundancy, a broken engagement, a serious operation involving an amputation, and so on. We can best meet sorrow and grief by recognising that, in this world, we will all have to come face to face with loss; some, of course, have to face more serious loss than others. If some loss has occurred, and you say, 'Why should this have happened to me?' then that attitude will soon drag you down into self-pity. The idea that you are being singled out for bad treatment brings a martyr's complex, and this produces unhappiness. Trouble comes, but grace comes with it.

Gracious Father, I realise that loss comes to everyone at some time or other. Some it sweetens, others it sours. With your help I will use it to sweeten my spirit. For your own dear name's sake. Amen.

FOR FURTHER STUDY – Jn. Ch. 14; Rom. 8:11, 16; Gal. 4:6

1. What name does Christ give to the Holy Spirit? / 2. How does he carry out this ministry?

We are not exempt

FOR READING AND MEDITATION – 2 CORINTHIANS 1:3–11

'This means that if we experience trouble it is for our comfort and spiritual protection …' (v. 6: J.B. Phillips)

We are seeing the need to realise that because we are Christians this does not mean that we are going to be exempt from the ordinary ills that afflict humanity. If a Christian falls from a height, he is just as likely to break a leg as a non-Christian. Believers in Christ have financial losses, lose loved ones, and maybe have to undergo major surgery – just like unbelievers.

While it is true that a special providence operates in the lives of Christians, that providence will not intervene to cancel out a law, such as gravity, but will work to ensure that nothing happens to a believer that cannot be used for God's glory and the person's good. Richard Baxter wrote of the Great Plague, 'At first so few of the religious sort were taken away, they began to be puffed-up, and boast of the great differences which God did make. But quickly after that they fell alike.'

We must make up our minds that one of the main differences between a Christian and a non-Christian is in the way they take what comes. Paul, as we have seen a number of times while studying this theme, made everything further him. He says: 'If I am in distress, it is in the interests of your comfort' (2 Cor. 1:6, Moffatt). He made his distress and difficulties contribute to other people's comfort. He found grace in the dungeon. Again he says: I have to suffer imprisonment as if I were a criminal. (But there is no prison for the word of God)' (2 Tim. 2:9, Moffatt). Note the word 'but' here. That 'but' was the hinge on which the doors of Paul's heart swung open. The Christian always has a 'but' to pit against any circumstance. 'I am in prison,' said Paul in effect, 'but the Word of God is not in prison. It is loosed by my very bondage, furthered by my frustration.'

O Father, forgive me that there is so little difference between those who do not know you and me. Deepen your work in me so that others will see your grace shining out through me. For Jesus' sake. Amen.

FOR FURTHER STUDY – Phil. Ch. 1; Eph. 6:19–20; Col. 4:3, 18

1. What did Paul say was the result of his imprisonment?
2. What was his personal attitude?

Are problems God's punishments?

FOR READING AND MEDITATION – LUKE 13:1–9

'…do you think they were more guilty than all the others … I tell you, no!' (vv. 4–5: NIV)

Many feel that when distressing circumstances come upon them, such as the loss of a loved one, redundancy, or any other tragic happening, it is God's punishment on them for some sin. This attitude is wrong. It is quite true that in a moral universe sin does bring trouble. But Jesus repudiated the idea that calamity and sin are always connected. In his comment on the tower of Siloam and on those 'whose blood Pilate had mixed with their sacrifices' (verse 1, NIV), Jesus said the victims were not worse sinners than all the others.

If something has happened to you to produce in your heart feelings of deep sorrow and grief, without being insensitive to your predicament, I would ask you to try to catch hold of the fact that there is grace flowing into your dungeon, which, if you absorb it, can transform the experience, and make you into an even better person. One poet said:

Why do I creep along the heavenward way
By inches in the garish day.
Last night when darkening clouds did round me lower,
I strode whole leagues in one short hour!
The darkening clouds serve to quicken your pace toward home.

Rabindrath Tagore, the great Indian poet, said, 'The bursting of the petals say the flowers are coming.' When your heart bursts with pain and grief, remember that the bursting is only the breaking of the constricting sheath petals to let the flower out. On a mission station in Northern India, they found that when the tops of certain plants were withered by the frost, they gave a second crop. The frost helped them to discover something. Now, after the plants have given one crop, they cut them back so that they give a second.

O Father, thank you for showing me that when the frost of sorrow and grief descend on my heart, they can, through grace, produce a second crop. Blessed be your wonderful name. Amen.

FOR FURTHER STUDY – Jn. 9:1–34; 2 Tim. 1:7; Psa. 91:5; Isa. 12:2

1. Why had blindness come upon this man? / 2. Why have we no need to fear?

Not 'back' but 'through'

FOR READING AND MEDITATION – LUKE 4:16–30
'But he walked right through the crowd and went on his way.' (v. 30: NIV)

We saw yesterday that God's grace, flowing into the dungeon of sorrow and grief, enables us to accept the fact that troubles come to us all. They are part of the human condition.

Another thing, however, that God's grace does is to strengthen us so that we can face issues, and not try to escape from them through the door of illusion and subterfuge. Illusions and subterfuges turn out in the end to be worse than the actual sorrow and grief. A minister told me that he had a person in his church who was blind, but she kept on insisting she was not blind. 'I can see,' she kept saying, 'hold up something in your hand and I'll tell you what you are holding.' He held up his Bible, and she said, 'You are holding a glove.' 'No,' said the minister, 'It's a Bible.' 'You say it's a Bible,' said the woman, 'but I know it's a glove.' He gave up after that. The woman lived in a make-believe world.

The passage we have read today says: 'They got up … in order to throw him down the cliff. But he walked right through the crowd …' (verses 29–30: NIV). Note: 'He walked right through the crowd.' Jesus didn't back off, or dodge them, or try to escape. He went straight through. The Christian way is always 'through'. It never tries to escape into illusions and subterfuges. It faces issues and moves straight ahead – 'through'. One Christmas day, long ago now, as a minister in a church, I had the task of informing a woman that her son would not return home, as he had been killed in an accident. She retreated at once into illusion. 'No,' she said, 'he will be here.' She made the Christmas dinner, and pretended he was there with her. Even at the funeral she shut out all reality. She walked away from the problem rather than through it, and became a backward rather than a forward-looking person.

Lord Jesus, I am grateful that you have shown me that the Christian way is 'through'. I surrender all my impulses to escape. Give me the spirit of reality – the will to go through. Amen.

FOR FURTHER STUDY – Josh. Ch. 1; Num. 13:26–30; Isa. 43:2, 54:10, 41:17
1. What was God's promise to Joshua? / 2. How did Caleb respond to the problem?

Jesus – God with a face

FOR READING AND MEDITATION – TITUS 2:1–15

'For the grace of God that brings salvation has appeared to all men.' (v. 11: NIV)

How wonderful it is to realise that our problems are solved and our questions answered, not merely by the application of certain principles, but by contact with a Person. Many of those who work in the helping professions are prepared to take the principles of Christianity, but push to the edge the Person. In Jesus we have a Person who puts content into the principles. The principles work only when he is in them.

Suppose a little child, crying for his mother, is told, 'Don't cry little child. I'll talk to you about the principle of motherhood.' The little child would cry, 'I want my mother.' You can't talk to a principle; you can only talk to a person. When we speak of grace flowing into the dungeon in which we are confined, that grace is not something that God tips out of a vessel in the sky. He himself is the grace. Our text for today tells us so. 'Jesus,' as someone has said, 'put a face on grace.' Grace is no longer something vague, nebulous and indistinct; it has form, tangibility and reality. Grace is Jesus.

A little girl complained of feeling lonely in her room at night. 'But your teddy is here,' said her mother. 'I know that,' said the little girl, but I want something with skin on.' When beset by life's problems, we want more than principles, we want a person – 'something with skin on'. Grace is 'God with a face'. So when you cry out for grace to help you deal with the pressing problems of life, remember it is not just a principle you receive, not just a vague inner trembling in your consciousness: you receive Jesus. His coming was not limited to that first century: he is with you today. Grace.

Blessed Lord Jesus, I am so thankful that when I think of grace, I need only think of you, for you are the embodiment of grace, and you never fail to make your way to me, whatever my circumstances and whatever my need. I am so thankful. Amen.

FOR FURTHER STUDY – Phil. 2:1–11; Jn. 1:1–14; Gal, 4:4

1. What does salvation mean to you? / 2. Why not share this with someone today?

A promise that gives hope

FOR READING AND MEDITATION – PSALM 119:49–64

'Remember thy promise . . . for thou didst bid me hope . . . thy promise puts life into me.' (vv. 49–50: Moffatt)

The one note I have been sounding on every page of this theme is this – don't just bear your problems, transform them, let them contribute to building your character.

A woman wrote to me recently and said, 'I read what you said about Josephine Butler who lost the only child whom she adored, and yet came through to become one of the greatest social reformers of her century. I haven't lost a child, but I have lost my husband. Your words challenged me out of my self-pity, and now I have found some service for the Lord which I know I could never have done were it not for the fact that my wounds deepened my sensitivity, and fitted me for this new task.' So, you see, sorrow and grief can be transformed. Robert Spear demonstrated victory over sorrow and grief when his gifted son was murdered. This is what he said, 'During more than forty-three years of incessant struggle, journeying to and fro throughout the world, I have never lost the assurance of Christ's living Presence with me. He is no mere vision. He is no imaginary dream, but a living Presence who daily inspires me and gives me grace.'

Difficult though it may be for you to understand, if you are right now in the dungeon of sorrow and grief, there will come a time, not too far ahead, when you will see that God gives most when most is taken away. Someone said that we can see further through a tear than through a telescope. Thousands of God's people have caught a vision of God in the midst of Sorrow and grief that they never had in times that were trouble-free. Your sorrow and grief are the burnishing powder that God will use to polish your soul.

Father, the hope that all my sorrow and sadness will contribute to building my character really does put life in me. Everything is sheer gain. Blessed be your name forever! Amen.

FOR FURTHER STUDY – 2 Cor. Ch. 1; Matt. 5:4; Psa. 86:17

1. Why are we comforted? / 2. How did Paul view his affliction?

The dungeon of silence

FOR READING AND MEDITATION – GALATIANS 1:13–24

'I did not consult any man … but I went immediately into Arabia …' (vv. 16–17: NIV)

We turn now to consider over the few remaining days left to us one final aspect of our theme – finding grace in the dungeon of spiritual silence. What do I mean? Well, from time to time many of us enter a situation where it seems that the heavens are silent, and God no longer speaks to us. We are not conscious of any sin, but it seems that God is far away, and nothing we do brings him closer to us. We enter a period of silence and inactivity; and this is sometimes harder to bear than positive suffering. Are you in such a position right now? I have been there many times, and take it from me – there is grace available to meet this situation.

Someone has said that pauses in music are 'music in the making'. There is a momentary pause, or silence, that produces a suspense, making the music that follows more lovely than before. Is it possible that these pauses in our spiritual experience, these enforced silences, may become music in the making? I believe it is.

We often talk of the public life and ministry of Jesus, but little is said concerning what theologians call 'the silent years'. The call to give his message to the world must have burned like fire in the heart of our Lord during those years of his teens and into his twenties. Just picture it – making yokes for the farmers of Galilee when he yearned to strike the yoke of sin from the neck of humanity! Making ploughs to till the soil when he longed to plough deep furrows in men and women's hearts! But he did not chafe. He could wait – yes, for thirty long years. Thirty years of silence: three years of song. But what a song; it was richer for the silence that preceded it.

O Father, help me yet again to absorb the grace that flows into my dungeon of silence so that when I am released, my life will be all the richer. For Jesus' sake. Amen.

FOR FURTHER STUDY – Lam. Ch. 3; Psa. 77:9, 88:8–9

1. List some of the feelings of the writer. / 2. List his affirmations concerning the Lord.

FOR READING AND MEDITATION – HABAKKUK 2:1–4

'Though it linger, wait for it; it will certainly come and will not delay.' (v. 3: NIV)

We said yesterday that a pause in music is 'music in the making'. Pauses produce suspense, which makes the music lovelier than it was before.

Let me share with you something that was said to me in a letter I received the other day: 'I thought that God had lost interest in me because he seemed not to hear my prayers, and answer me in the way that he usually did. But then what you wrote gave me the clue. You said, "Remember a dark tunnel is the best way of getting around a hill." I saw at once that the darkness was but the prelude to the light, and when the light shone, it was with a radiance I never thought possible. Just as darkness is the prelude to the dawn, so is silence the prelude to a divine symphony. God has music to play in your life that will not be as effective unless it is preceded by a silence in your soul.'

A missionary casualty I met in East Africa many years ago (a missionary casualty is someone who has to return from the mission field due to an inability to adjust), said to me, 'I decided to take a shortcut to learning the language by closing my books and going out among the people. I got to learn the language that way, but I found that when I got into the pulpit, I no longer had the ear of the people. They seemed to sense that my knowledge of the language was inferior to the other missionaries. Gradually it got to me and broke me down.' Chafing under the drudgery of months of digging at the language roots, and bypassing it, meant that he was greatly hampered in his missionary work. He sang broken music and lived to regret it.

O Lord, I see that if I refuse the necessary pauses of life, then when I sing, it is broken music. When I refuse the pause, there is no music in the making. Help me to lay hold of your grace so that even though I may chafe, I will not run away. Amen.

FOR FURTHER STUDY – Ex. Chs. 1–2; Ezek. 12:25; Matt. 5:18; Phil. 1:6

1. Why was there a pause in Moses' life? / 2. What was God teaching him?

It happened to me

FOR READING AND MEDITATION – HEBREWS 13:5–21

'… For God has said, "I will never, never fail you nor forsake you." ' (v. 5: TLB)

We continue looking at why God sometimes produces pauses or silences in our lives, and we are seeing that these suspensions from activity become 'music in the making'. The pause prepares us for further and finer music.

A couple of years ago I went through such a spiritual pause myself. It seemed for a while as if the heavens were brass, and I wondered whether or not God had lost his voice. Why wouldn't he speak to me? Why wasn't I hearing from heaven as I usually did? Then I remembered that, despite my feelings of isolation and abandonment, the promise that he would never leave me nor forsake me was unimpeachable. He was in my soul, whether my feelings registered it or not. Grace flowed into my dungeon, and I soaked it up.

During this period the time came around for me to sit down and write but day after day, as I put my paper into the typewriter and waited – nothing came. Some days I would sit before the typewriter for hours without typing a single word. It got to such a stage that I wondered whether God was drying up my ministry, and that he might want me to turn to other things. The silence in my soul would have been intolerable had I not realised that the pause was for a purpose. I waited, and then one day I heard his voice again. He said to me, as he said to John in Revelation, 'What thou seest … write.' I began to write, and what I wrote affected more people than many of my other writings put together. Now, whenever I sense a divine pause, I tremble with excitement, for I know that it is but 'music in the making'.

Father, help me to hold steady when my life goes into a spiritual pause, and help me to be patient under the restriction so that I may be richer when released. For Jesus' sake. Amen.

FOR FURTHER STUDY – Matt. 26:57–28:20; Jn. 2:18–22

1. How did the disciples respond to God's silence?
2. What happened when the silence was broken?

For the Body of Christ

FOR READING AND MEDITATION – 1 CORINTHIANS 14:26–33
'Let two or three prophets speak, and let the other judge.' (v. 29: NKJ)

Today I want to share with you what I believe is a word of prophecy God gave me as I began this page. As all prophecy has to be judged on its quality and tone, I offer it to you, the Body of Christ, in that spirit. This is the word the Lord gave me for you today:

'I know how your heart fears and trembles at silences, but do not be afraid, my child, for I am at its centre, as well as at its circumference. You feel as if you have been pushed aside, and that I no longer have any purpose for you. But that is not the case. You are precious to me, more precious than any of the world's resources; yes, more precious than the gold or silver that is buried in the mountains and in the hills. Do not let the silence of the moment persuade you that I am no longer interested in you, for you are mine and I am yours. Nothing shall ever break the bond that is between us, for I have washed you in my blood, and with my own hand have written your name in the Book of Life. In the hour of silence you shall know a serenity that you can never know in any other situation.

'The age that rushes by you is like a clap of thunder, and in it you will never find peace. I am not in the thunder of the world's busyness, but I am in the silence. And you shall find me there. I have watched your frantic efforts to achieve, your earnest desires to move ahead, but I have halted them for the moment that I might speak to you. Your time is mine and my time is yours. Let us share it together. The things you expected to happen have not happened because I have hindered them – purposely. Together, in the silence, we shall share, and you shall come forth, in the days that lie ahead, with renewed strength and vitality, and then my purpose for you shall be achieved.'

Thank you, dear Lord – thank you. Amen.

FOR FURTHER STUDY – 1 Ki. 19:9–21; Job 34:29; Eccl. 3:7
1. How did God speak to Elijah? / 2. What was the result?

Shut up to write immortally

FOR READING AND MEDITATION – PHILIPPIANS 3:1–14

'That I may know him ... and the fellowship of his sufferings ... ' (v. 10: NKJ)

We come now to the last day of a two-month study in which we have been seeing how faithfully God ministers to us whenever we are thrust by life's jailors into a dungeon from which, naturally speaking, we would do our best to escape. We have seen, however, that when confined in a situation from which we are unable to extricate ourselves, grace is provided to turn the situation to advantage.

Paul must have inwardly chafed at first when his liberty was taken away, and he was confined to various dungeons – confined for no other crime than announcing the Good News. The curtailment of his liberty must have been hard, but it was harder to be shut off from pronouncing and preaching the message of eternal salvation. What could compensate for that? As we look back, however, we see that grace flowed into every dungeon in which Paul was thrown. God allowed the good to be taken away (the preaching of the Gospel) so that the better might come (the writing of the epistles).

Paul's letters have enriched the world from the moment they were first sent out, and will do so for as long as the Church remains on earth; but it is my belief that they could never have been written with such effect were they not written in a dungeon. Paul dipped his pen into the blood of his suffering and wrote words that are deathless – words inspired by the Holy Spirit and mixed with grace. Through long days and nights of pondering on Jesus, and having, as he said, 'the fellowship of his sufferings', his thoughts crystallised into immortal phrases through which men have looked into the heart of a redeeming God. The good of preaching having been taken away became the better of written revelation.

O Father, thank you for showing me these past two months that all my restrictions can become revelations; all my denials, deliverances; and all my crosses, Easter mornings. I have found grace in the dungeon. Thank you, dear Father. Amen.

FOR FURTHER STUDY – Jer. 38:1–13

1. How did Jeremiah get out of the dungeon? / 2. What 'cords' has God lowered to us?

Out of weakness – strength!

FOR READING AND MEDITATION – HEBREWS 11:30–40

'…out of weakness were made strong…' (v. 34: NKJ)

For almost a year, I felt the urge to write on the theme, 'Strong at the broken places'. I had heard or read the phrase somewhere, but I had great difficulty in tracing its origin. Then a little while ago someone wrote to me, quoting the full phrase from the writings of Ernest Hemingway, who said, 'Life breaks us all… but many are made strong at the broken places.' I felt this to be a gentle nudge from the Holy Spirit, and began at once to put my thoughts together on this thrilling theme.

It is a principle of life that the place in which a bone breaks and then heals will be so strong that, generally speaking, it will never break there again. In the same way, when the skin is cut and scar tissue forms, the healed part becomes tougher than the surrounding skin. If this happens in the natural, why not in the spiritual? The writer to the Hebrews tells us, in the passage before us today, that God is expert at taking the weaknesses of his children and turning them into strength. What an encouraging truth! A traveller in the Netherlands tells how his guide pointed out an historic site. 'This is where the sea broke through,' he said, 'causing thousands to drown. But see – it is now so strongly reinforced that it will never break through there again.'

Have you been broken by life to such an extent that you feel an overwhelming sense of weakness? Are there areas of your personality, your marriage or your relationships in which you feel woefully weak and inadequate? Then take heart – God specialises in matching his ability to your disability. By his transforming grace, your frustration can become fruitful. You can be strong at the broken places.

O Father, this sounds fine as theory, but can it really become a fact? Your Word says it can. I am ready and eager to learn. Teach me, my Father. In Jesus' name. Amen.

FOR FURTHER STUDY – Psa. 34:1–22; Psa. 147:3; 1 Cor. 11:24

1. What is promised to the broken-hearted? / 2. Why was Jesus broken?

The 'inner-stances'

FOR READING AND MEDITATION – 2 CORINTHIANS 4:1–15

'We are hard-pressed on all sides ... we may be knocked down but we are never knocked out!' (vv. 8–9: J. B. Phillips)

We said yesterday, 'Life breaks us all ... but many become strong at the broken places'. Today we ask ourselves: why is it that while the same things can happen to us all, they may not have the same effect upon us all? The same thing happening to two different people may have entirely different effects. Why should this be so? It depends not so much on the circumstances, but on the 'inner-stances' – or, in other words, our inner attitudes. As someone has said, 'What life does to us in the long run depends on what life finds in us.' Life's blows can make some people querulous and bitter, others they sweeten and refine – the same events, but with opposite effects.

The Gospels tell us that there were three crosses set up on Calvary on the first Good Friday. The same event happened to three different people, but look at the different results. One thief complained and blamed Jesus for not saving himself and them; the other thief recognised his own unworthiness, repented of it and found an open door to Paradise. Jesus, of course, saw it as the climax of his earthly achievements and made it the fulcrum on which he moved the world.

What counts, therefore, is not so much what happens to us, but what we do with it. The same sunshine falling on two different plants can cause one to wither up and die, while the other will blossom and flourish. And why? It all depends on the response the plants make. Although, of course, they both need water, one plant is more suited to hot sunshine than the other, and therefore responds with more life and growth, while the other shrivels up and dies.

Gracious heavenly Father, write this precept upon my heart so that I shall never forget it: it's not so much what happens to me, but what I do with it that is important. Thank you, Father. Amen.

FOR FURTHER STUDY – 2 Cor. 11:21–29; 2 Tim. 4:7; Psa. 37:28; Prov. 2:8

1. What was Paul's testimony? / 2. How did he sum up his life?

Are Christians exempt?

FOR READING AND MEDITATION – MATTHEW 5:38–48

'He causes his sun to rise on the evil and the good, and sends rain on the righteous and the unrighteous.' (v. 45: NIV)

We are meditating on the theme, 'Strong at the broken places', and we are discovering that although life deals blows to us all, those who meet life with the right responses and the right inner attitudes are those who turn their weaknesses into strengths.

I know some Christians who believe that they ought to be exempt from the cruel blows of life. I heard of a young man who was stunned after failing his examination and said, 'I cannot understand. I prayed very hard before the examination, and I lived an exemplary life for the Lord. Why, oh why, should he fail me at this important moment?' Later he confessed to a friend, 'As a result of God letting me down, my faith in him has been shattered.'

I can sympathise with the young man's feelings, of course, but I cannot agree with his conclusions. Suppose prayer alone could enable us to pass examinations – what would happen to the human race? Prior to examination time, classrooms would be deserted, and everyone would flock to the churches for prayer and meditation. Not a bad situation, you might think. But what would happen to the minds of young people if prayer alone brought success? They would become blunted by lack of study. I suspect the young man I have just referred to was depending more on prayer than on diligent and painstaking study. Now prayer and study make a good combination, but prayer without study never helped anyone pass an examination. Christians are not exempt from the natural laws that govern the universe. We may through prayer be able to overcome them, but we are not able to avoid them.

Father, thank you for reminding me that even though I am a Christian, I am still governed by natural laws that apply equally to everyone. I cannot be exempt, but through you I can overcome. I am so grateful. Amen.

FOR FURTHER STUDY – Jas. 2:14–26; 1 Tim. 4:9–16; 2 Tim. 2:15

1. What is James teaching us? / 2. How does Paul apply this to Timothy?

How do you respond?

FOR READING AND MEDITATION – HEBREWS 12:4–15

'Be careful that none of you fails to respond to the grace of God, for if he does there can spring up in him a bitter spirit…' (v. 15: J.B. Phillips)

Today we must examine an issue that may be extremely challenging to us as Christians, but we must face it nevertheless. The matter can best be presented in the form of a question: why is it that many non-Christians, though broken by life, succeed in becoming 'strong at the broken places', while many Christians go through similar experiences and come out crippled and bitter?

A few years ago I watched a television programme in the United States in which a famous Jew, Victor Frankel, talked about his experiences in a concentration camp in Nazi Germany. When he was brought before the Gestapo, they stripped him naked and then, noticing that he was still wearing his gold wedding ring, one of the soldiers said, 'Give it to me.' As he removed his ring, this thought went through his mind, 'They can take my ring, but there is one thing nobody can take from me – my freedom to choose how I will respond to what happens to me.' On the strength of that, he not only survived the Holocaust, but also developed his whole psychiatric system called Logotherapy, which states that 'when you find meaning in everything, then you can face anything'.

Frankel, a non-Christian, survived the horrors of the Holocaust because he was sustained by an inner conviction that he would come through it, and be able to use the suffering to good effect. His system of Logotherapy is now being used to help thousands who have mental and emotional problems. If a non-Christian, bereft of redemptive grace, can respond to life in this way, then how much more those of us who claim to be is children?

O Father, whenever you corner me like this, you know my tendency to wriggle and try to get off the hook. Help me to face this issue and take my medicine, however bitter it tastes. For Jesus' sake. Amen.

FOR FURTHER STUDY – Heb. Ch. 4; 2 Cor. 12:9–10; Lam. 3:22–23

1. Why can we come boldly to God? / 2. What was Paul's inner attitude to his problem?

Two men – different reactions

FOR READING AND MEDITATION – 2 CORINTHIANS 12:1–10

'... "My grace is sufficient for you, for my power is made perfect in weakness."' (v. 9: NIV)

We must spend another day examining this very important issue of why it is that some non-Christians seem to respond better to life's problems than many Christians.

Just recently I heard of two different people whose business ventures collapsed. One was a Christian and the other an agnostic. The agnostic responded to the situation by saying, 'I cannot determine what happens to me, but I can determine what it will do to me. It will make me better and more useful.' He struck out in another direction, and his new venture prospered to such a degree that he won an award. The Christian responded to the collapse of his business by saying, 'Life is unjust. What's the point of trying? I shall withdraw from the cut-throat world of business and concentrate on my garden.' He had to undergo some in-depth counselling before he was on his feet again, and after six months he felt strong enough to rebuild a new and now prosperous business.

What can explain the different reactions of these two men? We could explain it in terms of temperament, upbringing, and so on, but there is one thing that must not be overlooked – the Christian had access to the grace of God which, if utilised, should have enabled him to view the situation even more positively than the non-Christian. As a counsellor, I understand why people respond wrongly to life's situations. However, my understanding of it does not prevent me from recognising that the true Biblical response to life's problems is to take full advantage of the grace of God and turn every setback into a springboard.

Gracious Father, help me to respond to everything in the way a Christian should. Help me to see that not only do you lift the standard high, but you also supply the strength for me to attain it. For Jesus' sake. Amen.

FOR FURTHER STUDY – Jas. 1:1–15; Eph. 3:16; Isa. 41:10

1. What does James teach us about trials? / 2. What was Paul's prayer for the Ephesians?

Doing what is right

FOR READING AND MEDITATION – PHILIPPIANS 2:5–16

'…continue to work out your salvation…for it is God who works in you to will and to act according to his good purpose.' (vv. 12–13: NIV)

We ended yesterday by saying that the Biblical response to all of life's problems is to take advantage of the unfailing grace of God, and turn our setbacks into springboards. I know that some will respond to that statement by saying, 'It sounds good in theory, but it's hard to put it into practice. What about the hurts and wounds that some people carry inside them, that make it difficult or sometimes impossible for them to make use of God's grace to turn their problems into possibilities?'

No one who has been a reader of *Every Day with Jesus* could accuse me of failing to understand or be sympathetic to the hurts and wounds that people have, which sometimes militate against their desire to respond to life in a Biblical way. I know from firsthand experience the arguments that people can put forward to avoid doing what God asks in his Word. However, I must take my stand, and so must you, on the authority of Scripture, and affirm that God never asks us to do what we are incapable of doing.

Much of evangelical Christianity, I am afraid, is man-centred. We need a return to a God-centred position which does exactly what God asks, whether we feel like it or not. I freely confess that there are times when I don't feel like obeying God. I know, however, what is right – that God has redeemed me and that I belong to him – and I do what he wants me to, whether I feel like it or not. What controls you in your Christian life – your feelings, or what you know God asks and expects you to do? Your answer will reveal just who is in the driving seat!

Gracious and loving heavenly Father, teach me the art of responding to life, not with my feelings but with a clear mind and a clear resolve. Help me to do what is right – whether I feel like it or not. For Jesus' sake. Amen.

FOR FURTHER STUDY – Jn. 14:15–31; Lk. 12:11–12; 1 Cor. 2:13

1. How do we express our love for Christ? / 2. How are we enabled to do this?

Get hold of this!

FOR READING AND MEDITATION – ROMANS 8:28–39

'And we know that in all things God works for the good of those who love him, who have been called according to his purpose.' (v. 28: NIV)

We have been meditating this past week on the thought that although 'life breaks us all … many are made strong at the broken places.' Before going on to examine some of the major ways in which life breaks us, we pause to review what we have been saying over these past few days. We said that while the same things may happen to us all, they do not have the same effect upon us all. Life's blows make some people querulous and bitter; others, they sweeten and refine.

We also saw that the reason why some respond to life positively and turn their problems into possibilities is because of right inner attitudes. There are many non-Christians who put us to shame when it comes to the question of rightly responding to life, and it is high time, therefore, that we Christians got our philosophy of living sorted out once and for all.

If, as the Scripture teaches, God will let nothing happen to one of his children without supplying the necessary grace to turn the stumbling block into a stepping-stone, then we ought to be ahead of the world in demonstrating how to meet whatever life sends us with confidence and faith. Be quite clear about this: no one can fully represent the Christian way of living until they commit themselves to believing that, though God may allow what appears to be a disaster in the life of one of his children, he does so only if he can turn it to good effect. If transformation is not possible, then God would never have allowed it to happen in the first place. So let this truth sink deep into your spirit – God only allows what he can use.

Father, I come to you now to ask that this truth be so impressed upon me during the weeks ahead that never again will I have to be reminded of it. For your own dear name's sake. Amen

FOR FURTHER STUDY – 1 Pet. Ch. 4; Psa. 30:5, 40:1–3; Isa. 43:2

1. What is God's promise during trials?
2. How does Peter encourage us to respond to them?

Never soar as high again?

FOR READING AND MEDITATION – 1 PETER 1:3–9

'These have come so that your faith...may be proved genuine and may result in praise, glory and honour when Jesus Christ is revealed.' (v. 7: NIV)

We turn now to examine some of the ways in which our lives become fractured, and what we can do to become 'strong at the broken places'.

We begin by looking at the brokenness that comes about through failure. It is quite likely that someone reading my words at this moment is caught up in a vortex of pessimism and gloom due to a recent or long-standing failure. You may be feeling like the man who said to me recently, 'I am stunned by my failure. My stomach, my insides ... twist and turn. I am so upset that I cannot sleep. My life is shattered into smithereens. I read somewhere that "the bird with the broken wing will never soar as high again". Does this mean I can never rise to the heights in God that once I knew?'

I reminded him of Simon Peter – a man with one of the worst track records in the New Testament. He was prejudiced, bigoted, stubborn and spiritually insensitive. Again and again he got his wires crossed, such as the time when he attempted to divert Christ from going to his death in Jerusalem (Matt. 16:22), or his insistence that they should stay on the Mount of Transfiguration (Matt. 17:4). Then what about that time, on the eve of Christ's crucifixion, when he denied and even cursed his Lord? I can imagine Satan whispering in his ear, 'Now you're finished. Burned out. A failure. You'll be forgotten ... replaced.' But by God's grace, Peter rose from failure to success. He became 'strong at the broken places'. Because he refused to live in the shadow of his bad track record, his two letters are enshrined forever in the Scriptures. Failures, you see, are only temporary tests to prepare us for more permanent triumphs.

O Father, I see so clearly that no failure is a failure if it succeeds in driving me to your side. All things serve me – when I serve you. Amen.

FOR FURTHER STUDY – Ex. Chs. 2, 3

1. How did Moses fail God? / 2. How did God deal with him?

Incisive questions

FOR READING AND MEDITATION – ECCLESIASTES 7:21–29
'So I turned my mind to understand, to investigate and to search out wisdom …' (v. 25: NIV)

Today we ask ourselves: what are the steps we must take, when broken by failure, to ensure that we become strong at the place of weakness? Keep in mind, too, that the principles we are considering in these readings are not only corrective, but also preventative.

The first thing we should do, whenever we have failed in anything, is to analyse the reason for the failure. These are some of the questions you should ask yourself: have I contributed in any way to this failure by such things as inattention to detail, lack of preparation, naivety, wrong timing, failure to weigh up the pros and cons, disregard of moral principles, or insensitivity to other people's feelings? Another question you should ask yourself is this: what does God want me to learn from this failure? It is difficult, of course, to sit down and question yourself like this when failure strikes but as soon as possible after the event, try to assess the lessons that can be learned by honestly facing your emotions – such as hurt, anger, anxiety and so on. Remember, when we stop learning we stop living.

Yet another question to ask yourself is this: has God allowed this failure so that his purposes for me might be made clear? I know a man, well known in evangelical circles, who, when he was in his teens, mapped out a career for himself. Although a brilliant student, he failed the entrance examination into his chosen profession. When the news was broken to him, he simply said, 'Lord, I just know you are involved in this: what do you want me to do?' This was the moment God had been waiting for, and he showed him a new path that has made him Christ's ambassador to millions.

Father, help me to face my failure in the knowledge that some good can be wrested from even the most depressing circumstances. Show me that incisive questions can bring incisive answers. In Jesus' name. Amen.

FOR FURTHER STUDY – Jas. Ch. 3, 1:5; Prov. 2:1–5, 3:13–14
1. What are the characteristics of earthly wisdom? / 2. How are we to obtain wisdom?

Looking failure in the face

FOR READING AND MEDITATION – JOHN 13:12–32

'…"Now is the Son of Man glorified and God is glorified in him."' (v. 31: NIV)

We continue meditating on the steps we must take in order to become strong at the broken places of failure. The second thing we should do when failure strikes is to face it in the knowledge that with God, something can be made out of it.

The account before us today tells of Christ's betrayal by Judas. Notice how Jesus first accepted the situation before he went on to make something out of it. The Master said: 'What you are about to do, do quickly' (verse 27). He made no attempt to ignore the situation, sweep it under the carpet, or pretend it was not there – instead he calmly and deliberately faced reality. Before we go any further, make up your mind to face up to all of life's problems, because if you try to ignore them, you will become inwardly demeaned and deprived. The account continues: 'As soon as Judas had taken the bread, he went out. And it was night. When he was gone, Jesus said, "Now is the Son of Man glorified and God is glorified in him"' (verses 30–31).

Not only did Jesus accept the situation, but he moved on to turn it into victory. Look again at what he says: 'Now is the Son of Man glorified …' No self-pity, no egotistical concern – he took charge of the situation and made the betrayal contribute to his victory. Was Jesus hurt by Judas' betrayal? I should think so. But instead of spending the night wallowing in self-pity, he looked at the situation from God's point of view and quietly affirmed: 'Now is the Son of Man glorified.' It may take you a little while to be able to respond to difficult situations in the way Jesus did, but remember this – the resources on which the Master drew are yours for the asking.

Father, I see that my life will be made or broken at the place where I acknowledge and deal with my failures. Help me not to run away from them, because in you I am more than a match for anything. Thank you, Father. Amen.

FOR FURTHER STUDY – Matt. 26:58–75; Lk. 24:12; Jn. 21:15–19; Acts 2:14

1. What was the progression of Peter's failure? / 2. How did he face his failure?

A Biblical mentality

FOR READING AND MEDITATION – 1 THESSALONIANS 2:1–12

'You know, brothers, that our visit to you was not a failure.' (v. 1: NIV)

Today we examine yet another principle which we must develop in our lives if we are to become strong at the broken places of failure: cultivate a Biblical perspective on everything. In the passage before us today, I want to emphasise several points that will help us to see how effectively Paul believed and practised spiritual principles.

Firstly, his words and preaching, despite strong public opposition, were not the result of his own thinking – they were the result of the Gospel of God (verse 2). Secondly, the very foundation of his life and character were not based on error or deceit, but rather on the truth of the Gospel (verse 3). Thirdly, he considered God's Word as something 'entrusted' to him, and it gave him such security that he didn't feel the need to compromise or become a 'people pleaser' (verse 4).

It may sound old-fashioned and naive to some, but I believe with all my heart that the secret of surviving life's crushing defeats and blows is to develop a spiritual and Biblical perspective on everything. 'It is blessed,' wrote C.H. Spurgeon, 'to eat into the very soul of the Bible until, at last, you come to talk in Scriptural language, and your spirit is flavoured with the words of the Lord, so that your blood is Bibline and the very essence of the Bible flows from you.' Descriptive, isn't it? I find this is idea of being committed to a Biblical mentality so rare among modem-day Christians that I sometimes tremble inwardly with concern. Someone said, 'Time spent with the Bible knits up the ravelled sleeve of care.' It does.

O Father, help me, also, 'to eat into the very soul of the Bible…until my spirit is flavoured with the words of the Lord.' Give me a biblical mentality. For Jesus' sake I pray. Amen.

FOR FURTHER STUDY – Psa. 119:97–104; Josh. 1:8; 2 Cor. 10:1–5; Rom. 12:2

1. How can we cultivate a Biblical perspective? / 2. How is our mind renewed?

I didn't

FOR READING AND MEDITATION – HEBREWS 12:1–13

'Let us fix our eyes on Jesus ... who for the joy set before him endured the cross ...' (v. 2: NIV)

We continue meditating on the principles we must develop in our lives if we are to cope with the problem of failure. Another principle is this: if the thing in which you failed is clearly the right thing for you to do, then dedicate your energies to God, try again and don't give up.

A father, trying to encourage his teenage son after he had failed an examination, said, 'Don't give up, try again.' 'What's the use?' said the son. 'It's easier to quit.' His father remonstrated with him, saying, 'The people who are remembered in life are the people who, when they failed, didn't give up, but tried again.' He went on, 'Remember Churchill? He didn't give up! Remember Thomas Edison? He didn't give up!' The boy nodded. His father went on, 'Remember John McCringle?' The boy looked nonplussed. 'Who is John McCringle?' he asked. 'You see,' said the father, 'you don't remember him – he gave up.'

I saw a poster recently that impressed me deeply. It was a picture of a man sitting on a park bench looking depressed and disconsolate. His arms were folded across his chest, and there was a look of resignation in his face. The caption read, 'I gave up.' When I first saw this poster, I looked at it for a few moments and turned away, but then my eye was attracted to something in the right-hand corner of the poster. It was a picture of a black hill and on it a very tiny cross. These words, barely perceptible, were printed beneath it: 'I didn't.' Feel like giving up at this moment? Then lift your eyes to the cross. The one who triumphed over all obstacles holds out his hands towards you. Take his hand, and in his strength and power – try again.

O God, help me to link my littleness to your greatness, my faintheartedness to your boldness, my fear to your faith. Then nothing can stop me. Amen.

FOR FURTHER STUDY – Phil. Ch. 3; Jas. 1:6–8; Matt. 6:22

1. What was Paul's attitude? / 2. What happens when our eye is single?

Grace – greater than failure

FOR READING AND MEDITATION – 2 CORINTHIANS 9:6–15

'And God is able to make all grace abound to you, so that in all things at all times…you will abound in every good work.' (v. 8: NIV)

Another principle we must develop in our lives if we are to cope with failure is this: however disappointing and discouraging our failures, grace covers them all. No fear need creep in today from yesterday's failures, for grace has wiped them out and works to turn them to good effect. This does not mean that we evade the consequences of our failures, but providing we respond correctly and with honesty, grace flows in to take over and transform. Emerson says, 'Finish every day and be done with it. You have done what you could. Some blunders, some failures, some absurdities will have crept in. But forget them. Tomorrow is a new day.'

This is good advice, but not quite good enough. We cannot just 'forget them', especially if our failures have brought distress to others also. However, when we face things honestly and determine to learn from our failures, then God transforms those failures by his grace. He wipes away the burning memories of shame and self-disgust so that our failures, seen through grace, do not paralyse us but propel us forward.

I have mentioned before that the Old Testament ends with a curse (Mal. 4:6), but the New Testament ends with grace (Rev. 22:21). What does this suggest? It suggests that grace does not simply look back at past deeds: it looks forward to hold that future steady. You are under grace today, and you will be under grace tomorrow. What a prospect! The past can't hurt you, and both today and tomorrow are secure. Our failures, therefore, make us sing – sing at the redemption that grace draws from them.

O Father, I am so thankful that grace holds the keys of yesterday and tomorrow. You lock the one – and open the other. And there is grace for today too! I am eternally grateful. Amen.

FOR FURTHER STUDY – Rom. Ch. 5, 3:23–24; 2 Tim. 2:1; Tit. 3:7

1. What are the characteristics of grace?
2. What is the result of being justified through grace?

Hallelujah – the pressure's off

FOR READING AND MEDITATION – 2 CORINTHIANS 1:12–22

'Now it is God who makes both us and you stand firm in Christ.' (v. 21: NIV)

We spend one more day examining the principles that can help us become strong at the places of failure. A further principle is this: strive not so much to succeed but to do the right thing.

Many years ago, when visiting the United States, I remember addressing a group of ministers in Atlanta, Georgia, on Pitfalls in the Ministry. I told them the story of my own failures, which at that time amounted to a great many, and I said, 'The lesson I have learned from my failures is that I don't have to succeed. I have to do the right thing under God's guidance, and leave success or failure in his hands.' One of the ministers came to me afterwards and said, 'I am a pastor of one of the largest churches in this area, and regarded by my peers as one of the most successful ministers in my denomination. But today you have helped me overcome the greatest pressure in my life – the pressure to succeed.'

In the early years of my ministry, I was extremely success-oriented: when I succeeded, I felt good, and when I failed, I felt devastated. Then God said to me quite bluntly one day, 'Are you willing to be a failure?' The question shook me rigid. It was a whole week later before I found sufficient grace to answer that question with a 'Yes', and when I did, I was instantly released from the two things that had crippled my life and ministry – the pressure to succeed and the fear of failure. Now, what matters is not succeeding or failing, but being true to him. Success and failure are in his hands. I am not on the way to success. I am on the Way. What a difference!

O Father, set me free today from these two crippling disabilities – the pressure to succeed and the fear of failure. Help me to do the right thing, and to leave success or failure in your hands. For Jesus' sake. Amen.

FOR FURTHER STUDY – Rom. Chs. 7, 8

1. What brought Paul through his despondent struggle?
2. Write down the number of times 'I' occurs in Ch. 7 and 'Spirit' in Ch. 8.

Men cry out against the heavens

FOR READING AND MEDITATION – PSALM 9:1–20

'God remembers those who suffer; he does not forget their cry…' (v. 12: TEV)

Having learned something about how to cope with failure, we turn now to face the issue of what to do when life breaks us with unmerited suffering and affliction. I get more letters on this subject than on almost any other. People write and say, 'My suffering is so great that I sometimes doubt the existence of a God of love. Can you say something that will help me regain my faith in this tragic hour?'

One of the most poignant elements in suffering is that there often seems to be no meaning in it – it seems so senseless, leading nowhere. One great writer said that anyone who was undisturbed by the problem of unmerited suffering was a victim of either a hardened heart or a softened brain. He was right. Everyone who is mentally alive, especially if he believes in a God of love, finds this problem difficult to solve. No wonder the poet cried out in these lines:

> My son, the world is dark with griefs and graves
> So dark that men cry out against the heavens.

I suppose there is nothing that makes men cry out against the heavens so much as the hurt and anguish which comes unbidden and unmerited. I say 'unbidden and unmerited', because some of our sufferings are the result of our own crassness and stupidity. But what about when life breaks us with sufferings that are not directly related to us? Does God remember us then? Our text today says that he does. This in itself should be enough to keep us brave, if not blithe, in peace, if not in happiness. Write it on your heart. God remembers you in your suffering. He really does!

Lord Jesus, you who experienced suffering in a way I will never know, hold me close to your heart so that my sufferings will not demolish me, but develop me. For your own dear name's sake. Amen.

FOR FURTHER STUDY – Rom. 8:17–26; 2 Cor. 1:7, 4:11–18; 1 Pet. 5:10

1. What is God's purpose in suffering?
2. What are some of the ways in which Christ suffered?

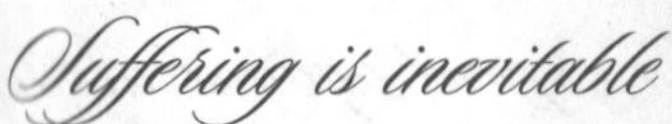
Suffering is inevitable

FOR READING AND MEDITATION – JOB 5:1–18

'Yet man is born to trouble as surely as sparks fly upward.' (v. 7: NIV)

Today we ask ourselves: how do we, as Christians, cope with the problem of unmerited suffering? What are the principles we need to employ if we are to become strong in the broken places of affliction? The first thing we must do is to recognise that in a universe whose balance has been greatly upset by sin, undeserved suffering is bound to come. Face this, and you are halfway to turning the problem into a possibility.

In an Indian palace, many years ago, a child was born whose parents decided to keep all signs of decay and death from him. When he was taken into the garden, maids were sent before him to remove all the decaying flowers and fallen leaves, so that he would be protected from all signs of suffering and death. One day, however, he left his home and, while wandering through the streets, came across a corpse. His reaction was so strong that he set about establishing the teaching that, as life is fundamentally suffering, the only thing to do is to escape into Nirvana, the state of extinction of self.

The young man was Guatama Buddha, whose beliefs are shared by millions of his followers, not only in India but around the world. His philosophy is a dramatic, and tragic result of trying to protect oneself from the realities of life, one of which is suffering. The Christian faith is the opposite of that: it exposes us to the very heart of suffering – the Cross. Then it takes that suffering, and turns it into salvation. This is why Christians should not be afraid to face the worst that can happen – because with God it can be turned into the best.

Father, I am so thankful for the cross – what is my suffering compared to that? And even if I have to bear similar suffering, I know that out of it will come to me what came to you – a resurrection. Blessed be your name forever. Amen.

FOR FURTHER STUDY – Isa. Ch. 53; Lk. 22:40; Heb. 2:9–10, 5:8, 8:1

1. Why was it necessary for Christ to suffer? / 2. How can suffering become positive?

The best out of the worst

FOR READING AND MEDITATION – 1 PETER 2:11–25

'Live such good lives among the pagans that, though they accuse you of doing wrong, they may see your good deeds and glorify God . . .' (v. 12: NIV)

We continue meditating on how to cope with the problem of unmerited suffering and affliction. Yesterday we said that the first attitude we should adopt toward unmerited suffering is to accept that it is bound to come. Sin has unbalanced the universe, and suffering is one of the inevitable results. To deny this is to deny reality, and the denial of reality is the denial of life. Arising out of this comes our second principle: God is able to turn all suffering to good and glorious ends.

J.B. Phillips translates the verse at the top of the page like this: '. . . although they may in the usual way slander you as evil-doers yet when disasters come, they may glorify God when they see how well you conduct yourselves.' Note the phrase, 'when disasters come'. They are bound to come to everyone – it's foolish to think that, just because we are Christians, we are exempt. We are part of a universe that has been unbalanced by sin, part of a mortal, decaying world. However, though we may fall victim to life's disasters, we are able, through the redemptive purposes of God, to turn them into doors of opportunity and step through them into richer, fuller and more abundant living.

A woman who was converted from one of the cults said in a testimony meeting in her church, 'They taught me that the first thing I should concern myself about is my happiness. You have taught me that the first thing is to "belong". That makes me feel safe.' Since she was safe, her happiness was safe too. Others are baffled by life's tragedies. Only the cross has an answer. Out of the worst, Christ brings the best, and makes life's victims victorious.

Father, the more I think about this, the more excited I get. You have given me such security. I can stand anything because I can use everything. Oh glory! Amen.

FOR FURTHER STUDY – Jn. 10:1–10; 2 Cor. 9:8; Eph. 3:20

1. What does the thief seek to do? / 2. What does Christ bring us?

Not comfort – but character

FOR READING AND MEDITATION – JOB 2:1–10

'"Shall we accept good from God, and not trouble?"' (v. 10: NIV)

We come today to one of the hardest and most difficult principles to understand in relation to suffering – but it must be grasped nevertheless. It is this – accept suffering as a gift from God.

This principle flows out of the verse that is before us today – a verse which one commentator describes as 'the most profound verse in the Bible'. It is obvious from reading this passage that Job's God is not a celestial Being who sits on the parapets of heaven, dropping nice little gifts into the laps of his children, at the same time saying, 'There, that will make you happy; that will surely please you.' If that is the picture you have of him, then you must learn that there is much more to God than that. The God of the Bible disposes and dispenses the things that bring most glory to his name. If, in achieving glory, he sees that adversity and suffering are the best means to that end, then that is what he will give. So before you go any further, mark this and mark it well – God is not under an obligation to make you comfortable.

Can you see the truth that is contained in the words of our text today? '"Shall we indeed accept good from God and not accept adversity?"' (NASB). You are ready to accept good, but are you just as ready to accept adversity? You see, God's goal is not our comfort, but our character. That is why it is wrong to tell a non-Christian, 'Trust God, and your troubles will all be over.' It's unfair, dishonest and downright unbiblical. In fact, becoming a Christian may mean that you will have more troubles than before. And why? Because character is formed in the furnace of affliction – no suffering, no character.

Father, if ever I needed your help I need it now. It's easy for me to accept good from your hand; help me also to accept adversity. Etch these words, not merely into my mind, but into my spirit. In Jesus' name I ask it. Amen.

FOR FURTHER STUDY – 1 Pet. 1:1–9; Psa. 66:10, 119:67; Isa. 48:10

1. What analogy does the Scripture draw? / 2. What is the result of enduring suffering?

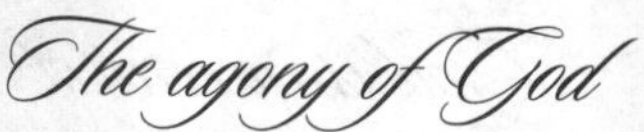

FOR READING AND MEDITATION – ISAIAH 53:1–12

'... he ... carried our sorrows, yet we considered him stricken by God, smitten by him, and afflicted.' (v. 4: NIV)

Yesterday we looked at a truth that many might find difficult to come to terms with – the acceptance of suffering as a gift from God. Today, therefore, I want to develop this point a little further. Dr E. Stanley Jones once said, 'Christianity is the only religion that dares ask its followers to accept suffering as a gift from God, because it is the only religion that dares say God too has suffered.'

Surely it must mean something to us, as Christians, to know that though living in this world is costing us pain, it is costing God much more. But just how much has God suffered? Some Christians think that the full extent of God's sufferings were the hours in which he watched his Son die upon the cross, but it means much more than that. The Bible tells us that Christ was 'the Lamb slain from the foundation of the world' (Rev. 13:8). That means that there was a cross set up in the heart of God long before there was a cross set up on the hill of Calvary.

God's sufferings began at the moment he planned the universe, and tugged at his heart-strings from the moment that he laid the foundations of the world. The pain of the cross must have pierced right through him as he waited for that awful moment when his Son would die on Calvary. How long did he wait? Centuries? Millenniums! Then finally it came – the awful, screaming agony of crucifixion. Was this the end? No. Now his sufferings continue in the world's rejection of his Son, and in the indifference of his children. I ask again: doesn't it mean something, even everything, to know that, though living in this world is costing us pain, it is costing God more? I find this thought deeply comforting. I pray that you will too.

Father, I realise that now I am looking into the heart of the deepest mystery of the universe – your sacrificial love. Help me to understand this fully, for when I see this I see everything. Amen.

FOR FURTHER STUDY – Matt. 26:36–42, Ch. 27; Isa. 50:6; Lk. 22:44; Heb. 2:10

1. List five aspects of the sufferings of Christ. / 2. What was the 'cup' Jesus had to drink?

God is in control

FOR READING AND MEDITATION – ISAIAH 46:3–13

'... I am God, and there is none like me. I make known the end from the beginning ... My purpose will stand, and I will do all that I please.' (vv. 9–10: NIV)

Another principle you will need to embrace if you are to become strong when life breaks you by suffering is this – recognise that because you are finite, you will never be able to fully understand the ways of God.

It was a wonderful moment in my life – I can even pinpoint the date, time and place – when I was delivered from the torment of trying to figure out the reasons why God behaves the way he does. I was reading the Scripture at the top of this page when these thoughts hit me like a bolt out of the blue: God is in control of the world. He is running the show. Don't try to grasp all the ramifications of this truth; just accept it. From that moment on, I have never spent a single moment trying to figure out why God does what he does. I accept his sovereignty without question – and I am all the better for it.

'One of the marks of maturity,' says Charles Swindoll, 'is the quiet confidence that God is in control ... without the need to understand why he does what he does.' Listen to what Daniel had to say on this subject: 'He does according to his will in the host of heaven, and among the inhabitants of the earth; and none can stay his hand or say to him, "What doest thou?"' (Daniel 4:35, RSV). There are, of course, many more Scriptures that make the same point – the Almighty is in charge. If you are in a turmoil of fear trying to figure out the reasons why God does what he does, then stop. You can't anyway. Feverishly trying to unravel all the knots can bring you to the edge of a nervous breakdown. The finite can never plumb the infinite. Face the fact that God's ways are unsearchable and unfathomable. Then you will start to live – really live.

My gracious Father, set me free today from the tyranny of trying to fathom the unfathomable. Quietly I breathe the calm and peace of your sovereignty into my being. No longer will I struggle to understand: I shall just stand. Thank you, Father. Amen.

FOR FURTHER STUDY – Isa. Ch. 55, 40:28–31; Rom. 11:33; Job 11:7

1. What has God promised instead of thorns and briers?
2. How are God's ways different to ours?

God tests before he entrusts

FOR READING AND MEDITATION – 1 PETER 4:12–19

'...those who suffer according to God's will should commit themselves to their faithful Creator and continue to do good.' (v. 19: NIV)

We spend one more day examining the principles we can put into effect when life breaks us by suffering and affliction. The final principle I would put before you is this: God seldom uses anyone unless he puts that person through the test of suffering and adversity.

Jesus, you remember, began his ministry in the wilderness of temptation, but it culminated in a garden in Jerusalem on Easter morning. Our lesser ministries, too, need the test of suffering. An ancient proverb says, 'He who is born in the fire will not fade in the sun.' If God lets us suffer in the fire of adversity, depend on it he is only making sure that we will not fade in the sun of smaller difficulties. Has life broken you by suffering and affliction? Are you feeling weakened and drained by the things that have happened to you? Take hold of the principles we have been examining this week, and I promise you that never again will life break you at the point of suffering.

This does not mean that you will never again experience suffering, but it does mean that you will respond to the suffering with a new and positive faith. Let me draw your attention once more to the text we looked at the other day: 'Although they may in the usual way slander you as evil-doers yet when disasters come, they may glorify God when they see how well you conduct yourselves' (1 Pet. 2:12, J.B. Phillips). Make no mistake about it – the world is watching how we Christians react to suffering. What do they see? People who struggle on in continual weakness, or people who have been made 'strong at the broken places'?

O Father, I am one of your followers, but so often I am afraid to follow you all the way. Yet I see that your way is right – nothing else is right. I know you will stand by me: help me to stand by you. For Jesus' sake. Amen.

FOR FURTHER STUDY – Rom. 5:1–11; 2 Thess. Ch. 1; Matt. 5:10–12

1. What are some of the results of suffering and affliction?
2. Are these being evidenced in your life?

When riches take wings

FOR READING AND MEDITATION – PROVERBS 23:1–8

'Do not wear yourself out to get rich…Cast but a glance at riches… for they will surely sprout wings and fly off…' (vv. 4–5: NIV)

We move on now to consider yet another way in which life can break us – through financial disaster or material loss. Some Christians speak scornfully against money. I have heard them quote Scripture in this way: 'Money is the root of all evil.' They forget that the text actually reads: '…the love of money is the root of all evils' (1 Tim. 6:10, RSV).

Money in itself is not evil. It lends itself to a thousand philanthropies. It feeds the hungry, clothes the naked and succours the destitute, and through it many errands of mercy are performed. Some years ago the Recorder at the Old Bailey made a statement that was taken up by the national press and reported in almost every newspaper. He said, 'A couple of pounds very often saves a life – and sometimes a soul.' It may be true that money cannot bring happiness but, as somebody said, 'It can certainly put our creditors in a better frame of mind.' Perhaps nothing hurts more than when life breaks us through a financial reverse, and we experience something of what the writer of the Proverbs describes – 'riches taking wings'.

The question we face is this: can we be made strong at the broken place of financial failure? We can. I think now as I write of a man I knew some years ago who lost all his assets. Such was his financial reverse that he lost everything – literally everything. Life broke him. He came out of it, however, with a new philosophy that changed his whole attitude towards money. I am sure of this; life will never break him there again. He was made strong at the broken place. And so, my friend, can you.

O Father, help me over this coming week to settle once and for all my attitude towards this complex problem of money. If it is a weakness, then help me make it a strength. For Jesus' sake. Amen.

FOR FURTHER STUDY – Matt. 6:19–34, 10:29–31; Lk. 12:15

1. What did Jesus teach about possessions? / 2. What is to be our priority?

Transferring the ownership

FOR READING AND MEDITATION – GENESIS 22:1–19

'…because you…have not withheld your son, your only son, I will surely bless you…' (vv.16–17: NIV)

We referred yesterday to the man who was broken by a financial disaster, but came out of it with a philosophy of life that enabled him to say, 'Never again will I be broken by material loss.' And why? Because he built for himself a Biblical framework which enabled him to see the whole issue of finances from God's point of view.

Here are the steps my friend took in moving from financial bondage to financial freedom. I recommend them to you.

(1) In a definite act of commitment, transfer the ownership of all your possessions to God.

Whether we acknowledge it or not, we do not in reality own our possessions. We are stewards, not proprietors, of the assets God puts into our hands. My friend told me that after reading the story of Abraham and his willingness to sacrifice his son, he got alone with God, pictured himself kneeling before God's altar and offered every single one of his possessions to the Lord. He said, 'I continued in prayer until every single item I had was laid on God's altar, and when it was over, I was a transformed man. That act of dedication became the transformation point in my finances.'

If, in reality, we do not own our possessions, then the obvious thing to do is to have the sense to say to God, 'Lord, I'm not the owner, but the ower. Teach me how to work out that relationship for as long as I live.' When you let go of your possessions and let God have full control, the whole issue of stewardship becomes meaningful. You are handling something on behalf of Another. Money is no longer your master, it becomes instead your messenger.

Father, I'm conscious that, once again, you have your finger on another sensitive spot. I wince, but I know I can never be a true disciple until I make this commitment. I do it today – gladly. For your own dear name's sake. Amen.

FOR FURTHER STUDY – 1 Ki. Ch. 17; 1 Cor. 4:1–2; Rom. 14:12

1. What can we learn from the widow at Zarephath?
2. What is the characteristic of a steward?

Hitched to a plough

FOR READING AND MEDITATION – COLOSSIANS 3:1–17

'Set your minds on things above, not on earthly things.' (v. 2: NIV)

We continue looking at the steps we can take in order to overcome financial disaster and so become strong at this place of weakness.

(2) Streamline your life toward the purposes of God's Kingdom.

Livingstone once said, 'I will place no value on anything that I have or possess, except in relation to the Kingdom of Christ. If anything I have will advance that Kingdom, it shall be given or kept, whichever will best promote the glory of him to whom I owe all my hopes, both for time and eternity.' Another great missionary said, 'That first sentence of Livingstone's should become the life motto of every Christian. Each Christian should repeat this slowly to himself every day: I will place no value on anything I have or possess, except in relation to the Kingdom of Christ.' If it advances the Kingdom it has value – it can stay. If it is useless to the Kingdom, it is valueless – it must be made useful, or go.

John Wanamaker, a fine Christian businessman, visited China many years ago to see if the donations he had made to missionary work were being used to their best advantage. One day he came to a village where there was a beautiful church, and in a nearby field, he caught sight of a young man yoked together with an ox, ploughing a field. He went over and asked what was the purpose of this strange yoking. An old man who was driving the plough said, 'When we were trying to build the church, my son and I had no money to give, and my son said, "Let us sell one of our two oxen and I will take its yoke." We did so and gave the money to the chapel.' Wanamaker wept! [11.]

Father, I feel like weeping too when I consider how little of my life is streamlined for Kingdom purposes. Help me to be willing to be hitched to a plough and know the joy of sacrifice. For Jesus' sake. Amen.

FOR FURTHER STUDY – Jas. 4:8–17; Rom. 14:8; Psa. 24:1; Hag. 2:8

1. How should we approach life? / 2. Is your value system Biblical?

Riches or poverty – so what?

FOR READING AND MEDITATION – PHILIPPIANS 4:4–13

'I know what it is to be in need, and I know what it is to have plenty. I have learned the secret of being content in any…situation…' (v. 12: NIV)

We are meditating on the steps we should take to rebuild our lives following a financial collapse.

(3) Recognise that you are free only when you are free to use either poverty or plenty.

There are two ways in which men and women try to defend themselves against financial disaster. One is by saving as much as possible in an attempt to avert it. The other is by renouncing money or material things entirely in order to be free from their clutches. Both methods have disadvantages. The first can cause miserliness and anxiety, and tends to make a person as metallic as the coins they seek to amass. The second seeks to get rid of the difficulty by washing one's hands off it, entirely. In each case, there is bondage – one is a bondage to material things, the other a bondage to poverty. The man who is free to use only plenty is bound by that, while the man who is free to use poverty only is also bound. They are both bound. But the person who, like Paul in the text before us today, has 'learned the secret of being content…whether living in plenty or in want' is free, really free.

While waiting for a train in India, a missionary got into conversation with a high-caste Indian. 'Are you travelling on the next train?' the missionary asked. 'No,' came the reply, 'that train has only third class carriages. It's all right for you, because you are a Christian. Third class doesn't degrade you and first class doesn't exalt you. You are above these distinctions, but I have to observe them.' Lifted above all distinctions! It's enough to make you throw your hat in the air!

O Father, what a way to live – lifted above all distinctions. Plenty doesn't entangle my spirit, and poverty doesn't break it. No matter how I have lived in the past – this is how I want to live in the future. Help me, dear Lord. Amen.

FOR FURTHER STUDY – Jas. 2:1–10, 5:1–8

1. Where does favouritism come from? / 2. What does James say about selfish living?

A need or a want?

FOR READING AND MEDITATION – PHILIPPIANS 4.14–23

'And my God will meet all your needs according to his glorious riches in Christ Jesus.' (v. 19: NIV)

Today we look at yet another step that will help us overcome financial disaster.

(4) Learn to differentiate between a need and a want.

Your needs are important, but not your wants. God has promised to supply all your needs, but not all your wants.

What are our needs? Someone defined it like this: we need as much as will make us physically, mentally and spiritually fit for the purposes of the Kingdom of God. Anything beyond that belongs to other people's needs. If this is true, then how do we decide what belongs to our needs? No one can decide that for you; it must be worked out between you and God. Go over your life in God's presence and see what belongs to your needs, and what belongs to your wants. Let the Holy Spirit sensitise your conscience so that you can distinguish the difference.

A fisherman tells this story. 'Yesterday I was on the lake. I pulled in my oars and let my boat drift. As I looked at the surrounding water, I could see no drift at all. Only as I looked at the fixed point of the shore line could I see how far I was drifting.' It is a parable! If you look around you to see what others are doing and merely follow, you will have no sense of drift. It is only as you fix your eyes on Christ, and watch for his approval, that you will know whether you are staying on God's course – or drifting away from it. One more thing: keep your needs strictly to needs, not luxuries disguised as needs. If you eat more than you need, you clog up your system. It is the same with other things. Needs contribute: luxuries choke.

Gracious Father, bring me under the sway of your creative Spirit. Sensitise my inner being so that I might hear your voice when I am about to go off course. This I ask for your own dear name's sake. Amen.

FOR FURTHER STUDY – Ex. Ch. 16; Psa. 23:5, 33:18–19, 37:25

1. How did God supply the needs of the Israelites?
2. List some of the needs God has supplied in your life.

Promises! Promises!

FOR READING AND MEDITATION – PROVERBS 20:1–22

'…"It's no good!" says the buyer; then off he goes and boasts about his purchase.' (v. 14: NIV)

We continue following the steps that help us become strong at the broken place of financial disaster.

(5) Ask God to help you resist the powerful pressures of this modern-day consumer society.

I once listened to a sermon in which the preacher likened Satan's conversation with Eve in the Garden of Eden with the subtle tactics of modem advertising. The main point he made was that if Eve could become discontented with all she had in that lush garden called Paradise, there is little hope for us unless we identify and reject modem methods of alluring advertising. What exactly is alluring advertising? One definition puts it like this: alluring advertising is a carefully planned appeal to our human weakness, which is designed to make us discontented with what we have so that we can rationalise buying things we know we do not need and should not have.

Not all advertising, of course, falls into this category, but much of it does. Charles Swindoll, an American author, claims that some advertising is not just alluring, but definitely demonic. I agree. He says that he and his family have developed a simple technique to overrule television commercials that attempt to convince us that we need a certain product in order to be happy. He describes it like this: 'Every time we feel a persuasive tug from a television commercial, we simply shout at the top of our voices, "Who do you think you're kidding!"' He claims it really works. God expects us to discipline ourselves in relation to many things, and not the least in the discipline of spiritual 'sales resistance'.

Father, help me, I pray, to see right through the alluring advertising of today's world, and develop within me the wisdom and strength to build up a strong spiritual 'sales resistance'. For your honour and glory I ask it. Amen.

FOR FURTHER STUDY – 1 Jn. 2:12–17; Gen. 3:6; Jas. 1:13–16

1. What are the three avenues which advertising exploits?
2. What is John's admonition?

Be a generous person

FOR READING AND MEDITATION – 1 TIMOTHY 6:6–19

'Command them … to be generous and willing to share.
In this way they will lay up treasure for themselves …' (vv. 18–19: NIV)

We have been discussing during this past week the steps we need to take to become strong at the place where life breaks us through a financial disaster. The friend I previously referred to claims that the principles we have been focusing on helped him to develop such spiritual strength and wisdom in relation to money that he was confident that, with God's help, he would never again be broken by a financial disaster.

The sixth and final principle he used, and which we need to practise too, is this:

(6) Become a generous person.

Look again at the text at the top of this page. It is so clear that it hardly needs any explanation. Woven through the fabric of these verses, as well as in many others in the New Testament, is one of the greatest definitions of Christianity I have ever heard, simply this: 'Give, give, give, give give …' When you have money, don't hoard it, release it. Let generosity become your trademark. This is not to say that you have to give all your money away, but give as much as you can, and as much as you believe God would have you give. Jesus once said: 'If your Eye is generous, the whole of your body will be illumined' (Matt. 6:22, Moffatt translation).

What does this mean? If your Eye – your outlook on life, your whole way of looking at things and people – is generous, then your whole personality is illumined, lit up. Jesus had little to give in terms of finances, but he was generous toward all – the sick, the needy, the maimed, the sinful and the unlovely. His whole personality was full of light. So be like Jesus – begin to see everybody and everything with a generous Eye. Don't be a mean person.

Lord Jesus, help me this day and every day of my life from now on, to make generosity the basis of all my dealings with people. Make me the channel and not the dead end of all your generosity to me. For your dear name's sake. Amen.

FOR FURTHER STUDY – Lk. 21:1–4, 6:38; Eccl. 11:1; Acts 4:32–35; Matt. 5:42

1. What did Jesus teach about giving? / 2. How did the early Church work this out?

When evil thoughts oppress

FOR READING AND MEDITATION – MATTHEW 15:1–20

'For out of the heart come evil thoughts . . .' (v. 19:NIV)

We turn now to focus on yet another place where life can break us – through the affliction of evil thoughts. I am thinking, not simply of an occasional wrong thought popping into one's mind, but those situations where people become oppressed by thoughts that are obsessive and repetitive. A letter I received some time ago said, 'My private discussions with Christians of all denominations has led me to believe that more are afflicted and oppressed by evil thoughts than we might imagine.'

When the late Dr Sangster, the great Methodist preacher, once visited Bexhill-on-Sea, he found a lovely avenue of trees. A nature lover to the core, he walked admiringly up and down the avenue, and then noticed a strange thing. Two of the trees were dead, and not only dead, but dismally and evilly offensive. Frost could not account for it; their neighbours were all healthy. He made enquiries, and found out that the gas main that ran underneath them had been leaking! Everything on the surface had been in their favour – the sea breezes, sunshine, rain...but they had been poisoned from beneath.

There are many Christians like that. Perhaps you are one. The circumstances of their lives all seem in their favour – a good job, a happy family, a pleasant environment, a fine church, yet their lives are mysteriously blighted by evil thoughts. Who can help us when our lives are spoiled by continual and oppressive evil thoughts? Jesus can! Christ can not only heal the brokenness but make you strong at the broken place.

O Father, I am so grateful that you are showing me your indomitable way. You can do more than sustain me in my weakness; you can turn my weakness into strength. Make me strong in this area. For Jesus' sake. Amen.

FOR FURTHER STUDY – Matt. 5:27–28, 6:19–34; 2 Cor. 10:5; Eph. 4:22–24

1. List eight ways in which Satan seeks to attack our minds.
2. What is the Christian antidote?

Be careful, little eyes

FOR READING AND MEDITATION – MARK 9:42–50

'And if your eye causes you to sin, pluck it out.' (v. 47: NIV)

Today we come to grips with the question: what are the principles we must follow if we are to move from weakness to strength in relation to this matter of evil thoughts? The first principle is this: take steps to ensure that you are not contributing to the problem by the literature you read or the things you watch.

One great philosopher said that if you want to evaluate the moral tone of a nation or a society, just examine the literature they read. These days it is hardly possible to pick up a newspaper or a magazine that does not contain a picture or an article that is calculated to inflame our passions. We live in an age preoccupied with sensuality and hedonism (the pursuit of pleasure). Any discussion on this subject must inevitably be linked with sex, as this is one of the main ingredients in the problem of evil thoughts. Although sex is not evil in itself, few topics can so engross the mind or kindle our curiosity. People with a hot passionate nature, however high their ideals, often fight a battle in their minds and imaginations with sexual fantasies. These, in turn, make them the kind of people of whom Montaigne speaks with much contempt, 'Men and women whose heads are a merry-go-round of lustful images.'

Fix it firmly in your mind that the first step to victory over evil thoughts is to cut off the supply at the source. Burn any books or magazines in your possession that others might describe as 'really hot'. Turn off the TV when it violates biblical standards. Avoid newspapers that go in for nudity. Saying 'No' to sensuality is the same as saying 'Yes' to God.

Father, help me to realise that although Christianity is a privilege and not a prohibition – it does have prohibition in it. Today I am going to make up my mind to say a firm 'No' to the things that are not of you. Strengthen me in this resolve. Amen.

FOR FURTHER STUDY – 2 Sam. 11:1–17; 1 Jn. 2:16; Lk. 11:34; Eph. 1:18

1. What was the source of David's downfall?
2. List six ways in which Satan tempts us through our eyes.

The pathway to sin is short

FOR READING AND MEDITATION – ROMANS 8:1–17

'To set the mind on the flesh is death, but to set the mind on the Spirit is life and peace.' (v. 6: RSV)

We continue to look at the principles we can use when evil thoughts crowd unbidden into our minds. Although it may be impossible to prevent evil thoughts from entering your mind, make a conscious decision not to entertain them. A well-worn phrase, which I am sure you will have heard before, puts the same thought in this way: you can't stop the birds from flying into your hair, but you can prevent them from building nests.

Burns, the famous poet, said that when he wished to compose a love song, his recipe was to put himself on 'a regimen of admiring a beautiful woman'. He deliberately filled his mind with pictures that were extremely dangerous to his passionate nature. Shairp, his biographer, said of him, 'When the images came to be oft repeated, it cannot have tended to his peace of heart or his purity of life.' Augustine, one of the great early Christians, also trod this dangerous path. He came to Carthage with its tinselled vice and began at once to coax his own carnal appetites. He said, 'I loved not as yet, yet I loved to love; and with an hidden want I abhorred myself that I wanted not. I befouled, therefore, the spring of friendship with the filth of concupiscence, and I dimmed its lustre with the hell of lustfulness; and yet, foul and dishonourable as I was, I craved, through an excess of vanity to be thought elegant and vain. I fell; precipitately then.'

Augustine's experience, like that of many others, goes to show the folly of entertaining evil thoughts and desires. Make up your mind, then, that although you may not be able to stop evil thoughts crowding into your mind, you will not play host to them.

Father, although I know what I should do, it is often hard – though not impossible – to do it. I give my will to you again today. Take it and strengthen it, so that it will do your bidding. In Jesus' name I pray. Amen.

FOR FURTHER STUDY – Psa. 119:1–11, 139:23–24; Prov. 23:7; Matt, 22:37; Phil. 4:8

1. When do evil thoughts become sin? / 2. How can we use our thought life productively?

The law of reversed effort

FOR READING AND MEDITATION – HEBREWS 2:5–18
'But we see Jesus …' (v. 9: NIV)

Yesterday we stressed the folly of playing with evil thoughts and desires, and we said that although it is sometimes impossible to prevent them from entering our minds, we must make sure we do not entertain them. This sounds good in theory, but how does it work in practice? Build within your mind a strong picture of Jesus, and when an evil thought comes into your mind, turn and look at him.

Those who study the functions of the mind tell us that evil thoughts are not driven out by dwelling on them, even guiltily or prayerfully. It is bad tactics to direct sustained attention to them, even in penitence, for then you experience what is called the law of reversed effort. This law states that 'the more attention you focus on avoiding something, the more likely you are to hit it'. A simplified form of this happens when a cyclist sees a pothole ahead of him, and concentrates on avoiding it – only to run into it.

The longer things are held in the focus of attention, the deeper they are burned into the memory and the more mental associations they make. The way to overcome them is to outwit them by swiftly directing the mind to some other absorbing theme. It may be difficult to dismiss them, but they can be elbowed out by a different and more powerful idea. And what better idea than to hold a picture of Jesus in your mind, reinforced by daily Bible meditation and prayer, so that in the moment of overwhelming testing, the mind is turned towards him. One who developed this technique into a fine art, said, 'Christ in the heart and mind is the safeguard. To think of him is to summon his aid. Evil thoughts dissolve in the steady gaze of his searching eyes.'

O God, my Father, help me develop in my mind and imagination such a powerful picture of Jesus that it will become the saving focus of my being. Help me turn to him immediately whenever evil thoughts crowd my mind. For Jesus' sake. Amen.

FOR FURTHER STUDY – Jas. 4:1–8; 1 Pet. 5:8–9; Eph. 6:11

1. What are the three steps James gives for overcoming Satan's attacks?
2. How does this apply to wrong thoughts?

The Word to the rescue

FOR READING AND MEDITATION – PSALM 119:1–16

'I have hidden your word in my heart that I might not sin against you.' (v. 11: NIV)

Another important principle to follow in developing a plan to overcome oppressive and evil thoughts is this: store up the Word of God in your mind so that it becomes readily available in times of need.

This is one of the most powerful and successful principles of Christian living. Sometimes people write to me and say, 'Your practical suggestions are very interesting and intriguing, but do they work?' I have one answer: try them and see! They most certainly work for me, and I am absolutely sure that if you apply them in the way I am suggesting, they will work for you, too.

The church provided accommodation in one of the city's large hotels for a minister who was away from home on a preaching visit. One night in the lift, a woman accosted him and suggested that they should spend the night together. 'This was more than an evil thought,' said the minister, 'it was an evil thought clad in the most beautiful and attractive woman I have seen for a long time. I was lonely and she was available.' He went on, 'But do you know what immediately flashed into my mind? Not my wife and four children – at least not at first. Not even my position and reputation. No, and not even the thought that I might be found out. The thing that immediately rose up within me was an instant visual replay of Romans 6:11–12: 'Consider yourself dead to sin, but alive to God in Christ Jesus.' The memorised verse came to the rescue – right on time.

Gracious Father, help me to have your Word so deeply hidden in my heart that it triggers an automatic reaction within me whenever I am threatened by evil. For Jesus' sake. Amen.

FOR FURTHER STUDY – Psa. 119:17–40; Jer. 23:29; Eph. 6:17; Heb. 4:12

1. How can we hide God's Word in our hearts?
2. How can we use the weapon God has given us?

The last thought at night

FOR READING AND MEDITATION – PSALM 4:1–8

'I will lie down and sleep in peace, for you alone, O Lord, make me dwell in safety.' (v. 8: NIV)

Today we look at a principle that I want to deal with in a some detail. The principle is this: let your last thought at night be a thought about your Lord and Saviour Jesus Christ.

The last thoughts that lie on our minds at night are powerful and determinative, for the door into the subconscious is opening and they drop in to work good or evil. It's bad enough struggling with evil thoughts while you are awake: don't let them take control while you are asleep. Your conscious mind may be inactive while you are asleep; not so the subconscious. The last thoughts lying in your mind as you go to sleep usually become the 'playthings' of the subconscious, and it works on these during the hours you are asleep.

If it is true that your mind is active while you are asleep, and there certainly seems to be plenty of evidence to support this theory, then make your mind work in a positive and not a negative way. Satan delights to drop an evil thought into your mind during the moments immediately prior to sleep, because he knows that it will work destructively all through the night, influencing your attitudes and most likely preventing you from enjoying a peaceful night's sleep. Then when you wake, you find that not only do you have to face the problems of another day, but you also have to face them without having drawn fully on the resources available to you through sleep. Thus begins a recurring pattern that cannot help but drag you down. So learn to elbow out any evil thought that enters your mind when about to go to sleep, and let your last thought be a thought of Christ.

Father, if it is true that my mind works when I am asleep, then help me to make it work for good and not for evil. Teach me the art of holding a thought about you on my mind immediately prior to going to sleep. I shall begin tonight, Lord. Amen.

FOR FURTHER STUDY – Gen. Ch. 1, 24:63; Psa. 1:1–6, 63:6

1. When does God's day start?
2. Why is it important to meditate on God's Word at night?

Moving together into victory

FOR READING AND MEDITATION – 2 PETER 1:3–11

'...make every effort to add to your faith ... self-control.' (5–6: NIV)

We examine one more principle in relation to this matter of overcoming oppressive and persistent evil thoughts: God is willing to do his part in helping you in this battle with evil thoughts – but you must be willing to do yours.

There is a teaching in some Christian circles that if we discover a need for change in our lives, we should passively wait upon God until he accomplishes it. It sounds so spiritual, but actually it borders on profound error. A Christian man once said to me, 'I would like to be free from a certain sin I am involved in, but I find I am powerless to break away from it.' I asked him what he expected to happen in order for him to find deliverance. He said, 'I expect God to take away the desire for this sin and thus set me free.' Can you see what he was doing? He was saying, in effect, 'God is responsible for delivering me, and my task is to wait passively until he does so.'

Let me tell you, that view is unbiblical – and what is more, it doesn't work. Although deliverance comes from God, we are the ones that carry it out. Let that sink in! The principle is this – you supply the willingness, and he will supply the power. Do you really want to win this battle against evil thoughts? If so, you can. Show God you mean business by putting the principles you have learned this week into practice, and you will pave the way for his miraculous power to work in and through you. Once you have done this, life's oppressive and evil thoughts will never be able to break you again. Here, too, you can become strong at the broken place.

Gracious Father, thank you for reminding me that deliverance is a team effort. It involves the Holy Spirit and me. I supply the willingness: you supply the power. So let's team up, Father, and move together into victory. Amen.

FOR FURTHER STUDY – Dan. Ch. 1; Rom. 6:13; Eph. 6:13

1. How did Daniel and his friends deal with temptation?
2. What were the results of their resisting temptation?

Coming back from doubt

FOR READING AND MEDITATION – JOHN 20:19–31

'Thomas answered, "My Lord and my God!" ' (v. 28: NIV)

This week we consider another important place where some Christians are broken – the area of deep and disturbing doubts. All men and women who are entrusted with caring for people know of those who have received Christ as their Saviour and Lord, but yet are afflicted with paralysing doubts. Some of these people go through deep agony of soul as they wrestle inwardly with doubt, ending up spiritually exhausted.

I met someone like this recently. She told me that she was a scientist and had serious doubts about certain parts of the Scriptures. 'I'm afraid that one day I will wake up,' she said, 'and discover that science has disproved large chunks of Scripture.' I could sympathise with her problem, but really her doubts were quite unfounded. Science, that is, real science, will never disprove Scripture, only confirm it. Half-baked science may appear to discredit the truth of God's Word, but real science can only validate it.

I suppose the classic example of doubt is found in the disciple Thomas. We call him 'doubting Thomas' – an unfair label if ever there was one. It's sad how we pick out a negative in a person and label him for that one thing. Thomas had his moment of doubt, but he came back from that place of weakness to become strong at the broken place. How strong? Let history judge. A well-authenticated tradition has it that Thomas went to India and founded a strong church there. Even today there are Christians in India who call themselves by his name – the St Thomas Christians. They are some of the finest Christians I have ever met. Thomas had his doubts allayed in one glorious moment of illumination – and then he went places. So can you!

O my Father, just as you took Thomas and changed him from a doubter to a man of amazing faith and achievement – do the same for me. For your own dear name's sake I ask it. Amen.

FOR FURTHER STUDY – Psa. 37:1–40; Isa. 12:2; Lk. 12:29

List seven steps of trusting given in verses 1–9 of this psalm.

2. What are five results of trusting?

Truth – in the inner parts

FOR READING AND MEDITATION – PSALM 51:1–19
'Surely you desire truth in the inner parts ...' (v.6: NIV)

Today we face the question: what do we do when we find ourselves assailed by honest doubts? Well, firstly, we must learn to distinguish between honest doubts and defensive doubts.

Many of the doubts that trouble Christians concerning aspects of the Christian faith are made half-consciously into a screen to hide some moral weakness or failure. I am not denying that some people experience acute intellectual problems in relation to their faith, and it would be arrogant to suggest, or even hint that everyone troubled by doubts is consciously or unconsciously using them as a screen. But because experience has shown that some do, this issue has to be faced. So, difficult though it may be, ask yourself now: am I using my doubts as a 'defence mechanism' to cover up some weakness or personal defect? A 'defence mechanism', by the way, is a device employed by our minds to prevent us from facing up to reality.

Adam used a defence mechanism when he blamed Eve for his sin. It is called 'projection' – refusing to face up to personal responsibility, and projecting the blame onto someone else. Could it be that some of your doubts may be due to this? If you are willing to look at this issue objectively, or perhaps with the help of a wise and responsible Christian friend, then, I assure you, God will not withstand your plea. One hymn writer said:

Jesus the hindrance show,
Which I have feared to see
Yet let me now consent to know
What keeps me out of Thee.

Gracious Father, you know how difficult it is for me to see myself as I really am. Help me to be honest with myself – even ruthlessly honest. For I want to be as honest as you. Help me in this hour of challenge. For Jesus' sake. Amen.

FOR FURTHER STUDY – Gen. Ch. 3; 2 Cor. 2:11, 10:1–6, 11:3, Ch. 14
1. What was Satan's approach to Eve? / 2. How could Eve have overcome his strategy?

Dealing positively with doubt

FOR READING AND MEDITATION – ACTS 17:1–15

'...they ... examined the Scriptures every day to see if what Paul said was true.' (v. 11: NIV)

Today we face the question: what do we do when we find ourselves in the same position as the disciple Thomas – assailed by honest doubt? Well, first we must recognise that doubts can be valuable if they motivate us to search deep and long for the answers. Perhaps it was this thought that led Samuel Coleridge to say, 'Never be afraid of doubt...if you have the disposition to believe.'

Unfortunately, there is very little sympathy given to those who doubt in most evangelical churches. Doubters are about as welcome in some congregations as a ham sandwich in a synagogue! It was because of the lack of concern shown in many churches toward those with honest doubts that two American missionaries, Francis and Edith Schaeffer, set up their ministry in a remote Swiss village many years ago. They established a centre for those with doubts about their faith and called it *l'Abri*, which is French for 'The Shelter'. Hundreds have made their way there over the years, and have come back with their doubts resolved.

Have you ever heard of Frank Morrison? He was an agnostic who, many years ago, set out to demonstrate the validity of his doubts about the resurrection of Christ. The more he looked into the facts, however, the more convinced he became that Christ actually did rise from the dead. He finished up writing a book, entitled *Who Moved the Stone*? which is one of the greatest evidences for the resurrection I have ever read. There are clear answers to all the doubts you may have concerning the Christian faith. Search for these answers, and the more you struggle, the stronger will be your faith.

Father, help me today to understand that all things can contribute to my faith, including my doubts. When I realise this, then I will go far. Thank you, Father. Amen.

FOR FURTHER STUDY – Matt. 14:22–36, 21:21–22; Lk. 12:29; Heb. 11:6; Jas. 1:6–8

1. What did Jesus teach about doubt?
2. What causes doubt, and how should it be dealt with?

John's doubts about Jesus

FOR READING AND MEDITATION – MATTHEW 11:1–11

'…"are you the one who was to come, or should we expect someone else?"' (v. 3: NIV)

We continue meditating on the subject of doubt. An important thing to remember in relation to this issue is the fact that, although God would prefer us to believe, he is exceedingly loving and gracious toward those who struggle with genuine and honest doubts. Did you notice, when we were looking at Thomas the other day, that Jesus did not reject his doubting attitude, nor did he refuse his request for physical evidence that he was truly the Christ? Instead, Jesus said to him: ' "Put your finger here; see my hands. Reach out your hand and put it into my side. Stop doubting and believe" ' (John 20:27, NIV).

The passage before us today tells of another occasion when one of his followers became oppressed by doubt. John was in prison, and probably suffering great discomfort and disillusionment. John's messengers came to Jesus, wanting to know whether he really was the Messiah, or whether they should be looking for somebody else. John, you remember, had baptised Jesus and had introduced him to the world with these words:

'"Look, the Lamb of God who takes away the sin of the world!"' (John 1:29, NIV).

Does it not seem strange that John, who witnessed the descent of the Holy Spirit upon Jesus at his baptism, should now have doubts about who he was and the validity of his mission? How did Jesus respond to this situation? With tenderness and sensitivity, he said: ' "Go back and report to John what you hear and see: The blind receive sight, the lame walk, those who have leprosy are cured, the deaf hear…" ' (verses 4–5). Our Lord could have rebuked the doubting disciple with strong words of reproof, but he didn't. Although he cares about problems, he cares more about people.

Thank you, Father, for reminding me that you see me, not as a problem but as a person. I know you are concerned about my doubts, but you are more concerned about me. I am deeply grateful. Amen.

FOR FURTHER STUDY – Rom. 8:18–39; Jn. 3:16–17, 8:1–11; Rev. 12:10

1. Who condemns us? / 2. How did Jesus respond to the woman caught in adultery?

Decide to believe

FOR READING AND MEDITATION – JAMES 1:2–12

'…when he asks, he must believe and not doubt…' (v. 6: NIV)

Another important principle to employ when dealing with honest doubts is this: make a conscious decision to doubt your doubts and believe your beliefs. Living an effective Christian life, as we have been seeing, depends on how willing we are to exercise our wills in favour of God and his Word. To do this, of course, requires faith – faith in the fact that God has revealed himself in his Son and through the Scriptures.

As a teenager, I had many doubts about the Scriptures but, one night, I made a conscious decision to accept them as the eternal and inerrant Word of God. Notice, I said 'a conscious decision'. In other words, I decided by an action of my will to doubt my doubts and believe my beliefs. I then found an astonishing thing. Both doubt and faith are like muscles – the more you flex them, the stronger they become. I had been using the muscles of doubt to a great degree, but unfortunately, I had failed to exercise the muscles of faith. When I made up my mind to accept the truth of God's Word by faith, muscles I never thought I had began to function.

Now, nearly forty years later, those muscles are developed to such a degree that I find, where God is concerned, it is easier to believe him than to doubt him. I trace the beginnings of my own spiritual development to that day long ago, when I decided to take what one theologian calls 'the leap of faith'. Perhaps today might become a similar day of decision for you. I have asked you to make decisions about a lot of things – make one more today. Decide to doubt your doubts and believe your beliefs. Now!

O God, perhaps this is the secret: I have used the muscles of doubt more than the muscles of faith. From today, things will be different. I decide to take you and your Word on trust – now let it work. Amen.

FOR FURTHER STUDY – Heb. Ch. 11; Matt. 15:21–28, 17:20; Rom. 10:17, 12:3

1. What different aspects of faith are shown in Hebrews 11?
2. How did the Canaanite woman overcome the obstacles that confronted her?

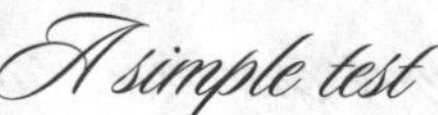

A simple test

FOR READING AND MEDITATION – PSALM 125:2

'As the mountains surround Jerusalem, so the Lord surrounds his people ...' (v. 2: NIV)

How good are you at trusting? The degree of your trust in God will be the degree to which you are secure as a person. One of the best tests I know to evaluate how secure I am in God is to examine my heart when I encounter an anxiety-provoking situation. Psychologists who study human reactions tell us that we have elaborate defence mechanisms built into us on which we can draw to guard ourselves against anxiety. They have names for these mechanisms, such as repression, denial, projection and displacement. The challenge for me as a Christian is to decide in times of anxiety whether to rely on my psychological defences to meet the situation or on God.

The psalmist says in Psalm 46:1: 'God is our refuge and strength, an ever-present help in trouble' (NIV). Lovely-sounding words, but are they true? Of course they are. It is on theology, not psychology, that I must base my trust. If you can't bank on anything else you can bank on what God says. Not to bank on it gives rise to insecurity.

O God, I would be a secure person. Forgive me that sometimes I have more confidence in my psychological defences than I have in you. Help me develop a deeper trust. In Jesus' name. Amen.

FOR FURTHER STUDY – Psa. 37:1–11; 118:8; Prov.3:5–6; Isa 26:4

1. What does the psalmist David exhort us not to do? / 2. What is his alternative strategy?

Do your emotions take over?

FOR READING AND MEDITATION – PSALM 103:1–22

'But the steadfast love of the Lord is from everlasting to everlasting upon those who fear him…' (v. 17: RSV)

We continue exploring ways in which we can become strong at the broken places caused by deep and disturbing doubts. Another point we should keep in mind in relation to this question of doubt is that some doubts are rooted more in the emotions than in the intellect.

Recently, I wrote on the whole subject of emotions, so I do not intend to go into this matter too deeply here, except to say that our emotions are an important part of our being, and they can do much to make our lives either miserable or meaningful. When emotions take over, they cause our thinking to waver, so that we can come to faulty conclusions about life. Ask yourself this question now: am I a person who is ruled more by my emotions than by my intellect? If you are, then it is likely that your doubts are rooted more in your feelings than in your mind.

Many years ago, a Christian university student came to me complaining that he had serious doubts about the inspiration and reliability of Scripture. As I counselled him, I heard the Spirit say, 'This is not an intellectual doubt, but an emotional one.' I explored with him the area of his feelings, and he confessed to me that he could never remember a time in his life when he ever felt that he was loved. When the emotional problem was resolved, his doubts vanished of their own accord. His problem was not intellectual, but emotional. Reason and emotion are both important in life, but decisions, especially decisions about the Christian life, must be built, not on what we feel to be true but what we know to be true.

My Father and my God, help me trace my problem to its roots and meet me at the point of my deepest need. This I ask in Jesus' Name. Amen.

FOR FURTHER STUDY – Job Chs. 1, 3

1. What were some of the feelings Job expressed?
2. Did he allow them to give rise to doubt?

Thomas, the doer

FOR READING AND MEDITATION – ACTS 1:6–14

'... "you will receive power when the Holy Spirit comes on you; and you will be my witnesses ... to the ends of the earth." ' (v. 8: NIV)

We spend one last day exploring the insights and principles that enable us to overcome doubt and develop our faith. The final principle we look at is this: recognise that if you could not doubt, you could not believe. So don't be threatened or intimidated by your doubts. Robert Brown put it like this, 'You call for faith: I show you doubt, to prove that faith exists. The more of doubt, the stronger faith, I say, if faith o'ercomes doubt.' Those who doubt most, and yet strive to overcome their doubts, turn out to be some of Christ's strongest disciples. We began this week by looking at Thomas the doubter, but we must end by looking at Thomas the doer.

One commentator points out that Thomas, being a twin, must have developed an early independence of judgment that made it possible for him to break with his brother and become a follower of Jesus. This is an assumption, of course, but I think it is a valid one. It was that independence, perhaps, that led him to reject the testimony of the other disciples when they said, ' "We have seen the Lord" ' (John 20:25, NIV).

Jesus did not reject Thomas because of his doubts, but said to him: ' "Reach out your hand and put it into my side. Stop doubting and believe" ' (John 20:27, NIV). Suddenly his doubts vanished, and he was transformed in that moment into one of Christ's most committed disciples. Up till then, no one had called Jesus 'God'. They had called him 'Messiah', 'Son of God', 'Son of the Living God' – but not 'God'. Here Thomas the doubter leapt beyond the others, and became the strongest believer of them all. And this faith of Thomas did not stop at faith – it resulted in mighty achievement. The doubter became a doer. And how!

O God my father, what a prospect – my faith, at first so tentative, can, through your illumination and my response, become a driving force. It can not only save me, but send me. May there be no limits! Amen.

FOR FURTHER STUDY – Matt. 8:1–13; Rom. 10:17, 14:23; Heb. 11:1

1. Where does faith come from? / 2. What did Jesus say to the centurion?

Danger in the home

FOR READING AND MEDITATION – MATTHEW 11:25–30

'"Take my yoke upon you and learn from me… and you will find rest…"' (v. 29: NIV)

We turn now to examine another area of life where many are broken – through troubles in the home. Life, as Hemingway put it, breaks us all, but perhaps nothing is quite as painful as being broken by difficulties in one's home. Have you been broken by pressing problems within your family circle? Then take heart – out of the brokenness, God can bring strength.

What kinds of troubles bring us to breaking point in the home? These are just some of them: incompatibility, disagreements, separation, threats or the action of divorce, insensitivity, bickering, rows, misunderstandings and violence. I haven't even mentioned such things as alcoholism, drug abuse, mental and emotional breakdowns, child and adolescent rebellion, or gross neglect of the aged members of the family. In some homes, even when they are Christian homes, things can get pretty desperate. A study completed at the University of Rhode Island described the American home as the most dangerous place to be – apart from a war or a riot. It's also getting like this in Britain.

I doubt whether any person reading these lines has not experienced, in one way or another, some hurt or trauma through broken relationships in the home. Many, out of loyalty to their families, face the world with a smile, but inwardly they are torn and bleeding. I know a woman who was heartbroken by her husband's adultery and the rebellion of her children, but today she has recovered and is busy staunching the bleeding wounds in other people's hearts. So it can be done. To those of you broken by troubles in the home, our Lord says, 'Learn from me: I will make you so strong at the broken places of your life that you shall minister to others out of that hidden strength.'

O God, you know how easy it is to blunder in this delicate and difficult business of relationships. I need someone to lead me in the right way. You lead me, Father – I will follow. Amen.

FOR FURTHER STUDY – Psa. 46: 1–11, 147:3; Lk. 4:18; Matt. 12:20

1. What did God say to the psalmist in the midst of upheaval?
2. What does God promise the broken-hearted?

Our three primary needs

FOR READING AND MEDITATION – COLOSSIANS 2:1–10
'... and you are complete in him...' (v. 10: New KJV)

We begin now by focusing on the first principle we must learn if we are to recover from the brokenness caused by troubles in the home: depend on God, and not on anyone else, to meet the deepest needs of your personality. Allow this truth to take hold of your innermost being and, I promise you, you will become a transformed person.

The needs of our human personality can be categorised in a number of ways, but the most basic ones are these: (1) the need to be loved unconditionally (security); (2) the need to be valued (self-worth), and (3) the need to make a meaningful contribution to God's world (significance). Human beings can function effectively only to the degree that these needs are met. If they are unsatisfied, our ability to function as a person is greatly hindered; if they are adequately met, then, other things being equal, we have the potential to function effectively.

Notice, however, this important point – our needs for security, significance and self-worth can be fully met only in a close and ongoing relationship with the Lord Jesus Christ. If we do not let Christ meet those needs, then because they have to be met in order for us to function effectively, we will attempt to get them met in and through others. Although many do not realise it, this is what draws many people toward marriage, because they see the possibility of having their needs met through their partner. But no human being, however loving, kind and considerate they may be, can fully meet these needs. I say again: they can be met fully only in a close and ongoing relationship with the Lord Jesus Christ.

Father, I sense that I am on the verge of something big and challenging. Help me to grasp this, for I sense that if I do, I shall become a transformed person. In Jesus' name I ask it. Amen.

FOR FURTHER STUDY – Eph. Chs. 1, 2
1.Where is Christ? / 2. Where are we?

Are you a manipulator?

FOR READING AND MEDITATION – JOHN 15:9–17

'My command is this: Love each other as I have loved you.' (v. 12: NIV)

Yesterday we touched on what is perhaps the biggest single problem in marital unhappiness – trying to get one's partner to meet needs that can only be fully met through a relationship with Jesus Christ. This issue is so important that I propose to spend another day discussing it.

What happens if we do not allow God to meet our basic needs? We will try to get those needs met in some other way. Some people try to find satisfaction in achievement or work. This, however, fails to bring lasting satisfaction, and whenever their inner discomfort reaches the threshold of awareness, they anaesthetise it with more activities, more achievement and more work.

Another way, as we have already said, is to attempt to get these needs met in marriage. Can you see the problem this produces? If we enter marriage as a way of getting our needs met, then we consciously or unconsciously become involved in manipulating our partner to meet our needs. Instead of following the Christian vision of marriage, which is to minister to our partners from a position of security in Christ's love, we begin to manipulate them to meet our needs. Thousands of marriages, perhaps millions, are caught up in this treadmill – each trying to get their partner to meet the needs that only God can fully meet. The best way to get our needs met is to depend on God to meet them. When we lock into him and focus on how much he loves and values us, and on his purpose for our lives, then and only then are we free to minister in the way he prescribes in his Word. Without that inner security, we become exposed and vulnerable to the likes or dislikes of our partner. We become puppets – not people.

O my Lord and Master, take me in your arms today and make me so conscious of your love that I will no longer manipulate others to love me, but minister to them with the love I already have. For Jesus' sake I ask it. Amen.

FOR FURTHER STUDY – 1 Cor. Ch. 13; Rom. 5:8, 8:35; 1 Jn. 3:16

1. List 15 qualities of love. / 2. Is their emphasis on giving or getting?

Making God more meaningful

FOR READING AND MEDITATION – 1 JOHN 4:7–21

'No one has ever seen God; but if we love one another, God lives in us and his love is made complete in us.' (v. 12: NIV)

We have been seeing over the past two days that the first principle to follow in healing the brokenness that comes through troubles in the home is to depend on the Lord to meet our basic needs. You might ask yourself: if the Lord can meet my needs for security, self-worth and significance, why do I need a human partner at all?

The answer to that question flows out of the next principle: in the relationship with your partner or your children, focus more on what you can give than what you can get. Now this can be exceedingly difficult, of course, if you are not allowing God to meet your needs, but once you are secure in him, everything he asks you to do becomes possible. Assuming our needs for security, significance and self-worth are being met in God, we are then in a position to fulfil God's true purpose for marriage, which is this: God, who is an invisible, intangible, eternal Being, has designed marriage to be a visible tangible demonstration of the reality of his love as we minister love and consideration to one another.

Just think of it – in marriage we have the marvellous privilege of demonstrating God's love to our partners in a way that they can feel, touch and understand. Our love will not add to the fact of their security in Christ, but it will add to the degree to which they feel it. No wonder Martin Luther said that marriage was the greatest way God had of teaching us the truths about himself. And the second greatest way? You've got it! The Church!

Father, to realise that I have the privilege of bringing the reality of your love to others, and thus making you more real to them, is so incredible that it almost blows my mind! But I know it is true. Make me worthy of this privilege. For Jesus' sake. Amen.

FOR FURTHER STUDY – Matt. 10: 1–8; Lk. 6:38; Prov. 11:25; Acts 20:35; 2 Cor. 9:6
1. What did Jesus teach his disciples? / 2. How can you demonstrate this today?

Accepting your partner

FOR READING AND MEDITATION – JOHN 13:12–20

'... whoever accepts anyone I send accepts me...' (v. 20: NIV)

Now that we have established the first two principles for healing the brokenness that arises from troubles in the home, we are ready to go on to the third. Incidentally, this third principle only works if the other two are firmly and clearly established: accept your partner or your children, and don't just endure them. Too difficult? Well, look again at the verse at the top of this page, where we are instructed to accept each other just as God accepts us. And remember what we said earlier – whatever God asks us to do, he also enables us to do. When we supply the willingness, he supplies the power.

There is quite a difference, of course, between accepting your partner and enjoying him or her; the former is a Scriptural requirement and the latter is something that is dependent on response and behaviour. Marriage sometimes involves living with an irritating, infuriating and obnoxious person: how can we accept, let alone enjoy such a person? Acceptance does not mean that we have to enjoy everything our partner does: it means rather that we see our partner as someone to whom God wants us to minister, and we pursue that ministry whether we feel like it or not.

Many Christians stumble over this. A lady who recently came through to victory on this point said to me, 'But how can I accept my husband, who is nothing more than a loathsome, alcoholic pig?' I said, 'It's impossible as long as you are depending on your husband to meet your need for security. Depend on God to meet that need, and then see what happens.' She did so, and found that when she no longer depended on her husband to meet her need for security, she saw him in a completely new light. Then she had no difficulty in accepting him.

O God this sounds too good to be true. Can life's difficulties be resolved so easily? Give me the courage not to dismiss anything until I've tried it, nor resist any principle that is in harmony with your Word. Amen.

FOR FURTHER STUDY – Eph. 5:21–33, 1:6; Rom. 15:7

1. How should the husband show his acceptance of his wife?
2. How should the wife show her acceptance of her husband?

A check-up for husbands

FOR READING AND MEDITATION – EPHESIANS 5:22–33

'Husbands, love your wives, just as Christ loved the church… (v. 25: NIV)

Over the next two days I want to establish two final principles for dealing with troubles in the home: one for the husbands and one for the wives. Today we begin with the men: be prepared to give yourself a spiritual check-up on how you are doing as a husband. Cross out whichever answer does not apply.

(1) Do you still 'court' your wife with an unexpected gift of flowers or chocolates? (Anniversaries and birthdays not included) (YES/NO)
(2) Are you careful never to criticise her in front of others? (YES/NO)
(3) Do you make an effort to understand her varying feminine moods and help her through them? (YES/NO)
(4) Do you depend on your wife to meet your basic personal needs? (YES/NO)
(5) Do you pray together? (YES/NO)
(6) Do you share at least half your recreation time with your wife and family? (YES/NO)
(7) Are you alert for opportunities to praise and compliment her? (YES/NO)
(8) Do you go to church together? (YES/NO)
(9) Is she first in your life – after the Lord? (YES/NO)
(10) Have you forgiven her for any hurts or problems she may have caused you? (YES/NO)

A YES score of 7 to 10 – excellent!
A NO score of 4 or more – you've got some work ahead of you.

Father, you who have set us in families, help me to be the person you intend me to be, both in my marriage and in my home. This I ask in Jesus' name. Amen.

FOR FURTHER STUDY – Eccl. 9:1–9; Gen. 2:23–24; Col. 3:18–21; 1 Pet. 3:7
1. What does the word 'cleave' mean? / 2. Why are our prayers often hindered?

A check-up for wives

FOR READING AND MEDITATION – 1 PETER 3:1–12

'Wives, in the same way be submissive to your husbands...' (v. 1: NIV)

Yesterday the men were asked to examine themselves using a simple questionnaire, as to how they were doing as husbands. Today a similar opportunity is extended to wives.

(1) Are you depending on the Lord to meet your basic needs for security, significance and self–worth? (YES/NO)

(2) Can you meet financial reverses bravely without condemning your husband for his mistakes, or comparing him unfavourably with others? (YES/NO)

(3) Do you dress with an eye for your husband's likes and dislikes in colour and style? (YES/NO)

(4) Do you keep up your own personal prayer life so that you may meet everything that arises with poise? (YES/NO)

(5) Do you avoid daydreaming or fantasising about other men you might have married? (YES/NO)

(6) Are you sensitive to your husband's moods and feelings and know when, and when not, to bring up delicate issues? (YES/NO)

(7) Do you respect your husband? (YES/NO)

(8) Are you careful never to criticise your husband in front of others? (YES/NO)

(9) Do you keep track of the day's news and what is happening in the world so that you can discuss these with your husband? (YES/NO)

(10) Are you a 'submissive' wife? (YES/NO)

A YES score of 7 to 10 – excellent!
A NO score of 4 or more – it's decision time.

My heavenly Father, I realise the tender relationships of home can be a shrine, or they can be a snarl. Keep my inner shrine from all wrong attitudes and from all worry. Let me approach today's challenge in the knowledge that 'I can do all things through Christ who strengthens me'. Amen.

FOR FURTHER STUDY – Prov. 31:10–31; 1 Tim. 3:11; Esth. 1:20

1. What are the characteristics of a virtuous woman? / 2. What do her children call her?

When broken by stress

FOR READING AND MEDITATION – PSALM 71:1 – 24

'You have let me sink down deep in desperate problems. But you will bring me back to life again, up from the depths of the earth!' (v. 20: TBL)

This week we shall examine together another major cause for brokenness in human life – stress. Often I get letters from people saying something like this: 'I feel I am on the verge of a breakdown. No one thing seems to be responsible for it, but I just can't cope. My doctor says I am suffering from stress. Can the Bible meet this need?' I am bold to say that it can. God can take people overcome by stress, and build into their lives insights and principles which will enable them to live above and beyond its paralysing grip.

We ask ourselves: what exactly is stress? One doctor defines it as 'wear and tear on the personality which, if uncorrected, can result in a physical or mental breakdown'. Donald Norfolk, a British osteopath who has made a special study of stress, claims that it comes from two main causes: (1) too little change, or (2) too much change. He says that to function at peak efficiency, we all need a certain amount of novelty and change. However, when changes come too fast for us to cope with, the personality is put under tremendous stress.

Dr Thomas H. Holmes, a recognised authority on the subject of stress, measures stress in terms of 'units of change'. For example, the death of a loved one measures 100 units, divorce 73 units, pregnancy 40 units, moving or altering a home 25 units and Christmas 12 units. His conclusion is that no one can handle more than 300 units of stress in a twelve-month period without suffering physically or emotionally during the next two years. Holmes, of course, was speaking from a strictly human point of view – with God 'all things are possible'.

Father, you have taught me much on how to turn my weaknesses into strengths. Teach me now how to handle stress. I cannot change my surroundings – but I can change my attitude. Help me to do this. For Jesus' sake. Amen.

FOR FURTHER STUDY – Lk. 10:38–42; Phil. 4:6; Psa. 127:2; Matt. 6:25

1. What was Jesus' response to Martha?
2. How did it differ from his response to Mary?

Find the cause – find the cure

FOR READING AND MEDITATION – PSALM 139:1–24

'Search me, 0 God, and know my heart; test me and know my anxious thoughts.' (v. 23: NIV)

Were you surprised to discover yesterday that Christmas earned 12 points on Dr Thomas Holmes' stress scale? Let me tell you that in the week leading up to Christmas, there are more suicides and breakdowns than in any other week of the year. This is because the gaiety and festivity of the Christmas season stands out in such marked contrast to the melancholy feelings of the depressed that these people are easily pushed over the edge into suicide or a breakdown.

What then is the first step toward recovery from, or prevention of, stress? This: identify what causes you to feel stress. No two people react to stress in quite the same way. One person may revel in frequent change, while another may be thrown into a state of disquiet if a piece of furniture is moved around in a room. Dr Hans Selye, a world-famous expert on stress, says, 'The mere fact of knowing what hurts has a curative value.' Get alone in the presence of God with a pen and a sheet of paper, and ask the Lord to help you identify the causes of your stress.

You can help prime the pump of questioning by asking yourself the following: what one thing above all others makes me jumpy and irritable, or gives me the feeling I can't cope? (That could be stress factor No. 1.) How do I react to change, easily or with difficulty? How much competition can I take? Keep on questioning yourself until you pin down the things that produce stress in your system. It is only when you establish the origins of stress in your life that you can set about the task of building up biblical principles that will not only modify its impact, but enable you to turn your weaknesses into strengths.

Father, teach me how to respond to life so that, instead of a breakdown, I may experience a breakthrough – a breakthrough into a new way of living. For Jesus' sake. Amen.

FOR FURTHER STUDY – Mk. 4:35–41; 1 Pet. 5:7; Matt. 13:22; Lk. 12:29

1. Why were the disciples full of stress when Jesus was not? / 2. How did Jesus respond?

What a waste!

FOR READING AND MEDITATION – PHILIPPIANS 4:1–13

'Do not be anxious about anything, but in everything, by prayer and petition, with thanksgiving, present your requests to God.' (v. 6: NIV)

We continue meditating on the principles we can use when our lives are threatened by stress: recognise the symptoms of stress. No alarm bells ring in our homes or offices when we are suffering undue stress, but there are adequate warning signs. People under stress generally become irritable and over-react to relatively trivial frustrations. They show a change in their sleep patterns, and become increasingly tired and restless. They derive less pleasure from life, experience no joy while praying or reading the Bible, laugh less and become plagued with feelings of inadequacy and self-doubt. They sometimes develop psychosomatic complaints such as tension headaches, indigestion and other things.

Some people have what is known as 'target organs' – physical organs that are the first to suffer when they are under stress. Harold Wilson confessed that whenever he had to fire a colleague, he suffered acute stomach pains. Henry Ford suffered cramps in his stomach whenever he had to make an important business decision. Trotsky, when under pressure, used to develop bouts of high temperature, and frequently had to spend time in the Crimea recuperating. One businessman I know always has a glass of milk on his desk from which he takes frequent sips in order to calm his nagging peptic ulcer.

Are you able to recognise your own particular patterns of stress? You owe it to God and yourself to find out. The waste that goes on in Christian circles through believers channelling their energies into coping with stress, rather than into extending the Kingdom of God, is appalling.

O God, sharpen my ability to recognise the things I do that contribute to stress in my life, so that all my energies can be channelled into spiritual activity, not self-activity. For Jesus' sake. Amen.

FOR FURTHER STUDY – Lk. 12:15–34; 2 Tim. 1:12; 2 Cor. 11:22–33, 12:7–10

1. What was the key to Paul's trust under stress?
2. List six reasons Jesus gave for not worrying about tomorrow.

Stop and smell the roses

FOR READING AND MEDITATION – MATTHEW 6:25–34

'... Consider the lilies of the field, how they grow...' (v. 28: RSV)

Another principle that helps us cope with stress is this: seek to overcome any rigidity in your personality. You can best understand rigidity by comparing it with its opposite – flexibility. A more formal definition of rigidity is this: 'The inability or refusal to change one's actions or attitudes even though objective conditions indicate that a change is desirable.'

The rigid person clings to certain ways of thinking and acting, even when they are injurious to the personality and burn up their emotional energy. Someone described it as similar to driving a car with the brakes on. Take the housewife who worries herself into a migraine attack because she cannot maintain a scrupulously tidy home while her grandchildren are visiting. Or the businessman who triggers off another gastric ulcer because he falls behind with his schedule when his secretary is away sick.

Inflexible goals can be crippling fetters. It's no good saying, 'But there are things that have to be done, and if I don't do them, they just won't get done.' Perhaps you need to rearrange your priorities, adjust your lifestyle and learn to say 'No'. As someone put it, 'We must not drive so relentlessly forward that we cannot stop and smell the roses by the wayside.' You may be caught up in the midst of one of the busiest weeks of the year, but pause for a moment and ask yourself: am I driving, or am I being driven? Am I in control of my personality, or is it in control of me? Today, decide to take a step away from rigidity by pausing to 'smell a rose'.

O God, I am now at grips with the raw material of living: out of it must come a person – your person. Help me to be rigid only in relation to you, and flexible about everything else. For Jesus' sake. Amen.

FOR FURTHER STUDY – Gen. Ch. 1, 2:1–3; Heb. 4:1–11; Psa. 37:7; Matt. 11:29

1. What was man's first day? / 2. How can we enter into God's rest?

Don't push the river!

FOR READING AND MEDITATION – ECCLESIASTES 3:1–4

'There is a time for everything, and a season for every activity under heaven.' (v. 1: NIV)

We examine yet another principle that can help us cope with stress: refuse to be obsessed with time. Notice, I say 'obsessed'. It is right to be concerned about time, but it is not right to be obsessed with it. Do you live life by the clock? Then you are a candidate for stress.

Have you noticed that when filmmakers want to create tension, they show recurrent shots of a clock relentlessly ticking away? These 'High Noon' tactics are pointless when they are applied to the ordinary issues of everyday life. Nervous glances at a watch will generate tension when you are caught in traffic, but they will not make the traffic move any faster. Fretting and fuming will do nothing to alter the situation. So learn to relax, and do not become intimidated by time.

Some people live life as if they are on a racing track, and set themselves rigid lap times for the things they want to accomplish during the day. A test I read about recently showed how two motorists were given the task of covering a distance of 1 700 miles. One was asked to drive as fast as he could without breaking any speed limits; the other was told to drive at any comfortable pace. At the end of their journeys, it was found that the faster driver had consumed ten gallons more petrol and doubled the wear on his tyres by driving at a speed that, in the end, proved to be only two mph faster than the other driver! A man said to me in a counselling session when I advised him to slow down, 'The trouble is that I'm in a hurry – but God isn't!' Learn the wisdom of letting things develop at their own pace, and follow the maxim that says, 'Don't push the river – let it flow.'

O Father, save me from being obsessed by time. Help me to see that I have all the time in the world to do what you want me to do. And when I am over-concerned, I am overwrought! Help me, dear Father. Amen.

FOR FURTHER STUDY – Eph. 5:1–21; Col. 4:5; Jas. 4:14

1. How can we redeem the time? / 2. To what does James relate this?

Jesus – God with us

FOR READING AND MEDITATION – JOHN 1:1–14

'The Word became flesh and lived for a while among us…' (v. 14: NIV)

Over the past few weeks we have been looking at the principles by which we can turn our weaknesses into strengths. We now pause for a moment to absorb the wonder and joy of our Lord's coming to this world.

Just imagine what life would be like if all we had were 'principles'. Principles are good, but they fail to meet our need unless they are embodied in a person. Suppose you go to a child who is crying. for its mother, and say, 'Don't cry, little one, follow these principles and you will feel better. Would its tears dry and its face light up? Hardly. The child would brush aside your 'principles' and continue to cry for its mother. How glad I am, therefore, to point you, not merely to a principle but to a Person. We have learned much over the past weeks by looking at the various principles by which we can cope with life's problems and difficulties, but now the point must be made that principles by themselves are inadequate – those principles must be caught up in a Person. 'The Impersonal laid no hold on my heart', said Tulsi Das, one of India's great poets. It never does, for the human heart is personal and wants a personal response.

One Christmas Day, a little boy stood in front of a picture of his absent father, and said wistfully, 'I wish father would step out of the picture.' The little boy expressed the deepest yearning of the human heart. We have gazed at many principles and we are grateful – grateful, but not satisfied. We want our Father to step out of the picture and meet us, not as a principle, but as a Person. But listen! Listen! He has! That is the meaning of our Lord's birth. Jesus is Immanuel – God with us.

My Father and my God, just as you stepped out of the picture, help me this day to do the same, and let someone see in me the meaning of your principles when they are embodied in a person. For your own dear name's sake. Amen.

FOR FURTHER STUDY – Matt. Ch. 1, 2:1–12; Gal. 4:4; Phil. 2:5–7; 1 Jn. 4:10

1. What gift will you give to Jesus today? / 2. Share Jesus with someone today.

Keeping fit for Jesus!

FOR READING AND MEDITATION – 1 TIMOTHY 4:1–12

'... physical training is of some value, but godliness has value for all things...' (v. 8: NIV)

We spend one last day meditating on the ways by which we can overcome stress in our lives: engage in as much physical exercise as is necessary.

One laboratory experiment took ten under-exercised rats, and subjected them repeatedly to a variety of stresses shock, pain, shrill noises and flashing lights. After a month, every one of them had died through the incessant strain. Another group of rats was taken and given a good deal of exercise until they were in peak of physical condition. They were then subjected to the same battery of stresses and strains. After a month, not one had died.

More and more Christians are waking up to the fact that God has given us bodies that are designed to move, and the more they are exercised, the more effectively they function. Studies on how exercise helps to reduce stress are quite conclusive. Exercise gets rid of harmful chemicals in our bodies, provides a form of abreaction (letting off steam), builds up stamina, counteracts the biochemical effects of stress and reduces the risk of psychological illness. The Bible rarely mentions the need for physical exercise, because people living at that time usually walked everywhere and therefore needed little admonition on the subject. In our world of advanced technology, however, common sense tells us that our bodies need to be exercised, and we should not neglect it. It may not be a spectacular idea, but often God comes to us along some very dusty and lowly roads. We must not despise his coming just because he comes to us along a lowly road.

Lord, help me not to despise this call of yours to exercise my body. Forgive me that I am such a poor tenant of your property. From today I determine to do better. For your own name's sake. Amen.

FOR FURTHER STUDY – 1 Ki. Ch. 19; 1 Cor. 3:16–17; 1 Cor. 6:19

1. What caused stress in Elijah's life? / 2. How did God help him?

Transformed!

FOR READING AND MEDITATION – PSALM 32:1–11

'Blessed is he whose transgressions are forgiven, whose sins are covered.' (v. 1: NIV)

We come now to the final days of our theme. I have pondered for some hours on what issue to focus, and after much prayer and meditation, this is the subject which has come to me. I want to speak to all those who have been broken, or are on the verge of being broken, by the memory of some deeply grievous sin.

I am not thinking so much of those who have committed sin and have not come to Christ for forgiveness, but of those who, though they have been forgiven by God, are unable to forgive themselves. A man came to me recently at the end of a meeting at which I had spoken, and told me the details of a particularly horrendous sin in which he had been involved. He said, 'I know God has forgiven me, but the memory of what I have done is constantly with me. It is quietly driving me insane.'

This brought to mind a story I heard many years ago of a father who taught his son to drive a nail into a board every time he did something wrong, and then to pull out the nail after he had confessed the wrong and had been forgiven. Every time this happened, the boy would say triumphantly, 'Hurray! The nails are gone!' 'Yes,' his father would say, 'but always remember that the marks made by the nails are still in the wood.' The message I want you to get hold of and build into your life in these last few days is this: the Carpenter of Nazareth can not only pull out the nails, but so varnish and beautify the wood that the marks become, not a contradiction, but a contribution.

Lord Jesus Christ, you who once were known as a carpenter's son take the stains and blemishes of my past and work through them so that they contribute, rather than contradict. For your own dear name's sake. Amen.

FOR FURTHER STUDY – 1 Jn. Ch. 1; Psa. 103:3; Acts 5:31; Eph. 1:7

1. How can we know full forgiveness? / 2. Why not ask for it today?

Grace – greater than all our sin!

FOR READING AND MEDITATION – ROMANS 5:12–21

'But where sin abounded, grace abounded much more . . .' (v. 20)

We are meditating on how to recover from the brokenness caused by the memory of some deeply grievous sin. By that we mean a sin that God has forgiven but which, for some reason, still burns in our memory. What principles can we use to cope with this distressing situation – a situation by which many are hurt and broken?

The first principle is this: realise that God can do more with sin than just forgive it. I heard an elderly minister make that statement many years ago, when I was a young Christian, and at first I resisted it – as you may do at this moment. I said to myself, 'How can God use sin? Surely it is his one intolerance?' Then, after pondering for a while, I saw what he meant. God uses our sin, not by encouraging us to gloat over it, but by using it to motivate our will toward greater spiritual achievement, to quicken our compassion toward sinners and to show God's tender heart for the fallen.

We must be careful, of course, that we do not fall into the error which Paul refers to in Romans 6:1–2: 'Shall we continue in sin, that grace may abound? God forbid!' (AV). If we sin in order that God may use it, then our motive is all wrong and we fall foul of the eternal purposes. If, however, we commit sin, but then take it to God in confession – really take it to him – then he will not only forgive it, but also make something of it. Is this too difficult for you to conceive? Then I point you to the cross. The cross was the foulest deed mankind ever committed; yet God used it to become the fulcrum of his redemption. It was our nadir – our lowest point – but it was God's zenith. Hallelujah.

O Father, I am so relieved to know that you take even my sins and make them contribute to your purposes. Grace turns all my bad into good, all my good into better and all my better into the best. Hallelujah!

FOR FURTHER STUDY – Heb. 10:1–22; Isa. 43:25, 44:22, 55:7

1. What will God not remember any more? / 2. What is the 'full assurance' we can have?

Why do I do these things?

FOR READING AND MEDITATION – 1 JOHN 1:1–10

'If we confess our sins, he is faithful and just and will forgive us our sins and purify us from all unrighteousness.' (v. 9: NIV)

We continue meditating on the principles that enable us to recover from the brokenness caused by the memory of some dark and grievous sin. A second principle is this: understand the major reason why you tend to brood on the past. People who brood on the past, and keep the memory of their sin alive, do so for several reasons: they are not sure that God has forgiven them; they are in the grip of spiritual pride; they have not forgiven themselves.

Let's take them one by one. They are not sure that God has forgiven them: If you have this kind of doubt, then you must see that the doubt is really a denial. It is taking a verse, like the one before us today, and flinging it back into God's face, saying, 'I don't believe it.' You see, if you don't accept God's forgiveness, you will try to make your own atonement in feelings of guilt and self-debasement. Once you confess your sin, then, as far as God is concerned, that's the end of it. Believe that – and act upon it. It's the Gospel truth!

They are in the grip of spiritual pride: You could be saying to yourself, at some deep level of your mental and emotional life: how could *I* have ever done a thing like that? (Note the stress on the 'I'.) What this really amounts to is that you have too high an opinion of yourself. And that's about as bad as too low an opinion of yourself.

They have not forgiven themselves: It might help to stand in front of a mirror with your Bible open at the verse at the top of this page, reassure yourself that God has forgiven you, and say to yourself, by name, '.............................., God has forgiven you – now I forgive you too!'

Gracious Father, although I understand many things, I fail so often to understand myself. Teach me more of what goes on deep inside me, so that, being more self-aware, I may become more God-aware. For your own dear name's sake. Amen.

FOR FURTHER STUDY – Psa. 51:1–19; Eph. 4:32; Col. 3:13; Mk. 12:33

1. Why can we forgive ourselves? / 2. Forgive yourself today.

Remembering to forget

FOR READING AND MEDITATION – PHILIPPIANS 3:1–14

'…forgetting what lies behind and straining forward to what lies ahead, I press on toward the goal…' (vv. 13–14: RSV)

We examine one more principle in relation to this highly important matter of recovering from the brokenness caused by the memory of some dark and grievous sin: forget the matter by reversing the process of remembering. Puzzled? Then let me explain. Memory works like this: one revives an image of some past event (or sin), holds it in the mind for a certain length of time, and then this process is repeated again and again until it is locked into the memory for good. Now begin to reverse that process. Don't revive the image. The matter has been forgiven by God, so don't let your mind focus on it. When it rises to the surface by itself, as it will, turn the mind away from it immediately.

Have in your mind a few interesting themes 'on call' – a favourite Bible character, or a text which has special meaning. We are told that the mind, like nature, abhors a vacuum – so think of another and more profitable theme. I know a Christian man, involved in one of the deepest sins imaginable, who has learned to blot out unwanted memories the moment they rise to the surface by focusing his thoughts on the cross. It does not matter what the substitute image is so long as it is wholesome and can thrust the unwanted memory from your attention.

Another thing you can do when the memory of your sin returns – even if it is only for a moment – is to turn your mind to prayer. Don't pray about the sin itself – that will keep it in the memory – but pray that God will build into you love, forgiveness, peace and poise. Images that are consciously rejected will rise less and less in your mind. When they do occur, they will occur only as fact: the emotions will no longer register a sense of burning shame.

O my Father, how can I cease thanking you for the answers you give – they are so right. Everything within me says so. Now help me to put the things I am learning into practice. Amen.

FOR FURTHER STUDY – 2 Sam. 12:1–14; Mk. 2:5; Col. 2:13; Heb. 8:12

1. What was Nathan's message to David? / 2. What does God do besides forgive?

A new approach

FOR READING AND MEDITATION – 2 CORINTHIANS 2:12–3:11

'…thanks be to God, who always leads us in triumphal procession in Christ…'
(v. 2:14: NIV)

Today we come to the end of the theme on which we have been meditating over these past two months, 'Strong at the broken places'. Although this is the end of the theme, I pray that, for many of you, it will be the beginning – the beginning of a new approach to handling your weaknesses.

How thankful I am that, in the early years of my Christian life, God impressed into my spirit the truth that my weaknesses could be turned into strengths. I can almost pinpoint the day on which this truth was borne home to my heart. With just a few years of Christian experience behind me, I stumbled and fell. The temptation was to lie in the ditch and wallow in self-pity. But by God's grace, I got up, brushed myself down, and said, 'Devil, you won that round, but I'll work on that problem until it is no longer a weakness, but a strength.' I did work on it, and today I can testify that the weakness that caused me to stumble has indeed become a strength. I say that humbly, recognising that the strength I have is not my own, but his.

Tomorrow you begin a new month. How will you face it? Are you ready to face your weaknesses in the assurance that, no matter how life breaks you, you can draw out from each experience a lesson that will live on inside you and help you to find victory in a future situation? Just as a bone, when it is healed, becomes stronger at that place than it was before it was broken, so you can become stronger by your very weaknesses. Thus when you stumble, you stumble forward; when you fall, you fall on your knees and get up a stronger person. When we are Christians, everything is 'grist to our mill'.

O Father, I sense today that this is not the end, but the end of the beginning. From now on, I shall face the future knowing that, however life breaks me, in you I can become strong at the broken places. All honour and glory to your peerless and precious name. Amen.

FOR FURTHER STUDY – Eph. Ch. 3; 2 Cor. 12:9; Isa. 40:31, 41:10

1. What was Paul's testimony? / 2. What is your testimony?

A prescription for health

FOR READING AND MEDITATION – MATTHEW 5:1–11

'... His disciples came to him, and he began to teach them ...' (vv. 1–2: NIV)

Today we begin a study of one of the most powerful and profound passages in Scripture – the Beatitudes. In more recent years it has been my custom to focus annually on a well-known Biblical passage, and expound it phrase-by-phrase or verse-by-verse.

We begin our theme by laying down the thought that the eight principles that comprise the Beatitudes are the best prescription for mental and spiritual health it is possible to find. Dr James Fisher, a well-known and widely travelled psychiatrist, went throughout the world looking for the positive qualities that make for good mental health. He said, 'I dreamed of writing a handbook that would be simple, practical, easy to understand and easy to follow; it would tell people how to live – what thoughts and attitudes and philosophies to cultivate, and what pitfalls to avoid in seeking mental health. And quite by accident I discovered that such a work had been completed – the Beatitudes.'

What an amazing admission! I would go as far as to say that once a person absorbs the principles which underlie the Beatitudes – and lives by them – then that person will never again fall prey to serious depression or despair. How sad that so often the Christian Church has to refer its depressed and discouraged people to the mental experts of the world when we hold in our hands the blueprint for healthy and abundant living.

My Father and my God, help me to come to you at the beginning of these studies just like a little child – open and receptive. Show me how to open my heart and my hands to receive your prescription for mental and spiritual health. In Jesus' name I pray. Amen.

FOR FURTHER STUDY – Luke 6:20–38; Psa. 32:1–2, 41:1

1. What does 'blessed' mean to you? / 2. How would you define the word 'beatitude'?

The psychology of Jesus

FOR READING AND MEDITATION – JOHN 2:12–25

'He did not need man's testimony about man, for he knew what was in a man.' (v. 25: NIV)

We touched yesterday on the statement of a psychiatrist, Dr. James Fisher, who said that when searching for the positive attitudes which made for good mental health, he came across the Beatitudes and realised that he need search no longer.

Listen to his conclusion after close on fifty years' experience of working with people with mental, emotional and physical problems, 'If you were to take the total sum of all authoritative articles ever written by the most qualified of psychologists and psychiatrists on the subject of mental hygiene – if you were to combine them and refine them and cleave out the excess verbiage – if you were to take the whole of the meat and none of the parsley, and if you were to have these unadulterated bits of pure scientific knowledge concisely expressed by the most capable of living poets, you would have an awkward and incomplete summation of our Lord's Beatitudes – and it would suffer immeasurably through comparison.'

Dr Raymond Cramer, a minister and a Christian psychologist, says something similar when he describes the Beatitudes as 'the psychology of Jesus'. Some may find that expression unacceptable when applied to the Beatitudes, but remember, this is a scientist who is speaking. In studying the laws of human behaviour and seeking to discover what it is that brings a person to his highest point of integration, he came to see that the words of Jesus in the Beatitudes reveal more succinctly and more clearly than any other section of literature the principles by which a person can know contentment and inner happiness. In an age fascinated with the study of human behaviour, there is only one true psychology – the psychology of Jesus.

Father, I see that psychology, and all other '-ologies', are valid only as they are brought to your feet. Show me, dear Lord, not just how to live, but how to live abundantly. In Jesus' name I pray. Amen.

FOR FURTHER STUDY – Col. 1:1–20, 2:9–10; John 1:16; Eph.1:22–23

1. Where is fullness found? / 2. What does this mean for us?

The beautiful attitudes

FOR READING AND MEDITATION – ROMANS 13:7–14

'But put on the Lord Jesus Christ ...' (v. 14: RSV)

We continue meditating on the fact that the Beatitudes are the finest prescription for mental and spiritual health that has ever been given to man. It is helpful to keep in mind at this stage in our meditations that the Beatitudes are be-attitudes, not do-attitudes; the doing comes out of the being. Some ministers and commentators refer to them as 'the beautiful attitudes' – a phrase I find greatly appealing.

Our attitudes have a tremendous and powerful influence upon every part of our being – physical as well as emotional. A missionary from the Philippines tells how, during the war, he and his wife were ordered into prison camps by the Japanese, and were instructed that they could take with them all they could carry in their suitcases and no more. His wife, weighing just over 100 pounds, and not at all strong, carried a load of 200 pounds, mostly tinned food, a distance of five miles – a load neither of them could even lift after they arrived.

Mannheim, a famous scientist, says that we normally use about one-eighth of our physical reserves, and that these other reserves are only called upon when we employ the right attitudes. If our attitudes can help tap hidden physical reserves, then think of what our experience can be if we adopt the 'beautiful attitudes', which our Lord expounds for us in his Sermon on the Mount. We can maximise our potential and multiply our effectiveness, not only in the physical area of our being, but in our mental and emotional areas also. Many doctors and scientists agree that it is not our arteries but our attitudes that have the biggest say in our personal well-being.

Loving heavenly Father, help me to do as your Word commands and 'put on the Lord Jesus Christ'. Show me how to have his attitudes – the 'beautiful attitudes' – so that I might live fully and abundantly. Amen.

FOR FURTHER STUDY – 1 Pet. 2:21; Matt. 11:29; John 13:15; Heb. 12:2

1. What did Jesus do besides expounding these attitudes? / 2. How should our lives be?

Inner attitudes affect outer aspects

FOR READING AND MEDITATION – 1 CORINTHIANS 6:12–20

'"All things are lawful for me"? Yes, but not all are good for me…' (v. 12: Moffatt)

We must spend another day focusing on this important thought that our attitudes play an important and determinative part in our physical health. One doctor told me that immediately he receives the current edition of *Every Day with Jesus*, he quickly scans it to see if I have written anything along the line of the relationship between attitudes and health – a favourite topic of mine – and then orders a small supply for those of his patients who need to have their attitudes changed. He wrote to me on one occasion and said, 'Keep coming back to this subject every time you can – you just don't know how much good you are doing in my medical practice.'

According to an article in the *British Medical Journal*, 'there is not a tissue or organ in the body that is not influenced by the attitude of mind and spirit'. Dr Frank Hutchins, a nerve specialist, said, 'Seventy per cent of the medical cases I see need new mental and spiritual attitudes for health.' Man is a unit made up spirit, soul and body, and he cannot be sick in one part without passing on the sickness to other parts. The attitudes we hold in our minds do not stay merely as attitudes – they pass over into definite physical effects.

God has so designed our beings that the right attitudes produce the right effects in our bodies. Suppose they produced the wrong effects? Then the body and morality would be alien to one another. An outstanding surgeon said, 'I've discovered the kingdom of God at the end of my scalpel; it's in the tissues. The right thing morally is always the right thing physically.' The laws of morality and the laws of health are written by the same God for the same purpose – healthy and happy living.

O Father, you have made us so that we can either damage or deliver ourselves in this matter of health. Help me to have your attitudes in everything I say and everything I do. For your own dear name's sake. Amen.

FOR FURTHER STUDY – 2 Cor. 4:1–16; Prov. 20:27; Matt. 15:18–19; Mark 7:21

1. How did Paul need to be daily renewed? / 2. What is it that defiles a man?

Not altitude – but attitude

FOR READING AND MEDITATION – JEREMIAH 17:5–14

'…blessed is the man who trusts in the Lord…
He will be like a tree planted by the water …' (vv. 7–8: NIV)

We must spend another day meditating on the importance and power of right attitudes. Someone put the point most forcefully in the following lines:

As man's created spirit
Up the ladder, God-ward mounts
He finds it isn't altitude,
But attitude that counts.

The greatest source of power for physical health is the absence of inward clash and strife in the spirit. Many people could be well physically if they were well spiritually. Other things being equal, a Christian should be healthier and happier than a non-Christian, for he or she has access to the attitudes that contribute to health.

We said yesterday that God has designed our beings in such a way that right attitudes in the mind produce right effects in the body. William James says, 'The greatest revolution in my generation was the discovery that human beings, by changing their inner attitudes of mind, could alter the outer aspects of their lives.' We could say that any results in life, any evidence of good mental health (and perhaps even physical health), any spiritual growth and maturity hinge on our understanding of the truths which our Lord expounds for us in the Beatitudes. They are the gateway to health and happiness. Let's decide here and now that no matter how much effort we have to make to understand and absorb these powerful and important principles, we will not give up until they become part of our daily thinking and our daily living.

Father, I am so grateful that you have set before me this gateway to health and happiness. Help me to walk through it – carefully, prayerfully and expectantly. This I ask in and through your peerless and precious name. Amen.

FOR FURTHER STUDY – Psa. 1:1–6; John 15:5; Rom. 6:22; Heb. 12:11

1. When is a man blessed? / 2. What are the results?

Christ's first word...

FOR READING AND MEDITATION – 1 THESSALONIANS 5:12–24

'Be happy ... at all times.' (v. 16: J.B. Phillips)

Now that we have spent a few days meditating on the fact that the Beatitudes provide us with the right mental and spiritual attitudes we need for healthy and abundant living, we are ready to begin focusing on the first of these profound statements of our Lord: 'Blessed are the poor in spirit, for theirs is the kingdom of heaven.'

Some translations read, 'Happy are the poor in spirit...' and one goes as far as to say, 'Congratulations to the poor in spirit...' It is important to keep in mind as you go through the Beatitudes that the word 'happy' (Greek: makarios) carries a far richer tone than we commonly attach to the word. It suggests a deep, abiding happiness, not just a temporary emotional lift.

In the very first words of the Sermon on the Mount, therefore, Jesus puts his finger on one of life's most vital issues – individual and personal happiness. We all want to be happy – and rightly so. The longing for deep, lasting happiness is a deep-rooted instinct that has been built into us by the Creator himself. The God who made the sunset, painted the rose, put the smile on a baby's face, gave the gift of playfulness to a kitten and put laughter in our souls is surely not happy when we are unhappy. The universe is on the side of the old saying that goes, 'Down with the coffee-pot face, up with the teapot face.'

Although it is a God-given instinct to be happy, we must also see that it is only God who can make us happy. Apart from him and his redemptive love as expressed through the cross and the resurrection, we would be 'most miserable' (1 Cor. 15:19). As someone once put it, 'Now that I know Christ, I'm happier when I'm sad than before when I was glad.'

Thank you, my Father, that you not only command me to be happy but provide me with the resources to make it gloriously possible. One touch of your gladness and my heart sings forever. I am so deeply, deeply thankful. Amen.

FOR FURTHER STUDY – Rom. 14:1–18; Isa. 12:3; John 16:24; 1 Pet. 1:8

1. What is the kingdom of God? / 2. What is this joy full of?

You cannot make happiness

FOR READING AND MEDITATION – MARK 6:45–51

'And he saw them toiling in rowing …' (v. 48: AV)

We said yesterday that we all want to be happy – and rightly so. This is a deep-rooted instinct that God has built into us. But happiness, as someone has pointed out, is not something you make but something you receive. You cannot make happiness any more than you can make love. Despite the wide currency of the phrase, I repeat: you cannot make love. The phrase is an anachronism. You can express love, you can make a pretence of love, but – you cannot make love.

So it is with happiness. You cannot make it. She is a coquette: follow her and she eludes you; turn from her and interest yourself in something or someone else and you may win her. There is no escaping – it is a law of our very being. Psychology and the Scriptures are at one here, and the experience of millions confirms their findings. The most miserable and fed-up people I know are those who are most bent on being happy. They are saying to themselves what the old lady said to the frightened child whom she had taken to the circus, 'Now enjoy yourself, do you hear? I brought you here to have a good time, so make sure you do' – as she shook him till his teeth rattled.

In the passage before us today, it is said that the disciples were toiling, rowing in the dark and getting nowhere. The wind and the waves were against them and the whole thing was ending in futility. Then Jesus came. In John's account of the same event, we are told that they took him into their boat – and immediately the boat was at the land where they were going (John 6:21). This is the way it is with happiness. We strive to achieve it, but we 'toil in rowing'. Then we let Christ in – and lo, we are at the land where we were going.

Father, I see that to get happiness, I must forget it. It is not an achievement, but a by-product – a by-product of knowing you. Help me to know you better, not just today but every day. In Jesus' name I pray. Amen.

FOR FURTHER STUDY – Isa. 61:1–10; Luke 10:21; John 15:11; Psa. 16:11; Neh. 8:10

1. What was Isaiah's testimony? / 2. Where does our strength come from?

Poor enough to receive

FOR READING AND MEDITATION – MARK 10:13–31
'"I tell you the truth, anyone who will not receive the kingdom of God like a little child will never enter it."' (v. 15: NIV)

Today we ask ourselves: if happiness is not something we can create but something we receive, how do we go about receiving it? Listen again to the words of Jesus: 'Blessed are the poor in spirit, for theirs is the kingdom of heaven.'

What does it mean to be 'poor in spirit'? There are those who tell us that the words should read, 'Blessed in spirit are the poor' – an idea derived from Luke 6:20, which reads: 'Blessed are you who are poor, for yours is the kingdom of God.' Our Lord, however, is not thinking here of material poverty, but spiritual poverty: 'Blessed are the poor in spirit'. The word for 'poor' in the Greek is ptochos and means a chosen poverty. It implies a voluntary emptying of the inner being and refers to those who by choice are so poor that they become poor enough to receive. One translation puts it: 'Blessed are those who are receptive in starts' – those who are willing to empty their hands of their own possessions and have them filled with the riches of God.

Jesus' first prescription for happiness, then, is a voluntary act of self-renunciation. This reverses the usual prescriptions for happiness, which begin with words such as 'assert', 'take', 'release' or affirm'. Which prescription will the universe back? I have no doubt myself – it is the prescription of Jesus. The first step, then, toward mental and spiritual health is self-renunciation. It is the decision we must take to reach out and receive Christ – with empty hands. Note that – with empty hands. The reason why so many fail to find Christ is because they are unreceptive – Christ cannot give himself to them because they do not give themselves to him.

O Father, help me to fling everything else away so that I might find you. I will take this first prescription: I will be humble enough to acknowledge my need and receive. In Jesus' name I pray. Amen.

FOR FURTHER STUDY – Mark 9:30–37; Matt. 10:40; Luke 8:40; John 1:12
1. What was the attitude of the disciples? / 2. What was Jesus' response?

Receptivity – the first law of life

FOR READING AND MEDITATION – JOHN 1:1–14

'...as many as received him, to them gave he power to become the sons of God ...' (v. 12: AV)

We ended yesterday by saying that the first step toward mental and spiritual health is self-renunciation and receptivity. When I am willing to acknowledge my need of Christ and stop striving to find happiness but receive him into my life – then lo, like the disciples we talked about the other day, we have reached the land where we were going.

It ought not to be considered strange that the entrance into the kingdom of God begins in receptivity – isn't that where all life begins? Our scientists tell us that the ovum and the sperm have to receive each other before they can begin the positive business of producing active life. The seed in the ground receives moisture and nutrition from the earth before it can begin to give forth in flower and fruit. If it doesn't begin with receptivity, it doesn't begin. The scientist who does not sit down before the facts as a little child and who is not prepared to give up every preconceived notion and follow to whatever end nature will lead him will know nothing. He has to know that he doesn't know in order to know.

The first law of life is receptivity, and that is also the first law of the kingdom of God. Look at our text once again: 'As many as received him, to them gave he power to become the sons of God'. How do we get power? First, by receptivity – 'as many as received him'. At the very threshold of Christ's kingdom, then, we are met with the demand for self-emptying and receptivity. Have you made your own personal response to this demand? If not, I urge you to do it today. If you are not willing to do this, then nothing else can follow – if you are willing, then everything else follows.

O God, you who wrap me around as the atmosphere wraps itself around my body, help me to respond to you as my physical body responds to its environment and lives. I receive you into my being – spirit, soul and body. Through Jesus Christ my Lord. Amen.

FOR FURTHER STUDY – Matt. 13:1–23; Acts 17:11; 1 Thess. 2:13

1. To what must we be receptive? / 2. What was said of the Bereans?

Flinging away your garment

FOR READING AND MEDITATION – MARK 10:46–52

'And throwing aside his garment, he rose and came to Jesus.' (v. 50: NKJ)

We are seeing that the first step to mental and spiritual health is receptivity – we must be willing to empty our hands of whatever we are holding and receive Christ.

Someone has defined life as response to environment. You and I live physically when we respond to our physical environment – we take in food, light and air. When response is shut off, we die physically. Our spiritual environment is the kingdom of God. When we respond to it, surrender to it, adjust ourselves to it, receive our very life from it – then we live happily and abundantly. Take a plant – how does it live? By being proud, self-sufficient, unrelated and unresponsive? No; it lives by surrendering, adjusting, receiving. Suppose a plant tried to live by asserting itself, by trying to 'lord' it over the other plants – what would be the result? It would lose its life, for it lives only as it responds to its environment. When it is properly adjusted, it takes in from the air, sun and soil and lives abundantly. Plant 'sin' is anything that hinders that receptivity and response.

The plain truth of what Christ is saying, then, in the words, 'Blessed (or happy) are the poor in spirit', is that we must choose to give up whatever we are holding and allow him to fill our lives with his forgiveness, love and power. A highly cultured and beautiful woman, after reviewing her life, said with a sigh, 'I have everything – and nothing.' Everything in the way of comforts and riches – yet empty in heart. To find happiness, we must find Christ. And how do we find him? We do what the blind man did in the passage today – fling away our 'garment' and run to Jesus.

Blessed Lord Jesus, where else can I run? If I run from you, I shall run away from life, from release, from forgiveness, from freedom and from eternal happiness. So I come, humbly, willingly – and receive. Amen.

FOR FURTHER STUDY – Matt. 19:16–29, 16:25; John 12:24

1. What was the young man's problem? / 2. What did Jesus teach must come before life?

As many as touched him ...

FOR READING AND MEDITATION – LUKE 8:40–56

'She came up behind him and touched the edge of his cloak ...' (v. 44: NIV)

We continue meditating on Christ's first prescription for happiness: 'Blessed are the poor in spirit, for theirs is the kingdom of heaven.' Over the past few days we have seen that the phrase 'poor in spirit' means, not material poverty, but spiritual poverty; a willingness to throw away our own self-sufficiency and open our hands to receive Christ.

The passage before us today shows how on one occasion as Jesus passed along the road, a multitude thronged around him. A woman in deep need came timidly through the crowd and touched his garment. 'Who touched me?' asked Jesus as he felt power go forth from him. The disciples replied: 'Master, the multitudes throng you, so why do you say, "Who touched me?"' 'Somebody touched me', said Jesus. He knew that there was a great difference between thronging him and touching him. Those who throng Jesus get little; those who touch Jesus get everything.

Sunday after Sunday, thousands of people go to church and listen; they throng Jesus but never touch him. Some go to church for a lifetime and never really touch him. If you are one of those people who constantly throng Jesus but never touch him, then I pray that over these few days in which we are meditating on the opening words of the Beatitudes, you will reach out and touch Christ in a definite and personal way. Touch him now – today – touch him for forgiveness, for cleansing, for power over temptation, over fears, over anxieties, over everything that stands in the way of your personal happiness. As Christ gave himself to those who needed him when he was here on earth, so he does today. Cease thronging him – touch him.

O Lord Jesus, as you pass by I move up from those who throng you to boldly touch you – and I do it now. By the touch of faith I receive into my being your forgiveness and your power. Thank you, dear Lord. It's done. Amen.

FOR FURTHER STUDY – Mark 10:1–16; Matt. 14:35–36, 8:3, 15, 9:29–30; Luke 6:19

1. What are some of the occasions when Jesus touched people? / 2. What was the result?

Come... today

FOR READING AND MEDITATION – LUKE 19:1–10

'For the Son of Man came to seek and to save what was lost.' (v. 10: NIV)

We spend one more day meditating on the first of the Beatitudes: 'Blessed are the poor in spirit, for theirs is the kingdom of heaven.' Dr Raymond Cramer, the minister and counsellor whom I mentioned earlier, says that in the psychology of Jesus, it is the one who has a problem that gets the Master's attention.

When our Lord was here on earth, everyone needed him, but only those who realised their need got his attention. It is often said that God rushes to the side of a person in need. That is not quite true. It would be more correct to say – God rushes to the side of the person who recognises and acknowledges their need. Those who recognise their need are to be congratulated, they are to be envied – they are candidates for the kingdom of heaven.

We could almost translate this first Beatitude in the following manner without doing any injustice to the original statement of Jesus: 'Congratulations to those who are humble and willing enough to recognise their need – for then they are candidates for the help of God.' Take it from me, there is no one in the kingdom of God who is not 'poor in spirit'. You cannot be filled until first you are empty. Salvation is not something earned, but something received. It is by grace we are saved, through faith, and that not of ourselves, it is the gift of God (Eph. 2:8). The old hymn puts it in a way that is powerful and effective:

Nothing in my hand I bring,
Simply to thy cross I cling . . .
Foul, I to the fountain fly,
Wash me, Saviour, or I die.

Father, thank you for helping me understand that to be 'poor in spirit' is recognising my utter helplessness in trying to save myself. I have nothing to give, but everything to receive. Humbly I bow my heart and receive you now. Amen.

FOR FURTHER STUDY – Phil. 3:1–9; Mark 10:28; Luke 5:27–28, 18:29–30

1. What was Paul's attitude? / 2. What did Jesus require of the first disciples?

Not just a code of ethics

FOR READING AND MEDITATION – GALATIANS 2:15–21
'I have been crucified with Christ and I no longer live,
but Christ lives in me …' (v. 20: NIV)

We turn now to consider the second of our Lord's Beatitudes: 'Blessed are those who mourn, for they will be comforted.' It is important to note that there is a very definite order in these sayings of Christ. Our Lord does not present them in an haphazard or accidental manner. Every one is carefully thought out and is given a precise and proper place in the spiritual sequence. Once we see that the entrance into the kingdom of God is through the acknowledgement of one's spiritual poverty and the acceptance of Christ's riches and resources, we are then ready to consider the next: 'Happy are those who know what sorrow means, for they will be given courage and comfort' (J. B. Phillips).

Before pondering the meaning of this Beatitude, we pause to make clear that the Beatitudes must not be viewed simply as a code of ethics, but as a description of character. Many people view these sayings of Jesus, as well as the rest of the Sermon on the Mount, as a set of regulations which they must follow in order to become a Christian – a kind of New Testament 'Ten Commandments'.

The simple truth is that to try to live out these principles in our own unaided strength would be about as possible as trying to move the Rock of Gibraltar with a pea-shooter. Dr Martyn Lloyd Jones says, 'We are not told, "Live like this and you will become a Christian", but rather, "Become a Christian and you will live like this." ' Advocates of the 'social gospel' – the belief that we become Christians by attempting to live out Christ's principles – are seriously in error. We must first know Christ as a Person before we can fully live out his principles.

Father, how tragic that, down the centuries, so many have got your truth the wrong way round – they try to follow your principles before first knowing you in person. Help me never to go wrong here – ever. Amen.

FOR FURTHER STUDY – Eph 3:1–19; John 14:20; Col. 1:27; 1 John 3:24
1. Of what does the indwelling Christ bring a full knowledge?
2. What is the 'hope of glory'?

The purpose of sorrow

FOR READING AND MEDITATION – 2 CORINTHIANS 1:1–11

'…the Father of our Lord Jesus Christ … who so wonderfully comforts and strengthens us in our hardships and trials …' (vv. 3–4: TLB)

We continue meditating on our Lord's second Beatitude: 'Blessed (or happy) are those who mourn, for they will be comforted.' The word 'mourn' has reference to more than just sorrowing over the death of a loved one – it includes all those experiences in life where we may feel crushed, broken or sorrowful. I feel the best translation of this verse is the one given by J. B. Phillips, which I quoted yesterday. Permit me to quote it once again: 'Happy are those who know what sorrow means, for they will be given courage and comfort.'

Why should people who are caught up in the throes of distressing and sorrowful experiences be congratulated? The conclusion of the verse gives the answer – 'for they shall be comforted'. And what then? Out of the comfort they receive, they are able to give comfort to others. Examine the text at the top of this page again, or read it as J.B. Phillips paraphrases it: 'For he gives us comfort in all our trials so that we in turn may be able to give the same sort of strong sympathy to others in their troubles'.

I have mentioned before that one of the things which often intrigues me in my work of training Christian counsellors is the fact that the best counsellors are those who have known the deepest hurts. Has the Lord allowed you to go through deep waters? Congratulations! You are a candidate for receiving divine comfort, which, in turn, will deepen your sensitivity to others and enrich your ministry in the Body of Christ. Don't, whatever you do, ask God to deliver you from painful or sorrowful experiences – they are worth much, much more than they cost.

Blessed Lord, help me to grasp this fact, not just with my mind, but with the whole of my spirit. I see that if I can learn this truth, my entire approach to problems can be transformed. In Jesus' name I pray. Amen.

FOR FURTHER STUDY – John 16:1–16, 14:26, 15:26; 1 Cor. 14:31; 1 Thess. 5:11–14

1. From where do we receive our comfort? / 2. What does the word 'comfort' mean to you?

It's not worth an argument

FOR READING AND MEDITATION – JAMES 1:1–12

'Dear brothers, is your life full of difficulties and temptations? Then be happy.' (v. 2: TLB)

We are meditating on the second of Christ's Beatitudes: 'Blessed are those who mourn, for they will be comforted.' We saw yesterday that the meaning of this statement is that when we are willing to experience sorrow and grief, then God is able to use these encounters to sensitise our spirits and make our ministry to others more effective and more fruitful.

I am afraid, however, that the majority of Christians greatly fear this truth. Honesty compels me to admit that at times I shrink from it myself. Some years ago, I wrote along this same line and a woman wrote to me thus, 'I am terribly afraid of what you said concerning grief and sorrow being the means in God's hands of deepening our sensitivity to others. I have not found this to be so. I find that grief and sorrow make me more concerned about myself than about others. Thus I cannot pray the prayer you suggested: "Lord, put all the pressure on me you want; I know that the pressure you permit is all part of your purpose – to make me the kind of person you want me to be." '

We must always be careful that we do not interpret Biblical truth by human experiences; we must interpret human experiences by Biblical truth. Scripture tells us that God permits pressure for a purpose, and that sorrow and grief will produce tremendous benefits in our lives – providing we let them. There's the rub! Whenever Biblical principles don't seem to work for us, then don't question the principle. Question whether or not you are open to it, and whether you are applying it in the way God directs. There is very little point in arguing with him – he's always right.

O Father, help me to see that whenever things are not working out the way your Word decrees, the problems are not on your side – but on mine. And help me to side for you and against myself in such issues – for you are always right. Amen.

FOR FURTHER STUDY – 1 Pet. 1:1–9; Job 23:10; Isa. 48:10; 2 Cor. 4:17

1. What was Job's testimony? / 2. What does our suffering bring about?

The dangers of denial

FOR READING AND MEDITATION – PSALM 51:1–12

'Surely you desire truth in the inner parts ...' (v. 6: NIV)

We are looking at the Beatitudes as containing the principles and attitudes that enable us to experience good mental and spiritual health. I cannot think of anything more psychologically in harmony with the best thinking of today's social scientists than the words of Jesus in the second Beatitude: 'Happy are those who mourn, for they shall be comforted'. We would not be taking any undue liberty with the text of Matthew 5:4 if we translated it thus: 'Congratulations to those who are willing to face and feel sorrow, for they will discover in and through the comfort that I impart to them a new ministry and a new joy.'

A mentally and spiritually healthy person is someone who is willing to face and feel sorrow, and recognise that it can be made to deepen one's life – not devastate it. You are familiar, I am sure, with the terms 'neurotic' and 'psychotic'. These are words used by the mental health experts of our day to describe certain attitudes and certain psychological conditions. A 'neurotic' is someone who is afraid to face reality, while a 'psychotic' is someone who is unaware of reality.

If we draw back from being willing to face and feel any emotion that rises up within us, then the denial of this feeling will have negative results within our personality. A woman once said to me, 'I have problems with the second Beatitude because I don't know how to mourn; I am too happy to mourn.' As we talked, it became clear to her that it wasn't so much that she didn't know how to mourn, but that she didn't want to mourn. She was afraid to face or feel any negative emotions – grief, sorrow, etc. – and thus, despite her claim to happiness and light-heartedness, she was a stunted soul.

Loving heavenly Father, how wonderfully you help me to put my finger on my need. Help me, I pray, to be willing to feel and face my emotions, and show me that when you are by my side I need be afraid of nothing – myself included. Amen.

FOR FURTHER STUDY – Psa. 139:14–24; 1 Chron. 28:9; Jer. 17:10

1. What was Daniel's prayer? / 2. Make that your prayer today.

Why pretend?

FOR READING AND MEDITATION – HEBREWS 4:12–16

'For we do not have a high priest who is unable to sympathise with our weaknesses …' (v. 15: NIV)

We ended yesterday with the case of the woman who said that she didn't know how to mourn, but her real problem was she didn't want to mourn. Whenever we are unwilling to face a negative emotion that reverberates within us, it implies that we are not in control of it, but that it is in control of us.

Christians are often taught to pretend that they feel joyful and happy when really they are miserable. Our text today, however, tells us that we have a great High Priest who can sympathise with us in our weaknesses. How pointless and purposeless it is to conceal our weaknesses from the Lord and deny ourselves the comfort of his uncritical and compassionate understanding. This is terribly important, for in my experience I would say that eight out of ten Christians have a completely wrong view of how to handle the hurts and sorrows that come into their lives.

The typical Christian reaction to negative emotions is either denial or expression. We dealt yesterday with the issue of denial – refusing to face them and feel them – so let's consider for a moment what we mean by the term 'expression'. The expression of emotions is the act of letting our emotions out. This is a popular approach with many of today's counsellors and therapists. They say when you feel upset, hurt or angry, then shout and scream or punch a pillow until you have released those pent-up emotions. There is no doubt that some relief can be gained in this way, but it is not a very Biblical or mature way of dealing with our negative feelings. The right way of handling negative feelings is neither to deny them or express them, but to acknowledge them. But more of that tomorrow.

O Father, I see that this whole issue of emotions is a minefield in which I must tread carefully and cautiously. Take my hand as I move through this area, and lead me to clear and Biblical conclusions. For Jesus' sake. Amen.

FOR FURTHER STUDY – Luke 10:25–36, 7:13; Matt. 9:36, 20:34; Mark 1:41
1. What was Jesus always demonstrating? / 2. How did he graphically illustrate this?

Moving toward maturity

FOR READING AND MEDITATION – PSALM 139:1–24

'Search me, O God, and know my heart; test me and know my anxious thoughts.' (v. 23: NIV)

We continue meditating on the right way to handle our negative feelings. We said yesterday that the two wrong ways to handle hurting emotions are to deny them or express them. Denial pushes them down inside us, where they reverberate and work to produce psychosomatic disorders, while expression clumps them on to other people or things. Neither of these, in my view, is a Biblical way of dealing with negative emotions. In fact, recent research by some psychologists shows that the uncontrolled expression of negative feelings can compound, rather than clear up, one's emotional difficulties.

In my judgment, the correct and Biblical way to handle negative emotions is to acknowledge them fully before God and share with him how we feel. Now understand clearly what I am saying, for at this point many have responded to this advice by coming to God when they are hurt or sorrowful and saying, 'Lord, please forgive me for feeling hurt.' That misses the point entirely. A Christian psychologist puts the issue most effectively when he says, 'We are not to pretend that we feel penitent when we feel hurt.'

When our stomachs are churning with grief, sorrow or hurt, we must come before the One who sees and knows everything, and pray a prayer something like this, 'Lord, right now I am hurting more than I think I can endure. I feel like screaming, running away or hitting somebody. I don't want to feel like this, dear Lord – but I do. Thank you for loving me as I am, not as I should be. Help me now to handle my feelings in a way that glorifies you and honours your name.' When we pray a prayer like that – and mean it – we are on the way to maturity.

O Father, help me not just to receive this concept into my mind and do nothing about it, but enable me to put it to work in my daily Christian living. I ask this for the honour and glory of your peerless and precious name. Amen.

FOR FURTHER STUDY – Psa. 51:1–19, 69:1–36, 46:1–11

1. How did David deal with his feelings?
2. Write a short psalm expressing your true feelings.

Wounded healers

FOR READING AND MEDITATION – ISAIAH 51:1–16
'"I, even I, am he who comforts you" ...' (v. 12: NIV)

We spend one last day meditating on Jesus' words in the second Beatitude: 'Blessed (or happy) are those who mourn, for they will be comforted.' Facing and being willing to feel negative feelings such as grief, sorrow, hurt and emotional pain may not be something that excites us, but it is essential if we are to know our Lord's purpose for our lives. When we are willing to go down into the hurt and feel it, then something glorious and transformative happens – we experience the loving comfort and compassion of our Lord. 'Blessed are those who mourn, for they shall be comforted.' Comforted? By whom? By the Triune God. He comes alongside us in our pain, and through the comfort he pours into our beings, enables us to become more sensitive to him, to ourselves, and to others.

After a lifetime of dealing with people and their problems, I have no hesitation in saying that the happiest people on earth are those who have been hurt but have had those hurts healed through the power of Christ's transforming love. They are what someone has called 'wounded healers'. Having been healed themselves, they go out to heal others. Going down into the pain of hurt feelings is not a very pleasant journey, but coming back from it with the comfort of God in your soul is an experience that is positively exhilarating and enriching. You return, not only with a new sensitivity in your soul, but with a new potential for ministering to others.

Remember this: great sorrow leads to great happiness – and without the sorrow, there can be no genuine happiness. This might sound to many like a contradiction in terms. It is not a contradiction, but a paradox – and a blessed one at that!

O Father, I take again this second prescription for happiness and ask that you will enable me to take the 'medicine', not just today, but every day of my life. Then I will be whole – truly whole. In Jesus' name I pray. Amen.

FOR FURTHER STUDY – 2 Cor. 1:1–7; Psa. 86:17; Isa. 12:1, 66:13
1. What has God promised? / 2. How are we to respond?

Subdued puppies?

FOR READING AND MEDITATION – PSALM 149:1–9

'For the Lord taketh pleasure in his people: he will beautify the meek with salvation.' (v. 4: AV)

We come now to Christ's third prescription for happiness: 'Blessed are the meek, for they will inherit the earth.' How we have shied away from that word 'meek'. We have thought of meekness as weakness and thus have a totally wrong concept of what Jesus meant. The *Amplified Bible* translates it thus: 'Blessed are the meek (the mild, patient, long-suffering), for they shall inherit the earth.'

The dictionary defines 'meek' as 'humble, compliant and submissive'. Does this mean that Jesus expects the children of the Kingdom to be like subdued puppies that crawl into their master's presence and cower at his feet? Or to become the type of people who lack inner fortitude and gumption, who can easily be pushed around and manipulated?

The truly meek person – in the Biblical sense of the word – is not timid, shy, hesitant and unassuming, but trusting, confident and secure. The root meaning of meekness is that of yieldedness or surrender – a characteristic without which no real progress can be made in the Christian life. What happens, for example, to the scientist who approaches the mysteries of the universe in a manner that is aggressive and belligerent? He discovers nothing. But what happens to the scientist who approaches the mysteries of the universe in a spirit of meekness? He finds its richest secrets unfolding themselves to him and he is able to harness mighty forces around him to advantage. The Christian who approaches life in the same spirit – the spirit of meekness and submission – discovers the true meaning of his existence and the purpose of God in all his affairs.

Gracious Father, help me to understand clearly the difference between meekness and weakness. And show me how to apply this principle in all I say and in all I do. This I ask in Christ's powerful and precious name. Amen.

FOR FURTHER STUDY – James 1:12–2; Zeph. 2:3; Gal. 5:22–23; 1 Pet. 3:4

1. What are we to receive with meekness?
2. Does the Biblical definition of meekness fit you?

Meekness – a spiritual quality

FOR READING AND MEDITATION – 1 CORINTHIANS 6:1–11

'And such were some of you. But you were washed, you were sanctified …' (v. 11: RSV)

We touched yesterday on the point that the universe will not respond to aggressive people who approach it in a demanding spirit. It is the meek – those who are yielded, submissive and compliant – who inherit the earth. Thomas Huxley is quoted as saying something which we commented on earlier, 'Science says to sit down before the facts like a little child, be prepared to give up every preconceived notion, be willing to be led to whatever end nature will lead you, or you will know nothing.'

Today we must focus our thinking on the fact that the quality of meekness described in the Beatitudes is not the result of natural temperament, but comes from knowing Christ and abiding in him. That goes, of course, for all the qualities enunciated in the Beatitudes – they are spiritual characteristics, not natural ones. This point needs elaborating, for there are many Christians who say, 'I am aggressive by nature, so it is not possible for me to be a meek and mild person. This is how nature has endowed me and I must be the person I am.'

Every Christian, whatever their natural temperament, is meant to be meek. It is not a matter of natural disposition; it is a quality produced by the Spirit of God. Think of the powerful and extraordinary nature of a man like David – and yet observe his meekness. Look at a man like Paul the apostle, a mastermind, a powerful and outstanding personality, yet consider his great humility and gentleness. How did these men get to be like this? Not because of a natural proneness toward meekness, but because they were indwelt by Christ and the Holy Spirit. It is not a matter of genes; it is a matter of grace.

My Father and my God, help me to face up to the fact that whatever I am by nature, I can be changed by the power of your grace. Show me how to absorb that grace so that I become more and more like you. For your own dear name's sake. Amen.

FOR FURTHER STUDY – Num. 12:1–13; Psa. 22:26, 147:6; Luke 6:29

1. What was Moses' great characteristic? / 2. How does meekness reveal itself in practice?

What meekness is not

FOR READING AND MEDITATION – 1 PETER 3:1–12

'…the unfading beauty of a gentle and quiet spirit, which is of great worth in God's sight.' (v. 4: NIV)

We are seeing that meekness is not a natural quality, but a spiritual one, and by reason of this all Christians should possess it. Over the past couple of days we have examined the importance of meekness and seen something of its nature; today, we examine what meekness is not.

Firstly, meekness does not mean indolence. There are people who appear to be spiritually meek, but really they are not so at all – they are indolent. And this is not what Jesus is talking about in the Beatitudes. Again, meekness does not mean an easy-going type of attitude – the attitude seen in those who just take life as it comes. That is not meekness; that is flabbiness. There are some Christians who have such a casual air about them that one can easily mistake this for the quality that Jesus is referring to in the Beatitudes. We must learn to differentiate, as we said yesterday, between that which is bestowed upon us by nature, and that which is bestowed upon us by grace.

Another thing that meekness ought not to be confused with is – niceness. There are people who are nice by nature. Dr Martyn Lloyd Jones says of such people, 'Natural niceness is something biological, the kind of thing you get in animals. One dog is nicer than another, one cat nicer than another.' Finally, meekness is not passivity, or a desire to obtain peace at any price. How often is the person regarded as meek who adopts the attitude that anything is better than a disagreement. This is the kind of passivity that does not make for good mental or spiritual health. The most greatly used men and women of God down the ages have been people who were meek without being weak – strong men and women, yet meek men and women. They were meek enough to absorb the resources of God.

O Father, I see that so much depends on my understanding of what meekness really is. I pray yet again for your continuing light to be shed around me as I pursue these thoughts day by day. I ask this in Jesus' name. Amen.

FOR FURTHER STUDY – 2 Tim. 4:1–16; Psa. 37:11, 149:4; Isa. 29:19

1. How did Paul display meekness? / 2. What does meekness increase?

The meek are the assured

FOR READING AND MEDITATION – COLOSSIANS 3:1–15
'Put on then, as God's chosen ones … meekness …' (v. 12: RSV)

It is time now to focus more precisely on what Jesus meant when he said: 'Blessed are the meek, for they will inherit the earth.' Meekness, as Jesus is using the word here, refers to an attitude of heart and mind that is entirely free from a spirit of demandingness and accepts the will of God in its entirety.

I think J.B. Phillips gets close to the meaning in Jesus' mind when he translates his statement thus: 'Happy are those who claim nothing, for the whole cart will belong to them.' I must stress once again that the thought here is not of passivity, but of active compliance and obedience to the will of God. If I might be permitted to embark upon a translation of my own, I would put it this way: 'Congratulations to those who do not feel a need to be over-assertive, for they shall inherit the earth.'

The meek are so sure of their resources and their goals that they can afford to be meek. Others have to become aggressive simply because they are unsure of themselves and their goals – hence the universe is closed to them. The meek could be called the assured, for they are meek enough to rest confidently in the resources of God. I realise, of course, that this is directly opposite to the world's view of things. The man of the world would say to this, 'What? Abounding happiness and universal possessions given to the meek? How ridiculous!' The world thinks in terms of strength, power, ability, self-confidence and self-assurance as the keys to success. The more you assert yourself and the more you affirm yourself, says the worldling, the more you will get. But such people do not inherit the earth; they just inherit dirt.

O Father, more and more as I hang upon your words, I realise that you have 'hid these things from the wise and prudent, and revealed them unto babes'. Unfold your truth in even more new and exciting ways to my heart. In Jesus' name. Amen.

FOR FURTHER STUDY – Isa. 53:1–7; Matt. 26:62–63, 27:14; Luke 23:9
1. How did Jesus display meekness? / 2. How do you display meekness?

All things serve

FOR READING AND MEDITATION – JAMES 3:1–18

'…By his good life let him show his works in the meekness of wisdom.' (v. 13: RSV)

We continue meditating on the meaning of the word 'meek' as used by Jesus in his third Beatitude. 'Meekness', said one commentator, 'is essentially a true view of oneself, expressing itself in attitude and conduct with respect to others.

If that is so, then it means it is two things: (1) our attitudes toward ourselves, and (2) our attitudes toward others. The meek person is so sure of himself that he does not need to demand anything for himself. He does not see his rights as something to be rigidly held on to, but follows the spirit of Jesus as outlined in Philippians 2:6–7: 'Who, although being essentially one with God … did not think this equality with God was a thing to be eagerly grasped or retained; but stripped himself of all privileges … and was born a human being' (*Amplified Bible*).

That is the place to which you and I must come if we are to understand and practise the principle of meekness. The Christian who is meek will not be over-sensitive about himself, or defensive; he realises that he has no rights at all and delights to leave everything in the hands of God. When he is called upon to suffer unjustly, he remembers the word of the Lord that says: 'Vengeance is mine; I will repay', and trusts God to work out the situation in his own time and in his own way. He leaves himself and any cause in which he is involved in God's hands, believing that as he adopts a quiet mind and a meek spirit, the outcome will be the one that God appoints. The poet Browning puts the same truth in these words, 'He who keeps one end in view makes all things serve.' When that one end is the purpose of God, then indeed – all things serve.

O Father, instil into me such a spirit of meekness that irritation, distrust, suspicion and unbelief may become decaying forces within me. Help me to see that only meekness must survive. And not just survive – but thrive. For Jesus' sake. Amen.

FOR FURTHER STUDY – Pet. 2:18–25; Matt. 11:29, 26:52

1. What was Peter's Exhortation? / 2. Why was Jesus able to display meekness?

What an example!

FOR READING AND MEDITATION – MATTHEW 11:28–30

'Take my yoke upon you . . . for I am gentle and lowly in heart, and you will find rest for your souls.' (v. 29: RSV)

Today we ask ourselves: what is there about this famous saying of Jesus that engenders good mental health? Mental health, after all, is more than a medical term. It is a concept that goes beyond the walls of a hospital or a doctor's clinic and applies also to the home, the church and the world of everyday living.

Mental health is concerned with the dynamics of relationship and adjustment – the way we handle such things as anxiety, hostility and frustration. 'Mental health', says one authority, 'concerns itself with the everyday troubles of everyday people – helping them to solve their problems or face them bravely when they cannot be warded off.' The statement of Jesus we are focusing on at the moment contributes to good mental health because it encourages us to be free from the attitude of demandingness – the attitude that says, 'Things must go my way', 'I ought to have some consideration', 'People should respect my rights.'

One psychologist goes as far as to say that if we could eliminate the *shoulds* and the *woulds* from our vocabulary and our inner attitudes, we could become transformed people overnight. He was not referring, of course, to the moral compass which God has placed within us that cries out for obedience to that which is right, for example, 'I ought not to lie', 'I should always do right', but to the attitude of demandingness that insists on having one's rights irrespective of any other considerations. One of the biggest causes of mental and emotional illness is the attitude of demandingness and over-concern. Do we wonder any longer why Christ congratulates the meek and promises them the earth?

Blessed Lord Jesus, deliver me, I pray, from a spirit of demandingness that insists on having my rights rather than being willing to give them up for the sake of others. Help me to take your yoke upon me and learn of you. Amen.

FOR FURTHER STUDY – 2 Cor. Ch. 10, 11:18–21; Phil. 4:11–12

1. Why could Paul be bold?
2. How did Paul highlight the difference between weakness and meekness?

Sand in the machinery

FOR READING AND MEDITATION – COLOSSIANS 1:15–27

'…for in him all things were created, in heaven and on earth … all things were created through him and for him.' (v. 16: RSV)

We spend one more day meditating on the text: 'Blessed are the meek, for they will inherit the earth.' Today we ask ourselves: what did Jesus mean by the phrase, 'for they will inherit the earth'? It means, so I believe, that when we develop the attitude of meekness, the whole universe is behind us and throws itself on our side. If, for example, we decide to manifest attitudes of anger and hostility rather than cultivating a meek and quiet spirit, then the anger and hostility becomes, as someone put it, 'sand in the machinery of life'.

The universe has been made in a Christ-like fashion and is not designed to support such things as hatred, hostility or lies. Our text for today shows that when God made the world, he made it to work in a certain way, and that way is the way of Christ: 'All things were created through him (Christ) and for him.' Edison, the scientist, tried eleven hundred experiments, all of which turned out to be failures. Someone said to him, 'You must feel that you have wasted your time.' 'Oh, no', said Edison, 'I simply found out eleven hundred ways how not to do things.'

This is what is happening in the world right now – humanity is finding out how to live. We are discovering that there are some things that the universe will not approve and some things it will approve. The meek are those who have come to terms with reality and know that they cannot twist it to their own ends or make it approve of what cannot be approved. Whoever has the first word in this universe must always remember that the universe has the last word. The Christian who adopts the attitudes of his Master finds the universe backing him in everything he does.

Father, thank you for reminding me that life only works in one way – your way. When I live life as you designed it, then the whole universe works with me. I inherit all things – all that is yours is mine. Blessed be your name forever. Amen.

FOR FURTHER STUDY – Phil. 2:1–11; John 1:3; 1 Cor. 8:6; Heb. 1:1–2

1. How did Jesus demonstrate meekness? / 2. How does this apply to you?

What's your goal?

FOR READING AND MEDITATION – MATTHEW 6:19–34

'But seek first his kingdom and his righteousness, and all these things will be given to you as well.' (v. 33: NIV)

We turn now to the next of our Lord's Beatitudes: 'Blessed are those who hunger and thirst for righteousness, for they will be filled.' One of the axioms of life is this – everyone thirsts after something. Some thirst for success, some thirst for fame, some thirst for stable relationships, and some thirst for financial security. But there is a thirst that is common to every human heart – the thirst for happiness. Notice, however, that Jesus does not say: 'Happy are those who thirst for happiness', but 'Happy are those who thirst for righteousness.'

Happiness, therefore, is a by-product – to get it, you must focus on something else. We touched on this thought at the beginning of our meditations, but now we must give it some further attention. Dr W. E.Sangster, the famous Methodist preacher, when dealing with this point in one of his sermons, put it like this, 'Do you enjoy a game of golf or tennis? Then your pleasure is strictly proportioned to the degree to which you lose yourself in the game. While it lasts, it must absorb you: your whole mind should be on the game. If you stop in the midst of it and ask yourself precisely what degree of pleasure you are deriving from this particular stroke, the pleasure will evaporate and you will begin to feel rather foolish in following a wee white ball over a mile or two of turf.'

To experience happiness, one must forget it and focus on something other than its pursuit. Those who reach out for happiness are forever unsatisfied – the more they strive, the less they find. Happiness, I say again, is a by-product; it is not something you find, but something that finds you.

My Father and my God, I see so clearly that if my goal is wrong, then all of life turns out wrong. Help me to make my goal, not the pursuit of happiness, but the pursuit of righteousness. In Jesus' name I pray. Amen.

FOR FURTHER STUDY – John 4:1–14, 6:35; Psa. 36:8; Isa. 55:1

1. What did Jesus promise? / 2. What do you thirst for?

An important key to living

FOR READING AND MEDITATION – COLOSSIANS 1:1–14
'And we pray this in order that you may live a life worthy of the Lord and may please him in every way…' (v. 10: NIV)

We saw yesterday that when we make it a goal to hunger and thirst after happiness, we get nowhere, but when we make it our goal to hunger and thirst after righteousness, we get everywhere.

Once again Jesus touches on an aspect of good mental health when he teaches us through these words to focus on right goals. Those who study human behaviour tell us that everything we do has a goal. 'We are not conditioned animals that act automatically and unthinkingly in programmed response', says a psychologist, '… neither are we the hapless victims of internal forces that drive us relentlessly in unwanted directions.' Everything we do has a goal. It may sometimes feel as if we do things we don't want to do, but the truth is that everything we do represents an effort to reach a goal that somehow, albeit at an unconscious level, makes sense. In fact, one of the ways in which you can better understand why you do the things you do is to ask yourself, 'What's my goal?'

A woman I once counselled and who was extremely frustrated because her husband would not change to meet her requirements said to me, 'My husband is so stubborn and obstinate that I just can't see any future for us together.' I shared with her the concept that everything we do represents a goal, and asked her to put into words what she thought her goal might be in her marriage. Without a moment's hesitation she replied, 'To change my husband.' Her daily prayer was, 'Lord, you love my husband and I'll change him.' I suggested she altered her goal to, 'Lord, you change my husband and I'll love him.' She did, and instantly found a new freedom – and a new happiness in her marriage.

O Father, I see what I need – I need to bring my goals in line with your goals. Unfold more of this important truth to me as I pursue it over the next few days. In Jesus' name I ask it. Amen.

FOR FURTHER STUDY – Eph. 5:1–16; Rom. 6:4; 2 Cor. 5:7; Gal. 5:16
1. How are we to live? / 2. What does 'circumspectly' mean?

Why we get angry

FOR READING AND MEDITATION – 1 CORINTHIANS 9:15–27

'... Run in such a way as to get the prize.' (v. 24: NIV)

We continue meditating on the idea that everything we do represents a goal. In fact, most of the frustration we experience in life comes from wrong goals and blocks to those goals. Let me illustrate. Cast your mind back to the last time you were angry. If you can find your goal and what blocked your goal, then you have the clue to what produced your anger and frustration.

A man asked me recently if I could explain what it was that caused his deep-seated anger. I listened to him for a while and soon it became apparent – his anger was due to a blocked goal. His goal in life was to make money. The conviction he held in his mind was this: 'If can make plenty of money, then everyone will see I am a successful and important person.' Believing that, he pursued the goal of making as much money as he could (our goals and behaviour are usually the result of our beliefs), and when he encountered blocks to his goal, such as his wife's insistence that he cut down on the amount of time he was spending in his business, he would erupt in anger.

I pointed out to him that the way to deal with the anger was to establish a goal that no one could block. And what was that? To please the Lord. He resisted that idea at first, but when he came to realise that his goal in life was unbiblical and that his anger resulted from others blocking his unbiblical goal, he surrendered his whole being to God in a new commitment and found a happiness and a release he never thought possible. From then on his goal was not to make money, but to please the Lord. I hasten to point out that there is nothing wrong with wanting to make money – it is a legitimate human desire – but it must remain a desire and never become a goal.

O God my gracious Father, help me never to turn what can be a legitimate human desire into a life goal. Save me from pursuing unbiblical objectives, and guide me towards the truth that alone can make me free. In Jesus' name. Amen.

FOR FURTHER STUDY – James 1:9–20; Psa. 37:8; Prov. 14:17, 16:32

1. Who will 'take the city'? / 2. What does a foolish man do?

Desires versus goals

FOR READING AND MEDITATION – HEBREWS 12:1-13

'... who for the joy that was set before him endured the cross, despising the shame ...' (v. 2: RSV)

We ended yesterday by saying that some things in life, such as the desire to have money, can be legitimate concerns but they must be looked upon as desires and never become goals.

Permit me to differentiate between the two. A goal is a purpose to which a person is unalterably committed and something for which he or she assumes unconditional responsibility. A desire is something wanted and which cannot be obtained without the co-operation of another human being. A desire must never become the motivating purpose behind our behaviour, for if it does, then it becomes a goal – and a goal that is likely to be blocked, causing negative emotions to arise and erupt within our being. Remember the man we talked about yesterday? His goal, we said, was to make money. Once he changed his goal to pleasing the Lord and then saw his concern to make money as merely a desire, he found instant release.

Keep in mind that what causes emotional problems to arise within us is invariably a blocked goal. Take another illustration that might help to mark the difference between goals and desires more clearly. Have you ever found yourself talking to other Christians who seem to have difficulty in applying to their lives what seems to you a simple Biblical principle? You point out the need to do as God says, but your friends fail to see the truth that to you is as clear as daylight. If you get frustrated at that point, the chances are that you are allowing a desire to become a goal. To want your friends to listen is a legitimate desire, but to get frustrated over it means you are determined to make them listen – and that becomes a goal.

Gracious Father, I come to you again to help me sort out this important issue of desires versus goals. I see that if I can resolve this problem, then a new chapter in my life is about to be written. Help me, dear Lord. In Jesus' name. Amen.

FOR FURTHER STUDY – Psa. 37:1–11, 21:2, 73:25; Prov. 10:24

1. What was the psalmist's desire? / 2. What happens when we delight ourselves in the Lord?

Happiness a by-product

FOR READING AND MEDITATION – PSALM 16:1–11

'... in your presence is fullness of joy, at your right hand there are pleasures for evermore.' (v. 11: *Amplified Bible*)

Having seen over the past few days the importance of differentiating between goals and desires, we return now to the thought that we can experience happiness only as a by-product. If we make the obtaining of happiness a goal, it eludes us like a will-o'-the-wisp but if we give up the chase and hold it only a desire, then it comes home and takes up residence in our hearts.

Let me repeat: there is nothing wrong in wanting to be happy; it is a natural and valid desire – but the paradoxical truth is that I will never be happy if I am primarily concerned with becoming happy. My overriding goal in every circumstance and situation must be to respond biblically, to put the Lord and his righteousness first and seek to behave as he would want me to. The wonderful truth is that as we devote our energies to the task of becoming what Christ wants us to be – righteous – he responds by filling us with unutterable happiness and joy. I must, therefore, firmly and consciously by an act of the will, refuse to make the obtaining of happiness my goal, and instead adopt the goal of becoming more like the Lord.

An obsessive preoccupation with happiness will obscure our understanding of the biblical route to eternal peace and joy. And what is that route? Our text for today tells us: 'At your right hand there are pleasures for evermore.' It follows that if we are to experience those pleasures, then we must learn what it means to be at God's right hand. Paul tells us that Christ has been exalted to God's right hand (Eph. 1:20). Can anything be clearer? The more we abide in Christ, the more we shall experience true happiness.

O God, forgive us that we have made the pursuit of happiness our goal, and the pursuit of righteousness merely a desire. Help us to get our values straightened out, and to set our goal on becoming more and more like you. In Jesus' name. Amen.

FOR FURTHER STUDY – Psa. 139.1–12, 140:13; Ex. 33:14; Isa. 43:2

1. What did the psalmist feel about God's presence?
2. How much time are you spending in his presence?

At God's right hand

FOR READING AND MEDITATION – HEBREWS 6:1–12

'Therefore let us … go on to maturity … ' (v. 1: NIV)

Quietly we are coming to see the stupendous truth that it is only as we learn to dwell at God's right hand in fellowship with Christ that we can experience true happiness and joy. Despite the clear teaching of Jesus that happiness is a by-product of righteousness (becoming more and more like Christ), there are still multiplied thousands of Christians paying no more than lip service to this truth. Happiness is their goal, righteousness merely their desire.

I am speaking generally when I make this next point, but sit down with any Christian who does not experience true happiness and you will find, deep within that person's heart, that they have never come to a clear understanding of this important principle uttered by Jesus in his Sermon on the Mount: 'Blessed are those who hunger and thirst for righteousness, for they will be filled.' The same condition can be noted in nine out of ten people who seek help through Christian counselling. Ask them what they want to experience as they go through counselling, and they say, 'I want to feel good', or 'I want to feel happy'.

I imply no criticism or condemnation of these people, for I know that the same tendency exists in my own heart. Whenever I am struggling or hurting over some issue, my immediate desire is to get rid of the negative feelings and recover my lost happiness. But to try to find happiness is like trying to fall asleep. As long as you consciously and zealously try to grasp it, it never comes. There is only one way: it is to do whatever you have to do in the situation to glorify Christ. Then happiness inevitably bubbles upward – as it must.

Father, I am so grateful that, as my Lover and my Redeemer, you corner my soul. Don't let me wriggle and apologise and slip past your redemptions. Help me to take my medicine, however bitter to the taste of self it may be. In Jesus' name. Amen.

FOR FURTHER STUDY – Phil. 3:1–11; 2 Cor. 13:11; Eph. 4:13, 1:28

1. What was Paul's desire? / 2. What was Paul's goal?

Spiritual/psychological problems

FOR READING AND MEDITATION – PHILIPPIANS 3:7–21

'... that I may know him and the power of his resurrection ...' (v. 10. RSV)

Today we ask ourselves: what happens to those who hunger and thirst after righteousness? The answer is clear: they will be filled. Make righteousness your goal and you will be eternally satisfied. This fourth Beatitude carries us a step further in our understanding of Jesus' formulae for good spiritual and mental health. If, once again, I might venture upon a paraphrase of my own, I would put it like this: 'Congratulations to those who ardently crave and desire to become more and more like me and to know my righteousness, for they shall find a satisfaction that will never vanish or be destroyed.'

May I be permitted to ask you this personal question: what are you most hungering and thirsting for? Is it health? Is it relief from pain? Is it freedom from anxiety? Is it financial security? All of these are legitimate cravings, but if your primary hunger and thirst is not to become more and more like Christ, then you will experience an inner emptiness that nothing can fill.

Let me point out one more thing – something that might astonish you: to the extent that your deepest hunger and thirst are not toward God, to that extent will you experience spiritual and psychological problems. If you are not hungering and thirsting after him, you will hunger and thirst after something else. When we make it our goal to glorify God, then we will enjoy him. We must not make it our goal to enjoy him in order to glorify him. Remember the goal of happiness is elusive, regardless of how well thought-out is our strategy. But the by-product of happiness is freely available to those whose goal is to know God and be found in him.

O my Father and my God, you are teaching me your ways – written in your Word and also in me. My flesh, my nerves, my very being cry out that your way is the right way. Help me to surrender to your purposes so that I might be the vehicle of victory. Amen.

FOR FURTHER STUDY – Isa. 26:1–9; Psa. 38:9, 73:25; 1 Pet. 22–3

1. What was the psalmist's confession? / 2. What did Isaiah's desire cause him to do?

The meaning of mercy

FOR READING AND MEDITATION – PSALM 85:1–13
'Mercy and truth are met together ...' (v. 10: AV)

We continue our study of the Beatitudes – the study of 'the happy ones'. Today we come to the fifth of Christ's famous sayings: 'Blessed are the merciful, for they will own mercy.' The true disciple of Jesus, according to our Lord, manifests not just the characteristics we have previously considered, but he is merciful also.

What does our Lord mean when he uses the word 'merciful'? The thought underlying the word is that of compassion and concern for the plight of others. The original word used in this fifth Beatitude is also used to describe the High Priestly ministry of Christ in Hebrews 2:17. One authority, W.E. Vine, says that a merciful person is 'not simply possessed of pity but is actively compassionate'.

It is important to stress once again that the characteristic of being merciful of which our Lord spoke here, is not something that arises from our natural temperament, but something that is endowed on us when we abide in Christ. As Dr Martyn Lloyd Jones says, 'This is not a gospel for certain temperaments – nobody has an advantage over anybody else when they are face to face with God.' Again, mercy is not the turning of a blind eye to moral violations – the attitude that pretends not to see things. This can be seen most forcefully when we consider that the term 'merciful' is an adjective which is applied especially and specifically to God himself. This means that however the word applies to God, it applies equally to man. God is merciful, but he is also truth: 'Mercy and truth are met together.' If we think of mercy at the expense of truth and law, then it is not true mercy; it is merely a caricature.

O God, help me, I pray, to have within me the right blend of mercy and truth. Save me from becoming a lopsided Christian, someone who manifests one characteristic at the expense of another. In Jesus' name I pray. Amen.

FOR FURTHER STUDY – Titus 3:1–7; Psa. 103:17, 108:4; Lam. 3:22
1. What is the quality of God's mercy? / 2. How merciful are you?

Grace and mercy

FOR READING AND MEDITATION – LUKE 10:25–37

'…and when he saw him, he had compassion, and went to him…' (vv. 33–34: RSV)

We continue focusing our thoughts on what it means to be merciful. One of the best ways to understand the word is to compare it with grace. Have you ever noticed, when reading Paul's epistles, that in the introduction to every one of his epistles, from Romans through to 2 Thessalonians, he uses the words: 'Grace and peace to you from God our Father and the Lord Jesus Christ.' The phrase usually appears in the second or third verse of every one of his epistles. However, when he comes to what are described as the pastoral epistles (1 and 2 Timothy and Titus), he changes the phrase to read: 'Grace, mercy and peace from God the Father and Christ Jesus our Lord.'

When Paul inserted the word 'mercy' after the word 'grace', he implied an interesting distinction. Someone has defined the two words thus: 'Grace is especially associated with men in their sins; mercy is especially associated with men in their misery.' While grace looks down upon sin and seeks to save, mercy looks especially upon the miserable consequences of sin and seeks to relieve. This helps us to see mercy in a wider dimension. Mercy is compassion plus action.

A Christian who is merciful feels such compassion and concern that he is not content until he does something about the plight of the one with whom he comes in contact. The story of the Good Samaritan is a classic illustration of being merciful. Others saw the man but did nothing to help him in his plight. The Samaritan, however, crossed the road, dressed the man's wounds, took him to an inn and made provision for his comfort. I say again: mercy is compassion plus action.

Merciful and loving heavenly Father – make me in your own image. One thing is sure – I cannot be a merciful person without your help. So come and think in me, love in me and live in me. For your own dear name's sake. Amen.

FOR FURTHER STUDY – John 8:1–11; Prov. 3:3, 11:17; Micah 6:8

1. What does the Lord require?
2. How did Jesus show mercy without compromising truth?

A most misunderstood Beatitude

FOR READING AND MEDITATION – LUKE 6:27–40
'Give, and it will be given to you ...' (v. 38: NIV)

Someone has pointed out that the fifth Beatitude – 'Blessed are the merciful, for they will be shown mercy' – is unique and quite different from the ones that precede it. In the first four, there is a contrast between the need and the fulfilment. The 'poor in spirit' receive the kingdom; those 'who mourn' are comforted; 'the meek' inherit the earth; those who 'hunger and thirst' are satisfied; but in the fifth Beatitude, the theme changes – 'the merciful will be shown mercy'. It is as though we cannot receive mercy without first giving it.

We must move carefully here, for no Beatitude has been more misunderstood than this one. There are those who take these words to mean that we can only be forgiven by God to the extent that we forgive others. They bring alongside this Beatitude such passages as: 'Forgive us our sins, for we also forgive everyone who sins against us' (Luke 11:4, NIV), and 'This is how my heavenly Father will treat each of unless you forgive your brother from your heart' (Matt. 18:35, NIV).

Putting all these Scriptures together, they claim that it is the clear meaning of the Bible that we are forgiven by God only to the extent that we forgive others. If this is so, then salvation is by works and not by grace. We must never interpret Scripture in a way that contradicts other Scriptures. What our Lord means in this fifth Beatitude is that when we demonstrate mercy to others, we make it possible for God's mercy to penetrate deeper into our own lives and personalities. The act of giving makes us more able to receive.

O Father, help me not to stumble over this truth. Show me even more clearly that although my forgiveness of others is not a condition of salvation, it must be a consequence of it. In Jesus' name I pray. Amen.

FOR FURTHER STUDY – 2 Cor. 9:1–6; Prov. 11:25, 22:9; Matt. 10:8
1. What is the law of sowing and reaping? / 2. What was Jesus' instruction to the disciples?

Forgiven!

FOR READING AND MEDITATION – EPHESIANS 4:17–32
'...forgiving one another, as God in Christ forgave you.' (v. 32: RSV)

We must spend another day considering whether or not it is a condition of our salvation that we first forgive those who have sinned against us. We said yesterday that to believe this contradicts the teaching which is to be found everywhere in Scripture, that we are saved by grace, through faith. What, then, is Scripture getting at when it seems to encourage us to forgive in order that we might be forgiven? I think it refers to the matter of realised forgiveness.

I know many Christians, as I am sure you do, who, although they have been forgiven by God, are never really sure of it. And one of the major reasons for this is that they have never taken the steps to get rid of the bitterness and resentment they hold in their hearts toward others. The problem they experience in not feeling forgiven is not God's fault, but their own. He has forgiven them on the basis of their own personal repentance, but his forgiveness is unable to reach the centre of their spirit and dissolve their feelings of guilt because they harbour an unforgiving attitude toward others.

C.S. Lewis says something similar in relation to praise. He explains that we do not really receive something until we give thanks for it. The very action of saying 'thank you', and meaning it, opens up the spirit to a true sense of appreciation. In giving thanks, something moves inside the centre of our spirits and allows the wonder of what has been done for us to invade us to the depths of our being. It is the same with mercy and for forgiveness. When we adopt these attitudes toward others, we not only express mercy and forgiveness – we experience it.

O Father, I see that you have fashioned me in my inner being for mercy and forgiveness, and when I demonstrate it, I allow it to invade me to my deepest depths. I am so grateful. Amen.

FOR FURTHER STUDY – Luke 17:1–4, 23:34; Mark 11:25; Col. 3:13
1. How often should we forgive? / 2. How did Jesus set us an example?

Some things bitter to digest

FOR READING AND MEDITATION – ISAIAH 3:1–11

'... Woe to them! For they have brought evil upon themselves.' (v. 9: RSV)

We pause now to ask ourselves how this fifth Beatitude, when practised, engenders within us good mental and spiritual health. Psychologists have shown that those who lack the qualities of mercy and compassion in their disposition are more likely to develop physical problems than any other group of people. Harsh, judgmental attitudes may bring a sense of satisfaction to the person who does not know the meaning of mercy, but it is a false sense of satisfaction.

A verse that, strictly speaking, does not really apply to what I am saying here, but nevertheless has some application, is this: 'It did taste sweet, like honey, but when I had eaten, it was bitter to digest' (Rev. 10:10, Moffatt). That is what happens whenever we adopt any attitude that is not in harmony with Jesus Christ. At first it does 'taste sweet, like honey' – its beginnings are apparently sweet, but it is 'bitter to digest' – it cannot be assimilated. Our human constitution is not made to function effectively on any attitude that is foreign to the spirit of Jesus Christ.

A Christian doctor says, 'We are allergic to wrong attitudes just as some people are allergic to shrimps.' I am physically allergic to red and green peppers. I have tried them scores of times, but it always has the same result – I get sick. I am just as allergic to harsh, judgmental attitudes. I can't assimilate them. They disrupt me – body, soul and spirit. And what goes for me goes also for you. When we fail to practise the principles that our Lord outlined for us in the Beatitudes, then our sense of well-being is lowered, depleted and poisoned. Goodness is good for us – spiritually, mentally and physically.

Father, something is being burned into my consciousness: there is only one healthy way to live – your Way. When I break with you, I break with life. Help me to maintain a close connection with you in everything I do and everything I say. In Jesus' name. Amen.

FOR FURTHER STUDY – Psa. 23: 1–6, 31:9; Ex. 34:6; Gal. 5:22; Eph. 5:9

1. Of what is goodness a characteristic?
2. Can you make the same declaration as the psalmist?

Getting back what you give

FOR READING AND MEDITATION – PROVERBS 11:16–31

'He who seeks good finds goodwill, but evil comes to him who searches for it.' (v. 27: NIV)

Those who know how to be merciful are men and women to be envied. They get back what they give. Psychologists are always pointing out that our attitudes and emotions are contagious. Scripture puts the same truth in these words: 'A man that hath friends must show himself friendly' (Proverbs 18:24, AV). And what's more, a merciful attitude can encourage others to themselves be merciful. People who are merciful are not so apt to arouse harsh feelings or awaken enmities – they receive what they give.

Within the act of mercy is the power to effect change. When you demonstrate mercy toward someone, it calls forth the same feeling tones from the other person and there will be an exchange that will reinforce the importance of the quality of mercy in your own spirit. So you do not lose anything, for they, in turn, give you something of themselves that can enrich your life and become your own inner possession.

It does not always happen, of course, that the demonstration of mercy evokes a positive response in others, but whether it does or not, you are all the better for being merciful. The pay-off is in you.

Have you noticed how people with this quality always seem to have good personal relationships? And when he or she has need of mercy from others, then it is instantly forthcoming – for as we give, so shall we receive. And not only do they enjoy good personal relationships – they enjoy (other things being equal) good physical health. The right thing morally is always the healthy thing physically. For morality is one – whether it is written in our tissues, or whether it is written in the Testaments.

Gracious Father, I am finding your way amid my own ways. Daily, hourly, it is being disclosed before my astonished gaze. Help me to follow your way, your attitudes, and your lifestyle, for all other ways defeat me. Yours develops me. Amen.

FOR FURTHER STUDY – Matt. 18:23–35, 6:15; Rom. 1:31; James 2:13

1. What was Jesus teaching in this parable? / 2. How is this sometimes a picture of us?

Through Christian eyes

FOR READING AND MEDITATION – PHILIPPIANS 2:1–13

'Each of you should look not only to your own interests, but also to the interests of others.' (v. 4: NIV)

On this, the last day of a week in which we have been studying the phrase: 'Blessed are the merciful, for they will be shown mercy', we ask ourselves what would happen if we really put this important attitude into practice? It would mean that we would look through Christian eyes. We would see sinners, not merely as the dupes and victims of sin and Satan, but as men and women who are to be pitied. We would see a fellow Christian who falls by the way, not as someone to be clobbered, but as someone to be lifted.

Far too many of us in the Christian Church walk about with judgmental attitudes, and whenever anyone slips up, we either bang him over the head with a Bible text or wither her with a look of scorn. We have the philosophy of an eye for an eye and a tooth for a tooth. Failure is met with derision and wrong is met with contempt. I have no hesitation in saying that such attitudes ought not to be found among the people of God. Wherever they are present, they will eat like acid into the soul. Being merciful means letting Christ have control of our lives, so that his gentleness overcomes our vindictiveness, his kindness our unkindness and his bigness our littleness.

Are you a merciful person? Do you look upon those who have fallen with concern and compassion – or is your attitude one of contempt, derision and scorn? Can you feel pity for those who have been duped by the world, the flesh and the devil? If so – congratulations! You have passed the test showing mercy, and are on your way to experiencing spiritual health and happiness. Blessed indeed those who are merciful – for they shall obtain mercy.

O my Father, with all my heart I cry out – help me to be a merciful person. Touch my whole being today by your blessed Holy Spirit so that I might be changed into your image. In Jesus' name I pray. Amen.

FOR FURTHER STUDY – Luke 18:1–14; 2 Cor. 8:1–9; Heb. 2:17–18

1. How did Jesus show mercy? / 2. How do you show mercy?

Spiritual heart surgery

FOR READING AND MEDITATION – MATTHEW 15:1–20

'But the things that come out of the mouth come from the heart, and these make a man "unclean".' (v. 18: NIV)

We continue examining the positive attitudes which make for good mental and spiritual health, and today we come to the one which is considered by many commentators to be the most sublime of them all: 'Blessed are the pure in heart, for they will see God.'

We begin by asking ourselves: what is meant by the term *heart*? According to the general use of the word in Scripture, it has reference to what goes on in the core of our being. It means more than just the seat of the affections and emotions; it is the fount from which everything proceeds. In the passage before us today, our Lord puts it thus: 'Out of the heart come evil thoughts, murder, adultery, sexual immorality…' and so on. Dr Oswald Chambers says, 'If a sinner really wishes to understand his heart, then let him listen to his own mouth in an unguarded frame for five minutes.'

Someone has pointed out that the gospel of Jesus Christ is a religion of new things. It offers to men a new birth, a new life, a new hope, a new happiness – and, at the end of time, a new name. However, out of all these fascinating new things which Christ offers his children, none is perhaps more intriguing than his offer of a new heart. The promise is first given in the prophecy of Ezekiel: 'A new heart I will give you, and a new spirit I will put within you' (36:26, RSV). Quite clearly, when it comes to spiritual things, the heart of the matter is the matter of the heart. Christ's offer of changing our hearts is, without doubt, one of the greatest promises of the Bible. Be encouraged – our Lord is not content with tinkering about on the surface of our lives – his goal is to purify our hearts.

My Father and my God, slowly but surely I am coming under the sway of your 'beautiful attitudes'. But I see you have more for me to discover. Hold me close as I go through these next few days of spiritual heart surgery. In Jesus' name I pray. Amen.

FOR FURTHER STUDY – Psa. 51:1–10, 19:12–13, 79:9

1. What was the psalmist's prayer? / 2. Make it your prayer today.

Purity – not a popular thought

FOR READING AND MEDITATION – ACTS 15:1–11

'…purifying their hearts by faith.' (v. 9: AV)

Now that we understand what Scripture means by *heart* – the central and inner core of our being – we ask ourselves another question: what does our Lord mean when he uses the word 'pure'? 'Blessed are the pure in heart, for they will see God.'

The term *pure* (Greek: *katharos*) means a heart that is clean or clear. Unfortunately, purity is not a popular word in contemporary Christianity. The emphasis nowadays is more on power than purity. Most Christians I talk to want to *know* how they can possess and develop spiritual gifts. Few, generally speaking, want to know how to experience the blessing of what our text today calls a heart purified by faith. Someone has said of modern-day Christians that they 'long to be good the easy way'. The attitude of many toward the subject of purity can be summed up in the couplet:

Won't somebody give me some good advice
On how to be naughty – and still be nice.

Nearly 1 600 years ago, St Augustine expressed the same thought in words that may contain the thoughts of many – thankfully, not all – in today's Church, 'Lord, make me pure … but not just yet.' Most of us would be willing to identify ourselves with the conditions in the first five of our Lord's Beatitudes, but how do we feel about the condition of being pure in heart? Are we ready and willing to pray:

I want, dear Lord, a heart that's true and clean
A sunlit heart, with not a cloud between.
A heart like thine, a heart divine.
A heart as white as snow.
On me, dear Lord, a heart like this bestow.

O yes, dear Father, from the depths of my being I cry – make me clean. I have come so far with you – how can I turn back now? I'm a candidate for both power and purity. Give me the deep inner cleansing I need – today. For Jesus' sake. Amen.

FOR FURTHER STUDY – John 13:1–17; 2 Cor. 7:1; James 4:8; 1 John 3:3

1. What was Peter's request? / 2. Make it your request today.

Whiter than snow!

FOR READING AND MEDITATION – PSALM 51:1–15

'Cleanse me with hyssop, and I shall be clean; wash me, and I will be whiter than snow.' (v. 7: NIV)

We continue discussing the issue of what it means to be pure in heart. Today we ask: how do we go about ensuring that our hearts are made pure? Great controversy has raged around this in every century of the church. Those who see sin as having made deep inroads into human nature say that all God can do with sin is to forgive it. Others see the soul as a battleground on which a long, drawn-out war takes place between the flesh and the spirit. And there are those who claim, as did John Wesley, that inner purity can be imparted by a sudden influx of divine grace. These three main views in the Church can be presented in this way: those who believe that purity is imputed; those who believe that purity is imparted; those who believe that purity is developed.

Those who believe purity is imputed say that Christ flings his robe of righteousness around a sinner and then God forever sees him in the spotless garments of his Son. Those who believe purity is imparted claim that there is an experience awaiting all believers, usually subsequent to conversion, whereby, through a crisis experience, God imparts the gift of purity. This belief received great prominence under John Wesley. Those who believe purity is developed see the work of God in the soul proceeding along the lines of a slow but steady improvement.

Which of these is right? I believe that each view has something to contribute; it is when the emphasis is disproportionately placed that problems arise. God both imputes and imparts purity, and then helps us apply and develop these truths in our daily life and experience.

O God my gracious Father, I am so thankful that you have provided for my deepest needs – and especially my need for inner cleansing. Wash me so clean on the inside that I will be whiter than the whitest snow. Amen.

FOR FURTHER STUDY – 1 Pet. 1:1–22; Psa. 24:3–4; 1 Tim. 1:5, 5:22

1. What was Paul's exhortation to Timothy? / 2. To what else does Peter relate purity?

Lord – make me clean

FOR READING AND MEDITATION – ROMANS 7:14–8:4

'...through Christ Jesus the law of the Spirit of life set me free from the law of sin and death.' (v. 2: NIV)

We ended yesterday by saying that God can impart purity as well as impute it, and he then helps us apply it in our daily life and experience. Permit me to share my own personal experience in this connection, not as a model for you to follow, but simply to illustrate how God revealed himself to me.

Following my conversion in my mid-teens, friends assured me that I ought to ask God to baptise me in his Holy Spirit. This, they told me, would give me the power I needed to become an effective witness for him. I asked God to do this – and in a remarkable encounter with him, I found the power I sought. But although this experience transformed me overnight from a shy, timid follower of Christ into a fearless witness for him, I still felt deeply troubled by the sinful forces that continued to stir deep within me. I fought hard with such things as lust and sensuality until one night, worn down by the inner conflict, I got down on my knees and prayed, 'Lord, reach deep inside me and make me truly clean.'

Again, something wonderful took place in my inner being – not so much an invasion of power as an invasion of purity. It did not result, I found, in placing me beyond the possibility of a carnal thought, a stab of pride, a trace of envy, but it meant that from that moment to this, I have been more conscious of the Holy Spirit's presence than I have been of sin's presence. Evil was not eradicated in me, as some proponents of imparted holiness believe, but I found that the eagerness for it had gone, the appetite for it was brought under control and the hunger for it was no longer a clamour. Now, close on forty years later, I never cease to thank God for his Spirit's cooling and cleansing touch.

My Father and my God, although I know I have to walk my own personal path to holiness and inner cleansing, help me to know at last that same cooling, cleansing touch in the depths of my heart. I ask this for your own dear name's sake. Amen.

FOR FURTHER STUDY – Gal. Ch. 5; Matt. 5:29; Rom. 6:6, 13:14

1. How did Paul exhort the Galatians? / 2. How drastically did Jesus put it?

A divine catharsis

FOR READING AND MEDITATION – ISAIAH 9:1–7

'…And his name will be called Wonderful Counsellor …' (v. 6: NASB)

We continue meditating on the word 'pure' as used by Jesus in his sixth Beatitude. One of the interesting things I discovered when researching this theme was the fact that the term *catharsis* – meaning to cleanse or make pure – is derived from the same Greek root as the word 'pure'.

In psychology, a catharsis describes the feeling of release and cleansing a person experiences in the presence of a trusted friend or counsellor when he or she empties out a lot of repressed feelings or ideas. In the right circumstances and under the right conditions, a person who does this often feels purged, renewed and released. I have seen this happen myself on countless occasions when counselling. People come with deep hurts and when they are sure they are in the presence of someone who understands them, someone they can trust, they open up their repressed feelings in such a way that afterwards they sit back and say, 'I feel so different. It's like someone has reached deep down inside me and scraped my insides clean.'

What produces this feeling of purging and release? It is difficult to explain, because the inner release they feel is not obtained simply by sharing – it comes only in the atmosphere of mutual confidence and trust. When a counsellor shows signs of disapproval or shock, then no deep release is experienced. If, as mental health experts claim, catharsis happens only when a counsellor is warm and accepting, as opposed to harsh and judgmental, then it becomes immediately obvious that in the presence of Jesus, the Wonderful Counsellor, we have the possibility of experiencing the deepest catharsis it is possible to know.

Blessed Lord Jesus, my Counsellor and my Friend, help me to open up the whole of my being to you, so that I might experience a divine catharsis. I long not just to be clean – I long to be wholly clean. For your own dear name's sake. Amen.

FOR FURTHER STUDY – 1 John 1:1–7; Psa. 65:3; Ezek. 36:25; Zech. 13:1

1. How are we to walk? / 2. What does this result in?

No condemnation now I dread

FOR READING AND MEDITATION – JOHN 8:21–36

'So if the Son sets you free, you will be free indeed.' (v. 36: NIV)

We saw yesterday that the phenomenon of catharsis comes about, not simply through telling someone else our troubles, but only when that someone else is a warm, accepting and understanding person. Psychologists believe the explanation for this to be the fact that the warm, accepting manner of the helper is so directly opposite to the harsh, judgmental attitudes of those who caused the hurts that repressed feelings easily surface and are released.

What does this law of the personality have to do with the subject now under discussion? A great deal, I believe. In Jesus Christ we find someone who not only yearns for our trust, but also is worthy of our trust. To sit in his presence is to hear, not words of harshness and judgment, but similar words to those he spoke to the woman caught in adultery: 'Neither do I condemn you; go, and sin no more.' Such acceptance, such compassion, such concern, cannot fail to produce within the depths of every heart a willingness to open up those hurts and fears which have been so deeply repressed.

As I said yesterday, I have witnessed on countless occasions this strange and mysterious phenomenon of catharsis take place as, in the presence of love and acceptance, repressed hurts and ideas are discharged from the personality. But beautiful and wondrous as this natural phenomenon is, to behold it is as nothing compared to the glory and radiance of standing in the presence of Jesus Christ, the Wonderful Counsellor, and experiencing a catharsis that reaches, not merely into the outer regions of the heart, but to its deepest depths. To have such an experience is not just to be free – it is to be free indeed.

My Father and my God – slowly things are coming into focus. I am beginning to understand what you mean when you say: 'If the Son sets you free, you will be free indeed.' Purge me to the deepest depths of my being. In Jesus' name. Amen.

FOR FURTHER STUDY – John 3:1–18, 5:24; Rom. 8:1, 34; Rev. 12:10

1. Who brings condemnation? / 2. What is the promise to the believer?

Seeing God

FOR READING AND MEDITATION – PSALM 24:1–10

'Who may ascend the hill of the Lord? Who may stand in his holy place?' (v. 3: NIV)

We spend one more day meditating on the words of the sixth Beatitude, and we focus today on the phrase: 'Blessed are the pure in heart, for they will see God.' The concluding words of this Beatitude are often misunderstood. Many believe it to have reference to the saints' eternal reward in heaven. Tennyson expressed this thought in his famous lines:

> I hope to see my Pilot face to face
> When I have crossed the bar.

The thought contained here, however, is not so much related to seeing God in heaven, but to seeing God now. Seeing God means seeing God in everything. Let me put it another way: not to see God is to fail to find the meaning of life and to see no purpose in anything. Such a condition, one must admit, produces an emotional overload on the personality that leads inevitably to despair. Some who fall prey to this mood end up committing suicide. As someone put it, 'Those who can't see the *why* have little energy to cope with the *what*.'

Seeing God is being acquainted with him, sensing his acceptance, comprehending what it means to be forgiven and made anew. Raymond Cramer puts it beautifully when he says, 'To the pure in heart, seeing God is viewing a stained glass window from the inside rather than the outside. The pure in heart are aware of a reality that most people miss. They are sure of God.' Seeing God must irrevocably be connected with purity of heart, for we must see and sense God first in our own inner being before we can see him and sense him elsewhere. See him within and you will not fail to see him without.

Gracious and loving Father, I see that an uncleansed heart causes more ill health and more unhappiness than anything else. Help me take the prescription you have given me this week – for I am going all the way with you. Amen.

FOR FURTHER STUDY – Isa. 6:1–8; Psa. 99:9; Heb. 12:14; Rev. 15:4

1. What was Isaiah's experience? / 2. What is a prerequisite for seeing the Lord?

Peace in our time

FOR READING AND MEDITATION – ROMANS 5:1–11
'Therefore, since we have been justified through faith, we have peace with God through our Lord Jesus Christ ...' (v. 1: NIV)

We come now to the seventh positive attitude that makes for good spiritual and mental health: 'Blessed are the peacemakers, for they will be called sons of God.' This Beatitude seems to have a special relevance to the age through which we are passing, for if there is one thing the world needs at this moment, it is – peacemakers.

Our generation has never known peace on a worldwide basis. One authority says, 'During most of recent history the air has been filled with rumblings of pending war until today, at the so-called peak of scientific enlightenment, the menace of a global conflict threatens our atomic age with suicide.' The uncertainty of being constantly on the brink of nuclear confrontation is taking its toll on the people of all nations, spiritually and psychologically. Studies show that living in a generation that has the power to annihilate itself in global destruction, has a crippling effect upon the minds of thousands, if not millions of people.

There was never a time when peacemakers were as important as they are now. And more and more are standing up to be counted on the side of peace. Organisations report increasing memberships and their attempts to alert the world to international treaties continues to gain the attention of every section of the media. Yet how strange that most of those who are so concerned for peace between nations, fail to see the need for peace between themselves and their Creator. The solemn truth is that no man or woman can become a peacemaker – at least in the Biblical sense of the word – until peace can be found in the innermost being.

O my Father, help humanity to come to the realisation that before they can enjoy the peace of God, they must first enjoy peace with God. Show them, dear Lord, that you will peace. And help them accept the will that wills their peace. In Jesus' name. Amen.

FOR FURTHER STUDY – Rom. 12:9–18, 14:19; Prov. 12:20; Mark 9:50
1. What are we to do? / 2. Are you a peacemaker?

How much do we 'project'?

FOR READING AND MEDITATION – PSALM 139:1–24

'Search me, O God, and know my heart; test me and know my anxious thoughts.' (v. 23: NIV)

We ended yesterday by saying that no one can become a peacemaker – in the Biblical sense of the word – until peace can be found in the innermost self. We said also that most of those who are concerned for peace on an international level fail to see the need for peace in their own hearts and minds.

As we are looking at the Beatitudes from the point of view of how effective they are in producing good spiritual and mental health, it is interesting to see how the psychology of Jesus is always ahead of the findings of those who study human behaviour. The view of many psychologists and psychiatrists is that much of the talk and activity by the masses in relation to international peace is actually a projection whereby they take the pressure off themselves. I am not convinced that all the concern can be dismissed in this way, but a lot of it can be explained in terms of the mechanism known as psychological projection.

Listen to what Louis Linn and Leo Schwartz say in their book, *Psychiatry, Religion and Experience*, 'A psychological origin of an adolescent's social idealism lies in his yearning for peace within himself. He tends to project his feelings of helplessness and turmoil onto the outer world, so that his yearning for peace may take the form of a wish for world peace.' Many of the activists who work for world peace may find this difficult to accept, but the truth is that if they did not have a world crisis on which to project their feelings, they would have to create some other condition. As long as we are not at peace within ourselves, we will create situations onto which we project our insecure feelings.

Dear Father, help me to understand this strange mechanism of projection. For I see that I can do the right things for the wrong reasons. Only you can probe my heart. I pray today with the psalmist, 'Search me, O God, and know my thoughts.' Amen.

FOR FURTHER STUDY – Lam. 5:1–5; Isa. 48:22, 57:20; Deut. 28:67

1. Which of these statements could be written about this generation?
2. Make this a matter for prayer today.

Discord within – discord without

FOR READING AND MEDITATION – ISAIAH 48:12–22

'"There is no peace," says the Lord, "for the wicked."' (v. 22: NIV)

We are seeing that the reason why people get caught up in activism, gaining the attention of world leaders in relation to the need for securing international peace is in part, the mechanism of projection. If we do not know peace within, then we will tend to focus on finding ways of securing peace in our outer circumstances and environment.

I hasten to add that not everyone who is involved in peace movements is motivated by this reason. I know a number of genuine Christians – people who already have the peace of God in their hearts – who are active in the peace organisations and have a genuine concern to bring pressure on world governments to do everything that must be done to avoid the horrors of a nuclear war. Nevertheless, I have no hesitation in saying that the majority of those involved in the peace organisations are motivated by the strange mechanism we introduced into our discussions yesterday – 'projection'. Since they do not possess peace within themselves, they talk at length about international peace.

It is easier to blame the world leaders, the political parties, the Presidents and Prime Ministers than to look into one's own heart and accept individual accountability. Actually the reason why there is so much war and hostility in the world is that, generally speaking, we do not have peace within ourselves. We create an environment that reflects our inner conflicts – the outside world reflects our inner world. Peace between nations does not guarantee peace within nations, nor does peace between two people guarantee peace within an individual.

Gracious and loving Father, I bow my head and my heart in deep gratitude for the exquisite peace you have given me in the depths of my spirit. Now that I am at peace with you, help me to be at peace with others – and to bring peace to others. In Jesus' name. Amen.

FOR FURTHER STUDY – John 14:15–27; Psa. 29:11, 119:1–65; Isa. 26:3

1. What keeps us in peace? / 2. What does the peace of Christ resolve?

What a beautiful day!

FOR READING AND MEDITATION – EPHESIANS 2:11–22

'For he is our peace, who has made us both one, and has broken down the dividing wall of hostility …' (v. 14: RSV)

Our meditations over the past few days have shown us that before we can become peacemakers in the true sense of that word, we must first know peace in our own minds and hearts. There can be no peace until we find peace with God.

The Bible is not content to leave the nature of the peace that Christ purchased for us, in doubt. Our text today tells us that Christ made peace by the blood of his cross. He bore the sins of men so that those who know him and accept his meritorious sufferings on the cross need no longer be troubled. The greatest message the world has ever heard – or will ever hear – is this: Christ interposed himself between sinful humanity and a holy God so that men and women could be eternally redeemed. Have you been redeemed? Have you accepted Christ's sacrifice for you on the cross? If so, good – your mission now in life is to be a peacemaker. You are to share his peace with others.

A little girl who a few weeks earlier had become a Christian, came down from her bedroom one morning and said to her mother, 'What a beautiful day.' The surprised mother said, 'What do you mean? It's raining like I've never seen it rain before, and the weather forecast is that we are going to have several more days of this. How can you call such weather beautiful?' 'But mother,' the little girl replied, 'a beautiful day has nothing to do with the weather.' In those simple but powerful words, she reconciled her to the weather – and her mother had a more beautiful day. You see, this is what peacemaking is all about. The peacemakers make a new world around them and within them.

O Father, help me today to be a peacemaker wherever I go, and to reconcile people, not just to the weather – but also to you. That which reaches the heart must come from the heart. Let the peace in my heart overflow. In Jesus' name. Amen.

FOR FURTHER STUDY – Matt.11:20–30; Ex. 33:14; Psa. 116:7; Heb. 4:3

1. What did Jesus promise? / 2. What must we do?

Let every Christian begin ...

FOR READING AND MEDITATION – JAMES 3:1–18

'...those who are peacemakers will plant seeds of peace and reap a harvest of goodness.' (v. 18: TLB)

We continue making the point that we cannot be peacemakers until we first find peace within ourselves. A psychiatrist was interviewing a man full of conflicts. In the middle of the interview the telephone rang, and because the receptionist had put a call through to him when he had given instructions not to be disturbed, the psychiatrist swore. He lost his peace and he lost his patient. For the patient saw that he had little to give except verbal advice.

The fact is that when we lose our peace with others, it is usually the projection of an inner conflict within ourselves. The one who is constantly out of patience with the family or the people with whom he works is usually out of patience with himself. A church in the Far East has this statement engraved over the door: 'Let every Christian be in the work of union within himself.' This is the place to begin – within yourself. For, as the Chinese saying puts it, 'He who has peace in himself has peace in the family; he who has peace in the family has peace in the world.'

A prominent member of a peace movement in the British Isles who said he was dedicated to peace, wrote a stinging letter to a member of the British Parliament, which was published in the Press. As a result, his advocacy of peace was blurred. People said, 'This man's idea of peace needs an overhaul. It is simply verbal, and not vital.' A missionary said, 'God and I are not at peace; we seem to be at cross-purposes. And my relationships with others are becoming more and more difficult.' Of course – for when we are not in harmony with God, then we are not in harmony with anyone else.

O Father, I long to become so harmonised with you that my life becomes a harmony to others. I cannot afford to live with conflict within, for if I do, then inevitably I will have to live with conflict without. Make me a peaceful and peaceable person. For Jesus' sake. Amen.

FOR FURTHER STUDY – John 16:25–33; Luke 1:78–79; Rom. 8:6, 14:17

1. What does peace spring from? / 2. Why can we be of good courage?

What peacemaking is not

FOR READING AND MEDITATION – TITUS 2:1–15

'…use your full authority as you rebuke your hearers. Let none of them look down on you.' (v. 15: TEV)

Today we go a step further in our meditations on the seventh Beatitude, and affirm that no one can be spiritually or mentally healthy until they know what it means to have peace in their inner beings. A psychologist says, 'If we could only measure the amount of emotional energy that is dissipated within the human personality by lack of peace, we would be surprised to find that physical, mental and emotional loss would represent our greatest deficit within the human economy. He is simply saying that inner conflict tears us apart – physically, mentally and spiritually.

The intriguing thing is that as, we make peace with God, a change comes into our own lives and this, in turn, is reflected in the lives of other people. We are not only at peace – we become peaceable. But even more – we become peacemakers. To be a peacemaker means, quite simply, that we become reconcilers. We reconcile people to God and to each other.

We should be careful not to misunderstand the meaning of the word 'peacemaker', so let's examine for a moment what it is not. Peacemaking is not just keeping the peace. Some strive to keep the peace because they do not wish to risk any unpleasantness that might be involved in trying to put matters right. They avoid a conflict by smoothing over the surface, but this is not peace. The true peacemaker sometimes has to be a fighter. Paradoxically, he or she is called, not to a passive life, but an active one. Peacemaking, at times, can be exceedingly difficult – especially within the Christian Church. Those who pursue this ministry must realise that peacemaking is not patching things up, but getting to the root of the problem. Peacemakers sometimes have to stir up trouble before they can resolve it.

Father, thank you for reminding me that peacemaking is not cowardice or the love of quiet. Give me the courage I need to risk any unpleasantness that may be involved in the cause of putting matters right. In Jesus' name I pray. Amen.

FOR FURTHER STUDY – Eph. 6:1–15; Psa. 119:165; Phil. 4:7

1. What is the essence of the Gospel? / 2. What keeps our hearts and minds?

Like our Father

FOR READING AND MEDITATION – 1 JOHN 2:28–3:11

'Behold what manner of love the Father has bestowed on us, that we should be called children of God!' (v. 1: New KJV)

Peacemaking is a positive attitude that produces good spiritual and mental health, and the one who has this attitude, according to Jesus, is to be envied and congratulated. The promise of the seventh Beatitude is that peacemakers 'will be called sons of God.' Why 'called'? Because they are sons of God. This is their lot in life. Sons are those who in character and life resemble God in closest similarity. Dr Martyn Lloyd-Jones puts it like this, 'The meaning of being called "the sons of God" is that the peacemaker is a child of God and that he is like his Father.'

If I were to pick out the one verse that most perfectly expresses the meaning of the Christian Gospel, it would be this: '… in Christ God was reconciling the world to himself … and entrusting to us the message of reconciliation' (2 Cor. 5:19, RSV). Ever since man sinned, God has been engaged in the positive business of an outgoing love – seeking to reconcile those who did not want to be reconciled. God wants us to do what he does – he commits to us the same word of reconciliation. This attitude enables us to live life to the full – a life free from mental, emotional and spiritual problems.

Those who are inwardly reconciled to God and seek to reconcile others to him and to each other will never suffer from psychological problems. They are the healthiest and the happiest people on earth. In two outstanding passages in the Bible, we are called sons of the Father – and for the same reason: Matthew 5:9 and Matthew 5:45. What do we conclude from this? We are most like God when we are bringing people together in reconciliation. And those who try to reconcile others are doing the work of heaven – for it is heaven's work to reconcile us.

O God my Father, I pray that you will help me become more and more like you. You are a Father who reconciles – make me into your own divine image. Help me to breathe 'peace' upon all I meet. For your own dear name's sake. Amen.

FOR FURTHER STUDY – Gal. 4:1–7; John 1:12; Rom. 8:14; Heb. 2:10

1. As sons, what have we become? / 2. How are we led?

When society kicks back

FOR READING AND MEDITATION – PHILIPPIANS 1:12–30

'For it has been granted to you on behalf of Christ not only to believe on him, but also to suffer for him ...' (v. 29: NIV)

We come now to Christ's eighth and final prescription for good spiritual and mental health: 'Blessed are those who are persecuted because of righteousness, for theirs is the kingdom of heaven.' The inevitable result of bringing our attitudes in line with Christ's attitudes is that our lives become a silent judgment upon others. And men and women do not like to be judged, so they kick back in persecution. 'Society', said someone, 'demands conformity: if you fall beneath its standards, it will punish you; if you rise above its standards, it will persecute you. It demands an average, grey conformity.'

The true Christian, however, does not conform – he stands out. His head is lifted so high above the multitudes that, not surprisingly, he gets hit. 'Woe to you', said Jesus, 'when all men speak well of you' (Luke 6:26, NIV). If they do speak well of us, then it could be that we are too much like them. Let there be no mistake about this, the righteous will be persecuted – inevitably so. Once we adopt the attitudes and principles that Christ presents so clearly for us in his Sermon on the Mount, the men and women of the world are going to react with hostility and indignation.

Dr E. Stanley Jones was close to the mark when he said that the first thing a person must get used to on becoming a Christian is the sight of his or her own blood. Are you being persecuted for righteousness' sake at the moment? Is the world venting its hatred and hostility upon you because of your stand for the Lord Jesus Christ? Then take heart – the persecution is the final proof, if one is needed, that you are a true disciple of your Master, a child of God and a citizen of heaven.

My Father and my God, help me not to miss the deep underlying truth in this, the last of your prescriptions for happiness. Strengthen me so that I am unafraid of seeing my own blood. In Jesus' name I ask it. Amen.

FOR FURTHER STUDY – Matt. 10:16–42, 24:9; Luke 21:12

1. How are we sent out? / 2. What was Jesus' promise?

Collision course

FOR READING AND MEDITATION – 2 TIMOTHY 3:12–17

'…everyone who wants to live a godly life in Christ Jesus will be persecuted…' (v. 12: NIV)

We continue from where we left off yesterday in saying that persecution is one of the proofs that we are true disciples of the Lord Jesus Christ. Many Christians find great difficulty in coming to terms with this issue of persecution, and because they have never understood that those who reject Christ will also reject those who follow Christ, they become entangled in such things as conciliation and compromise.

If you have never done so before, face the fact right now that when you identify yourself with Jesus Christ, the world will persecute you. The degree of persecution differs from one Christian to another, but always remember that a close relationship with Jesus Christ will cause the world, in one way or another, to react against you with hostility and contempt. Once you face this fact, you are nine-tenths of the way toward overcoming the fear that cripples so many Christians – the fear of witnessing

Not long after my conversion to Christ, an old Welsh miner gave me some advice that greatly helped to overcome my fear of rejection. He said, 'Keep ever before you the fact that those who reject Christ will reject you. And the more like Christ you become, the more the world will resent you. Remember also that when they do reject you, it is not you personally whom they are against, but Christ who is alive and who is being seen in you.'

Never shall I forget the release that came to me through those wise words. Once I understood that becoming identified with Christ meant I was on a collision course with the world, I came to terms with the inevitability of this fact and was set free from fear. And what happened to me can happen to you – today.

Lord Jesus Christ, I bring to you my fear of persecution and ask you to set me free from it right now. Help me to face the world's hostility in the knowledge that just as it could not overcome you, it cannot overcome me. In you I can endure all things. Amen.

FOR FURTHER STUDY – John Ch. 17, 15:20, 16:2

1. How did the world respond to the first disciples? / 2. What was Jesus' prayer?

My neighbours won't talk to me

FOR READING AND MEDITATION – MATTHEW 10:1–20

'… be wise as serpents and innocent as doves.' (v. 16: RSV)

We are saying that many Christians are ineffective witnesses because they attempt to water down their testimony so as to avoid misunderstanding or persecution – and they end up achieving nothing. Once we understand and accept the fact that those who reject Christ and his principles will also reject us, we will then be free to throw our whole weight on the side of Christ and become fully identified with him.

In following this principle, however, we must be careful that our freedom from fear of rejection or objectionable persecution does not lead us to become objectionable. I know some Christians who have a hard time from their non-Christian acquaintances, not because of their likeness to Christ, but because of their tactlessness and lack of wisdom. I once knew a man who told me he had convincing evidence that he was a true disciple of Christ. I was intrigued to know his reason for thinking this way, and in answer to my question, 'Why are you so sure?' he replied, 'My neighbours won't talk to me and cross to the other side of the road when they see me coming. I take this persecution as proof that I am a true citizen of the kingdom.'

Some time later, I had occasion to talk to some of this man's neighbours, who told me that the reason they avoided him was because he continually accosted them with questions like, 'Do you know you are going to hell?' or 'What if you were to drop dead at this moment – where would you spend eternity?' The neighbours thought it good policy to avoid him rather than to be faced continually with his belligerence. The man was suffering, not for Christ's sake, but for his own sake.

O God my Father, I see how easy it is to bring suffering and persecution upon myself by my own tactlessness and folly. Help me to object without being objectionable and to disagree without being disagreeable. In Jesus' name. Amen.

FOR FURTHER STUDY – 2 Tim. 3:1–13; 1 Cor. 13:3; Rev. 2:10

1. What is the result of living a godly life? / 2. What is promised for faithfulness?

No compulsions in Christianity

FOR READING AND MEDITATION – 1 PETER 4:7–19
'If you suffer, it should not be as a murderer or thief or any other kind of criminal, or even as a meddler.' (v. 15: NIV)

We continue focusing on the fact that many Christians suffer persecution, not because of their identification with Christ, but because of their own tactlessness and folly. This eighth Beatitude – 'Blessed are those who are persecuted because of righteousness, for theirs is the kingdom of heaven' – does not apply to such people. Let us be quite clear about that.

There is a great difference between being persecuted for the sake of righteousness and being persecuted for the sake of self-righteousness. Many Christians are foolish in these matters. They fail to realise the difference between prejudice and principle, and thus bring unnecessary suffering upon themselves. The same applies to those who are over-zealous in their witnessing. They make a nuisance of themselves and interpret the persecution that comes as a result as persecution for righteousness' sake.

The Scripture teaches us to be 'wise as serpents and innocent as doves'. The writer of the Proverbs puts it powerfully when he says: 'He who wins souls is wise.' We are not told in this eighth Beatitude, 'Blessed are those who are persecuted because they are over-zealous', neither are we told, 'Blessed are those who are persecuted because they are fanatical.' I was once asked by a church to counsel one of their members who had a compulsion to witness. The man got into so many difficulties because of this that the church threatened to discipline him unless he agreed to receive counselling. I found his compulsion to witness came not from Christ, but from is own inner drives. He needed to witness so as to feel significant. Witnessing should be a constraint, never a compulsion.

O Father, show me how to distinguish between what is a compulsion and what is a constraint. And help me to see that if I don't find my significance in my relationship with you, then I will attempt to find it in other ways. Save me, dear Lord – or I shall go astray. Amen.

FOR FURTHER STUDY – Acts 9:1–29; 1 Cor. 4:12; 2 Cor. 4:9

1. Who was Saul really persecuting?
2. What was his early experience of proclaiming Christ?

A martyr complex

FOR READING AND MEDITATION – COLOSSIANS 2:1–15
'... you are complete in him ...' (v. 10: New KJV)

We are seeing that a lot of the suffering and persecution we experience in our Christian lives can be due to our own tactlessness and folly. Today I want to take this matter a stage further, and suggest that in relation to this matter of suffering and persecution, some Christians have developed a 'martyr complex'.

A martyr complex is an attitude of mind that finds some strange emotional satisfaction in being persecuted. Why should this be? Well, if, for example, a person does not experience a good sense of personal worth, he becomes motivated to secure that worth in other ways. And one of those ways can be that of making an impact upon the immediate environment or society through taking a stand on some 'Christian' issue.

Now I am not saying, of course, that all of those who take a stand on such issues as pornography, violence and other serious moral problems in our nation are motivated to do so because of a martyr complex. That would be foolish to suggest and foolish to deduce. But it must be seen that some Christians strike out on issues, not because of an overriding concern for Christian values, but because of the satisfaction they get out of being noticed. And when being noticed leads to severe persecution, they draw from this the emotional charge they need to compensate for their low sense of worth. Such people almost court suffering and persecution, but it has to be said that they are not suffering for righteousness' sake – they are suffering for their own sake. May God give us grace and wisdom to understand when we are doing things to meet our own emotional needs, rather than out of love for him.

Father, I see even more clearly that unless my needs are met in a close relationship with you, then I am a vulnerable person – and prone to go astray. Draw me closer to you this day, so that I am conscious you are meeting all my deepest needs. In Jesus' name. Amen.

FOR FURTHER STUDY – 2 Cor. 11:16–33; 2 Tim. 2:8–9, 3:10–11
1. List some of Paul's sufferings. / 2. What was Paul's testimony?

Xenophobia

FOR READING AND MEDITATION – JOHN 15:12–27

'…you do not belong to the world, but I have chosen you out of the world. That is why the world hates you.' (v. 19: NIV)

We continue meditating on the eighth and final Beatitude. One of the questions that has often puzzled people concerning this matter of suffering and persecution is this: why is it that Christians, when they do good, are often persecuted, while non-Christians who do the same kind of good are adulated and adored?

One commentator suggests the reason for this is that when non-Christians do good, other non-Christians find it easy to identify with them and say to themselves, 'These people are just like me when I am at my best.' The thinking that goes on below the threshold of a non-Christian's mind when he sees other non-Christians doing good is along the line of, 'I am probably capable of the same thing myself if the opportunity came my way.' The admiration that is then given is a way of paying a compliment to oneself.

The Christian who does good has about him or her the atmosphere of another world, and because of this, the non-Christian observes, not just the act of good, but the different motivation that underlies the act. They sense that there is something different about this person, and because they cannot understand or explain the difference, they react with fear and the fear then turns to hostility. Psychologists have a name for extreme forms of this fear – xenophobia. It means a fear of someone we do not know or understand. This is why the scribes and Pharisees hated our Lord so much. It wasn't because he was good; it was because he was different. This is the effect Jesus Christ always has upon the world. And to the extent that you reflect his spirit, to that extent you will experience the same reaction.

O Father, I see that if I just try to do good, the world will applaud me, but if I try to become Christ-like, it will hate me. Nevertheless I long to be Christ-like. Help me, dear Father, for apart from your grace, I know it is not possible. Amen.

FOR FURTHER STUDY – Phil. 1:1–14; Col. 4:3; 2 Tim. 1:7–8

1. How did Paul view persecution? / 2. What was his charge to Timothy?

Stand – and be healthy

FOR READING AND MEDITATION – DEUTERONOMY 30:1–20

'...I have set before you life and death, blessings and curses. Now choose life...'
(v. 19: NIV)

We spend one last day meditating on the eighth and final Beatitude. Some feel that the verses that follow this Beatitude (verses 11 and 12) constitute a ninth Beatitude, but really they are an amplification and enlargement of what our Lord has been saying in verse 10. It must be pointed out in passing that more is said about this eighth Beatitude than is said about the others – a fact that surely underlines its supreme importance.

The question we ask ourselves today is this: how does this eighth Beatitude contribute to good mental and spiritual health? It does so by encouraging us to stand up and be counted. The famous missionary doctor and scientist, Dr Albert Schweitzer, when addressing a group of medical men in Africa many years ago, is reported to have said, 'You cannot be healthy unless you stand for something – even at a cost.'

The person who unashamedly identifies with Christ and stands up for him, knowing that the stand will produce, in one form or another, inevitable persecution, experiences an inner release from fear that affects every part of the personality in the most positive way. The positive may be persecuted, but they are also the most productive – they survive when others fall by the way. So stop wearing out your nervous system. Cease using up precious energy trying to find ways to make it through this world. Follow God's blueprint as laid out in the eight Beatitudes and yours will be a life which, through the psychology of Jesus, will bring you maximum effectiveness with minimum weariness. Choose any other way and you will experience minimum effectiveness with maximum weariness. I choose life.

Father, I too, choose life. Help me to absorb and assimilate your attitudes until they become my attitudes. Then life will always have to be spelt with a capital 'L'. With your help, dear Lord, I'm on my way to real living. Hallelujah!

FOR FURTHER STUDY – Philemon Ch. 1; Eph. 3:1; 1 Pet. 3:15–16
1. How did Paul view his imprisonment? / 2. When were you last persecuted?

How do I rate?

FOR READING AND MEDITATION – 2 CORINTHIANS 13:1–14

'Examine yourselves to see whether you are in the faith; test yourselves…' (v. 5: NIV)

Before embarking on our last theme together, we take a simple test. Ask yourself the following questions and see how many of Christ's 'beautiful attitudes' have been assimilated into your life:

(1) Am I trying to grasp things from God's hands or are my hands relaxed and empty so that I might receive?

(2) Do I shrink from painful experiences or do I welcome them, in the knowledge that they will make me a more sensitive person?

(3) Am I so sure of God and his resources that I am free from a spirit of demandingness and over-concern?

(4) Is my goal to be happy, or is it to be holy? Am I more taken up with getting pleasure out of God than I am with giving pleasure to God?

(5) Do I have a deep compassion and concern for the plight of others?

(6) Is my heart clean and pure? Have I experienced an in inner cleansing that has reached to the deepest depths?

(7) Am I a reconciler – one who seeks to reconcile others to God and, where necessary, to each other?

(8) Am I so identified with Christ that I experience the hatred the world gives to those who remind them of him?

Don't be discouraged if you can't see all of these 'beautiful attitudes' at work in your life. Remember, we grow in grace. Ask God, however, to help you absorb more and more of his 'beautiful attitudes' day by day. The more you have, the more you are to be envied. Possess them all – and you are truly blessed.

Lord Jesus, I see that as you came… so I must go. I have listened to your words and I realise now the Word must become flesh – in me. I want the balance of my days here on earth to reflect, not my attitudes, but ours. Help me, my Lord and Master. For your own name's sake. Amen.

FOR FURTHER STUDY – Eph. 4:1–15; Heb. 6:1; 2 Pet. 3:18

1. What are we going to go on to? / 2. What 'beautiful attitude' will you reflect today?

Spiritual sure-footedness

FOR READING AND MEDITATION – PSALM 18:16–33
'He makes my feet like hinds' feet, and sets me upon my high places.' (v. 33: NASB)

We begin a theme that I hope will add greatly to your spiritual life and experience – 'Hinds' feet on high places'. The urge to write on this theme came to me after reading the story of a man who spent a few weeks holidaying on a ranch in Wyoming, USA. While he was there he was given the use of one of the horses that belonged to the ranch – the fastest he had ever ridden.

One day a group of cowboys who worked on the ranch invited him to join them for a ride up into the mountains, at which time he discovered that while speed might be important on the plains, something more was needed on the steep mountain slopes. As they climbed into the hills they came to a dangerous ascent, and the foreman turned to the newcomer and said, 'I think you would be well advised to take the longer, but less dangerous trail to the top. Your horse is not dependable on the hills. Our horses are true climbers – their rear feet track exactly where their front feet are planted. Your horse has spent so many years on the plain that its rear feet could miss the track by inches, and one slip could mean serious injury – perhaps even death.'

When I read those words, my thoughts turned immediately to the verse before us today, for no animal has such perfect correlation of its front and rear feet as the deer. When it leaps from rock to rock, its back feet land exactly where its front feet had been placed. If we are to climb higher with God that we have ever gone before, then more is needed than just speed – we must know spiritual sure-footedness also. Let's determine on this, that we will let nothing stand in the way of making our feet like hinds' feet and climbing with God to the 'high places'.

My Father and my God, hear my prayer as I begin a new month and perhaps a new chapter in my spiritual experience. Help me to climb higher with you than I have ever gone before, and do it not only with speed, but with sure-footedness also. In Jesus' name. Amen.

FOR FURTHER STUDY – Phil. 3:1–14; Isa. 54:2; Eph. 3:17–19
1. What was the deep desire of Paul's heart? / 2. What did he pray for the Ephesians?

Climbing higher with God

FOR READING AND MEDITATION – HABAKKUK 3:12–19

'... He has made my feet like hinds' feet, and makes me walk on my high places.' (v. 19: NASB)

We continue unfolding the thought that if we are to climb higher with God than we have ever done before, we must learn how to become as sure-footed in the spiritual realm as a deer is in the natural realm. There are numerous references in Scripture where the pursuit of God is likened to a deer climbing steadily and sure-footedly toward the high mountain peaks – today's text being just one of them – and the more we consider the simile, the more rich and rewarding are the truths that flow out of it.

Why does God liken the pursuit of himself to a deer making its way upward to the high places? And why does he focus so much attention upon the deer's feet? Well, as we said yesterday, the deer has an amazing ability, when climbing a steep mountain slope, of ensuring that its back feet alight on the exact spot where its front feet were positioned. This perfect correlation between its front and back feet enables the deer to avoid the dangers that would befall a less coordinated animal.

The Bible writers, in drawing attention to the sure-footedness of the deer, are attempting to show (so I believe) that what the deer experiences in the natural realm, we can experience in the spiritual realm. Do you really want to climb higher with God than you have ever gone before? Is there a deep longing in your heart to ascend, like the prophets and seers of old, into the mountain of the Lord? Then take heart – you can. This can be the greatest time of spiritual advance you have ever known. You supply the willingness, and I promise you – God will supply the power.

O Father – I long more than anything to ascend into the mountain peaks with you. I am willing – now send the power. In Jesus' name I ask it. Amen.

FOR FURTHER STUDY – Isa. Ch. 55; Psa. 42:2, 63:1, 143:6

1. What did the psalmist express continually? / 2. What does God promise?

God has the biggest part

FOR READING AND MEDITATION – PSALM 40:1–17

'…He set my feet upon a rock making my footsteps firm.' (v. 2: NASB)

We are meditating in these first few days of a new month on the way that God has designed the deer. I hope I am not labouring the point, but the more we are acquainted with the way a deer functions in its natural habitat, the more clearly we can see the spiritual lessons that God wants to bring home to our hearts. No animal has such perfect correlation of its front and rear feet as the deer. While the male deer, the hart, is a wonderful example of sure-footedness, still more wonderful is the female, the hind. Those who have watched it leading its young into the hidden fastnesses of the mountain peaks say it is the most perfect example of physical coordination that God ever made.

Why is this physical coordination so important? Well, when a deer moves upwards over a steep mountain slope, it proceeds by leaping from one spot to another and for this reason, it needs to be certain that its back feet will land on something that is solid and unlikely to move or slide. Thus, by positioning its front feet on something that is secure, it instinctively knows that if its rear feet land there also, it will proceed upwards in safety. If this were not so, and the deer's back feet were to land on a loose rock or stone, then it would slip and meet with serious injury – perhaps even death.

This sense of perfect coordination is not something the deer learns; it is an instinctive ability given to it by its Creator. And what God has done for the deer in the natural realm, he is able to do for us in the spiritual realm. Listen again to the words of the Psalmist: 'He makes my feet like hinds' feet.' Note the word 'makes'. I find that deeply encouraging. It is not something I have to achieve on my own; he has a part in it too. And, may I add – the biggest part.

O Father, help me understand that although you have the biggest part in making my feet like hinds' feet, it cannot be accomplished unless I, too, do my part. Thus I willingly surrender to your divine purposes. In Jesus' name I pray. Amen.

FOR FURTHER STUDY – Isa. 26:1–4; Psa. 92:15, 61:2; Matt. 7:24–29

1. What did Isaiah declare? / 2. What was Jesus teaching?

Togetherness

FOR READING AND MEDITATION – MARK 11:12–26

'…whoever says to this mountain, "Be removed…", and does not doubt in his heart, but believes … will have whatever he says.' (v. 23: NKJ)

Today we ask ourselves: what is the spiritual lesson we can draw from the deer's amazing ability to ensure that its back feet land on the exact spot where its front feet had been positioned? I believe it to be this: just as the creature which has the most perfect correlation between its front and rear feet makes its way swiftly and safely to the mountaintop, so the Christian who has a perfect coordination between the head and heart will rise to new heights with God. For you see, unless the head and heart are properly coordinated and move purposefully together, it is possible to miss one's step on the steep slopes of Christian experience and become a spiritual casualty.

I have known many Christians in my time who, because they lack coordination between what they ask for with their lips and what they want deep down in their hearts, stay in the same place spiritually year after year after year. They are not bad people' they just lack spiritual coordination and thus never know what it is to ascend into the mountain peaks with God.

Perhaps nowhere in Scripture is this truth more clearly portrayed than in the verse before us today. We are told that things happen in the spiritual realm when there is a perfect coordination between what we ask for with our lips and what we believe in our heart. When our mind and our heart are in alignment, when they track together with the sure-footedness of a mountain deer, then nothing shall be impossible to us. How many of us, I wonder, miss our step on the slopes of the Christian life because our hearts and minds are not properly and perfectly coordinated?

Gracious and loving heavenly Father, slowly I am beginning to see the truth that underlies your promise to make my feet like hinds' feet. Show me how to be as coordinated in the spiritual realm as the deer is in the natural realm. In Jesus' name. Amen.

FOR FURTHER STUDY – Isa. 58:1–11; Matt. Ch. 23

1. Why was the Lord displeased with Israel? / 2. How did Jesus depict the Pharisees?

Not just what you say

FOR READING AND MEDITATION – PROVERBS 4:10–27

'Keep your heart with all diligence, for out of it spring the issues of life.' (v. 23: NKJ)

We continue thinking about the question we ended with yesterday: how many of us miss our step on the slopes of the Christian life because our hearts and minds are not properly coordinated? I am convinced myself that one of the major reasons why so many of us fail to receive from God the things we ought to be receiving lies in this very fact – our hearts and minds are not properly correlated.

Do you find yourself continually praying for things you never receive? I don't mean things about which there may be some doubt, but things you definitely know the Almighty longs to give you – love, joy, peace, wisdom, patience, the Holy Spirit, and so on. This could be the reason – your mind is asking for one thing and your heart another. You see, it is possible to want something with the mind that is not supported by the heart. The mind is a much easier part of the personality to deal with than the heart, but as our text for today states so clearly: 'Keep your heart… for out of it spring the issues of life.'

We can approach God with our minds and think that because we have a clear idea of what we want, God will give it to us, but the heart may contain hidden doubts and fears that prevent us from being fully integrated people. We fail to receive because we are not asking out of a fully integrated personality. As someone has put it, 'God does not just answer prayer – he answers you.' Those who wish to achieve proficiency in prayer and receive from God the things he delights to give ought always to remember that who we are is just as important (if not more so) than what we ask. God is not just listening to your words; he is listening to you.

O Father, the more I meditate on the need for heart and mind to be in perfect coordination, the more I am set on fire to become a fully integrated person. I know you are eagerly reaching down to me; help me to be as eager to reach up to you. In Jesus' name. Amen.

FOR FURTHER STUDY – Matt. 15:1–20; Prov. 3:5, 23:7; Luke 6:45

1. What did Isaiah prophesy? / 2. How did Jesus respond to Peter's request?

The seemingly trivial inches

FOR READING AND MEDITATION – JEREMIAH 29:1–14

'...you will seek me and find me, when you search for me with all your heart.' (v. 13: NKJ)

We must hold steady at this point in our meditations as we are looking at what I consider is one of the greatest truths about prayer and receiving from God that we can ever discover: God does not just answer prayer – he answers you.

The Almighty does not just listen to the words we weave into the air when we pray; He listens also to the attitude of the heart. If the two are not properly correlated, then we miss out on many of God's blessings. And this missing out is not because God is niggardly about the way he dispenses his blessings, but because we short-circuit our own spiritual system and become bad or imperfect receivers. To put it another way, our failure to receive isn't due to the fact that God is not good at giving, but because we are not good at receiving. The fault is always in us, never in him.

We are far enough along in our meditations, I believe, for me to ask you this personal question: are you a fully integrated person? When you present your requests to God, are your heart and mind at one? Is what you ask with your lips fully supported by what you are saying in your heart? If not, then when you attempt to climb higher with God, you will not have the precise coordination you need to scale the precipitous heights. The awesome fact that has to be faced by all those who want to climb the mountains of God is this – it is possible to miss your step on those steep slopes, not by yards, not by feet, but merely by inches. And it is in those seemingly trivial inches that our spiritual direction is often determined.

O Father, I am seeing more and more the perils that come from being inwardly at cross-purposes. Help me, however, to see that although the challenge is great, the power behind me is greater than the challenge in front of me. In Jesus' name. Amen.

FOR FURTHER STUDY – Joel 2:1–13; Deut. 6:5; Psa. 119:2

1. What was God's message through Joel? / 2. When are we blessed?

The peril of a missed step

FOR READING AND MEDITATION – PSALM 18:32–50

'You enlarged my path under me; so my feet did not slip' (v. 36: NKJ)

We ended yesterday with the thought that it is possible to miss our step on the steep slopes of the mountains of God, not by yards, not by feet, but merely by inches. In my research into the ways of the mountain deer, I came across an interesting but sad tale of a hunter who one day came across a deer, grazing at the foot of a high mountain. He took aim with his rifle but the bullet seemed to miss its mark. The startled animal raced towards the mountains and the hunter watched in amazement as he saw it leap from crag to crag and rock to rock with consummate skill and ease. Higher and higher went the animal, but suddenly its back feet appeared to slip and although it struggled frantically to regain its footing, it fell hundreds of feet into a ravine and was instantly killed.

When the hunter arrived at the spot where the animal lay, he noticed a small burn on its flank caused by the bullet he had fired, which had simply grazed the animal without penetrating its flesh. The hunter says, 'It was obvious what had happened. The graze had affected the deer's coordination and in a moment when it needed to move swiftly and safely to the mountain height, it did not proceed with its usual perfect correlation. Its back feet did not land on the precise spot where its front feet had been, and although it was only an inch off, it was enough to bring about its fall.'

The illustration I have used must not be pushed too far and made to mean that a missed step on the mountain of God will bring about our spiritual death. A missed step, however, will undoubtedly hinder our spiritual progress and prevent us from climbing as swiftly as we ought into the heights of God.

O Father, make me the kind of person whose heart and mind move forward into your purpose with perfect unity and coordination. Help me not to miss my step – not even by inches. In Jesus' name I pray. Amen.

FOR FURTHER STUDY – Psa. 40:1–5; Isa. 52:7; Eph. 6:15

1. What was the psalmist's testimony? / 2. What are we to have on our feet?

Commitment means cohesion

FOR READING AND MEDITATION – LUKE 11:14–28

'…a house divided against itself will fall.' (v. 17: NIV)

We have been seeing over the past few days that one of the reasons why we may not be receiving as much as we ought spiritually is because there is no proper correlation between the heart and the mind. Today we look at a Scriptural illustration of this, based on the life of the Old Testament character, Amaziah. In 2 Chronicles 25:2 we read: 'He did what was right in the eyes of the Lord, but not wholeheartedly' (NIV). His mind gave itself to doing right in the sight of the Lord, but his heart did not support his actions.

This lack of coordination proved to be his undoing: 'When Amaziah returned from slaughtering the Edomites, he brought back the gods of the people of Seir… set them up as his own gods, bowed down to them and burned sacrifices to them' (verse 14). Now look at how the life of Amaziah ends: 'From the time that Amaziah turned away from following the Lord, they conspired against him … and … sent men after him to Lachish and killed him there' (verse 27).

Notice the steps:
(1) outwardly correct but inwardly uncoordinated
(2) the inner disunity shows itself in outer disloyalty
(3) failure and death.

At the beginning, Amaziah does not appear to be a particularly bad individual – he just failed to be wholehearted in his commitment. He did all the right things outwardly, but his heart was not in them – hence spiritual ruin. We could say he missed his step by inches, but his fall was one of the worst ever recorded. If we are not held together by a single-minded devotion, our spiritual life can quickly go to pieces. Commitment to God demands cohesion – the cohesion of heart and mind.

O God my Father, help me to live a life of single purpose, with heart and mind moving together as one. Let me will the highest with all my being. In Jesus' name I ask it. Amen.

FOR FURTHER STUDY – James 1:1–8, 4:8; Heb. 13:9

1. What makes us unstable? / 2. What was the word of the Lord to the Hebrews?

Spoiled by ulterior motives

FOR READING AND MEDITATION – JAMES 4:1–12

'When you ask, you do not receive, because you ask with wrong motives . . .' (v. 3: NIV)

We come across many people in the Scriptures who appear to be spiritually minded but whose hearts harbour deeply unspiritual motives. Take the mother of the sons of Zebedee, for example, who according to Matthew 27:55 was one of the women who followed Jesus from Galilee for the purpose of ministering to him and doing whatever they could to make his load lighter.

Most commentators believe this small band of women were devotees of Christ and assisted him and the disciples in the preparation of meals, washing and repairing of clothes and so on. Those looking on would have classified them as deeply spiritual women, willing to give up their time and energy to minister to Jesus – and of course, in the main, they were. However, in one place the Scripture draws aside the veil over the heart of one of them, the mother of James and John, and shows her approaching Jesus with this request: 'Grant that these two sons of mine may sit, one on your right hand and the other on your left, in your kingdom.' Jesus replied: 'You do not know what you ask' (Matt. 20:21-22, NKJ).

She served Jesus, of that there can be no doubt, but she had a secret and selfish motive in her heart – a privileged position for her sons. It is easy to excuse her action, as many have done, on the grounds that she was doing only what any other concerned mother would have done – attempting to get the best for her children. But Jesus saw right into her heart and said: 'You do not know what you ask.' How sad that her beautiful ministry to Jesus was spoiled by ulterior motives.

My Father, help me to see that I cannot be a fully integrated person when I harbour within me two mutually exclusive loves. I cannot love you fully when I love my own interests fully. Set me free, dear Lord, to live only for you. Amen.

FOR FURTHER STUDY – James Ch. 2; Eph. 2:3; 1 John 2:15–16

1. What motive was James exposing? / 2. What did he say about the law?

The heart of the matter

FOR READING AND MEDITATION – PROVERBS 3:1–18

'Trust in the Lord with all your heart and lean not on your own understanding. (v. 5: NIV)

Today we ask ourselves: what is the essential difference between the heart and the mind? Many believe there is no difference and that they are really one and the same thing. I myself see a clear difference between the heart and the mind that I would describe in this way: the mind is the part of us that thinks and reasons; the heart is the part of us that contains our deep longings and desires. Although the mind is important, the heart is even more important because it is the engine room of the personality – the part from which comes our drive and motivation. That is why our Lord says: 'For out of the overflow of the heart, the mouth speaks' (Matthew 12:34, NIV).

Christ said that the words he spoke were the words given to him by his Father (John 14:24). Does that mean the Father wrote out the words he wanted Christ to say and got him to learn them by heart? No – the motivating centre of the heart of Jesus Christ was the very heart of God the Father, consequently the words Christ spoke were the exact expression of God's thought. In our Lord, the tongue was always in its right place. He spoke not just from his head, but from his heart. His heart and mind were one.

Oswald Chambers put it like this, 'The heart is the central altar and the mind the outer court. What we offer on the central altar will show itself in due course through the outer extremities of the personality.' In the search for unity of purpose and integration, there is no doubt that the heart of the matter is the matter of the heart.

O God, help me to be like Jesus and to pass on to others, not just the things that come into my head but the things that flow out of my heart. Bring my heart in closer contact with your heart, dear Father. In Jesus' name I pray. Amen.

FOR FURTHER STUDY – Mark 7:14–23; Prov. 4:23; Rom. 10:10

1. What comes from the heart? / 2. What was Jesus teaching?

An honest look

FOR READING AND MEDITATION – LUKE 8:1–15

'...they are those who, hearing the word, hold it fast in an honest and good heart, and bring forth fruit with patience.' (v. 15: RSV)

Having spent several days opening up our theme, we turn now to consider some of the steps we must take in order to bring about a more perfect coordination between heart and mind. The first step is this – prepare to take an honest, straightforward look at what is going on beneath the surface of your life.

Over the years in which I have been writing, I have from time to time invited my readers to take a good, honest look at themselves. The reactions I have received to this suggestion have been quite interesting. Some Christians hear in my words a call to self-preoccupation and become concerned that I am pushing people toward becoming engrossed with their personal aches and pains. One of my readers put it like this, 'What people need is to forget about themselves and concentrate on reaching out to others, then their personal problems will quickly be forgotten.' Others have taken an opposite position and said, 'We need more and more of this, for our hearts are so self-deceived that unless we are constantly challenged in this way, we will never get through to a close relationship with God.'

I want to state clearly that I am unhappy about both those reactions, for both are unbalanced positions. The first one fears that taking a look beneath the surface of our lives leads to unhealthy self-preoccupation, and the second assumes that constant self-examination is the only way forward. An occasional honest and straightforward look at what is going on beneath the surface of our lives contributes greatly to our spiritual progress, providing it is done in a proper and balanced way.

O God, help me to see that in inviting me to examine myself, you are not seeking to demean me, but to develop me – not to take away from my spiritual stature, but add to it. Make me an honest person – honest with you, honest with myself and honest with others. Amen.

FOR FURTHER STUDY – Psa. 51:1–6, 15:1–2; Rom 8:27

1. Where does God require truth? / 2. What must we allow God to do?

Going below the water line

FOR READING AND MEDITATION – PSALM 51:1–17
'...You desire truth in the inward parts...' (v. 6: NKJ)

We are considering the proposition that an honest, straightforward look at what is going on beneath the surface of our lives is something that contributes greatly to our spiritual health and progress – providing it is done in a proper and balanced way.

It will help you to see the point I want to make over the next few days if you think of your life as an iceberg. We are told that the visible part of an iceberg, that is, the part we see above the water line, is about one-tenth of its total size. Its bulk lies hidden beneath the surface and is revealed only to those who are equipped to go down below the water line. Our lives are like that; there is much more to them than we see on the surface. Think of the visible part above the water line as representing the things you do, the thoughts you consciously think, and the feelings you sense going on within you. Let the mass below the water line represent the things that go on inside you that cannot be clearly seen or understood, such as motives, attitudes, impulses and so on.

Facing what goes on above the water line, our visible behaviours and actions, is a whole lot easier than delving below the surface, and this is why many Christians (not all) concern themselves with only what they can see, know and understand. These people can be described as 'surface copers', who cope with life by dealing with whatever they can see and ignoring all the rest. If, however, we are to enjoy a deeper relationship with God, then we will do so only as we come to grips with the tough issues that lie beneath the surface of our lives.

God, help me this day to stand before you in complete and utter honesty. Save me from becoming a 'surface coper' and give me the grace I need to face the things that I would normally avoid. In Jesus' name I pray. Amen.

FOR FURTHER STUDY – Isa. Ch. 11; 1 Kings 3:1–10; John 5:30
1. How does Jesus judge and reprove? / 2. What did Solomon ask for?

More needed than performance

FOR READING AND MEDITATION – PROVERBS 23:12–28

'My son, give me your heart, and let your eyes observe my ways.' (v. 26: NKJ)

We said yesterday that many Christians live on the surface of life and rarely, if ever, look below the water line. Their answer to the inner longings they sometimes feel to climb higher with God is to focus their attention on what goes on above the water line – the area of performance and behaviour. So they try harder in terms of more Bible reading, more prayer, more giving, more Christian activities.

There is nothing wrong with greater obedience, of course, and I would be the last person to view this as unimportant, but it is not the only, or indeed the final answer. A great mistake made by many Christians, who recognise they are not receiving from God the things they ought to be receiving is to think that the solution lies solely in more spiritual effort, the assumption being that as we do more above the water line, the problems that lie below the water line will all come right.

Now sometimes, greater obedience and more responsible effort do have this result. I have often found, for example, that when a man who falls out of love with his wife chooses a change in behaviour and deliberately sets out to do loving things for her, the loving behaviour can trigger loving feelings. I would be a fool to deny that, for I have seen it work all too often. However, there is more to spiritual change that a change on the surface. It can begin there, but it is not complete until the focus moves from the surface down into the depths. Those who remain above the water line in their Christian living and resist the invitation to look beneath the surface soon become legalists – good at performing but bad at being.

My Father and my God, I see that if change is to take place in me, then it must take place in all of me. Help me to see even more clearly that while what I do is important, what I am in the depth of my being is even more important. In Jesus' name. Amen.

FOR FURTHER STUDY – 2 Tim. 3:1–5; Isa. 29:1–13

1. What did Paul say would be a characteristic of the last days?
2. What was the Lord's complaint against the children of Israel?

There must be no pretence

FOR READING AND MEDITATION – MATTHEW 23:13–28

'...you are like whitewashed tombs which... appear beautiful outwardly, but inside are full of dead men's bones...'(v. 27: NKJ)

We ended yesterday with the thought that Christians who live on the surface and refuse to take a look below the water line soon become legalists. A legalist is someone who is more concerned about doing good than being good.

The Pharisees of Jesus' day were like that. They specialised in looking good and focusing only on those things that appear above the water line. Sin was defined by them in terms of visible transgressions, and as long as they did nothing to violate the standards which they so carefully defined, they regarded themselves as being free from sin. And there can be little doubt about it – they were good performers. Their level of disciplined conformity to external expectations was very high. They impressed many by their performance, but there was someone they failed to impress – Jesus. He told them that they were nothing more than whitewashed tombs and called them 'blind leaders of the blind' (Matt. 15:14, NKJ).

In his rebuke to the Pharisees, our Lord established a principle that must guide us in our effort to become the people he wants us to be, and that principle is this – there must be no pretence. Christ's teaching seems to be that we can't make it as his followers unless we are willing to take an honest and straightforward look at what is going on beneath the surface of our lives. To look honestly at those parts of our being which we would rather not know about is not, as some would have it, a sign of morbid introspection but a sign of healthy spirituality. Always remember, our Lord reserved his harshest criticism for those who like the Pharisees, made pretence and denial into a trademark.

O Father, you are boring deep – help me not to wriggle and squirm. Love me enough to overcome all my resistances, all my antipathies and all my fears. For I don't just want to be a better person – I want to be a whole person. In Jesus' name. Amen.

FOR FURTHER STUDY – Col. 2:1–20; Isa.1:11–17; Gal.4:10

1. What did Paul bring to the Colossians' attention?
2. How similar was it to Isaiah's word centuries before?

The awful consequences of pretence

FOR READING AND MEDITATION – ACTS 5:1–11
'When Ananias heard this, he fell down and died.
And great fear seized all who heard what had happened.' (v. 5: NIV)

We said yesterday that in his rebuke to the Pharisees, our Lord established an important principle of living – namely that there must be no pretence. Today we look at a couple who forfeited their lives because they pretended to be more spiritual than they were.

Ananias and Sapphira were highly respected members of the Early Church and appeared on the surface to be deeply committed disciples of the Lord Jesus Christ. I have no doubt myself that they had a fairly high degree of dedication, and easily went along with the idea of selling their possessions and putting the proceeds into the treasury of the Early Church. Their mistake, of course, was to pretend they had given their all when they hadn't, and the consequences of this pretence were, as our passage for today shows, swift and dramatic.

God deals harshly with pretence and dishonesty, but he is most gentle and compassionate to those who see themselves as they really are, confess that to him, and request his help in becoming the person they know he wants them to be. I have known people who have stood up in front of a Christian audience and talked about how wonderful it is to live a victorious Christian life when in reality they were inwardly messed up and pulled one way and another by conflict. And I have known others get up before their brothers and sisters, confessing that though they love the Lord, they are experiencing great struggles and difficulties in seeking to live for him. Who do you think is the closer to God? I will tell you – it is the one who is honest and open. Pretence repels God – openness and honesty draws him quickly to our side.

Father, help me to be a sincere and transparent person. Save me, I pray, from adopting an air of pretence and masquerading as someone I am not. You delight in openness and honesty – help me to delight in it too. Amen.

FOR FURTHER STUDY – Acts Ch 19; Eph. Ch.1; Rev. 2:1–5
1. Why did the word of the Lord spread rapidly in Ephesus?
2. What words did Christ bring to them some years later?

Ostrich Christians

FOR READING AND MEDITATION – PROVERBS 20:15–30

'The spirit of a man is the lamp of the Lord, searching all the inner depths of his heart.' (v. 27: NKJ)

Most of us (and I include myself) are not good at observing ourselves and reflecting honestly on what goes on beneath the surface of our lives. Why is this so? I think one of the reasons is fear – fear of the unknown, fear of losing control, fear of spoiling a comfortable existence or fear of having to face some unpleasant discoveries about ourselves. I have met many Christians in my time who adopt the attitude: however things are, good or bad, they could be worse, so it is better to leave well alone. I have heard the same attitude expressed in these words, 'Poking around in one's life is an unproductive exercise and it would be far better if people spent more time in God's Word and got their minds off themselves.'

When we read the Bible, however, what do we find? We discover texts like the one before us today, showing us that God has designed us with the ability to explore our deepest parts. Also we hear men like the psalmist crying out to God: 'Search me thoroughly, O God, and know my heart! Try me and know my thoughts! And see if there is any wicked or hurtful way in me, and lead me in the way everlasting' (Psalm 139:23–24, *Amp. Bible*).

I want to stress once again that too much introspection is unhealthy, but occasionally and in proper doses, it is 'good medicine'. Those who resist this and pretend everything is well when it isn't, are what a friend of mine calls 'ostrich Christians'. They have peace, but it is a peace built on unreality. When they lift their heads out of the sand, the peace they possess somehow falls to pieces. God's peace can keep our hearts and minds intact while we face whatever is true – outside and inside.

Father, save me from becoming an 'ostrich Christian' – someone who pretends everything is well when it isn't. Nothing, dear Lord, must be allowed to hinder the work that you want to do in my heart. Corner my soul and make me what you want me to be. Amen.

FOR FURTHER STUDY – Mark 2:1–8; Matt. 12:25; Luke 6:8; John 2:25

1. How deeply did Jesus see into people's lives?
2. How deeply do you let him penetrate into your life?

Why take an inside look?

FOR READING AND MEDITATION – ISAIAH 33:10–24

'Such a man will dwell on the heights; his place of defence will be the fortresses of rocks ...' (v. 16: *Amplified Bible*)

We spend one more day meditating on the thought that before we can have feet like hinds' feet, we must be prepared to take an honest and straightforward look at what is going on beneath the surface of our lives. Doing this, of course, can be dangerous unless it is approached in the right attitude. Some Christians use the process of self-examination as a means of avoiding rather than assuming responsibility. They look at what is going on inside themselves and allow what they discover there to develop into a cynical negativism which hinders rather than helps their Christian lives and experience.

Those who do this fail to understand the purpose of godly self-examination, which is to bring what is discovered to the Lord so that he can deal with it and remove it from our personalities. Many commentators have pointed out, in the incident when the Israelites in the wilderness were bitten by the snakes, that when they looked at themselves and recognised their condition, they were then highly motivated to look to the brass serpent for help (see Numbers 21:4–9).

The purpose of taking an honest look at what is going on beneath the surface of our lives is to promote a deeper dependence on the Lord and thus contribute to our spiritual effectiveness. Recognition of our true condition provides a strong motivation to look away from ourselves and turn in simple faith to the Lord Jesus Christ. As, in the weeks ahead, we take this journey into the core of our beings, let me encourage you to be willing to face yourself in a way that you have never done before. I cannot promise you it will be painless, but I can promise you it will be profitable.

Father, give me the courage to overcome all those fears that would rise within me and say, 'I am not sure that I can face it.' Deepen the conviction within me that with you, I can face anything. In Jesus' name. Amen.

FOR FURTHER STUDY – 1 Cor. 11:23–33; Lam. 3:40; Gal. 6:4

1. How does Paul admonish us? / 2. How does the writer of Lamentations put it?

Honesty put to the test

FOR READING AND MEDITATION – PSALM 15:1–5

'He who walks and lives uprightly…who works rightness and justice and speaks and thinks the truth in his heart' (v. 2: *Amplified Bible*)

Now we have seen that the first step toward producing a perfect coordination between the head and the heart is to be willing to take an honest look at what is going on beneath the surface of our lives; we must put our honesty to the test. Today we move to the second step by facing the question: when I pray or seek the Lord, is my heart fully and enthusiastically behind what I am asking for with my lips? If not, I will fail to surmount the heights of God 'with all four feet'.

One of the things that used to puzzle me greatly in the early days of my pastoral ministry was to sit down with people who were not getting what they longed for spiritually and, after hours of counselling, sometimes discover that although they were asking God for something with their lips, they were not really desiring it deep down in their hearts. I am thinking as I write of a woman I knew who prayed earnestly (and loudly) in church for the conversion of her non-Christian husband.

One day, however, in a moment of great openness and honesty (such as often occurs in counselling) she admitted that deep down in her heart, she didn't really want her husband to be converted because she was afraid that if he was, the attention and sympathy she was getting from her brothers and sisters in the church would no longer be there. Once she realised what was going on inside her, she was able to deal with it and became one of the most spiritually released woman I have ever known. Her whole life (not just her prayer life) became one of deep, quiet conviction and eventually, many years later, she had the joy of seeing her husband surrender to Christ.

My Father, one thing is clear – such are the subterfuges of the human heart that without your light and guidance, I can be self-deceived. Help me to apply the test of honesty and openness to my own spiritual life. In Jesus' name. Amen.

FOR FURTHER STUDY – Jer. 17:1–10, 23:24; 1 Cor. 3:20

1. How does Jeremiah describe the heart?
2. How does the Lord view the thoughts of the worldly wise?

Preferring the safety of the old

FOR READING AND MEDITATION – MATTHEW 7:1–14

'"Ask, and it will be given to you; seek, and you will find; knock, and it will be opened to you."'
(v. 7: NKJ)

We ended yesterday with the illustration of how a Christian woman with an unconverted husband came to see that what she was asking for with her lips was not what she desired in her heart. Once she was willing to take a deep inside look, she recognised what was going on in her heart, put it right and became a released woman.

Although, in her case, she had the joy of seeing her husband become a Christian, this must not be taken to mean that we have here a guaranteed formula for bringing a non-Christian spouse to the Lord. It is right to pray with passion and desire for those in our families who are not converted, but we must remember that it is not our prayers that save them. Our prayers help, of course, but each of them must personally surrender their wills to Christ if they are to be converted. People are admitted into the family of God only as they give up their commitment to independence and say, in effect: 'Heavenly Father, I can do nothing to save myself; save me, in Jesus' Name.'

Let me tell you about a man I knew who came to me complaining that he was not getting what he wanted spiritually. He told me that he had a deep sense of unworthiness and although he prayed desperately for God to take it away, the sense of unworthiness stayed with him. After many hours of talking, praying and heart-searching, he came to see that although in his head he was asking for God to take the feeling away, deep down in his heart he did not desire it. He had lived with it for so long that he was afraid of the new positive feelings he would have to face if the negative feelings were not there. He preferred the safety of the old to the adventure of the new.

Father, day by day I am seeing more clearly than ever the subtle devices of the human heart. Give me the insight I need to probe my own heart and track down those things that may be preventing me from climbing into the heights with you. In Jesus' name I pray. Amen.

FOR FURTHER STUDY – Luke 18:1–8; Deut. 4:29; Prov. 8:17
1. What characteristic did the woman display? / 2. How can we be sure of finding God?

Why we cling to unforgiveness

FOR READING AND MEDITATION – PSALM 86:1–17

'... give me an undivided heart, that I may fear your name.' (v. 11: NIV)

Today we look at another example of how we can ask for one thing with our lips but something completely different with our hearts. A friend of mine who is a minister and Christian counsellor shared with me just recently about a woman who told him that she spent thirty to forty-five minutes every day asking God to take away from her an unforgiving spirit. She told him that what she wanted more than anything in the world was the ability to forgive those in her family who had brought her hurt.

The minister joined her in prayer, but as they sat together in his study, the Holy Spirit spoke to his heart and showed him that deep down, the woman did not want a forgiving spirit. The minister waited for the Spirit to show more, but nothing came. Realising that he had enough information to pursue the matter, the minister invited the woman to explore the possibility that what she was asking for with her lips was not what she was asking for in her heart.

At first, the woman seemed annoyed and upset by the suggestion that deep down she might not want what she was asking for, but gradually she agreed to take an inside look. In the hour or two that followed, this came out – despite her claim that she wanted to forgive, deep down in her heart she clung to an unforgiving spirit, as it gave her the justification she felt she needed when she was the cause of hurt to someone else. In other words, she was saying to herself, 'Other people have hurt me, so it won't matter so much when I hurt them.' When she saw what she was doing, she immediately surrendered to God and found inner release and freedom.

God, I am deeply challenged by this, yet deeply relieved to know that whatever might elude me can never elude you. I open up my heart right now for inspection and examination. Search me and make me whole. In Jesus' name. Amen.

FOR FURTHER STUDY – Luke 17:1–5; Mark 11:25; Eph. 4:32

1. How did the apostles respond to Christ's challenge?
2. How did Paul admonish the Ephesians?

Why so many slip and fail

FOR READING AND MEDITATION – LUKE 11:1–11

'"Forgive us our sins, for we also forgive everyone who sins against us"...' (v. 4: NIV)

I was about to move on to another illustration of how we can ask God for something with our lips but want another thing in our hearts, when the Holy Spirit gently nudged me to stay with what I was talking about yesterday. You will remember I drew your attention to the Christian woman who asked God to deliver her from an unforgiving spirit, yet deep down in her heart, she held on to it because of the way in which it served her unconscious purposes.

I want to suggest that you read the next sentence carefully, for in it lies the secret of the failure of many Christians to walk with 'hinds' feet' to the high places which God has prepared for them. If you harbour resentment or hatred toward just one individual in the world, by that much you are separated from God himself. By just that much do your rear feet fail to track with your front feet and, in the pursuit of God, you are in danger of slipping over the edge to spiritual failure. Let me put it even more clearly – if anyone has sinned against you and you have not forgiven him from the depths of your heart, then the attitude of unwillingness is a sin against God.

Listen to what the apostle John says about this: 'If anyone says, "I love God", yet hates his brother, he is a liar. For anyone who does not love his brother, whom he has seen, cannot love God, whom he has not seen' (1 John 4:20, NIV). The very first thing we must do if we are to climb higher with God is make sure there is no bitterness or resentment lingering in our hearts. If you have not done so before, turn now in thought to all those who have trespassed against you and forgive them – fully and completely.

God, once again I plead for the insight and courage to see myself truly, for I may be cloaking my resentments with garments of piety. I would harbour no dangerous Trojan horses within me. Help me to be free of all resentment. In Jesus' name. Amen.

FOR FURTHER STUDY – 1 John Ch. 4, 3:14–24; John 15:12

1. What was Christ's commandment? / 2. Why not memorise 1 John 3:16?

The familiar feelings of failure

FOR READING AND MEDITATION – PSALM 145:1–21

'The Lord is near to all who call on him, to all who call on him in truth.' (v. 18: NIV)

Today we look at another example of how the head and the heart can lack spiritual coordination, thus preventing us from having 'hinds' feet' and scaling the mountain peaks with God. Many years ago, when I pastored a church in the centre of London, a young man came to see me and said, 'I am not making a success of my life spiritually. I want with all my heart to become a successful Christian, but I seem to be failing in everything I do.' At that time I was not as aware of the subtleties of the human heart as I am today, and I encouraged him to keep trying. I said, 'Responsible effort and dogged obedience will bring you what you need; keep going no matter what.' I am convinced that the advice I gave him was good, but it was not complete.

About a year later, after God had allowed me to see the subtleties and deceptions of my own heart, and after putting some personal things right before him, I sat down once again with the young man and asked him how things were going. 'A little better,' he said, 'but even though I keep asking God to help me become a successful Christian, I am still failing.'

I took a deep breath and tentatively suggested that perhaps, deep down in his heart, he preferred failure to success. He looked at me in amazement and after a few seconds said, 'Say some more about that. I feel you are touching something very vulnerable inside me.' We talked for hours and he told me how all his life he had lived with failure, and it soon became obvious that he preferred the familiar feelings of failure to the unfamiliar feelings of success – even spiritual success. That one insight was all he needed to open up the whole of his being to God.

O Father, if I, too, need something to trigger off a deeper openness and self-awareness in my heart, then give it to me today. I want nothing more than to be an honest person – honest, not only on the surface but also at the depths. Help me – in Jesus' name. Amen.

FOR FURTHER STUDY – Ex. 16:1–3; Num. 11:1–6, 13:17–33

1. What was the problem of the children of Israel?
2. Why were they not prepared to move forward?

The danger of denial

FOR READING AND MEDITATION – JOHN 8:21–36

'And you shall know the truth, and the truth shall make you free.' (v. 32: NKJ)

One of the biggest difficulties some of you will experience as you follow me through the concepts I am now presenting will be to make the admission that perhaps your heart and your head may not be spiritually coordinated. Permit me to come back to the point I made the other day, that many Christians are content to live above the water line and insist that it is quite unnecessary to wrestle and struggle with the things that go on deep inside us. Their motto is: just trust, persevere and obey. This is fine as far as it goes, but in my opinion it does not go far enough.

The effect of this teaching is to blunt the painful reality of what the Bible says about the condition of the human heart: 'The heart is deceitful above all things, and desperately wicked; who can know it? I, the Lord, search the heart' (Jer. 17:9–10: NKJ). It is possible for even mature Christians to be self-deceived, and this is why we must live in constant dependence on God and invite him from time to time, as did the psalmist, to 'search me…and know my heart' (Psalm 139:23, NKJ).

There is a word to describe the attitude of those who ignore what may be going on deep inside them and concentrate only on what they can see above the water line, and that word is – denial. In many Christian circles, maintaining a comfortable distance from what may be going on deep down inside is strongly encouraged. But nothing can be gained from denial. In fact, I would say it is one of the major reasons why our feet are not like 'hinds feet' and why we slip and slide on the slopes that lead upward to a deeper understanding and knowledge of God.

God, I realise I am dealing with something too devastating to pass over quickly or lightly. Help me to be aware of the tendency that is in me to deny that I deny. Stay close to me at this moment, dear Father, for without you I can do nothing. Amen.

FOR FURTHER STUDY – Gal. Ch. 6; Rom. 6:16–23

1. What was Paul's word to the Galatians? / 2. How are we to walk?

The stark choice facing us

FOR READING AND MEDITATION – LUKE 16:1–13

'...unless you are honest in small matters, you won't be in large ones...' (v. 10: TLB)

I want to spend another day nailing down what I consider to be one of the most damaging things in the Christian life – denial. What is denial? It is the attitude that avoids looking realistically at issues and pretends that things are not the way they are.

What I am going to say may sound like a sweeping statement, but it is based on over forty years of Christian experience: most Christians, including me, are, to varying degrees, held together by denial. Deep down we sense that if we were to face the realities of life openly and honestly, we might not be able to cope, and so we pretend things are not what they are. I know Christians who pretend that what they have satisfies more than it does, or pretend they haven't been hurt as badly as they have. They refuse to face and feel what is going on inside them, due to the strange belief that it is lack of faith on their part to admit to anything that is negative.

The teaching that we ought to ignore what is going on inside us instead of facing it and dealing with it, is responsible for more casualties in the Christian life than anything I know. A Christian psychologist says, 'I am convinced that much of what we admire as spiritual maturity is a fragile adjustment to life based on the foundation of denial.' My own observation would lead me to say that I have found some non-Christians to be more open and honest in facing what is going on inside them than some Christians. Is denial a wise plan for life? Absolutely not. The choice, then, is stark: either to deny and live comfortably, or face every issue painfully – and go on to climb the heights with God.

Father, help me to see that I need never be afraid to face anything, for in you I have the resources to resolve all problems, not just skirt them. Show me how to blast denial right out of my life – once and for all. In Jesus' name. Amen.

FOR FURTHER STUDY – Eccl. 5:1–7; Isa. 29:13; Matt. 15:1–9

1. What do fools do? / 2. What prophecy was fulfilled by the Pharisees?

A heart that pants for God

FOR READING AND MEDITATION – PSALM 42:1–11

'As the deer pants for the water brooks, so pants my soul for you, O God.' (v. 1: NKJ)

Today we look at the third step we must take if we are to have feet like 'hinds' feet' and be able to pursue God with a coordinated heart and mind – be willing to get in touch with the deep thirst for God which resides at the core of your being. Believe me, you will never pursue God 'with all four feet' until you become aware of this deep inner thirst – and not just aware, but intensely aware. The thought underlying the word picture in our text today is that of a deer craving for water during a prolonged drought or after having been chased by a hunter or a marauding animal. The psalmist said his heart panted for God, and the strong Hebrew word used here suggests a desire so intense that it is audible.

Permit me once again to ask you a personal question: do you pant after God in the way the psalmist described? Do you pursue him in such a way that everything else in your life takes second place? I have to confess that I don't. Oh yes, I long after God. I can even say I yearn for him. But I know I don't pant after him in the way the psalmist described. And neither, I am convinced, do most other Christians.

Now don't react defensively and say, 'Whatever does he mean? My heart pants after God and I will not let anyone try to tell me differently.' Let me ask you to reserve any judgment you have on the statement I have just made, and I think I will be able to show you over the next few days that although you have a deep desire to know God, you might still not have got to the place where your heart pants after him in the way the psalmist described. But take heart – you can. You can.

God my Father, I would be rid of all that hinders my pursuit of you. Help me to see clearly into my heart, for I am so prone to defend myself. If there is something here that I need to know, then help me to look at it – openly and honestly. In Jesus' name. Amen.

FOR FURTHER STUDY – Psa. 73:15–28, 27:4; 2 Chron. 15:15

1. What was the psalmist's confession?
2. What happened when Israel sought the Lord wholeheartedly?

The DIY syndrome

FOR READING AND MEDITATION – DANIEL 5:13–28

'…the God who holds your breath in his hand and owns all your ways, you have not glorified.' (v. 23: NKJ)

Yesterday I made what some might consider a startling statement when I said that most Christians do not pant after God in the way the psalmist described in Psalm 42:1. Now and over the next few days, I must attempt to make clear what I mean.

Firstly, let me pull into focus the major problem with which we all struggle as soon as we arrive in this world. When God created us in the beginning, he designed us to have a relationship with himself. This means that deep within our being is a thirst for God that will not go away. It can be ignored, disguised, misunderstood, wrongly labelled or submerged under a welter of activity, but it will not disappear – and for good reason. We were designed to enjoy something better than this world can give us, particularly in the sphere of relationships. No human relationship can satisfy in the way that a relationship with God satisfies.

This deep thirst for God that resides within us makes us dependent on God for satisfaction, and that is something our sinful human nature deeply resents. You see, due to Adam and Eve's sin in the Garden of Eden, we have all been left a legacy called, 'Do It Yourself'. By this I mean there is something within every single one of us that wants to take charge of our own affairs and have a hand in bringing about our own salvation. So here is the problem: to face the fact realistically that we inwardly thirst after God puts us in touch with a level of helplessness from which our sinful human nature shrinks. It reinforces the conviction that we are dependent on someone outside of ourselves for satisfaction. And that is something we don't care to acknowledge.

O my Father, I recognise this elemental drive in my nature which causes me to resist standing in utter helplessness before you. But I sense that there can be no breakthrough in my life until I face the issue and deal with it. Help me Father. In Jesus' name. Amen.

FOR FURTHER STUDY – Psa. 143:1–6, 42:2, 63:1

1. What did the psalmist recognise? / 2. What does it mean to 'thirst'?

Looking in the wrong places

FOR READING AND MEDITATION – JEREMIAH 2:1–13

'My people have committed two sins: they have forsaken me, the spring of living water, and have dug their own cisterns, broken cisterns ...' (v. 13: NIV)

The points I am making to support the statement I made a couple of days ago, that very few people pant after God in the way described in Psalm 42:1, must be followed with great care. It will take several days of close reasoning to make clear the thrust of what I am saying, but I hope the rewards will be worth the effort.

I said yesterday that the major problem with which we are all confronted when we come into this world is that we have at the core of our being a deep thirst for God which makes us entirely dependent on God for satisfaction. Our sinful human nature resents this because it dislikes the feeling of helplessness that such dependence brings, and prefers to have a hand in bringing about its own satisfaction. This terrible tendency of the human heart to try to satisfy its own thirst independently of God is brought out most clearly in the passage before us today. The prophet Jeremiah indicts the people of God for depending on broken cisterns in their efforts to quench their spiritual thirst, cisterns which they themselves made but which can hold no water.

Note carefully the two observations our text for today suggests: first, the people were thirsty, and second, they moved in the wrong direction to satisfy their thirst. God said it was as if they walked right past the clear waters he provided and chose instead to dig their own wells. They wanted to run their own lives and refused to come to God and allow him to quench their deep thirst. This stubborn commitment to independence is responsible more than anything else for preventing us having feet like 'hinds' feet'.

Gracious Father, I see that the problem you had with the nation of Israel is my problem too. For far too often I try to dig my own well. You are searching deeply into my life. Help me not to evade or avoid any issue. In Jesus' name. Amen.

FOR FURTHER STUDY – Judges 17:1–6, 21:25; Prov. 28:26; 1 Cor. 10:12

1. How does the book of Judges sum up the human heart?
2. What was Paul's admonition to the Corinthians?

How problems occur

FOR READING AND MEDITATION – JOHN 7:32–44

'...if anyone thirsts, let him come to me and drink.' (v. 37: NKJ)

Yesterday we put our finger on what in my opinion is the biggest single preventative to us having feet like 'hinds' feet' – a stubborn commitment to independence. This reflects itself in every one of our lives – even those who have been on the Way for several decades. The problem all began, as we saw, in the Garden of Eden when Adam and Eve, who were designed to experience life and fulfilment by being dependent on God, decided to act independently of him. Sin can be summed up in the phrase, 'A Declaration of Independence' – an attempt to do for ourselves what only God can do for us.

What happened in the Garden of Eden is duplicated millions of times daily, not only in the lives of unbelievers, but in the lives of Christians also – Christians who use self-centred attempts and strategies to satisfy the deep thirst that is in their hearts for God. Almost every spiritual or psychological problem that exists has at its roots this condition – the person is failing in some way to let God satisfy the deep inner thirst.

This might sound a simplistic explanation to some, but after many years of experience working in the field of counselling, I am convinced that it is this which underlies such conditions as anorexia, sexual perversions, worry, hostility, depression, homosexuality, and so on. You see, if we are not conscious that God is meeting the deep thirst that we have for him on the inside of our being, then the inner emptiness will move us in one of two directions – to work to fill the emptiness in any way we can, or to withdraw and protect ourselves from the possibility of any further pain.

Father, I see yet again that until and unless my deep thirst for you is being quenched, I am in deep trouble and vulnerable to all kinds of problems. I simply must get this issue straightened out. Help me, dear Father. In Jesus' name. Amen.

FOR FURTHER STUDY – Matt. 5:1–6; John 4:1–42

1. What was the message of Jesus to the woman?
2. How was this reinforced through the teaching of the Sermon of the Mount?

The purpose of living

FOR READING AND MEDITATION – LUKE 10:25–37

'..."Love the Lord your God..." and, "Love your neighbour as yourself."' (v. 27: NIV)

We ended yesterday with the thought that if God is not meeting the thirst for life which exists at the core of our beings, then we will strive to dig our own wells and slake our thirst in some self-centred way. The energy behind most of our behaviour (particularly strange or abnormal behaviour) is an independent attempt to satiate the deep longings that God and God alone can satisfy. If you want to know a Biblical reason why people do the things they do, then keep these thoughts in mind.

A man said to me some time ago, 'Why do I browbeat my wife and make demands on her which I know are not loving? And why, despite my best efforts to change, do I fall back into my usual patterns?' I told him, 'Your legitimate longings for impact and respect are not being met by God, and as you can't function very well when these longings go unmet, you set about trying to get your wife to meet them.' He saw the point, asked God to forgive him for drinking at the wrong well and turned in a fresh way to Christ for life and power and reality.

But what about the people who go in the other direction and withdraw from others, manifesting such symptoms as extreme shyness and some forms of depression? These people have little awareness of their thirst being quenched by God – hence a degree of inner emptiness – and are motivated to avoid moving toward loving involvement with others for fear they may be rejected. Self-enhancement (a selfish attempt to quench our own thirst) or self-rejection – these are the two styles of relationship that characterise many Christians' lives. And both are a violation of the law of love.

Loving Lord, your Word is crystal clear – the purpose of living is simply to love as I am loved. If I am not loving others, then quite simply, I am not allowing you to love me. I am sinning in both directions. Help me, my Saviour. Amen.

FOR FURTHER STUDY – John 12:1–35; 15:12; Matt. 22:39; 1 Thess. 3:12

1. How do we show that we belong to Jesus?
2. What was Paul's desire for the Thessalonians?

Much easier to pretend...

FOR READING AND MEDITATION – JOHN 5:24–40

'...you are not willing to come to me that you may have life.' (v. 40: NKJ)

Today we return to the issue I raised a few days ago when I stated that, in my opinion, most Christians (myself included) do not pant after God in the way described by the psalmist. Why is this so? Because to pant after God means we have to get in touch with the deep thirst which is at the centre of our being, and acknowledge our basic helplessness and dependence – a feeling which our fallen human nature deeply dislikes.

Most of us instinctively draw back from facing and dealing with this stubborn commitment to independence, and pretend we are all right as we are. It is much easier to pretend we are thirsting after God than it is to face the challenge of giving up our commitment to independence. Even while writing these lines, I have been conscious that the challenge I am putting before you is one I want to deny in my own life. There is something in me that would like to think – and would like you to think – that I have a heart that pants after God. But I know that if I stop short of examining my independent strategies for finding life on my own, identifying them and giving them up, I will never get in touch with the deep thirst for God that exists at the core of my being.

What is the answer? I must ask God to search my heart, expose my self-centred motivations, and help me see just where it is that I stop short of panting after him. You see, the more deeply we sense our thirst, the more passionately we will pursue water – but we will never sense that thirst until we are willing to face the fact that we may be drinking more from our own self-constructed wells than from the wells of God.

Father, I tremble as I recognise this terrible tendency within me to walk right past the fountain of living water and drink from a well of my own making. But help me to recognise it for what it really is – not just a terrible tendency, but also a terrible sin. In Jesus' name I pray. Amen.

FOR FURTHER STUDY – Ex. 32:1–9; Isa. 28:12, 30:15; 2 Chron. 24:19

1. How did God describe the children of Israel?
2. What is said of them time and time again?

The word that irritates

FOR READING AND MEDITATION – 2 CHRONICLES 7:11–22

'If my people … will humble themselves and … turn from their wicked ways, then will I hear from heaven and will forgive their sin …'(v. 14: NIV)

We spend one more day on the question: do we really pant after God? As I have said, I am convinced that most Christians never allow themselves to come too close to the deep thirst for God that exists at the core of their being, for if they did, they would be compelled to get in touch with their basic helplessness and independence – a fact which our fallen human nature helps us to deny.

Why would we want to deny our basic helplessness and independence? Because to recognise it puts us in a position where we have to repent of it – and that is something our fallen human nature pulls back from doing. Believe me, the one word that grates and irritates our carnal nature is the word 'repent'. It is much easier to be given advice like, 'Read a few more chapters of the Bible every day', 'Add another fifteen minutes to your prayer time', or 'Seize more opportunities to share your faith', than to be told to repent. All these things I have just mentioned may be excellent in themselves, but more is required if we are to get in touch with the deep thirst for God which exists at the core of our being – we must repent.

But repent of what? Our stubborn commitment to independence; the awful desire and practice of choosing to dig our own wells – a passionate pursuit of God demands this. Believe me, no matter what we say with our lips, we will never begin to pant after God until we are prepared to repent of the self-sufficiency that has made its home deep within our hearts. This, in my opinion, is the biggest single step we can take in our pursuit of God and the experience of having feet like 'hinds' feet'.

Gracious and loving heavenly Father, help me to repent deeply. May I know at this moment a turning from self-dependence to God-dependence. I give you my willingness – now give me your power. In Jesus' name I ask it. Amen.

FOR FURTHER STUDY – Psa. 34:1–18; Joel 2:12; Luke 13:1–3

1. What was the central message of Jesus? / 2. How does the psalmist express it?

Faith in two minds

FOR READING AND MEDITATION – MATTHEW 21:18–27

'…if you have faith, and do not doubt …you can say to this mountain, "Go, throw yourself into the sea," and it will be done.' (v. 21: NIV)

We move on now to consider the fourth step we must take if we are to have feet like 'hinds' feet' – learn how to face and handle any doubts that may arise in your heart. Most of us have to face the problem of doubt at some time or another, and unless we have a clear understanding of what is involved when we doubt and how to deal with it, our pursuit of God can be greatly hindered.

What exactly is doubt? My research into the word gave me this information: 'Our English word doubt comes from the Latin *dubitare*, which is rooted in an Aryan word meaning "two".' To doubt means to take two positions on something or to have a divided heart. A major misconception concerning doubt – and one that has brought great anxiety to many a Christian's heart – is to view doubt as the opposite of faith, which clearly it is not. Doubt is not the opposite of faith; unbelief is the opposite of faith. Os Guinness puts it like this, 'To believe is to be "in one mind" about accepting something as true; to disbelieve is to be "in one mind" about rejecting it. To doubt is to waver between the two, to believe and disbelieve at once, and so to be "in two minds".'

Donald Bridge, in his book *When Christians Doubt*, refers to doubt as 'faith asking questions'. Some might think this definition elevates doubt to a position it does not deserve and masks its true nature – but not so. It is only when we understand what doubt really is that we can deal with it in the way we should. So let me spell it out once again – doubt is not a betrayal of faith, nor the surrendering of the soul to unbelief. It is, as Os Guinness puts it, 'faith in two minds'.

My God and Father, I would be at my best – at your best. But your best cannot get across to me if doubt remains in my heart. Show me the steps I must take to overcome doubt. In Jesus' name I pray. Amen.

FOR FURTHER STUDY – Mat. 14:22–33; Luke 24:13–35

1. How does Peter illustrate the principle of being in two minds?
2. What did Jesus mean by 'slow of heart'?

The true nature of doubt

FOR READING AND MEDITATION – MATTHEW 28:1–20
'When they saw him, they worshipped him; but some doubted.' (v. 17: NKJ)

We said yesterday that one of the things which has brought anxiety and bondage into many a Christian's life is a wrong understanding of doubt. A man whom I regarded as truly converted said to me some years ago, 'I am riddled with so many doubts that I sometimes feel I am not a Christian at all.'

When I pointed out to him the nature of doubt – that it is not the same as unbelief – I saw a new light come into his eyes and a new expression appear on his face. He grasped me by the hands and said, 'How can I ever sufficiently thank you? You have released a pressure that has been building up inside me for years.' I met him years later, and he told me that the simple insight I had given him concerning the nature of doubt was all he needed to face his doubts and deal with them in a spiritual way. I say again, no misunderstanding causes more anxiety and brings more bondage to the heart of a Christian than that which concerns the nature of doubt.

Let's put unbelief under the microscope for a moment, for by doing so we will see the nature of doubt still more clearly. 'Unbelief is a wilful refusal to believe, resulting in a deliberate decision to disobey. It is a state of mind that is closed against God, an attitude of heart that disobeys God as much as it disbelieves the truth. It is the consequence of a settled choice.' Doubt is not a wilful decision to disbelieve, but a suspension between faith and unbelief. To believe is to be in one mind, to disbelieve is also to be in one mind, but to doubt is to be caught in the halfway stage between the two – suspended between the desire to affirm and the desire to negate.

Father, while I am relieved to discover that doubt is not the same as unbelief, I nevertheless long to live a doubt-free existence. Break down any barriers within me that would hinder the flow of faith. In Christ's name I ask it. Amen.

FOR FURTHER STUDY – John 20:24–29, 11:16, 14:5, 21:2; Matt. 10:3
1. How did Thomas display his total commitment? / 2. Why then did he doubt?

Doubt must be corrected

FOR READING AND MEDITATION – MATTHEW 14:22–36

'…Jesus reached out his hand and caught him.
"You of little faith," he said, "why did you doubt?"' (v. 31: NIV)

We ended yesterday with the statement, 'To believe is to be in one mind (wholly positive), to disbelieve is also to be in one mind (wholly negative), but to doubt is to be caught in the halfway stage between the two.' While it is possible for us to distinguish between doubt and unbelief in theory, it is not so easy in practice. Doubt can eventually move in the direction of unbelief and cross the borderline, but when it does it ceases to be doubt. The idea of 'total' or 'complete' doubt is a contradiction in terms, for doubt that is total can no longer be classified as doubt; it is unbelief.

Os Guinness points out that when we attempt to undertake a Biblical analysis of doubt, we can come out with either a 'hard' or 'soft' view of the subject. Those who take a 'soft' view of doubt point to how vastly different doubt is from unbelief, and those who take a 'hard' view point out its similarities. Both views can be drawn out of the Scriptures. Error is usually truth out of balance and it is important, therefore, that we get a balanced view of what the Bible has to say about doubt. In my view it can be summarised like this – doubt is not the same as unbelief, but unless corrected, can lead naturally to it.

This view has helped me avoid what I consider to be the extremes of being too hard or too soft on doubt. It is a condition that must be regarded as serious but it need not be fatal. Don't allow your doubts to bring you into condemnation, for when faced and brought into clear perspective, they can be the catalyst to a deeper pursuit of God.

Father, when will I learn that in you all things serve – even doubt? Show me how to make my doubts into stepping-stones and use them to come into an even closer relationship with you. Amen.

FOR FURTHER STUDY – Matt. 8:1–26, 6:30, 16:8

1. What phrase did Jesus often use? / 2. What did he say of the centurion?

Doubt keeps faith in trim

FOR READING AND MEDITATION – JOHN 8:34–47

'...he is a liar and the father of lies.' (v. 44: NIV)

There are many things in life that at first glance appear to have no point, purpose or value. Fear is one such thing; doubt is another. I have heard it argued that all fear is of the devil and can serve no useful purpose in human life – but that is not true. Fear of being burnt helps us avoid coming in contact with hot metals. Fear of being run over produces within us a healthy caution as we negotiate a traffic-infested street. Fear can have a positive purpose – and so can doubt.

One of the values of doubt is that it can be used to help us detect error. We live in a world of which at the moment Satan is 'prince', and he tries his utmost to get us to believe his lies. Jesus was not being poetic when he described Satan as the 'father of lies'. The devil's stock in trade is half-truths, and half-lies where the half-lie masquerades as the whole truth. So because all things are not true, not everything should be believed. Some things ought to be doubted. One writer says, 'The inescapable presence of doubt is a constant reminder of our responsibility to truth in a twilight world of truth and half-truth.' It acts like a spur to challenge us to find out the truth about a situation.

It is precisely because all is not certain that we have to make certain. Francis Bacon put it like this, 'If a man will begin with certainties, he shall end in doubts; but if he will be content to begin with doubts, he shall end in certainties.' Doubt can act as a sparring partner both to truth and error; it keeps faith trim and assists us in shedding the paunchiness of false ideas.

Gracious and loving Father, thank you for reminding me yet again that I can take anything that comes and use it to positive ends – even doubt. Help me to use my doubts as a sparring partner to keep my faith trim. In Jesus' name I pray. Amen.

FOR FURTHER STUDY – 2 Peter 2:1–10; Titus 1:9–11; 2 Tim 4:1–5

1. What will come in the last days? / 2. How did Paul exhort Timothy?

The first thing to do

FOR READING AND MEDITATION – 1 TIMOTHY 2:1–15

'I want men everywhere to lift up holy hands in prayer, without anger or disputing.' (v. 8: NIV)

We looked yesterday at the way doubt could become a sparring partner to keep our faith trim. We must accept the fact, however, that although doubt can be turned destructively against error, it is also possible for it to be turned destructively against truth. This brings us to the question: how do we deal with the darker side of doubt? The first thing we must do is to bring every doubt into the open and examine it.

Most Christians I know fail to do this; they do nothing with their doubts and just hope that they will go away. The way people react to their doubts is an excellent indication of their attitude to doubt itself. Many feel ashamed when they experience doubt and thus push the doubts below the surface of their minds and refuse to recognise them. Some even regard doubt as the unpardonable sin. Others treat it as an unmentionable subject and never refer to any doubts they have for fear they are letting the side down. I myself sometimes struggle with doubt – even after over forty years in the Christian life.

In the months following my conversion, I had doubts about the inspiration and inerrancy of the Bible until, one night, I decided to accept it by faith. When I did, all my doubts concerning it were immediately dissolved, and from that day to this I have never had one doubt about the reliability of Scripture. But I have doubted other things – particularly in the area of personal guidance. I have learned, however, not to let doubts threaten or intimidate me, and when they come I simply look them in the face and say, 'I am going to put you in harness and make you work to bring me closer to God.' Now my doubts get fewer and fewer.

Father, how can I sufficiently thank you for showing me how to take the negative things of life and turn them into positives? Nothing need work against me when I have you within. I am so thankful. Amen.

FOR FURTHER STUDY – 1 John 2:1-20, 3:24; 1 Cor. 13:12

1. What did Paul admit to? / 2. What did John affirm?

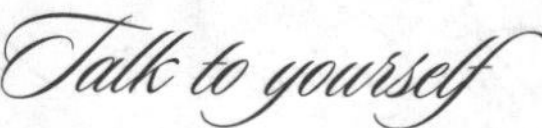

Talk to yourself

FOR READING AND MEDITATION – HEBREWS 4:1–13

'For the word of God is living and powerful…
and is a discerner of the thoughts and intents of the heart.' (v. 12: NKJ)

We continue looking at how we ought to handle doubt. Once we have acknowledged and faced any doubts that may be lurking within us, we must then seek to have them resolved as quickly as possible. Whatever we do, we must not let them go unchallenged. Pascal said, 'Doubt is an unhappy state but there is an indispensable duty to seek when we are in doubt, and thus anyone who doubts and does not seek is at once unhappy and in the wrong.'

How do we go about resolving doubts? One way is to bring them to the Lord in prayer and ask him to help you overcome them. If prayer does not dissolve them, apply the tactic Nehemiah adopted when he said: 'But we prayed to our God and posted a guard' (Neh. 4:9, NIV). Take a verse of Scripture that is the opposite of your doubt and hold it in the centre of your mind, repeating it to yourself many times throughout the day. Dr Martin Lloyd-Jones once said, 'Have you realised that most of your unhappiness in life is due to the fact that you are listening to yourself instead of talking to yourself? We must talk to ourselves instead of allowing "ourselves" to talk to us!'

In listening to our doubts instead of talking to them, we fall prey to the same temptation that caught Adam and Eve off guard in the Garden of Eden. The order of creation was stood on its head when the first human pair allowed themselves to be dictated to by the animal world (in the form of the serpent) when, in fact, they had been put in a position to dictate to it. Don't let your doubts dictate to you. Turn the tables and dictate to them. Talk to them with words from the Word of God.

Father, help me never to be nonplussed, for in you there are ways to overcome every problem. Drive the truth I have learned today deeply into my spirit so that I may apply it whenever I am faced with doubt. In Jesus' name. Amen.

FOR FURTHER STUDY – Gen. Ch. 3; Psa. 53:5; James 1:6
1. What was Satan's strategy? / 2. What did Adam confess?

The Doubter's Prayer

FOR READING AND MEDITATION – JOHN 20:19–29

'"Do not be unbelieving, but believing."' (v. 27: NKJ)

We spend one more day on the subject of doubt. If, after facing your doubts, praying about them and developing the habit of talking to yourself with a Scripture verse or passage that refutes them, they still persist, then seek the help of a minister or a Christian counsellor. God has given us three resources to help us whenever we get into spiritual difficulties: the Word of God, the Spirit of God, and the people of God. The final answer to doubt may come as you share with an experienced Christian the things that are going on in your heart.

If you are not able to get the kind of help I am suggesting, then get in touch with your nearest Christian bookshop and ask them to recommend some helpful reading on the subject. Whatever you do, don't allow yourself to settle down into a complacent attitude about your doubts. Adopt a positive approach and determine to do something about resolving them. This will ensure that even though your doubts may take some time to be resolved, they will not degenerate into unbelief. Let me remind you of *The Doubter's Prayer* compiled by Martin Luther:

> Dear Lord, although I am sure of my position,
> I am unable to sustain it without Thee.
> Help me or I am lost.

Remember this – if the only thing you are able to do is pray, then that by itself will prevent doubt from becoming unbelief. If you go further, however, and adopt the principle of 'talking to yourself' from the Word of God, then you have in your hands the strategy for overcoming every single doubt.

Father, help me, whenever I don't know what to do, to turn naturally to prayer. Then no moment will be empty or fruitless. But help me also to utilise the power of your Word, the Bible. Let these two things become my central strategy. Amen.

FOR FURTHER STUDY – Mark 9:14–29; Matt. 9:29–30, 21:21

1. What was the father's request? / 2. Do you need to pray that prayer today?

Another dip into the depths

FOR READING AND MEDITATION – PSALM 24:1–10

'Who may ascend the hill of the Lord?
...He who has clean hands and a pure heart...' (vv. 3–4: NIV)

It may be that as we pursue these suggestions of how we can have feet like 'hinds' feet' and ascend into the heights with God, you are saying to yourself, 'How many more steps do I have to take if I am to develop a rich relationship with the Almighty?' Well, I am afraid, once we agree to taking an honest and straightforward look at what is going on inside us, we must be ready for a number of strong spiritual challenges. But don't allow yourself to be disheartened, for we are soon coming to the end of what I consider are the major conditions for moving upwards into the mountains of God. The fifth suggestion I want to make is this – recognise the subtle and insidious nature of sin.

There is a view in the Christian church that as long as we focus on the sins that are obvious (i.e. sins of behaviour), then we can forget any hidden sins that may be in the heart and trust God to deal with them in his own way. Dealing with obvious sin is extremely important – don't hear me minimising this fact. Moral discipline is part of the Christian commitment. We are expected to resist the temptations that come our way and correct any spiritual violations that may occur, but to concern ourselves only with obvious sin and avoid facing the sins of the heart will cause us to miss our footing on the slopes of God.

Someone has put it like this, 'The grime has been so imbedded in the carpet that a simple vacuuming will not do the job. We need a scrubbing brush and a strong detergent.' Diligence in putting right the things that are obviously wrong is good, but without a clear understanding of how sin has penetrated our hearts, we will be nothing more than surface-copers.

Father, forgive me that I have been so content to live on the surface of life. Help me see that in turning my gaze to what is going on inside me, you are not seeking to demean me but to develop me. Give me grace not to shrink from the task. Amen.

FOR FURTHER STUDY – Jer. 17:1–11; Gen. 3:8; Prov. 28:13

1. What is the tendency of the human heart?
2. What is one condition for us to prosper spiritually?

A little-known sin

FOR READING AND MEDITATION – PSALM 7:1–17

'For the righteous God tests the hearts and minds.' (v. 9: NKJ)

We touched yesterday on the fact that while some sins fall into the category of the obvious, there are others that do not, and the pursuit of God demands that we give our attention to both. Focusing only on correcting obvious sin (i.e. sins of behaviour) without understanding what it means to deal with the issues of the heart will bring about a condition akin to that of the Pharisees – more smug than spiritual.

One of the things I have noticed about myself is that whenever I feel I am not pursuing God in the way I should, I tend to focus on the surface issues of my life, above-the-water-line problems, and work at them all I can. But sin involves far more than what goes on above the surface; there is also something going on in the deep recesses of my heart.

As there is little need for me to discuss the sins that are obvious, I want to focus now on those that are not. I imagine that those of you who have been Christians for some time will expect me at this stage to identify the hidden sins of the heart under such categories as resentment, lukewarmness, impatience, jealousy, and so on. My concern, however, is with a category of sin that is not easily recognised and not very well known. This sin is probably more deeply buried in our hearts than any other and acts, in my opinion, as a trigger to them. The sin I refer to is – demandingness. You won't find the word in the Bible, but you will certainly see it illustrated there. Demandingness is insisting that our interests be served irrespective of others. Clearly, if Christ is to live in us, then this has to die in us.

Father, I see that again you are about to face me with a strong and serious challenge. Forgive me if I draw back when your lance plunges deep. I have lived with demandingness for so long that I might not even be able to recognise it. Help me. In Jesus' name. Amen.

FOR FURTHER STUDY – Gal. 2:15–21; Isa. 29:15, 30:1–2; 1 Cor. 10:24

1. How did Paul describe demandingness? / 2. What were the children of Israel doing?

The example of Jacob

FOR READING AND MEDITATION – GENESIS 27:30–38, 28:10–22

'...If God will be with me and will watch over me...so that I return safely to my father's house, then the Lord will be my God...' (28:20–21: NIV)

We continue from where we left off yesterday with the thought that one of the things we discover about ourselves when we look deep into our hearts is a spirit of demandingness. We demand that people treat us in the way we believe they should. We demand that our spouses focus on ministering to our needs. We demand that people support us in times of trouble. We demand that no one comes close to hurting us in the way that we might have been hurt in childhood. Wedged tightly in the recesses of our heart is this ugly splinter which, if not removed, will produce a poison which will infect every part of our life. Let there be no mistaking this issue – if we are to pursue God wholeheartedly, then the spirit of demandingness that resides in every human heart must be identified and removed.

Jacob is probably one of the clearest Biblical illustrations of a demanding spirit. He insisted on having his father's blessing for himself and took advantage of his brother's hunger, buying his birthright for a plate of stew. Later, Jacob went through a kind of half conversion, making God his God and giving him a tenth and so on, but deep in his heart there was still the spirit of demandingness.

It shows itself again at Paddan Aram where, after marrying Rachel, Laban's daughter, he worked out a scheme to make himself rich at his father-in-law's expense (Gen. 30:41–43). He was still Jacob – the man who demanded to have his own way. He had talked about himself in terms of honesty: 'And my honesty will testify for me in the future' (Gen. 30:33, NIV), but it was nothing more than above-the-water-line honesty. His mind was changed, but not his heart.

O Father, I am so grateful that you have recorded in Scripture so many illustrations of the truths you want me to know. I see so much of myself in Jacob. Help me from this day forward to be less and less like him. In Jesus' name I pray. Amen.

FOR FURTHER STUDY – Luke 15:11–32; Matt. 20:1–16

1. How did the prodigal's brother display demandingness? / 2. How did Jesus illustrate it?

What is your name?

FOR READING AND MEDITATION – GENESIS 32:22–32

'So Jacob was left alone, and a man wrestled with him till daybreak.' (v. 24: NIV)

The way in which God helped Jacob to be rid of his spirit of demandingness is interesting and revealing – 'a man wrestled with him till daybreak.' Like the Hound of Heaven, the love of God pursued him down the years, awaiting the hour when he would be ready to admit that he was beaten, that his strength had turned to weakness and that he was all in.

God wrestled with him until Jacob's strength was diminished, at which point he asked him this question: ' "What is your name?" ' To us it seems a simple and innocent question, but in those days one's name was the expression of one's character; if the character changed, the name was changed. So Jacob, after a tremendous struggle, made the crucial confession. 'My name is Jacob – the supplanter', he sobbed. The depths were uncovered. Jacob's heart was naked before God. The real problem was identified.

If you have not reached this place in your spiritual experience, then I suggest you stop everything and tell God your name. You might have to confess, 'My name is Demandingness; I insist on having my own way in everything.' For some of you it will be hard to get that name out – you will choke on it. But get it out, no matter what the cost, for there will be no new name until you say the old name. The saying of the old name is a confession, a catharsis. When Jacob said his name, the angel said: ' "Your name will no longer be Jacob, but Israel" ' (v. 28, NIV) – a striver with God. It was after Israel, the crooked man made straight, that the new nation of Israel was named. Jacob was buried and Israel was alive for evermore.

God, help me to tell you my name – my real name. Help me to dodge no longer: the game is up. Take out of me the spirit of demandingness. Change my name and change my character. Save me from myself. In Jesus' name I pray. Amen.

FOR FURTHER STUDY – 1 John 1:1–9; Ezra 10:11; 2 Sam. 12:13

1. What are we to do with our sin? / 2. How did Nathan respond to David?

How demandingness flourishes

FOR READING AND MEDITATION – DANIEL 3:8–30

'But if not, let it be known to you, O king, that we do not serve your gods, nor will we worship the gold image . . .' (v. 18: NKJ)

Today we ask ourselves: how does demandingness manifest itself? Well, one way it shows itself is by an insistence that God answers our prayers in the way we think he should. Just recently I talked with a woman whose husband had abandoned her and left her with the responsibility of bringing up three small children. She seemed so buoyant in her spirit that at first I gave thanks to God for the way he appeared to be upholding her. But, as she talked, I grew more and more uncomfortable, for she told me, 'I know God is going to bring him back. If he doesn't, then he is not as faithful as he says he is. That can't be, so my husband will come back.'

Can you hear the spirit of demandingness in these words? I sympathised with her hurt to such a degree that it was painful for me to have to explain that faith is one thing, but demandingness is another. Her 'faith' in God was based, not on unconditional confidence in his character and sovereign purposes, but rather in the hope that he would relieve her suffering in the way she thought best.

Deep hurt and deep suffering is a most suitable environment in which to nourish a demanding spirit. Nothing convinces us more that God must answer our prayers in the way we think he should than when we are experiencing continued heartache. And the line between legitimate desiring and illegitimate demanding is a thin one that is easily crossed. How can we be sure our desiring does not turn to demanding? When we are willing to say: if God does not grant what I desire, then I can still go on because I know that he will never abandon me, and in his love I have all the strength I need to handle whatever comes.

O God, save me from an insistent and demanding spirit. You who are always reaching out to me in love and awakening me, help me to recognise the difference between a desire and a demand. In Jesus' name. Amen.

FOR FURTHER STUDY – Matt. 26:36–46; Psa. 40:8; Eph 6:6; Phil. 1:1

1. How did Jesus express desire without demandingness? / 2. How did Paul express it?

Faith is not demandingness

FOR READING AND MEDITATION – HEBREWS 11:1–16

'Now faith is the substance of things hoped for, the evidence of things not seen.' (v. 1: NKJ)

Whenever I talk about the condition of demandingness in a meeting, one of the questions that comes up is this, 'Doesn't what you say destroy the faith and confidence we ought to have when we approach God in prayer? Isn't powerful praying the ability to insist on God giving us the things we know we ought to be receiving?'

There is a world of difference between 'praying in faith' and demandingness. When we 'pray in faith', we have the assurance in our hearts that God wants to bring about a certain purpose for his own glory, whereupon faith reaches into heaven and pulls down the answer through fervent, believing prayer. Demandingness is another thing entirely – it insists on getting the answers that are in accord with its own desires rather than God's purposes. It is an attempt to bring God in line with our will rather than bringing our wills in line with his will.

Dr Francis Schaeffer, when advised that he was suffering from a terminal illness, became assured that his work on earth was finished and that soon he would leave this world and go to his heavenly home. Thousands of people prayed for his healing and when he himself was asked why he did not claim the Bible's promises concerning health and wholeness, he replied, 'When I am in the presence of God, it seems uniquely unbecoming to demand anything.' Some have interpreted these words as a lack of faith but I think I understand what the great man meant. It is one thing to plead and pray with passion for something very personal; it is another thing to demand that the will of the Almighty be one with our own.

Father, I see the line between demandingness and faith is so fine that I can easily cross from one to the other without knowing it. Tune my spirit so that I will always be able to discern the difference between these two things. In Jesus' name. Amen.

FOR FURTHER STUDY – Psa. 143:1–10; Matt. 12:50; James 4:1–15

1. What was the desire of the psalmist? / 2. How does James put it?

The cure for demandingness

FOR READING AND MEDITATION – HOSEA 14:1–9

'Take words with you and return to the Lord.' (v. 2: NIV)

How do we deal with demandingness? There is only one way – we must repent of it. Our passage today tells us exactly how to repent. First: 'Return to the Lord your God'. The key to ridding ourselves of anything that is spiritually injurious and defeating is to return to God. The pursuit of God involves at its core a shift away from dependence on one's own resources to dependence on God. Remember this – doing good and correcting wrong behaviour does not automatically make us good people. Obedience is important, extremely important, but it must be accompanied by the deep repentance of the heart.

Secondly, the passage says: 'Take words with you'. This phrase means, I believe, that we must put into words a clear description of what we are repenting of. If we are not clear what is going on inside us, how can we repent of it? Next: 'Forgive all our sins.' Repentance puts us in touch with the forgiveness of God. We can work to bring about change also, but the greatest catalyst for change is humbly positioning ourselves before God and asking for his forgiveness.

Then again: 'Receive us graciously, that we may offer the fruit of our lips'. The thought here is, 'Receive us that we may worship you more effectively.' That is the purpose of all restoration – to worship God. We will be drawn into true worship when we give up insisting on our own way and learn to trust God for our happiness. When repentance moves us from a spirit of demandingness to absolute trust in God, then we put ourselves in the position where God is able to make our feet like 'hinds' feet' and equip us with the ability to ascend into the heights with him.

Tender and skilful Invader of my heart, I yield my stricken being to you for healing. 'Be of sin the double cure': drain every drop of demandingness from my being. For I want not only to be better, but whole. In Jesus' name. Amen.

FOR FURTHER STUDY – Joel 2:12–18; Isa. 55:7; Psa. 34:18, 51:17

1. What does God not despise? / 2. What does it mean to 'rend your heart'?

Too good to be true

FOR READING AND MEDITATION – LUKE 24:36–53

'And while they still disbelieved for joy, and wondered, he said to them, "Have you anything here to eat?" ' (v. 41: RSV)

If we are to let nothing stand between us and the making of our feet into 'hinds' feet', then another step we must take is this – understand the nature of disappointment and how it works to hinder your pursuit of God. All of us have been disappointed. Living in a fallen world means we have been subjected to experiences where we have been let down by others and where even our loved ones have failed at times to come through for us. But this is not the problem – the problem occurs when we allow the hurts and disappointments of the past to prevent us from reaching out to God and to others in an attitude of love.

A dramatic illustration of what I mean is found in the passage before us today. It is the evening of the day of the Resurrection, and without warning, Jesus suddenly enters the room where his disciples are assembled and makes himself known to them. How did they respond? Listen to the words again, this time in the *New English Bible* translation: 'They were still unconvinced, still wondering, for it seemed too good to be true.' It was obvious that the disappointment of Christ's crucifixion and death still reverberated within them and now, faced with the reality of the resurrection, they did not want to believe it in case it was not true – and they would be disappointed again.

They wanted to believe but they had difficulty in doing so, because they knew that they could not cope with what would happen in their hearts if it turned out that what they were seeing was not true. Rather than take the risk of faith they preferred, for a little while at least, to withdraw into the safety of disappointment.

God, forgive me that so often I allow the disappointments of life to deter me from moving toward you, in case something might happen that will disappoint me again. Help me to put everything I am and have in your hands – with nothing held back. In Jesus' name. Amen.

FOR FURTHER STUDY – Luke 24:13–35; Job 30:26

1. How did the disciples express their disappointment? / 2. How did Jesus deal with them?

Surprised by joy

FOR READING AND MEDITATION – PSALM 30:1–12

'Weeping may endure for a night, but joy comes in the morning.' (v. 5: NKJ)

We continue examining the nature of disappointment to see how, unless correctly understood and handled, it can work within us to hinder our pursuit of God. We looked yesterday at the disciples, who struggled for a while with the problems of disappointment and were reluctant to believe in case what they were believing was not true.

What a distinctive and intriguing difficulty this was. They were grown men whose lives had been far from sheltered and protected, yet the experience of the crucifixion had been more harrowing than any of them cared ever to face again. Over and over again during the days in which Jesus lay in the grave, they must have racked their brains to try to find some explanation for why his life had ended on a grisly cross. Doubtless, in the closing hours of that fateful weekend, their thoughts would have turned naturally toward how they might go about restructuring their lives. Then, suddenly, Jesus appears to them. His appearance was everything they wanted, but such was the disappointment in their hearts that they considered it too good to be true. Thus they adroitly protected themselves against the risk of being disappointed again.

This is the tragedy of disappointment – it can, unless looked at and dealt with, reverberate inside us and hinder us in our pursuit of God. When disappointment is put into its proper perspective and faith comes into its own, far from being too good to be true, one discovers that there is nothing else so good and nothing else so true. God proves himself to be not just better than our worst fears, but better than our greatest dreams. Being surprised by joy quickly follows disbelieving.

Gracious and loving heavenly Father, give me insight into what I have been looking at today and show me how to press through all disappointments in the knowledge that beyond the hurts, I shall be 'surprised by joy'. Amen.

FOR FURTHER STUDY – John 21:1–22; Psa. 126:5; Isa. 35:10

1. How did Peter respond to his disappointment? / 2. What were Jesus' words to him?

It's OK to feel it

FOR READING AND MEDITATION – NEHEMIAH 1:1–11

'When I heard these things, I sat down and wept.' (v. 4: NIV)

Today we ask ourselves: why is it necessary to know how to cope with disappointment? Because if disappointment is allowed to reverberate in our hearts, however much we pretend with our minds that we do not care, the true feelings in our heart will prevent us from moving upward toward the peaks of God 'with all four feet'. Our back feet will not track where our front feet have been positioned, and thus we will miss our step on the steep slopes that lead upward to closer fellowship with God.

The first thing we should learn about disappointment is this – it's OK to feel it. I hope it is becoming crystal clear during the course of these daily meditations that the worst possible thing we can do with any problem that arises in our lives is to refuse to face it and feel it. Yet this is a typical response made by many Christians to life's problems.

A few years ago, I was involved in counselling a young, unmarried woman who had gone through some bitter disappointments, both in her childhood and in her adolescent years. Such was the pain these disappointments brought that the only way she could cope with them was to turn her mind to something else. She toyed with the idea of drink, sensual pleasures and several other things, but because she had a deep commitment to Christ, she decided to enrol in a Bible correspondence course. As we talked, it became clear to me that in doing this, her primary goal was not to learn more about Scripture but to relieve the pain of disappointment that was reverberating in her heart. Bible study became a way to escape from her problems rather than what it should have been – a way to confront them.

Father, help me to see that you have made me in such a way that I function best when I go through problems rather than around them. Show me that maturity is me being in charge of my feelings, not my feelings being in charge of me. In Jesus' name. Amen.

FOR FURTHER STUDY – Jonah Chs. 1–4; Prov. 16:32; Eccl. 7:9

1. Why was Jonah disappointed? / 2. How did demandingness come into it?

Let's not stay here too long

FOR READING AND MEDITATION – MATTHEW 26:36–46

'Then he said to them, "My soul is overwhelmed with sorrow to the point of death. Stay here and keep watch with me."' (v. 38: NIV)

We said yesterday, 'It's OK to feel disappointed.' By that we meant it is better to face disappointment and feel it than pretend it is not there. And when I say feel it – I mean exactly that. Most people, I find, just walk around the edges of their disappointment, in the way they would walk cautiously around the rim of a volcano, admitting they have been disappointed but working hard (often unconsciously) to blunt the feelings of disappointment with a 'let's not stay here too long' attitude.

Follow me carefully now, for I am entering an area where it is possible to be misunderstood. The usual response to what I am now saying is this: 'Surely there can be no good point or purpose in being willing to enter into all the pain of our disappointments? What possible value can this bring? What is past is past; isn't it better to forget the hurts and disappointments of the past and get on with life?' Sounds rational and sensible, doesn't it? However, it is not the best way to deal with life. The more deeply we are willing to face our disappointments, the readier we will be to turn to Christ and draw from him the strength we need to cope with them.

The danger when we are unwilling to face and feel as openly as possible the disappointments that come our way, is that we will come to depend on our own strategies to cope with them, and turn only partially to Christ for succour and strength. Facing and feeling disappointment is a sure way of coming to recognise that God, and God alone, is the only one who can help us cope with them. When we face and feel our disappointments, we will cling more closely to Christ.

Gracious and loving heavenly Father, I want to live fully and frankly. Help me to face whatever goes on inside me with complete honesty. Save me from all self-deception and subterfuges, for I would be a fit instrument for you. In Jesus' name. Amen.

FOR FURTHER STUDY – 1 Kings Ch. 19; Heb. 4:15

1. What was Elijah's disappointment? / 2. How did he respond to it?

The sin of self-protection

FOR READING AND MEDITATION – 1 JOHN 3:11–24

'And this is his command: to believe in the name of his son, Jesus Christ, and to love one another…' (v. 23: NIV)

Another advantage of being willing to face and feel one's disappointments is that it enables us to touch another hidden sin of the heart – self-protection. Let me explain what I mean. Whenever we are disappointed, we naturally feel hurt and experience inner pain. Some people are so affected by disappointment that a pool of pain builds up inside them, and they say to themselves something like this, 'People hurt: stay away from them and don't get too closely involved.' These people see non-involvement as the way to avoiding the pain of possible disappointment.

But this attitude is a violation of the law of love. Lawrence Crabb, a Christian psychologist, says, 'Deficient love is always central to our problems.' What does he mean? He means that behind most of our problems is a failure to love others as we love ourselves. If we refuse to move towards someone in the spirit of love because of the fact that he or she may disappoint us, then we are more interested in protecting ourselves from pain than we are in loving – and that is sin.

Did you ever think of self-protection as a sin? Well, it is, and in my estimation it is one of the subtlest of all. Many of our relationships are ruined by this – particularly marriage relationships. A man who shouts angrily at his wife early in his marriage is setting up a self-protective system that says, 'Disappoint me and you will have to suffer the consequences.' What is he doing? He is protecting himself more than loving his wife. And that, no matter how one might attempt to rationalise it – is sin.

Father, your challenges are sometimes more than I can bear, yet I see the sense and wisdom that lies behind them. Reveal to me my own self-protective devices and help me to give them up in favour of loving as I have been loved. Amen.

FOR FURTHER STUDY – Luke 10:25–37; Rom. 13:10; James 1:27

1. What did the priest and Levite display? / 2. What did the Samaritan display?

Enter here at your own risk

FOR READING AND MEDITATION – PHILIPPIANS 2:1–13

'Do nothing out of selfish ambition or vain conceit, but in humility consider others better than yourselves.' (v. 3: NIV)

We said yesterday that to love means moving toward another person without self-protection, or, as our text for today puts it – considering others better than ourselves. Our Lord is the supreme example of this. He 'made himself nothing, taking the very nature of a servant ... he humbled himself and became obedient to death – even death on a cross (Phil. 2:7–8, NIV)

Disappointed people sometimes find it difficult to move out towards others because they run the risk of being disappointed again. After all, people – even Christian people – can be rude, uncouth, obnoxious and sometimes downright disgusting. I sometimes think it might be helpful if we put a sign outside some churches saying, 'Enter here at your own risk.' Forgive my cynicism, but I have lived long enough to know that Christians can hurt! What are we supposed to do when we know that to move towards another person in love exposes us to the risk of being disappointed? We move forward in love: easy to say but more difficult to do. Making ourselves vulnerable to disappointment is frightening, but it is precisely this that has to happen if we are to love as we are loved.

Mature Christians are those who are willing to look fully into the face of disappointment and feel it, knowing that because they do, they will come to a deeper awareness that no one can comfort the heart like Jesus Christ. In the presence of such pain, one sees the uselessness of every attempt to find solace in one's own independent strategies. Let me make this point yet again – facing and feeling the pain of disappointment underlies more than anything else the gripping truth that only in God can we trust.

Father, at times your purposes seem to run diametrically opposite to my interests, but the more I ponder them, the more I see that you always have my highest interests at heart. Help me to trust you more – and myself less. In Jesus' name. Amen.

FOR FURTHER STUDY – Matt. Ch. 26; 2 Tim. 2:13

1. What disappointments must Jesus have felt? / 2. How often do you disappoint him?

Love is not blind

FOR READING AND MEDITATION – 1 CORINTHIANS 13:1–13

'Love never fails.' (v. 8: NKJ)

We spend one more day thinking through the issue of being willing to face and feel our disappointments. If we draw back from this, then a part of us will experience spiritual deprivation. The more deeply we enter into disappointment, the more thoroughly we will be able to see how committed we are to self-protection and turn from that in repentance to a more complete and utter dependence on our Lord Jesus Christ.

If I was to ask you where you have been disappointed the most, I wonder what your answer would be? Most people to whom I address that question tell me, 'My parents.' It's surprising, though, how so many will not admit to being hurt or disappointed by their parents, for fear they are failing to honour them or are being disloyal. Listen to what one writer has to say about this, 'When someone appreciates his parents only because he overlooks the pain they caused him, his appreciation is not only superficial, it is self-protective. Love is never blind to others' faults. It sees them clearly and is not threatened. It admits disappointment, but forgives and continues to be warmly involved.

Sadly for most of us, love is not the bottom line – self-protection is. When we can look into the face of every disappointment and be willing to feel the pain it brings, there is no more powerful way of motivating our heart to turn in full dependence toward the Lord. If we are unwilling to do this, then (as we saw) we might cling more to our own ways of handling disappointments than his. And if we do, then in no way can we climb to higher and more distant spiritual peaks 'with all four feet'.

Father, the more I become aware of what is involved in climbing higher with you, the easier it is to become discouraged. I am a dull, blundering disciple. Help me, dear Lord. Your grace works miracles. Work one in me today. In Jesus' name. Amen.

FOR FURTHER STUDY – 2 Cor. 12:6–10; Phil. 4:11; Eph. 3:16

1. What could have been a great disappointment to Paul?
2. What attitude did he take instead?

Deliverance from fear

FOR READING AND MEDITATION – 1 CHRONICLES 28:9–21

'"Be strong and courageous ... Do not be afraid or discouraged, for the Lord God, my God, is with you"' (v. 20: NIV)

We come now to the seventh and last step we must take if we are to have feet like 'hinds' feet' – ask God to rid your heart of all and every fear. I am convinced that thousands, if not millions of Christians are held back from pursuing God by reason of fear.

We saw earlier that not all fears are harmful. When fear is spelled with a small 'f' it may be contributive, for fear can have useful biological ends. Fear makes the frightened deer alert and fleet of foot; it makes the surgeon skilful, for he sees the dangers that beset him if he does the wrong thing. Fear harnessed to constructive ends may be constructive. When we use fear and control it, then it is good; when fear uses and controls us, it is bad. When fear becomes Fear, then it becomes fearsome. I am sure that you have known times, as I have, when God beckons to you, as he did with John in the Revelation, to 'come up hither' (Rev. 4:1, RSV), only to find that as your mind got ready to begin the journey, your heart suddenly became gripped with fear. You wanted to move upward but your progress was halted because you could not mount 'with all four feet'.

Overcoming the fears that sometimes grip our hearts ought to be one of the greatest objectives of our lives. The first word of the Gospel was the voice of the angel: 'Do not be afraid' (Luke 1:30). The first word of Jesus after his resurrection was, 'Do not be afraid' (Matthew 28:10). Between that first word and the last word, the constant endeavour of Jesus was to help us get rid of fear. We must learn his secret.

O God, give me deliverance from every harmful and unproductive fear. I know this is a prayer that you delight to answer, for you have fashioned me for faith, not for fear. Help me, then, to surrender to what I am made for. In Jesus' name I pray. Amen.

FOR FURTHER STUDY – Matt. 14:22–33, 17:1–8

1. What caused Peter to sink? / 2. What did Jesus say to the disciples on the mountain?

Jesus – God with a face

FOR READING AND MEDITATION – TITUS 2:1–15

'For the grace of God that brings salvation has appeared to all men.' (v. 11: NIV)

How wonderful it is, on this, another Christmas Day, to realise that our problems are solved, and our questions answered, not merely by the application of certain principles, but by contact with a Person. Many cousellors are prepared to take the principles of Christianity, but push to the edge the Person. In Jesus we have a Person who puts content into the principles. The principles work only when he is in them.

Grace is not something that God tips out of a vessel in the sky. He himself is the grace. Our text for today tells us so. 'Jesus,' as someone has said, 'put a face on grace.' Grace is no longer something vague, nebulous and indistinct; it has form, tangibility and reality. Grace is Jesus.

A little girl complained of feeling afraid in her room at night. 'But your teddy is here,' said her mother. 'I know that,' said the little girl, 'but I want something with skin on.' When beset by life's problems, we want more than principles, we want a person – 'something with skin on'. Christmas focuses on the fact that grace is 'God with a face'. So when you cry out for grace to help you deal with your fears, remember it is not just a principle you receive, not just a vague inner trembling in your consciousness: you receive Jesus. His coming was not limited to that first century: He is with you today.

Blessed Lord Jesus, I am so thankful that when I think of grace, I need only think of you, for you are the embodiment of grace, and you never fail to make your way to me, whatever my circumstances and whatever my need. I am so thankful. Amen.

FOR FURTHER STUDY – Phil. 2:1–11; Jn. 1:1–14; Gal, 4:4

1. What does Christmas mean to you? / 2. Why not share this with someone today?

Fear and cold feet!

FOR READING AND MEDITATION – 2 TIMOTHY 1:1–12

'For God has not given us a spirit of fear, but of power and of love and of a sound mind.' (v. 7: NKJ)

If we are to be free of unproductive fears, then we must take a few moments to examine fear's negative and pervasive influence. When Simon Peter stepped out of the boat and attempted to walk on the water to Jesus, we read: 'He was frightened, and … began to sink' (Matt. 14:30, *Amp. Bible*). Fear makes you sink. When Jesus healed the paralytic, he saw that his paralysis was rooted in fear, which in turn was rooted in sin. So his first word was: 'Take heart, my son', and his second, 'Your sins are forgiven' (Matt. 9:2, RSV). When Jesus lifted the guilt, that lifted the fear and that, in turn, lifted the paralysis.

When the disciples fell on their faces at the top of the Mount of Transfiguration, terrified because they had heard the voice of God, Jesus turned to his prostrate disciples and said: 'Rise, and have no fear' (Matt. 17:7, RSV). Fear puts you down; faith lifts you up. The man who buried his talent brought back the unused talent and said: '… I was afraid, and I went and hid your talent in the ground' (Matt. 25:25, RSV). His life investment was in a hole in the ground! Fear did it. Again, it was said of the disciples that they were gathered 'behind closed doors for fear of the Jews' (John 20:19, *Amp. Bible*). Fear always puts you behind closed doors; it makes you an introvert, an ingrown person. Joseph of Arimathea was 'a disciple of Jesus, but secretly for fear of the Jews' (John 19:38, *Amp. Bible)*. Fear always drives you underground.

I know a man who testifies to the fact that fear literally gave him cold feet. He says that prior to the Lord delivering him from fear, his circulation was so bad that he always had to wear his socks in bed. 'Now,' he says, 'my circulation is normal. God took away my fear and gave me warm feet.'

God, I see that fear is indeed costly. It is so costly that I dare not keep it. But I cannot easily get rid of it, for it has put its roots deep within me. Help me tear it up, root and branch. In Jesus' name I pray. Amen.

FOR FURTHER STUDY – Mark 4:35–41, 5:25–34

1. What had Jesus said to his disciples? / 2. What had this caused him to do?

Home-grown fears

FOR READING AND MEDITATION – MARK 4:35–41

'He said to his disciples, "Why are you so afraid? Do you still have no faith?"' (v. 40: NIV)

We continue meditating on the harmful effects of fear. Some social scientists maintain that there are no inherent fears except two; the rest are acquired. The two inherent fears, they say, are the fear of failing and the fear of loud noises. I read of some psychologists who examined five hundred people and found that, between them, they had about seven thousand fears. It is not a proven fact, of course, that we inherit just two fears, but if that is so, then those five hundred people were loading themselves down with hundreds of unnatural and useless fears!

Once when I was in India, I was told of a caste where the women, on their birthdays, add four rings of heavy brass, one on each ankle and one on each arm. By the time they are in middle age, they walk with great difficulty under this senseless burden. But this is no more senseless than weighting oneself down with useless fears; fear of failure, fear of rejection, fear of the future, fear of growing old, fear of what other people might think, and so on. Most of our fears are home grown – they come out of wrong home teaching and example. Parents who try to control their children by fear often succeed too well – their children grow up and are controlled by the fears themselves.

When I first began writing in 1956, one of the editions I put together was on the subject of fear. A woman wrote to me and said, 'All my life I have been a victim of fear. My nightly prayer was, "Lord, thank you for not letting anything too bad happen to me today." You said if I turned to Christ, I could be rid of all fear. Well, I have – and he did.'

Father, we have filled your world and our hearts with fear – needless, devastating fears. Help us, we pray, to find release from these fears, for they are not our real selves – they are an importation. In Jesus' name. Amen.

FOR FURTHER STUDY – Psa. 34:1–22, 23:4; Prov. 9:10, 19:23

1. What was David's testimony? / 2. How can we find freedom from our fears?

Two basic fears

FOR READING AND MEDITATION – HEBREWS 2:5–18

'– and free those who all their lives were held in slavery by their fear of death.' (v. 15: NIV)

Psychologists are at pains to point out that fear is different from anxiety. Fear has a specific object, whereas anxiety is a vague and unspecified apprehension. What, I wonder, is your biggest fear? Benjamin Rank, a social scientist, says that there are basically two forms of fear, the fear of life and the fear of death. The fear of life is the fear of having to live as an isolated individual. The fear of death is the fear of losing individuality. He says, 'Between these two fear possibilities, these poles of fear, the individual is thrown back and forth all his life.'

The first fear, the fear of life, is vividly illustrated by a small boy's comment on why his mother had given birth to twins, 'I suppose the reason for twins is because little children don't like to come into the world alone.' The fear of life makes many retreat into illness. Not all illnesses are due to this, of course, but many are. It is a refuge out of responsibility. Freud found the case of neurosis in the past – in childhood; Jung, a disciple of Freud, found it in the present. He said, 'I ask, what is the necessary task which the patient will not accomplish?' This backing out of life's responsibilities through fear of life is a major cause of problems.

But with many, it is not the fear of life that paralyses them; it is the fear of death. The verse before us today in the *New English Bible* reads like this: '...and might liberate those who, through fear of death, had all their lifetime been in servitude' (Heb. 2:15, NEB). Is it necessary to live under such servitude? Of course not – when Christ has all of you, then fear can have no part of you. It is as simple as that!

Father, I am so thankful that you have made it possible for me not to be enslaved by fear. I can be free, gloriously free – and free now. Touch me in the deepest parts of my being this day and set me free from all and every fear. In Jesus' name. Amen.

FOR FURTHER STUDY – 1 Cor. Ch 15; 2 Cor. 5:1; John 11:25–26

1. What is the hope of every believer? / 2. Is this your hope?

Steps out of fear

FOR READING AND MEDITATION – ROMANS 8:1–17

'For you did not receive a spirit that makes you a slave again to fear, but you received the Spirit of sonship.' (v. 15: NIV)

What are the things we have to do in order to be rid of fear? First, if you have any fear, don't be afraid to admit it. To try to conceal it is to reveal it in hurtful ways. Reveal it in a sound way and then you will not have it revealed in unsound ways. Bring all your fears out into the open and look at them. Secondly, give up all justification for your fears. Very often fear produces bodily sicknesses that help us get attention or gain power over others. We 'enjoy' bad health. This possibility has to be faced before you can ask God to deliver you from fear.

Thirdly, fix it in your mind that to be controlled by fear is a fool's business, so stop being a fool. Schoolteachers should have common sense as well as sense. Some do not. One schoolteacher said, 'I have been a teacher for thirty years, but I always have nervous indigestion a week before school begins.' He was afraid of the children and probably the children were afraid of him. And neither had anything to fear. There was nothing to fear except fear. Am I being too hard in urging you not to be a fool? No, I'm only echoing my Master, who said: 'O foolish ones, and slow of heart to believe…' (Luke 24:25, NKJ).

Fourthly, remember every fear you face has been defeated and overcome by Jesus Christ. When any fear rises up within you and threatens to beat you into submission by its overbearing presence, just calmly look it in the eye and say, 'I am not afraid of you. You have been decisively beaten by my Lord. Bend your neck! There, I knew it. There is the footprint of the Son of God upon your neck.' This confidence is your starting point. Nothing can touch you that hasn't touched him and been defeated.

Father, help me never to justify any unproductive fear, for when I do, I cut myself off from your redemption. I can live without all fear when I live with you. Set me free – gloriously free. In Jesus' name I pray. Amen.

FOR FURTHER STUDY – Luke 4:1–18; Isa. 61:1; John 8:31–32; Rom. 8:2

1. What was Christ's mission? / 2. Will you let him minister to you in this way today?

Love – stronger than fear

FOR READING AND MEDITATION – 1 JOHN 4:7–19
'There is no fear in love; but perfect love casts out fear…' (v. 18: NKJ)

We must spend one more day looking at the things we must do in order to be rid of fear. Fifthly, surrender all your fears into God's hands. This isn't as easy as it sounds, for it probably means the giving up of a whole life strategy. You may have been depending on your fears and using them as a crutch – now I am asking you to renounce them as a way to live.

Can you do that? You can if you are willing to depend on Christ for your life rather than depending on your own strategies and self-centred devices. This means reversal – a life reversal. You will be tempted to compromise – half give them up and half keep them in your hands. This halfwayness will mean a whole failure. If you surrender your fears into God's hands, this means he has them, not you. This shifts the basis – you are not struggling to overcome them; you and God are working it out together. To look at God creates faith; to look at yourself creates more fear – fear of fear.

Sixthly, keep repeating to yourself the verse at the top of this page: 'Perfect love casts out fear.' If there is no fear in love, then the obvious thing to do is to love. Fear can only come where love is not. Where love is, fear is not. How do you love? Well, don't try to work it up. Just open your heart to the love that is in God's heart. Remember his word that says: 'We love because he first loved us' (v.19, NIV). You will discover that as his love comes in, so fear will move out. Then, free of fear, your heart and mind will move, in a coordinated fashion, fleet-footed up into the hills of God.

Father, now all my fears are turned over to you, help me to open my heart to the great Niagara of your love. Pour your love into every corner of my heart until every one of my fears has been drowned. In Jesus' name. Amen.

FOR FURTHER STUDY – Psa. 118:1–6, 3:6, 27:3; Isa. 12:2
1. What did the psalmist declare? / 2. Why was Isaiah not afraid?

A final summary

FOR READING AND MEDITATION – ISAIAH 35:1–10

'Then the lame shall leap like a deer…' (v. 6: NKJ)

We come now to the final day of our meditations on the theme – 'Hinds' feet on high places'. Permit me to remind you of the seven things we have identified as being necessary to bring about a more perfect coordination between our hearts and our minds:

(1) Prepare to take an honest, straightforward look at what is going on beneath the surface of your life.
(2) Face the question: when I pray, is my heart fully and enthusiastically behind what I ask?
(3) Be willing to get in touch with the deep thirst for God which resides at the core of your being.
(4) Learn how to face and handle any doubts that may arise in your heart.
(5) Recognise the subtle and insidious nature of sin.
(6) Understand the nature of disappointment and how it works to hinder your pursuit of God.
(7) Ask God to rid your heart of all and every fear.

Attend to any one of these suggestions and your spiritual life will move into a new dimension. Attend to all of them and you are destined for the heights.

One word of caution, however – don't try to do too much all at once. Work on one suggestion before going on to the next. Remember, growth in Christ is not arriving but moving upward in a godly direction. And when the lips and the heart are in alignment, when they track together with the absolute certainty that the rear feet of the deer track with the front feet, then nothing is impossible, whether it be the climbing of mountains or the casting of mountains into the sea.

Father, what can I say? I have heard your call and I can never be the same again. I ask once more – make the coming year a time of rich and joyous discovery. Help me climb higher than I have ever gone before. In Jesus' name. Amen.

FOR FURTHER STUDY – 1 Cor. Ch.2; Rom. 8:6; Phil. 2:5; Eph. 4:23

1. What does the Spirit reveal to us? / 2. What has the Spirit revealed to you?